Adventures with Rare Coins

Adventures
with
Rare Coins

Q. David Bowers

Foreword by
John J. Ford, Jr.

Bowers & Ruddy Galleries, Inc.
Los Angeles, California

Also by Q. David Bowers:

Coins and Collectors
United States Half Cents 1793-1857
Early American Car Advertisements
Guidebook of Automatic Musical Instruments, Vol. I
Guidebook of Automatic Musical Instruments, Vol. II
How to Be a Successful Coin Dealer
Encyclopedia of Automatic Musical Instruments
How to Start a Coin Collection
Collecting Rare Coins for Profit
High Profits from Rare Coin Investment
Value Guide of Automatic Musical Instruments
Put Another Nickel In
A Tune for a Token

Library of Congress Card Catalogue Number: 78-71615
International Standard Book Number (ISBN): 0-914490-00-1

Copyright ©1979 by Q. David Bowers, Box 1669, Beverly Hills, CA 90210
Published by Bowers and Ruddy Galleries, Inc., Los Angeles, California

Contents

Acknowledgements

The author expresses appreciation to the many individuals who have provided assistance, photographs, historical data, and other information. The following were particularly helpful:

Amos Press (information concerning the 1913 Liberty head nickel); Mrs. Merrill D. Armstrong, St. Albans Historical Society, St. Albans, Vermont (material concerning the great Confederate raid in 1864); Aubrey Bebee (his experiences as a rare coin dealer in the field of silver dollars); Walter Breen (historical information, observations, and opinions concerning silver dollars); Kenneth Bressett (information from *A Guide Book of U.S. Coins*); Broadmoor Hotel, Colorado Springs, Colorado (Maxfield Parrish illustration); Dan Brown (recollections concerning silver dollars, including hitherto unpublished information pertaining to the 1964 Peace dollar).

Murray Clark, Clark's Trading Post, Lincoln, New Hampshire (historical information and suggestions); John J. Ford, Jr. (historical information and suggestions); Harry J. Forman (data concerning the 1962-1963 Treasury release of silver dollars); Wesley P. Mann (historical information); Cliff Mishler (historical information from the files of *Numismatic News*); James F. Ruddy (historical and business information); Larry Goldberg (silver dollar information); Eric P. Newman (information and illustrations, particularly pertaining to the Comstock lode).

Art Reblitz (information concerning Cripple Creek); Harvey Roehl and the Vestal Press (historical information and illustrations); Margo Russell (historical information, news clippings, and related details of the 1962-1963 Treasury release of silver dollars; back issues of the author's "Numismatic Depth Study" column in *Coin World*); Dr. Paul Rynearson (information concerning ancient coins); Harvey G. Stack (historical information).

Dr. Vladimir Clain-Stefanelli and the staff of the Smithsonian Institution Numismatic Department (illustrations and historical information); Adna Wilde and the Pioneer Museum of Colorado Springs (photographs pertaining to the early days of Cripple Creek; information concerning Lesher dollars).

Staff Acknowledgements

The author wishes to express appreciation to the following members of the Bowers & Ruddy Galleries staff who helped in the ways indicated:

Karen Andrews (graphic arts supervision and layout), Judy Cahn (technical information), James Clutterbuck (photography), Frank Draskovic (information relating to coins of the world), William D. Hawfield, Jr. (suggestions), Loren Jewitt (graphic arts and layout), James Jones (technical information), Mary Beth Johnson (typing of manuscript), Robert Korver (technical information), Richard Kosta (technical information), Kent Loose (photography), Bruce Lorich (technical information), Mar Miyazaki (graphics and layout), John Murbach (technical information), Christina Ozburn (graphic arts and layout), Phil Starr (project coordination and printing), Susan Thomas (graphic arts and layout).

About the Author

Q. David Bowers began his collecting interest in 1953 while a high school student in Forty Fort, Pennsylvania. In 1955, at the age of 16, he became the youngest person ever to have a bourse table at the American Numismatic Association's annual convention, held that year in Omaha. By that time his coin firm had become established and was gaining a reputation based upon Dave's knowledge and seemingly tireless research and study.

The author is now president of Bowers & Ruddy Galleries of Los Angeles, one of the world's largest rare coin firms. He was elected president of the Professional Numismatists Guild, the leading organization of rare coin dealers, for the 1977-1979 term, and is a recipient of that organization's coveted Founder's Award. Other memberships include the American Numismatic Association (life member 336), the Royal Numismatic Society, the American Numismatic Society, the Token and Medal Society, the Civil War Token Society, the Society of Paper Money Collectors, and many other groups.

His weekly column, "Numismatic Depth Study," has appeared in *Coin World* for many years and has earned several "Best Columnist" awards from the Numismatic Literary Guild. In addition he has written for all other major numismatic publications, including *The Numismatist, The Numismatic Scrapbook Magazine, Numismatic News, Coins Magazine, Coinage*, and many specialized journals. His articles and features on coins have also appeared in such diverse publications as the *Encyclopedia Americana, Reader's Digest*, and *Barron's*. A 1960 graduate of the Pennsylvania State University, the author in 1976 received the Alumni Achievement Award from that institution's College of Business Administration.

Dave's other activities include interests in coin-operated antique automatic musical instruments such as music boxes, nickelodeons, and orchestrions; old prints;

western Americana; antiques; and antique postcards. His 1,008-page book, *The Encyclopedia of Automatic Musical Instruments*, is the standard information source in the field, and it has been designated by the American Library Association as "one of the most valuable reference books," a rare honor. He is the author of over a dozen other volumes as well. In addition to his coin activities, Dave is a director of American International Galleries of Irvine, California, and of the Mekanisk Musik Museum in Copenhagen, Denmark.

Although Dave travels frequently, he and his wife Christie make Southern California their home.

While coins have their monetary aspects, both literally and figuratively, they offer an untold measure of art, history, and romance as well. In the spirit of these sentiments the present book was written.

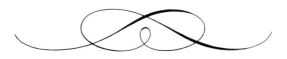

Foreword

by John J. Ford, Jr.

One hot June day in 1941, as a somewhat brash 17-year-old coin collector-trader, I made a periodic visit to the jewelry shop of I. Stupay, located in New York City's Times Square. Entering, I saw a tall gentleman, hatless but nattily attired in a crisp summer suit and sporting a thin mustache, his dark hair parted in the middle, who was chatting amicably with the proprietor. While waiting to inquire about what better grade coins my jeweler acquaintance had recently acquired, I gazed into the dusty display cases which contained, among other things, a tray of bust-type half dollars from the early 19th century priced at 65c each.

I couldn't help overhearing the conversation between Mr. Stupay and his customer; a discussion about how many different dates of Indian cents could be purchased at the marked price of three for 10c. When, a few minutes later, I. Stupay retired briefly to the rear of his little shop, the stranger turned to me and asked if I also had an interest in coins. When I replied in the affirmative he suggested that we have a cup of coffee together after he finished his business. Sensing the possibility of a sale, I readily agreed.

Subsequently, with a rather sheepish look on my face, I casually followed the man with the neat, almost pencil-thin mustache out of the shop. By chance I had three coins in my pocket, at least two of which were for sale. All three were 1845 large cents, more or less Mint State, two of which displayed considerable original red mint lustre. These had been purchased earlier in the day for $1 each from dealer Hans Sergl of 137 Fulton Street in downtown New York, another one of my regular stops I attended high school in 1941 and worked after school, evenings, and weekends as an usher in a local movie theatre. My pay was 25c per hour, the minimum wage at the time. The $3 I invested in the three 1845 large cents represented almost half a week's income. Therefore, when my newfound friend and I were comfortably settled in Horn & Hardart's nearby Automat it was not difficult for me to inform him how much better large cents were than small cents, even Indian heads! When I offered to deliver two of the cents for $3 he purchased the pair. Following a short conversation, during which I was told that the new owner of the two 1845 cents had never seen a "big penny" before, we exchanged names, addresses, and telephone numbers on slips of paper. Shaking hands, I said goodbye.

A few minutes later, while waiting for a train on a nearby subway platform, I took my slip from my pocket and read my new customer's name: Homer K. Downing, of 939 Woodycrest Avenue in the Bronx.

My friendship with Homer Downing grew rapidly despite an age difference of 25 years. I was buying and selling coins in a small way in order to finance the building of a collection; he had discovered a new hobby, complete with an active, eager, although youthful, advocate. Within weeks I was obtaining large cents on approval from Charles French (of Troy, New York) and M.H. Bolender (of Freeport, Illinois). Homer's appetite grew as I obtained more and more coins for him. Soon I obtained copies of the two standard reference books on large cents by Doughty and Andrews, a copy of each book for each of us. Many evenings were spent at his apartment carefully studying the varieties of the coins I had to sell him as well as other pieces he picked up in various local coin and curio shops. While Mrs. Downing was a bit overwhelmed by her husband's new activities, she prepared late snacks for us and often affectionately referred to me, in conversations with her husband and sister, as "the kid."

On Saturdays we visited the stores on 18th Street, went to see my old friends (of four years), the Stack brothers, Joe and Morton, and independently matched wits with Dave Bullowa, Abe Kosoff, "Izzy" Snyderman, and other established dealers.

That autumn we visited dealers outside of the city, always traveling in the Downing 1940 Packard, a considerable source of pride and joy to its owner. One crisp October day in 1941 we found ourselves in Pleasantville, New York, visiting old Tom Elder, who was supposedly retired. Mr. Elder had a reputation for being cantankerous, but we got along well with him. He sold us copies, with pictorial plates, of several of his publications, including Gilbert's work on half cents and thin, paper-covered texts on 1794 and 1796 large cents. We were given copies of many of his past auction catalogues with accompanying prices-realized lists. Homer Downing devoured all of this with relish. In time, we jointly skimmed the best from Abe Kosoff's auction offering of the Julius Guttag library. We encouraged each other in the eager pursuit of United States coin books of every variety, together with old and new auction catalogues, especially those with illustrations. It was

about this time that Homer and I discovered the importance of the famous auction sale catalogues of the Chapman Brothers.

Late in 1941 I started working part-time at Stack's, cataloguing the Gies collection of large cents and then selling them on behalf of my employer to Homer Downing. In 1942 I was at Stack's full time, and friend Downing was a constant visitor. Soon he was enlisted to attribute difficult die varieties of "big pennies" for the firm, utilizing his newly-acquired copies of Hays-Frossard (for 1794 large cents) and Howard Newcomb's work on the coppers of 1801, 1802, and 1803. It was during this period that Homer became actively involved with several of the local coin clubs and met a living legend in the large cent field, the aged and venerable Henry Hines.

When I entered the military service in January 1943 Homer Downing was visiting Henry Hines in Newark, New Jersey, weekly. In addition he was attributing die varieties for a well-to-do collector of coppers named Oscar Pearl. He became almost totally occupied with large cents, numismatic literature, and the people and institutions involved with them. When he wasn't checking out 1793 cents by Crosby numbers for Morton Stack, he was rearranging the American Numismatic Society's holdings for curator Bill Clark. During the war years he kept in touch with me wherever I was stationed. I learned of his meeting with Dr. William H. Sheldon and their collaboration on a monumental reference to be called *Early American Cents*. In 1945 Homer was deeply involved in the offering by Wayte Raymond and James Macallister of the Howard R. Newcomb collection. Today I number among my treasures Homer's personal bound copies of the two Newcomb catalogues, the only ones, to my knowledge, containing individually-mounted photographs of each cent variety from 1793 to 1814.

Following World War II, I was away from numismatics to some degree for several years, but I managed to keep myself aware of Homer Downing's far-ranging activities. If there was "large cent action" anywhere, he was involved in it one way or another! During this time he introduced me to Edmund Rice, of Prospect Plains, New Jersey, who had just purchased the remnants of the Henry Chapman estate. We got involved all over again with Chapman catalogues and with the fascinating material that went with them: correspondence, bid books, records, and just about everything else, not to overlook many coins, tokens, and medals. Homer seemed to know everyone, and everyone apparently knew him. By this time he had obtained almost all of Henry Hines' large cents and many colonial coppers, including many of great rarity. He met frequently with Fred Boyd, did business with the legendary Burdette G. Johnson of St. Louis, and generally was regarded by numismatists nationally as "Mr. Large Cent."

While my interest in coins never completely died, it was Homer K. Downing who rekindled my spirit in 1949-1950, which in turn led to my eventual long-time association with Charles M. Wormser and his New Netherlands Coin Company. Homer died in May 1951, less than ten years after becoming a serious collector. Happily, he lived long enough to see me established in the rare coin business as a full time professional and was able to lend encouragement and help as I struggled to compile my first two catalogues under the New Netherlands aegis.

Eighteen years after my initial meeting with Homer Downing I found myself happily and busily involved as a working numismatist. One day, while behind the counter at the old New Netherlands Coin Company office at 1 West 47th Street in New York, I attempted to wait on a customer who entered huffing and puffing. He must have grown impatient waiting for an elevator and had walked up the four flights of stairs. The man was of moderate height, stocky if not rotund, and wore glasses. When asked what he wanted, he inquired about obtaining one of the uncommon or scarce Lincoln cents, perhaps a 1914-S or 1931-S, that would be very difficult to find in circulation. Walking toward the back of the office to check the stock, I asked him if he wanted the coin in used or in Uncirculated grade. He paused, and his reply suggested that he didn't know the difference. As I recall, next to our main safe was a tray containing odd coins purchased earlier in the day in an over-the-counter transaction. On impulse, I selected a worn 1787 draped bust Connecticut copper coin from the assemblage, intending only to make a price comparison between it and the cheaper circulated Lincoln cent which I assumed would be selected. Being imaginative and secretly considering Lincoln cents (and their relatives) to be quite a bore, I thought it worthwhile to introduce our potential client to something numismatically *interesting*. Pricing both Lincoln cents competitively, I observed that there were other coins, much older and of greater historical importance, that could be bought for about the same price as a well-worn lowly Lincoln cent.

Producing the Connecticut copper, a coin which had seen many years of circulation, I patiently explained the meaning and significance of the legends on the coin, AUCTORI CONNEC and INDE ET LIB, and made much of the 18th century date. To my considerable surprise, he purchased both the circulated Lincoln cent *and* the shabby Connecticut copper. While writing up his invoice I learned that my customer's son collected Lincoln cents in a "penny board," but that the Connecticut coin and my explanation of it were more interesting. After he had left, I placed our office copy of his invoice and the payment into the cash box. Charles Wormser, who was

seated at his desk, and who could not help following, at least in part, my innocent machinations, looked up and asked, "Who was that?" Glancing at the sales ticket I replied, "The man's name is Ted Craige, spelled with an 'e' at the end."

Ted Craige returned a few days later. He wanted a book with something in it about his recently-acquired Connecticut cent, and he also asked about related coins. Years later he recalled that I had sold him a Whitman *Guide Book of United States Coins* for $1.50 and a Kentucky cent in Fine or so condition for $5. He remembered my telling him that he could buy a comprehensive reference on early American coins, but that it was rather expensive. I, of course, was thinking of a reprint of Sylvester S. Crosby's famous work about colonial issues. The attraction was almost magnetic. Ted was back the next day to see what a copy of Crosby's *Early Coins of America* looked like. I had picked up a copy of a reprint of the Crosby book from Aaron Feldman and invoiced it to Ted with the understanding that he could return it if he found it to be too detailed or otherwise not of interest. In addition to his book purchase, I sold him a small group of state coins, including a number of battered Connecticut coppers, a few New Jersey pieces, and a couple of 1788 Vermont cents. All of the coins were well worn, with Fine probably being the best grade represented. As an afterthought I threw in a handful of 2x2 paper coin envelopes with the suggestion that he attribute his latest purchases by using the Crosby work.

On his next visit I sold Ted a number of 1787 Fugio cents ranging in condition from Good to Very Fine. At that time New Netherlands Coin Company had a generous supply of Wayte Raymond's old publications, so I gave him with the firm's compliments a copy of the *Coin Collector's Journal* containing Eric P. Newman's monograph on Continental dollars and Fugio cents. Again, the idea was that he should look up his unattributed coins in the standard reference and identify them on the envelopes provided. I thought it a rather amusing exercise, but Charles Wormser considered it a bit strange. We were both surprised when our new customer showed up about a week later inquiring about the availability of the Miller-Ryder book on New England state coinage. It seems that he had spent the previous Saturday afternoon at the American Numismatic Society and had been introduced to that institution's marvelous library.

Homer Downing and Ted Craige, each in his own time, became close personal friends of mine. They had other things in common; both were electrical engineers, Homer having been employed at Western Electric and Ted having served as an executive at a small transformer plant in Brooklyn. Both, as soon as they got their bearings, chased numismatic literature simultaneously with the pursuit of coins themselves. Ted was fortunate to enter the hobby at the same time that Aaron Feldman (of "Buy the book before the coin" fame) took a booth at the Jewelers' Exchange a block from our offices. Genial Aaron specialized in all types of printed numismatic material. At the time he was selling discards and leftovers from the estate of David Proskey, a famous dealer who died during the early Depression years. Prominent among the Proskey remainders were a large number of late 19th and early 20th century auction catalogues, many unused, but the majority consisting of Proskey's personal sale copies, hand-priced and annotated, often with buyers' names. Ted Craige caught on quickly; what literature I didn't get went into his library.

While Homer Downing was *intrigued* by coins, Ted was *hooked*. Within two years of his first visit to New Netherlands Coin Company, Ted was buying $1500 and $2000 coins, expensive items at the time. In rapid succession I sold him a Bermuda sixpence, "New Yorke" tokens in both brass and tin, two 1785 Immune Columbia patterns in silver (one with a plain edge), a 1787 George Clinton cent, and similar coins.

Ted became a regular attendee at our auction sales and those of our competition, buying Uncirculated Continental dollars, choice Chalmers silver coins of Maryland, and related delicacies. He met George Fuld, Bob Vlack, and other specialists, became a close friend and confidant of Dick Picker (who lived nearby), made periodic visits to leading dealers all over the country, and rapidly became one of the foremost colonial collectors in the numismatic spectrum. During the 1960s his activities accelerated both in scope and intensity. One day I inadvertently introduced him to medals of the colonial period (to 1783, as listed in C. Wyllys Betts' reference), thereby creating a sort of "Frankenstein," in that I avidly collected the same series of medals myself. Ted almost overnight became my toughest and most knowledgeable competitor, a bittersweet situation which I secretly enjoyed. There was no one else nearby to discuss the medals with, to gloat with over a particular conquest, or to cry with when we had individually found out, unknown to the other, that we had both been outbid at an English sale.

Ted enjoyed the local coin shows, belonged to several coin clubs, and, like Homer Downing, actually "lived" coins. In 1970 his small company was absorbed by a much larger one and Ted was given a comparatively high position with the new firm. His recompense was to be commensurate with his new title. He was on top of the world in many ways, as he now would have more time and money to devote to his beloved numismatic avocation. Even so, it quickly became apparent that his new position was not enough. One damp November evening, shortly after he had found out about his new situation, we were seated in Ted's den surrounded by his comprehensive numismatic library. Over brandy and cigars

we discussed the possibility of his giving up his recently acquired title and place in the world of electronics; he confided to me that he really wanted to be a coin dealer, to be able to devote all of his waking hours to what he loved most outside of his family.

Ted Craige was already into part-time dealing, an activity many numismatists drift into as they upgrade their holdings, unless they wish to hold on to the duplicates that inevitably pile up. Ted knew his coins and medals, liked people, and was a born trader. I encouraged him, on the assumption that ideally everyone should really enjoy what they do every day for a living. While it was not mentioned, we both knew that he was not well, that he had a heart problem, and that the years remaining would be better spent anywhere but behind a desk in a high pressure conglomerate. Once a decision was reached, the question of capital arose. He realized that it would be desirable to sell off parts of his extensive holdings. Shortly thereafter he disposed of his cherished collection of Connecticut coppers, one of the finest extant, to our mutual friend, the author of this book, Q. David Bowers. Other groups of coins and individual rarities also went. By the time the two of us arrived in Los Angeles for the Numismatic Association of Southern California show in February 1971, Ted was in business. Unfortunately, Ted Craige never realized the full potential of his dream; he quietly passed away in his sleep the following June. My wife Joan and I were in Europe at the time, and the word of his death hit us both very, very hard.

In all the years I knew both Homer Downing and, later, Ted Craige, we never discussed coin investment as such. The word "trends" was either unknown or ignored; none of us, including myself, knew anything about newsletters or similar market reports. My friends had continual "adventures" with rare coins; they made their excursions, day by day, into numismatics, enjoying every minute of the experience.

Homer Downing was enamored with the provenance or numismatic origin of every rare large cent that he encountered. He felt compelled to establish the history of each and every rarity. Each pertinent auction sale catalogue in his library was given a number, as were all of his reference works and texts that had illustrations which permitted the coins to be specifically identified. These numbers were made part of an elaborate keying system involving pedigrees. Homer obtained huge loose-leaf binders and made a determined effort to create a photographic record of top-grade specimens of all of the early large cent varieties from 1793 to 1814. It was his plan to obtain photographic prints of the finest known examples of each variety, to mount them, and then to trace and enter the numismatic history and data concerning each piece.

All of this involved a large amount of effort. For each coin it was necessary to learn who first discovered or recorded the piece, the collectors who successively owned it, the authors who wrote about it, the sales in which the coin appeared, and the various price levels involved. Homer's efforts were the basis for the "Condition Census" data in Dr. William H. Sheldon's *Early American Cents* book, the first attempt at formally establishing and publishing such information in a standard work. I still remember the elation in his voice and the twinkle in his eye as he took me aside at a meeting of the New York Numismatic Club and told me that he had found a "Gilbert '94" pictured in an earlier auction catalogue which had annotations listing the buyers' names for the various lots. Hours and hours of patient research and study often went into such discoveries. Homer Downing's strong interest in the prior ownership or pedigree of his beloved large copper cents led him to people as well as to publications. He contacted either by mail or personal contact practically every large cent collector alive that he could find. It was truly an adventure for him to tie a particular coin to a specific owner, and it was even more gratifying if the collector in question was prominent and generally secretive about his holdings.

If adventure can be defined as a bold undertaking in which the outcome hinges upon unforeseen events, Ted Craige was, in his own way, every bit as adventurous as Homer K. Downing. While Homer had his Condition Census records, Ted Craige had his charts and records of die varieties. He devised systems of ready identification for almost every issue of colonial coin from the lordly NE shilling to the lowly Connecticut coppers. He incorporated this information into such concise form that whatever he didn't have in his head he had tucked under his arm. Ted's manner was engaging, his knowledge formidable. The Craige library became larger than that formed earlier by Homer K. Downing, as Ted continually attempted to broaden his horizons.

While in Scottsdale, Arizona, following the 1971 convention of the Numismatic Association of Southern California, during a brief vacation before getting home and down to business, Ted Craige told me of his hopes and plans. He wanted to extend his interests and knowledge. He talked of our visiting Virginia City and Carson City in Nevada and of traveling overland to San Francisco. He dreamed of visiting the Bancroft and Huntington libraries. He wanted to learn more about pioneer gold coins and assay ingots. Indian peace medals and 19th century American medals beckoned as well. Ted wanted to get into paper money; in fact, I remember selling him a large lot of colonial notes in Los Angeles and a small collection of obsolete currency in Scottsdale. Together, we studied the vignettes, signatures, ink, papers, printers, and other details of his new acquisitions. He couldn't wait to return home so he

could commence searching for the books and catalogues that contained these new interests. There was much to do; so many new worlds yet to conquer.

Clearly, to Homer Downing and Ted Craige, as well as to Dave Bowers, coins or any of the numismatic objects embraced by that term are much, much more than pieces of metal or paper with a monetary significance. They represent a great deal more than their dates, devices, legends, or composition might signify at first glance. They are, in fact, symbols—keys if you will—to almost unlimited knowledge. *These little pieces of history were there when it happened.* Where were they? Who put them there? What happened to the empires or countries which issued them? What about the king, president, duke, dictator, merchant, assayer, banker, stage line, or amusement machine manufacturer to whom they owe their existence? Who, as archeologist, antiquarian, or numismatist, found them? Who wrote about them? What collections have they been in? The answers to these questions and many others have to be sought; it is the search for them that constitutes true numismatic adventure!

Ted Craige once was offered a specimen of the extraordinarily rare "Washington and Columbia" medal. It fascinated him, and after establishing what it was, he located a book titled *Voyages of the Columbia to the Northwest Coast 1787-1790 and 1790-1793* by F.W. Howay. Early on, he and I discovered that the particular piece he had been offered was spurious, a cast copy, but Ted read the book from cover to cover (all 518 pages) anyway. Once he got started, he couldn't stop. Once he completed the book he couldn't bear to part with it; it just had to be in his library. He even wanted to keep the fake medal, but the price prohibited it. His enthusiasm grew as he researched the origin of the medal, the controversy concerning the die sinker, the purpose of issue, and other details. To my knowledge, he never owned a genuine specimen of this rare medal, but he certainly knew as much about it as any numismatist of my acquaintance.

Homer Downing and Ted Craige are gone, but their example lives on. Others have taken their places, and it is clearly the purpose of this book to increase their number. Dave Bowers compiled narratives and anecdotes, tells of his adventures, and presents pictorial evidence, all in an effort to induce others to follow in his footsteps of numismatic interest. He wants alert, intellectually curious collectors to venture beyond the somewhat plain world of the date, grade, and value of a coin. He knows, as do I, only too well, that once you take "what is it" *as far as you can go* "what is it worth" becomes elementary, very elementary. As a professional numismatist who must stay competitive, Dave often sells coins to investors. If one out of twenty investors who read this book is inspired by the fascinating background that coins offer, then Dave will have accomplished his purpose. He wrote it to *inspire,* and that is why I have added in this foreword the story of my two friends, both of whom rose from rank beginner to established authority within a decade. Both found that numismatics contributed immensely to their *enjoyment* of life.

There truly exists a wonderful and satisfying world of numismatic adventure—the world of the connoisseur, where one can learn to really enjoy and appreciate what one owns or what exists by being fully aware of its history and background. Nothing in numismatics is more rewarding.

John J. Ford.

Nickeldom

1

Recently I made the two hour drive from Santa Barbara to Los Angeles south along the California coastline. It was a dark evening, the moon was half full, and the firmament was spangled with stars. Looming in front of me was the great constellation Orion rising in the eastern sky. As I glanced at it through the windshield the thought crossed my mind that this vista is one which has remained unchanged for centuries, indeed millennia. The same Orion was seen by Julius Caesar, by David Rittenhouse (the first director of the United States Mint, and an accomplished astronomer), by me during my drive to Los Angeles, and it will be seen by others a thousand years from now. It was a warm and comfortable feeling to know that the universe is a link with tradition. There are few traditions left in today's society. One almost has to search for them. Likewise, one has to search for identity and uniqueness for society is going forward at the speed of light toward sameness.

Today's world is rush-rush, with emphasis on speed. An interstate highway enables one to drive from New York City to Boston in just four hours. Forgotten is the old Boston Post Road which winds along the Connecticut seashore, through Rhode Island, and ten or fifteen hours later into Boston—having passed innumerable quiet villages, old seaports and whaling outposts, and other interesting sights along the way.

On the other side of the continent, Route 1, the traditional scenic road which snakes along the Pacific seacoast from San Diego through San Francisco, is now relegated to sightseers. Anyone with any "intelligence" at all will take Route 5 which is nearly as straight as an arrow and which does not have such troublesome distractions as traffic lights, curves and twists, and, for that matter, scenery. After all, we can't wait for tomorrow to get here of its own accord—we must rush to meet it!

"Faster is better," so runs popular thinking. Everything is accelerated. Does your five-year-old child read at the seven-year-old level? Marvelous! Does your daughter at age 14 know what she wants to do as a career? Wonderful, she is ahead of her classmates!

I am reminded of a story a British travel agent told me of a client who never visited America and who was planning his first trip to the United States. Being a *busy* man he had little time. What he was saving his time for, I don't know. It was his plan to have breakfast at Niagara Falls, spend the afternoon at the Grand Canyon, and enjoy the evening at Disneyland in California! This in turn reminds me of the movie *If It's Tuesday, This Must Be Belgium.* Never mind stopping to poke along to see the scenery—just pick off the major tourist attractions in a rush to accomplish something. What, I don't know. Then there is the Concorde: Washington, D.C. to Paris in just four hours. Progress?

I collect old picture postcards. The other day I read the back of a postcard sent in 1908 from Wildwood, New Jersey, a spa on the eastern seashore, to a friend back home in Boston. The sender related that it took 10½ hours to reach Wildwood from Boston by a combination of steamship and railroad train—and that the trip had been delightful. "Getting there is half the fun," a travel ad used to say. Now, with today's speed before we can think about having fun we have already arrived!

So it is with shopping. When your parents or grandparents went to the "big city" a wonderland of interesting stores awaited them. This was an era of fine leathers, hand-crafted metal goods, and coffee measured out by the pound and run to your order through a bright red hand-cranked Enterprise coffee mill. Stores in Boston had their own characteristics. New York shops had different features, and those in Chicago or Los Angeles were different still. Not so today. We all have K-mart, Sears, McDonald's, and other stereotyped places whether we go shopping or eating in Northern Maine, Southern Florida, or Western California. Imagine traveling a thousand miles and writing home and saying, "I went shopping at Sears." What a laugh! Likewise, most of us use Crest toothpaste, eat Campbell's soup, and have a shelf full of Spice Islands condiments.

Remember the days when the postman would bring a three-page letter from your sweetheart? Now, instead,

we have push button telephone dialing. Coast-to-coast in just a few seconds.

Those few of us who want to use the mail to express sentiments don't have to think anymore. When Priscilla wants to let John know how she feels she can send him a pre-printed card on any subject from his birthday to sex. All she has to do is sign her name. It seems to me we've lost something.

Even collecting has become rush-rush. Why study to be a collector? Why read books about coins? Why bother subscribing to *Numismatic News, Coin World*, and other publications, or, if you do subscribe, why bother reading them? Why learn about grading? Why learn the difference between obverse and reverse? What difference does it make how dies were prepared in the year 1793 or 1836? Instead, send $25 per month, or $50 per month, or whatever, and receive a start on an instant "heirloom collection" of medals commemorating great events in American history, or famous comedians, or airplanes of the world. And, of course these are *rare*. There are *only* 10,000 other collectors, or 25,000, or 100,000 who have collections precisely identical to yours. Who is kidding whom?

It's becoming a plastic world. But, some of us are getting tired. There is a desire to return to the old ways.

The appreciation of nature, or what's left of it, has been on the increase in recent years. No two snowflakes are alike nor are two pine trees. The virtues of "virgin forests" and "lands unspoiled by man" are extolled, without realizing that we are calling ourselves our own adversary! "We have met the enemy, and they are us," comic strip character Pogo once said.

In recent years there has been a slump in the sales of prepackaged frozen food specialties. It is encouraging that sales of French-style food processing machines have been rising during recent years. Clearly, some of us are starting to make souffles again.

Books, magazines, and college courses on wines have become popular as people try to acquire this tradition in an effort to become different and to enjoy dining at the same time. Nestled in among the Sears and K-mart stores in shopping centers one can sometimes find craft shops selling candles, macrame, leather goods, or booklets of locally-written poetry. It is encouraging that some of us are indeed resisting being just a Social Security or credit card number.

Coin collecting offers the opportunity to be different. I have purchased hundreds of coin collections, perhaps even thousands, since my interest started in 1953, and no two collections have been identical. There is one marvelous thing about coins: although high values make spectacular news stories, the fact remains that numismatic interest is not dependent in any way upon the value of an item. Some of my clients have collected rare and expensive Proof double eagles by dates and have amassed series of them in the 1860s, 1870s, and 1880s, each coin a great rarity. Others have had as much fun if not more by collecting Civil War tokens for a few dollars each. John Ferreri, a Connecticut friend, collects broken bank notes of New England and can look appreciatively at a worn, limp "rag" with most of the lettering faded, a "prize" which might cost all of $10. In the same context, Nancy Ruddy collected $3 bills and spent countless hours corresponding with sellers, attributing varieties, and otherwise learning about them. The cost? For her entire group she paid less than the value of a single Proof double eagle—and yet she had one of the finest collections ever assembled.

John J. Ford, Jr., the well-known dealer, once became more excited over a crude Arizona token than I have ever seen him over an American rarity, and certainly he has sold more than just a few great high-priced coins. A worn 1909 V.D.B. cent purchased by a school boy at a coin shop for a few dollars can be infinitely more fascinating to its owner than a Proof 1895 Morgan dollar for which a successful businessman writes a check for many thousands of dollars.

Coin collecting can be as individual as you care to make it. There are no restrictions, no limits. And, once you get into it your collection will be unique. It will be reflective of your ideas, your personality, your thoughts.

Then there is the link with tradition. To me this is one of the greatest appeals of coin collecting. An ancient Roman bronze coin available today for a few dollars may have actually been held by Julius Caesar! A worn 1787 Connecticut cent may have been carried in Mint Director David Rittenhouse's pocket. Or, for that matter, George Washington's. Each and every coin has its hidden secrets and its own fascinating story to tell if it could only speak.

In today's world of sameness we have in our hobby the key to freedom, the key to individuality, the key to a return to the "good old days": numismatics.

I've found that one of the most enjoyable ways to participate in numismatics is not only to seek out individual coins but to learn their history and background. In some ways this is even more important than owning the coins themselves. One can draw an analogy to the world of art. Imagine being able to appreciate only paintings which one could buy and take home. Lost to you would be the great works of Rembrandt, Leonardo, Van Gogh, and others. One does not have to personally own a sculpture of Michelangelo to enjoy his artistry. Indeed, reading *The Agony and the Ecstasy*, the story of Michelangelo's accomplishments, can be one of the most enjoyable artistic experiences ever.

So it is with coins.

Combination Galloping Horse Carousell.
(PATENTED)

A HANDSOME machine which has all the features of the largest carousell. We have built more of this size than any other; they are quick to start and quick to stop and are easily handled in operation; some of these machines handle over one hundred passengers per trip regular during rush hours; the decorations permit of a beautiful light effect at night.

DIMENSIONS.

Diameter of platform, 44 feet; in 18 sections, each 3 horses abreast, 36 galloping horses, 12 standing horses, 3 double-seated chariots.

Complete with either steam or electric power.

Price, $7,000

There were all sorts of ways to spend a nickel around the turn of the century. Rides on a colorful Dentzel, Mangels, Herschell-Spillman, Parker, or other type of carousel cost 5c each. What nicer way could there be to spend an afternoon than with a handful of nickels at an amusement park? The five-cent cigar and nickel glass of beer are long gone, however the nickel pack of Chiclets stayed with us until relatively recent times.

"Put another nickel in," the old song goes. Nickels, by the millions, were used everywhere.

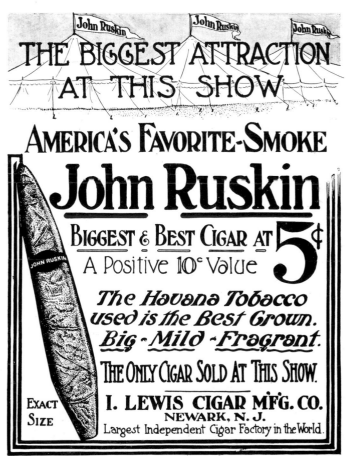

To me the nickel five-cent piece has always been interesting. The designs divide themselves into several basic types: the shield style minted from 1866 through 1883, the Liberty head nickel made from 1883 through 1913, the Indian or buffalo nickel made from 1913 through 1938, and the Jefferson motif made since that time.

The nickel has its roots in the Civil War when coins of all types were hoarded. First to disappear from pocket change were gold and silver issues because of their high intrinsic worth. As the outcome of the war became more uncertain, even copper-nickel Indian cents became rarities in circulation.

To fill the void and to provide a medium of exchange many new types of currency appeared. Most plentiful were Civil War tokens issued in many thousands of varieties. Many bore patriotic slogans such as THE HORRORS OF WAR, THE BLESSINGS OF PEACE, ARMY & NAVY, UNION FOREVER, and so on.

There were a few oddities. One token bearing a flag design had a legend intended to read IF ANYONE ATTEMPTS TO TEAR IT DOWN, SHOOT HIM ON THE SPOT. Instead, by some twist of diecutting fate, the word SPOT appeared as SPOOT!

Other tokens were privately issued by merchants and bore advertisements for boots and shoes, umbrellas, fish, beer, drugs, hotels, clothing, grain, and even rare coins. In the 1950s my firm purchased a magnificent collection of these pieces embracing thousands of different issues arranged by state of origin from Dr. George Fuld, leading authority in the Civil War token field. Included were many rarities such as pieces struck in silver using Liberty seated dimes as planchets!

Postage currency, later called fractional currency, was issued by the United States government during this time of coin hoarding. These thin paper notes were of various denominations from 3c to 50c. These pieces proved to be extremely popular.

At war's end in 1865 thought was given to producing a five-cent nickel alloy coin to replace fractional currency notes of the same denomination. Mint officials realized that there was little hope that half dimes, a silver issue of the time, would effectively circulate. Coins of this metal were hoarded, melted, or exported for profit as soon as they reached circulation as their metallic value was greater than their face value. Indeed, this situation prevailed for another ten years. It was not until 1876 that silver coins were once again seen in general circulation. Around that time a young man remarked that he had seen his first Liberty seated dime! The 15 years of his childhood had seen nothing but tokens and fractional currency used as small change; not a single official United States silver coin was among them!

Although some 1865-dated patterns for a nickel five-cent piece were made by James B. Longacre, mint engraver, studies for the new coin began in earnest the following year, 1866.

Longacre, a Philadelphia portrait engraver of renown and producer of *The National Portrait Gallery of Distinguished Americans*, was appointed to the position of mint engraver following the July 1844 death of Christian Gobrecht. Longacre's appointment, a political one made through the offices of Senator John C. Calhoun, was at first resented by Mint Director Robert M. Patterson. Longacre's experience dealt chiefly with portrait and scenic engraving on flat plates and not die sinking and medal work. Franklin Peale, assayer at the mint and an innovator who introduced new equipment and methods, was likewise resentful. In 1849, following the completion of Longacre's new double eagle design, Peale was especially vitriolic and dismissed the engraver's efforts as being unfit for coinage production. As a result Director Patterson sought a replacement for Longacre. Longacre persevered, and despite such insults as the suggestion that dies be made by private contractors outside of the U.S. Mint, he remained in his post until his death on January 1, 1869.

Because of Longacre's incompetence as a die cutter collectors are blessed with many interesting error varieties from the period of his tenure at the Mint. Such items as the 1846 over horizontal 6 half dollar (the last digit in the date was first cut horizontally in the die and then recut in the vertical position) and the fantastic 1858 half dime with the first date cut in the die upside down and then corrected can be traced to him.

A numismatic favorite for over a century has been the Indian cent first produced in pattern form by Longacre in 1858 and subsequently struck for circulation from 1859 through 1909.

In 1866 several dies were prepared for pattern nickel five-cent pieces. George Washington was the subject of three main styles; a small portrait with UNITED STATES OF AMERICA surrounding and, on another, IN GOD WE TRUST above, and a slightly larger bust with the motto GOD AND OUR COUNTRY.

Abraham Lincoln, whose portrait on an adopted United States coin design had to await the Lincoln cent in 1909, made an ephemeral appearance on a pattern 1866 nickel. For some reason Lincoln, martyred president and chief figure of the Civil War, received only passing consideration at the time. Still another obverse design featured a large shield with the date 1866 below. Reverse styles included the numeral 5 within wreaths of various shapes and sizes, the same numeral surrounded by a circle of 13 stars, and a variation of the last with resplendent rays added between the stars.

The 1913 Liberty head nickel, a coin of which just five specimens are known to exist, is perhaps the most famous American rarity. One dealer, the late B. Max Mehl of Texas, claimed to have spent over $1,000,000 in advertising to publicize this issue! Four are in private hands and one reposes in the Smithsonian Institution.

Shield type 1867-1883.
Reverse without rays.

Liberty head type of 1883.
Without CENTS on reverse.

Varieties of 1913 Indian/buffalo nickels. To the left is shown the Type I issue with the buffalo standing on a raised mound. This design was found unsatisfactory, and partway through the 1913 year the style was revised to a flat ground (Type II, illustration to right). The buffalo nickel was produced from 1913 to 1938, after which time it was replaced by the Jefferson style. Issues were produced at three mints: Philadelphia, Denver, and San Francisco.

Liberty head type 1883-1913.
Reverse with CENTS.

Buffalo or Indian type of 1913.
Buffalo on raised ground.

The first Liberty head nickel produced for circulation in 1883 had for an indication of value the Roman numeral V. Nowhere was the word "CENTS" to be found. Unscrupulous persons gold plated these and passed them as $5 gold pieces. The mint quickly recognized the design error. Later issues bore the word "CENTS" at the bottom of the reverse.

From late 1942 through 1945 nickel five-cent pieces were made of a special alloy containing 35% silver. To facilitate later redemption of these, each piece bore above the dome of Monticello an appropriate mint-mark: P,D, or S. This represents the only time that Philadelphia coins were issued with a distinctive mint letter.

Buffalo or Indian type 1913-1938.
Buffalo on level ground.

Jefferson type 1938 to date.

Following the Civil War, when silver coins were virtually unknown in circulation and were being hoarded, the nickel-alloy five-cent piece made its appearance. Acceptance was immediate, and the familiar "nickel" became a mainstay in American commerce. Shield-design nickels, with two variations, were minted from 1866 through 1883. Liberty head nickels appeared from 1883 through 1912, plus the 1913 which was issued under mysterious circumstances. Indian or buffalo nickels were struck from 1913 through 1938. Jefferson nickels have been with us since the latter year.

Throughout the nickel series many scarce and rare issues are sprinkled. Included are 1867 with rays, 1877, and 1878 in the shield series; 1885, 1886, 1912-S (San Francisco Mint), and 1913 in the Liberty head series; 1913-S Type II and 1918/7-D (overdate) in the Indian or buffalo series; and in the Jefferson series, 1939-D and 1950-D. There are numerous other die variations, overdates, and other curiosities sprinkled throughout the series.

At one time the nickel opened the door to a wonderland of treasures. Shortly after the turn of the century, for a nickel you could ride a merry-go-round, see a movie in a nickelodeon theatre, hear a violin played automatically in a Violano-Virtuoso, hear an entire mechanical orchestra play for you via the coin slot of an orchestrion, or buy a cigar, glass of beer, sandwich, or pack of gum.

Jefferson type 1942-1945.
Silver composition.

A mint error: this 1905 nickel was struck twice.

The multitude of obverses and reverses were combined in many different ingenious ways, not so much to seriously determine the merits of a new nickel five-cent piece design but, rather, to privately provide varieties for sale to collectors. An acidic commentary on this practice was printed in the *American Journal of Numismatics*, magazine of the American Numismatic Society, in August 1866:

"Though collectors have long ceased to regard the new issues of the 'government copper-head factory,' better known, perhaps, as the United States Mint, as of any value, they may be interested in the information that the ugliest of all known coins, the new five-cent piece, is out, as oysters are served in some places, 'in every style.'

"Though specimens are refused to societies and individuals, they are readily procured in Philadelphia through the agent of the young gentleman at the head of that department.

"At present the price of a set of four, struck in various metals, with the copper gold dollar included, is $35, although the expected purchaser is informed in every case that as the owner is very anxious to sell he will take $30. Collectors are advised to wait a little, when it is expected that the owner's anxiety will increase to such an extent that he will be glad to take any amount, however small, above their legal value."

This is a commentary on the mint practice of the time of creating rarities especially for collectors. The appearance of the motto IN GOD WE TRUST on United States silver coins of the same year apparently created quite an opportunity in this regard. Back-dated "patterns" were prepared in silver, copper, and aluminum of the various denominations going back to 1863.

At the suggestion of the director of the Mint at the time, James Pollock, the adopted design consisted of Longacre's obverse featuring a heraldic shield copied from his earlier two-cent motif but with certain features omitted due to the smaller diameter of the proposed nickel coin. The reverse consisted of a circle of 13 stars enclosing the numeral 5, with rays between each star.

The hardness of the nickel alloy, actually a composition consisting of 75% copper and 25% nickel, immediately caused coining problems. Soon Henry R. Linderman, who succeeded James Pollock (and Pollock's immediate successor, William Millward, who served several months following an appointment which was never confirmed by the Senate), complained that the nickel five-cent pieces caused tremendous problems at the mint. Dies wore out quickly and machinery was frequently broken.

In 1867 the rays were removed from the nickel reverse design in an attempt to make striking easier due to less metal flow in the dies. The rumor swept America that the new issues without rays were "counterfeit," causing some consternation among government officials.

Alternative designs, including an Indian maiden and the head of Liberty, were experimented with that year, but the shield design remained in official use. It was not until 1883 that it was discarded.

Copper and aluminum were considered as alternate coinage metals. In 1867 Longacre, after having experimented with many aluminum patterns of various denominations, favorably suggested that aluminum because of its lightness, ease of striking, resistance to discoloration, and relative value (at the time aluminum was a semiprecious metal), would be ideal for coinage. However, apparently Director Linderman had other thoughts, perhaps directed to private personal gain, for despite his frequent and loud complaints about the inadequacy of nickel alloy and the hardness of nickel metal, Linderman created a legislative proposal that cents and dimes be made not only of nickel alloy but nickel alloy containing up to 33% (instead of 25% as used earlier) of the hard metal! As historian Don Taxay relates, this "throws some doubt on his official motives."

From 1867 through 1883 the shield nickel remained constant in design. Slightly over 125 million shield nickels were produced. The high point in shield nickel coinage was reached with the 1867 without-rays design of which nearly 29 million were coined. The low point was 1877, a year in which no pieces were struck for circulation and only a few hundred Proofs were made for collectors.

The hardness of the nickel alloy and the resultant die breakage caused literally hundreds of different minute die variations to be produced. Broken and chipped dies are the rule, not the exception, especially among earlier issues. Finding a well-struck shield nickel completely free of die flaws is an unusual situation among business strikes of the earlier years.

At least two overdates exist among shield nickels, the 1879 with the last digit cut over a previous 8, a coin made in Proof grade, and the 1883 over 2. Additionally, some collectors consider an 1869 nickel with the last digit recut to be 1869 over 8, which it may indeed be (the under digit is not distinct so identification is controversial).

In 1881 Superintendent of the Mint Archibald L. Snowden directed engraver Charles E. Barber to prepare a new series of pattern designs so that the one-cent, three-cent, and five-cent pieces would be of uniform style. The resultant coins, issued in pattern form only, featured the head of Ms. Liberty on the obverse, modeled, some said, after the classical goddess Diana. The reverse depicted a wreath of cotton and corn enclosing respectively the Roman numerals I, III, and V.

Pattern Washington head nickel with IN GOD WE TRUST. Reverse with stars and rays similar to design adopted in 1866.

Washington pattern with UNITED STATES OF AMERICA on obverse. Reverse with inscription with delicate wreath.

Washington pattern with GOD AND OUR COUNTRY inscription. Reverse with 5 in wreath.

1866 shield pattern with date divided into two segments. Reverse with "Dutch" 5 in wreath.

Extremely rare Lincoln pattern nickel of 1866. Only a few of these were made.

PATTERN NICKELS. Beginning in 1865 patterns of various designs were made for the nickel five-cent piece. Adopted for circulation the following year, 1866, was a design featuring a shield on the obverse and stars and rays on the reverse. In 1866 several patterns featuring George Washington were produced. In the same year a few Lincoln patterns, today considered to be extreme rarities, were issued. Various other motifs including an Indian maiden and a Liberty head style similar to that used on the contemporary nickel three-cent piece were experimented with during the next several years. Beginning in 1881 Liberty head patterns were produced. In addition to patterns specifically made to test designs, different die combinations were produced to sell to collectors, often privately through mint employees and officials.

1866 pattern nickel with shield obverse similar to that adopted for circulation that year. Date is together and not divided. Pattern reverse with 5 within heavy wreath.

Pattern nickel by J.B. Longacre. Obverse features Liberty in Indian headdress. Reverse with letter V on shield. Like several other pattern nickel varieties of the earlier years, the word "CENTS" does not appear.

Liberty head style copied from that used on contemporary nickel three-cent pieces. Reverse with Roman numeral V heavier on the right side instead of the left, an error.

In 1884 and 1885 several varieties of pattern nickels with holes at the center were produced. Dr. Judd in his book, "U.S. Patterns," refers to these as "Eastman Johnson's holey designs" and notes that they probably represent an attempt to produce a nickel with a larger than usual diameter. In 1896 Charles E. Barber produced nickels featuring a shield motif on the obverse. Made only in pattern form, specimens were struck in pure nickel, nickel alloy, and aluminum.

Pattern nickels of the Liberty head type were made in a wide profusion of styles and die combinations during the 1881-1883 years. Shown above are three different obverse styles of 1882 and 1883. At the left is a coin with UNITED STATES OF AMERICA encircling the obverse. At the center is the design, subsequently adopted for circulation, with stars surrounding. To the far right is a design combining stars and LIBERTY around the periphery. The center coin above represents the design adopted for circulation the following year. The 1882 Liberty nickel, identical in every way to the regular-issue 1883 Liberty nickel without CENTS, is a transitional pattern. A number of years ago a single specimen of this coin, reposing in solitary splendor in a display case, won the Best of Show award at a Central States Numismatic Society convention. While the rarity at the other end of the series, the 1913 Liberty head nickel, is famous, the scarce 1882 (of which only a few dozen are known) has received very little publicity.

In 1881 Charles E. Barber, following a request by Colonel A. Loudon Snowden, director of the mint, produced designs for a uniform series of minor coins, each featuring the classical head of Liberty. The patterns for the one-cent and three-cent pieces were forgotten, but the nickel of this style eventually evolved into the Liberty head type produced for circulation beginning in 1883.

From the very beginning of coinage for circulation in 1866 the hard nickel metal produced problems in striking. Dies wore quickly and often broke after limited use. Accordingly, many experiments were made at the mint to test different alloys. In 1883 the above-pictured series was produced. Alloys ranged from pure nickel to a composition containing 33% nickel and 67% copper. In the end the composition used for circulating coins was unchanged. Standard issues contained 75% copper and 25% nickel. The relatively small proportion of nickel was sufficient to give all pieces a silvery color. It's interesting to note that, strictly speaking, our five-cent pieces should be called "coppers" rather than "nickels," for each contains three times as much copper as the latter metal!

In 1882 additional patterns of the five-cent denomination were minted. Most featured Barber's head of Liberty and differed from each other in the placement of stars and inscriptions. One interesting variation had five equally-spaced raised ridges on the edge so that blind persons could determine the denomination of the coin by its touch. The idea was never officially adopted.

In 1883 the new Liberty design nickel by Barber was adopted for circulation. In its final form the style consisted of the head of Liberty on the obverse surrounded by 13 stars and with the date 1883 below. The reverse depicted the Roman numeral V within a wreath with UNITED STATES OF AMERICA and E PLURIBUS UNUM surrounding. There was a slight problem: the word CENTS appeared nowhere on the coin. The only indication of value was the "V".

The inventive genius of the American mind very seldom lets an opportunity go unnoticed, and the new 1883 nickel was no exception. Many of these were gold plated, (some sophisticated entrepreneurs even added edge milling via a machine shop) and, presto, changed to "$5 gold pieces" of a new design. With the Roman numeral V as the only mark of denomination, who would know the difference? So, a deception was then created.

Unscrupulous persons would take a gold-plated 1883 Liberty nickel and offer it to a shopkeeper in exchange for an item valued at less than five cents; a cheap cigar or a piece of candy, for example. If the shopkeeper scrutinized the piece carefully and was familiar with the new five-cent design, then he either questioned the con artist about it or else routinely made change and gave the purchaser a piece of candy plus the correct change of three or four cents, never dreaming that the purchaser hoped the shopkeeper would value it at $5.

On the other hand, as often happened, if the shopkeeper glanced at the coin cursorily and mistook it for a $5 gold piece he would not give three cents back in change but a $4.98 refund on a two-cent purchase. When subsequently taken into court the coin passer had only to say to the judge, "I never said it was a $5 gold piece, I knew it was a five-cent piece, it was the storekeeper who made the mistake." This problem, which received wide notice in the press, plus the widespread notion that the omission of the word CENTS was a design error, caused the motif to be modified after about 5½ million coins were struck. From late 1883 onward all Liberty nickels bore the word CENTS at the bottom of the reverse, thereby hopefully preventing any further deception.

Piqued by the government "mistake" in coin design, the public hoarded 1883 CENTS-less nickels by the millions, so it seemed. Even today the coins are quite common. A few decades ago a dealer displayed a bushel basketful of this particular variety in his shop window!

Liberty head nickels were minted in an unbroken procession of dates from that time forward until 1912. In the latter year for the first time nickel five-cent pieces were struck at the branch mints at Denver and San Francisco. The same year marked the *official* end of the Liberty head nickel design. The official end was not the real end, as it turned out. In 1913 one of the most famous of all United States coin rarities was created: the 1913 Liberty head nickel.

Over the years my firm has had many wonderful rarities. The famous 1804 silver dollar, the exceedingly rare 1894-S dime (four of these), several 1838-O half dollars, several 1876-CC 20-cent pieces (including a dazzling group of four at one time), two 1907 MCMVII Extremely High Relief double eagles (including the Yale University specimen), and others are familiar to readers of popular numismatic literature.

Until 1974 the "rarest of the rare," at least in terms of nationwide publicity and fanfare, eluded me. Then it happened. John Hamrick, president of World-Wide Coin Company telephoned and offered me the chance to buy his 1913 Liberty nickel, a coin which earlier had been owned by a succession of prominent numismatists including Abe Kosoff, Edwin Hydeman, King Farouk of Egypt, B. Max Mehl, Fred Olsen, James Kelly, Burdette Johnson, Colonel Edward H.R. Green, August Wagner, and, in the beginning, Samuel Brown. After discussing the situation the purchase was made. What a thrill it was!

The 1913 Liberty nickel is the best known of all American coin rarities. Much of this fame is due to the late B. Max Mehl, the most colorful coin dealer on the American scene during the first part of the present century. In his catalogue description of the 1913 nickel in 1944, Mehl noted:

"I plead guilty to being responsible for making this coin so famous, having used it in all of my national advertising for a period of about a quarter of a century, during which time it appeared in advertising totaling an expenditure of well over $1 million! Certainly, this great coin will prove a most gratifying source of possession to the fortunate owner and also a profitable investment as well."

Sure enough, once the nickel was in our possession the limelight turned on Bowers & Ruddy Galleries! Nationwide newspaper and magazine articles, television coverage, and interviews came our way. The City National Bank, dedicating its impressive new headquarters in Beverly Hills, California, featured this coin as its opening attraction during a series of open houses and receptions. On request we displayed the famed nickel at the

SOME WELL-KNOWN 1913 LIBERTY HEAD NICKEL OWNERS.

Samuel W. Brown

The above advertisements mark the beginning of the 1913 Liberty head nickel's fame.

B. Max Mehl

King Farouk

Eric P. Newman

Louis Eliasberg

Hon. R. Henry Norweb

Aubrey Bebee

At the center of this photograph are Col. Edward H.R. Green and his wife Mabel. Col. Green, one of the most colorful figures in American numismatics, once owned all five specimens of the 1913 Liberty head nickel. Following Green's death the pieces were dispersed among various collectors, some of whom are shown on this page.

1975 American Numismatic Association convention exhibit. There were many other appearances as well.

The seven-page illustrated description of this coin and its history which appeared in Bowers & Ruddy Galleries' *Rare Coin Review* No. 22 in early 1975 was a record in terms of space devoted to a single coin. Thousands of collectors ordered copies just to read the fascinating story of this nickel!

Like many other things in the glare of publicity, a network of facts, some of them not accurate, arose concerning this coin over the years. In 1971 Courtney Coffing, Clyde Mervis, and others on the staff of the Amos Press delved into the subject in depth. An excellent article, "Liberty 1913 Nickel Offers Mystic Aura," was the result. Much of what I write here now and what is known to numismatists at present is the result of the efforts of these researchers.

At least 20 persons have owned from one to five of the 1913 Liberty head nickels. And yet, it is still not precisely known under what circumstances the pieces were struck, who made them, and how many were involved in the mintage.

In recent years attention has been focused on two specimens, the one sold when Omaha dealer Aubrey Bebee bid a final $46,000 at the American Numismatic Association convention in 1967 and bought the coin formerly owned by James V. McDermott, and the coin which I purchased in 1974, a piece which starred in many news and television features, as noted, and which was even the subject of a plot in the television series *Hawaii Five-O*. In 1977 I was called upon to evaluate for the Smithsonian Institution another specimen which they received as a gift in the following year from Hon. and Mrs. R. Henry Norweb of Cleveland, Ohio. For the first time the National Coin Collection owned a specimen of this famous American rarity.

Numismatists, writers, and editors have for years attempted to sift fact from legend.

On December 18, 1903, Samuel W. Brown, a Pennsylvanian, joined the staff of the Philadelphia Mint. He was proposed for membership in the American Numismatic Association in the April 1906 issue of *The Numismatist*, sponsored by Stephen K. Nagy and Dr. George F. Heath. Nagy, a Philadelphia resident, had joined the organization about six months before. Nagy had close ties to the Mint and was involved, among other things, in the private purchase from certain mint officials of restrikes and other delicacies from years earlier, including many Gobrecht silver dollars of the 1836-1839 period.

Nagy, whom I knew during the 1950s prior to his death, told me many stories of earlier days. Some of his stories, if true, will have a sensational impact on United States numismatics should the pieces ever come to light. One of these concerned the mintage of Proof restrikes of 1801, 1802, and 1803 silver dollars, coins of which just a few are known today. According to Mr. Nagy, one hoard located in Colorado had over 100 specimens!

I was impressed with this and other stories, including Mr. Nagy's assertion that he had bought and sold dozens of Gobrecht dollar patterns and had placed his "private mark" on each piece that went through his hands. I queried him as to the nature of this marking, and he said "perhaps you'll find out someday if you look at enough pieces." I still haven't found out.

In July 1909 *The Numismatist* reported on the sale of two different varieties of 1877 pattern $50 pieces struck in gold:

"The two unique United States 50-dollar gold coins, each of different design, which have long been regarded as the rarest coins in the world by American coin collectors, were purchased a short time ago by William H. Woodin, of New York City, for $10,000 each, which figure by far exceeds all recorded high premiums paid for any coin ever sold.

"The coins were bought of John W. Haseltine and Stephen K. Nagy, the Philadelphia coin dealers, establishing a new world's record . . .

"The newly-discovered gold pieces are included in the United States series of pattern coins and represent the most interesting pieces in the American series, the denomination being equivalent to five eagles, or the 'half union' recommended in 1854 by Secretary of the Treasury Guthrie. They illustrate the single case where United States coins of this value were struck in gold. They never emerged from the experimental stage, although declared by experts to be the the most handsome and striking coins ever issued at the United States Mint.

"These two gold coins have not been seen since the year of their mintage, 1877, and were supposed by all collectors to have been melted up."

A furor arose, and the government seized the $50 coins. Woodin obtained as a "refund" from Haseltine and Nagy "several crates" of other United States pattern coins. Presumably these other patterns came from "connections" at the Mint.

Following Nagy's sponsorship, Samuel W. Brown was assigned American Numismatic Association membership No. 808. At the Mint he performed duties as assistant curator of the Mint Coin Collection and later as a storekeeper.

His further connection with Nagy, if indeed there was one, is not known.

In 1912 much activity at the Mint centered around designs for the Indian head style five-cent piece being

prepared by James Earle Fraser, a new motif scheduled for circulation in 1913. The activity was initiated by Secretary of the Treasury Franklin MacVeigh who received a letter in 1911 from his son, Eames, which read:

"A little matter that seems to have been overlooked by all of you is the opportunity to beautify the design of the nickel or five-cent piece during your administration, and it seems to me that it would be a permanent souvenir of the most attractive sort. As possibly you are aware, it is the only coin the design of which you can change during your administration, as I believe there is a law to the effect that designs must not be changed oftener than every 25 years . . ."

By December 1912 Fraser, following much experimentation, had evolved a design depicting an Indian on the obverse and a buffalo on the reverse. While some modifications remained to be done, Mint and Treasury officials were satisfied with the new motif and decided to discontinue the old Liberty head style.

On December 13, 1912, Mint Director George E. Roberts instructed his Philadelphia staff: "Do nothing about five-cent coinage for 1913 until the new designs are ready for use." On that same day the last Liberty head nickel dated 1912 was officially struck at the Philadelphia Mint.

In March 1958, Lee Hewitt, founder and editor of the *Numismatic Scrapbook Magazine*, wrote:

"Various stories have circulated concerning issuance of the 1913 nickels, but actual proof of the circumstances surrounding their leaving the Mint has never been documented. As coinage of the buffalo type did not commence until February 21, 1913, the Mint had almost two months to strike the Liberty head type and supply all the demand from collectors, had the Mint been so inclined. Collectors, at least until recent years, have felt that the Mint was unethical in striking a few pieces instead of including both types in the 1913 Proof set, therefore the coin did not bring a price commensurate with its rarity.

"In addition to the five 1913 Liberty head pieces, there is a 1913 buffalo nickel in copper, and the Farouk catalogue, lot number 2029, listed a 1913 Buffalo without artist's initials.

"Stories, theories, rumors, or what have you concerning these coins boil down to three main versions:

"(1) They were struck to exchange for coins needed for the Mint Collection.

"(2) The coiner and engraver were amusing themselves and struck the pieces which years later found their way onto the numismatic market.

"(3) They were struck exclusively for a wealthy collector.

"Regardless of the 'why' of issue, under standard mint practices of the period all that was necessary for those who were responsible for their striking was to pay the Proof and Medal Fund eight cents for each coin and walk out of the Mint building with them."

In the September 1963 *Numismatic Scrapbook Magazine* Lee Hewitt further commented, "unless the order for the buffalo nickel design was received in mid-summer of 1912, the engraving department probably changed the 1912 hub to 1913 as a matter of routine, and the five specimens of the 1913 Liberty head nickel are die trials."

Don Taxay, writing in 1963, was the first to disclose that Samuel W. Brown, the first man to publish, set a price on, and display all five 1913 Liberty head nickels, was an ex-curator of the Mint collection who, in 1913, was still employed at the Mint as storekeeper. Taxay went on to say that in his opinion the 1913 Liberty head nickels were not trial pieces or set-up pieces to test the dies but, rather, they were made by or for Brown as a caprice.

Eric P. Newman, a former 1913 Liberty head nickel owner and one of America's best-known numismatic scholars, also wrote about the 1913 nickel in 1963:

"I still have the special leather case made for these nickels and formerly had the opportunity to study all five coins at one time. The important fact which I think should be further emphasized is that Samuel W. Brown, original owner of all five nickels, was guilty of deceptive practices from which one could conclude that the coins were improperly or unlawfully acquired by him.

"He worked for the Philadelphia Mint in various capacities from December 18, 1903, until his resignation on November 14, 1913. Although a coin collector and a member of the American Numismatic Association since 1906, he kept the nickels he obtained secret for seven years and told no one about them. [This is in reference to the fact that the existence of the 1913 Liberty nickel was not positively known until 1920.] He obviously feared disclosure of them He then advertised in *The Numismatist*, beginning in December 1919 to buy for $500 (later $600) 1913 Liberty nickels which were then unknown and which he knew no one else could have. Why should he want to buy such a coin when he already had five of them? . . . The reason was to build up the prices of the pieces he possessed.

"In the summer of 1920 he showed the pieces, privately, in the special case at the Chicago American Numismatic Association convention and said that the disclosure was off the record . . . When asked, he did not reveal how he obtained them . . ."

When the nickels were first shown publicly they caused quite a stir. The October 1920 issue of *The Numismatist*, reporting on the American Numismatic

Association convention in Chicago the preceding August, commented:

"Samuel W. Brown of North Tonawanda, New York, was present for a short time on Monday. He had with him a specimen of the latest rarity in United States coinage—the nickel of 1913 of the Liberty head type. It was among the exhibits during the remainder of the convention with a label announcing that it was valued at $600, which amount Mr. Brown announced he is ready to pay for all Proof specimens offered to him.

"An explanation of its rarity is that at the close of 1912, the Mint authorities not having received orders to use the dies of the buffalo type nickel at the beginning of 1913, prepared a master die of the Liberty head type dated 1913, and from this master die a few pieces—believed to be five—in Proof were struck. None of these are believed to have been placed in circulation."

Brown was again the subject of an article in *The Numismatist*, his obituary, in August 1944:

"Samuel W. Brown, 64, of North Tonawanda, New York, died on June 17th, after a year's illness. A native of Pennsylvania, he had resided in North Tonawanda for many years, taking an active part in civic affairs, serving as mayor for several terms, and for ten years was a member of the Board of Education. Before leaving his native state he was employed for a time as storekeeper in the Mint at Philadelphia, and afterwards located himself in New York State. He at one time was appointed a member of the Assay Commission. His former membership in the American Numismatic Association was acquired many years ago, his number being 808."

Considering Mr. Brown's record of public service in North Tonawanda and the fact that he openly advertised for 1913 Liberty head nickels in a national publication, one might think that Brown was secure in his position regarding the coins and risked no scandal or unfavorable investigation. It is certainly possible that he obtained the pieces legally, although perhaps not openly. In the same manner, Superintendent of the San Francisco Mint J. Daggett acquired two or three 1894-S dimes at the time of issue and gave one to his daughter, Hallie. Although the reasons may have been different, it is interesting to note that the existence of the 1894-S dime, today a great rarity, was not known or suspected by numismatists until the year 1900, six years after its issuance—which, coincidentally, was the nearly same length of time that the 1913 Liberty nickel remained a secret.

In 1924 August Wagner, a Philadelphia stamp dealer, offered the five coins for sale at $2,000 for the lot. The purchaser was Colonel Edward H.R. Green, who kept them until his death.

Green, born in England in 1868, was the son of Edward H. Green and Hetty Howland Robinson. Be-

fore he was 20 years of age his right leg was amputated seven inches above the knee. Even so, he was imposing in stature and stood six-feet four-inches tall and weighed 300 pounds.

Courtney Coffing and Clyde Mervis, historians of the 1913 Liberty head nickel, reported that just after reaching his 22nd birthday in September 1890, Green and "some of the boys" visited Chicago's red light district one evening. There he was charmed by Mabel Harlow, tall, redheaded, and attracted to money. She was variously known as Mrs. M. E. Staunton, Mrs. Wilson, Kitterage, de Vries, or Campbell.

Arthur H. Lewis, in *The Day They Shook the Plum Tree*, the biography of Hetty Green, prints a recollection of Mary Cammack, of Texas, concerning Mabel:

"Mabel was beautiful and had long, wavy, red hair which she would let down to her hips. She used to allow my older sister to comb it out for her. She used lots of makeup, but on her it looked good."

Green was given the Texas Midland Railroad by his mother, who made a fortune in Wall Street, to play with as other children play with electric and spring-powered trains. Green was never happier than when he rode in the cab of a steam engine on the TMRR. His palatial Pullman car was variously called *999, Mabel,* and *Lone Star.*

Hetty Green, his mother, died on July 1, 1916, and on July 10, 1916, Edward and Mabel were married, following a courtship of 26 years. Estates were established at Round Hill, near New Bedford, Massachusetts, and Star Island in Biscayne Bay in Florida. At Star Island was stored among other things a vault full of pornographic films, a collection considered to be the most extensive in the world.

Colonel Green died on June 8, 1938, at Lake Placid, New York, with Mabel at his side. William Snyder, a Philadelphia coin dealer, helped appraise the Green estate. He wrote, "What also bothered collectors was that he hung on to almost everything, even when he had a complete monopoly. Take the 1913 Liberty head nickels. If you were a coin collector when you were a kid you must have seen ads in magazines which read: 'will pay up to $10,000 for a 1913 Liberty head nickel.'

"Naturally kids went nuts when examining five-cent pieces whenever they saw them. The ad was probably placed by Colonel Green as a practical joke. The truth is that 1913 was the year the buffalo nickel was minted, and there weren't supposed to have been any more Liberty heads . . . He was simply having fun, providing excitement, and creating lots of new collectors."

Following dispersal of the Green estate the five 1913 Liberty nickels, still intact as a group, went to Burdette G. Johnson, a St. Louis, Missouri, dealer who did a large

wholesale business. He was known as "a dealer's dealer" in the trade. Johnson enlisted the assistance of Dayton, Ohio, dealer James F. Kelly, years later to be one of the founders of Paramount International Coin Corporation, to offer the nickels to collectors.

In 1967, when describing the 1913 Liberty head nickel in a catalogue, Kelly wrote:

"There has always been, and always will be, considerable mystery surrounding the origin of the 1913 Liberty head nickel. For what it may be worth, it is my opinion that these coins were struck at the Mint during the period when the dies for the buffalo nickel were being prepared. I base this opinion on extensive conversations with the late James Macallister, B.G. Johnson, and Ira Reed during that period when I handled three of these nickels.

"The reason for the person or persons involved in striking these coins and obtaining them from the Mint, along with withholding knowledge of their existence, can only be speculation and never a known fact . . ."

The coins were subsequently dispersed to various collectors, including King Farouk of Egypt, who obtained two of them. One specimen, the coin I offered for sale in 1975, was sold by Farouk a few years before he was ousted as king in 1952. In 1953 Farouk's properties were sold at auction. The royal treasures included the largest stamp collection in the world and a coin collection which comprised 8,500 specimens in gold and 164 in platinum, not to overlook silver, nickel, and copper pieces. The presentation, as it turned out, was haphazard, with many coins being put into large lots. The 1913 Liberty nickel was mixed in together with dozens of less valuable pieces! Purchasers were Sol Kaplan and Abe Kosoff who sold it to the Honorable and Mrs. R. Henry Norweb. In 1978 the Norwebs presented this specimen to the Smithsonian Institution.

All of the facts concerning the 1913 Liberty head nickel will never be known. Perhaps it is better this way, for certainly speculations and stories concerning the coin have provided fascinating reading for a long time!

The successor to the Liberty head nickel, the Indian or buffalo design, made its appearance in circulation on schedule in 1913. The portrait on the obverse is a composite of three Indians including Two Moons, Chief John Tree, and Irontail. Black Diamond, a bison in New York's Central Park Zoo, furnished the inspiration for the reverse.

It is interesting to speculate why the American Indian, who suffered terrible and unending abuse, discrimination, and appropriation of property during the nineteenth and early twentieth centuries, was selected by the government, main perpetrator of these abuses, as the subject for one-cent pieces (1859-1909), nickel five-cent pieces (1913-1938), and $10 gold coins (1907-1933). Likewise, the American Indian formed a beautiful motif for one of the most popular of all styles of American currency, the $5 Silver Certificate of 1899.

Following a minor alteration of the reverse ground beneath the buffalo in late 1913, the design remained constant until 1938.

Collectors today are enchanted by several interesting variations within the Indian or buffalo nickel series. One type of 1916 nickel has the date appearing twice, the result of a shift in the master hub die when the coining die was produced. Another variety is the 1918 Denver issue with 8 over 7 in the date. This overdate is exceedingly rare in higher grades for it was many years after 1918 when it was first called to the attention of numismatists, by which time the opportunity to easily obtain Uncirculated specimens had long since passed.

The problem of metal hardness surfaced throughout the buffalo nickel series, with the result that many issues in collectors' hands today, especially Denver and San Francisco coins of the 1920s, are weakly struck. 1926 Denver issues are particularly outstanding in this regard. A freshly-minted coin more often than not was so weakly struck that apart from the mint lustre on the surfaces it looked as though it had been in circulation for many years!

A famous variety is the 1937 Denver issue with three legs to the buffalo rather than four. The 1937 "three-legged buffalo" was the result of the front leg filling in on the die.

Two interesting incidents concerning this coin come to mind. The first involves Jim Ruddy when we were business partners in Johnson City, New York, many years ago. Parking in front of the Fair Store in nearby Binghamton, Jim was about to put a nickel into a parking meter. At the time buffalo nickels were plentiful in circulation, so little thought was given to parting with this particular one—except that a quick glance showed that it was slightly different. Wait a minute! It's a rarity! Jim, a moment before it went into the meter, rescued a sharp specimen of this prized 1937-D three-leg oddity, the only really rare issue of any coin he ever found in circulation.

The second recollection concerns Henry G. Spagenberger, "Hank," who was in charge of our United States Coin Department in the early 1960s. One afternoon he received a telephone call from a local lady who informed him that she had a "three-legged buffalo" and invited him to come to see it and make an offer.

The next day Hank, having called upon the lady the evening before, returned to the office with a twinkle in his eye. "I bought the three-legged buffalo," he said,

"and here it is." He then handed me a small statue of a buffalo with one missing leg! As it turned out, the lady thought we were in the antique business and was seriously offering us a three-legged buffalo without knowing that this was the name of one of America's most popular coin varieties!

Another interesting story concerning the early 1960s, not at all germane to the present discussion of nickels, but interesting anyway, was related to me by John Murbach:

Around 1961 there was a brisk trade in 1960 small date Proof coins. Sets with this feature contained a Lincoln cent with numerals ever so slightly smaller than those found on the large date variety. Whereas a 1960 large date set was worth scarcely more than a few dollars, a set with a 1960 small date cent commanded a price of $15 or more. The difference in the date sizes was very slight, and many people, even dealers, had difficulty differentiating them unless they checked the pieces carefully.

It seemed as though a particular dealer made a specialty in 1960 small date Proof sets and ran advertisements soliciting their purchase. In response to this, another dealer who had a couple dozen sets checked them rather carefully to determine they were 1960 small dates and then posted them to the prospective buyer. Instead of the anticipated check there came a check for a smaller amount plus the notation: "Sorry, some of these are large date Proof sets and are returned herewith."

Well, he could have made a mistake in checking, so he thought. Another shipment was ready to go to the same dealer for purchase, so before sending it the seller doublechecked so there would be no mistakes this time. A week or so passed, and instead of receiving the check in full a smaller check came with a similar notation: "Sorry, the large date sets we can't use and are returned herewith—we only kept the small date sets."

His suspicions aroused, the dealer decided to send one more shipment. First, he carefully put a secret mark on each Proof set packaging envelope. Sure enough, back came a check for a smaller amount plus several large date Proof sets with a note regretting that large date Proof sets weren't wanted. Upon examination the large date Proof sets proved indeed to be large date Proof sets, but they weren't the sets sent by the selling dealer!

The dealer, justifiably annoyed, came up with an interesting idea—one which is quite humorous, apart from the damage involved: A few weeks later he contacted the Proof set specialist and asked to buy a group of Proof sets of another scarce date, the 1955. The Proof set specialist, perhaps smug in the knowledge that his switching of small date for large date Proof sets hadn't been noticed and happy that the dealer still wanted to do business with him, complied quickly and sent a nice shipment of pristine 1955 sets, as nice as the day they left the Mint.

Our dealer friend, stung by the past fraud and deception, took an eating fork and stabbed the surface of each 1955 Proof set, scratching and disfiguring the coins therein.

The sets were then returned to the dealer who sent them, with the note, "I am sorry, but I cannot use these 1955 Proof sets for they appear to have *fork marks* on them!"

Back to nickels . . .

Occasionally during a discussion with a collector I am asked about numismatic research, a long-time interest of mine. I then will tell of the many discoveries that Jim Ruddy and I have made over the years, including quite a few overdates and other varieties not previously known to numismatists. "There is not much encouragement for the researcher today, for all of the important discoveries have already been made," is a comment I hear often.

Not so. In fact, this reminds me of the story in which it was suggested that the United States Patent Office close its doors in the 1840s shortly after its inception, for all of the things worth inventing had already been invented!

In 1978 the 1943/2 overdate nickel, a variety not previously known to numismatists, received coverage in coin publications, with the result that by April of that year several dozen were known! Several years earlier the variety had not even been dreamed of! Likewise, Rarcoa, the Chicago coin firm, disclosed the existence of an 1870-S Liberty seated half dime, a mint mark variety hitherto unsuspected. And, who knows, next year and the year after may see even more exciting discoveries.

For me one of the most significant such occurrences was the verification in 1961 of the 1938-D/S *overmintmark* buffalo nickel. Two Jamestown, New York dealers, C.G. Langworthy and Robert Kerr, discovered the variety, a coin with the letter D sharply punched over a previous letter S, and contacted *Coin World*, the weekly numismatic newspaper, about it. They called upon me to authenticate this startling issue, a coin which actually appeared to have two distinct and different mintmarks, both a D and an S!

While several overmintmarks have been discovered since then, in 1961 this was shocking news. No one had ever heard of, seen, or even suspected that such a variety existed. There were plenty of overdates, one date numeral punched over another, but no varieties of what were later designated as overmintmarks. This sensational news made exciting reading on the front page of *Coin World* shortly thereafter. It was one of the most spectacular discoveries of modern times.

TODAY!

Inside
COIN
WORLD

● BUFFALO BACKGROUND
Page 2

● MORE MESSMA FOR ANNIE
Page 3

● MILITARY DOCUMENTARY
Page 20

Coin World

THE WEEKLY NEWSPAPER OF THE ENTIRE NUMISMATIC FIELD

Vol. 3, Issue No. 100   SIDNEY, OHIO, FRIDAY, MARCH 16, 1962   Single Copy 25c

Coin World will pay for news tips which, in the judgment of the editor, merit it.

New Yorkers Uncover Major Variety Of Buffalo Nickel

Discoverer . . . Discovery . . .

C. G. Langworthy, discoverer of the 1938 D over S mintmark Buffalo nickel variety, checks his find with another lucky owner, Robert Kerr (left) in the Langworthy shop, Jamestown Coin Supply, Jamestown, N.Y., in the top photo. Bottom picture is an enlarged section of the 1938-D Buffalo nickel with the D mintmark punched over a previous S mintmark—labeled the numismatic find of the century.

U. S. Mint Asks For More Funds

Miss Eva Adams, director of the Mint, has asked the House Appropriations Committee to raise the mint's operating budget by $542,000 and to give it $560,000 worth of new equipment.

Miss Adams, according to testimony made public recently, detailed to congress a series of reasons for the increase.

Miss Adams, according to news dispatches, said the demand for coins has more than doubled since 1958.

In that year, about 1.5 billion new coins were needed—about the same as 100 years before.

In 1958, however, the figure jumped to 2.5 billion coins, in 1960 to 3 billion and last year to 3.3 billion.

She was quoted as saying that the budget increase will provide for production of 3,370,000,000 cents, nickels, dimes, quarters and halves in 1963.

As she asked Congress for more money so she can make more money, Miss Adams detailed:

Americans are spending money so fast even the U. S. Mint can't keep up.

Banks in the New York area ran out of nickels just before Christmas last year.
(Continued on Page 3)

Experts Label 1938-D/S Mintmark 'Find' Of Century

Discovery of a major United States coinage variety—a 1938-D Buffalo nickel with a D over S mintmark—has been reported by two men in Jamestown, N. Y.

C. G. Langworthy, 35, a coin dealer, and Robert Kerr, 37, a fireman, both of Jamestown, made the find which electrified the numismatic world.

Q. David Bowers, partner in the Empire Coin Co., Inc., Binghamton, N. Y., was the first recognized numismatic authority to authenticate the coin.

The variety has been described as the "find of the century." It is said to be without parallel in domestic coinage history.

Four of the coins with the superimposed mintmark are known to exist. Langworthy found three, and Kerr, one. Bowers bought one from the Jamestown dealer.

"I personally examined and found to be genuine and unequivocal in all respects a 1938-D Buffalo nickel with the D mintmark punched clearly and sharply over a previous S mintmark," said Bowers in Binghamton. He also tested the coin to see if it was an electrotype; this test was negative.

He said the Langworthy coin was in nearly uncirculated condition, which aided him in making the identification positive.

"As a coin with two different mintmarks, each clearly distinguishable, the 1938-D/S nickel is unique in American numismatics," said Bowers.

"It will certainly come to be known as the most outstanding error on a U. S. coin."

Although only four of the rarities are known at the present time, this picture was expected to change as soon as news of the find reached the public, and the thundering herd of collectors and pseudo-collectors begin a battle of the buffalos across the nation in a search of counterparts.

The discoverers of the variety, Langworthy and Kerr, were schooled in varieties of coinage, but they were totally unprepared for the find.

For 24 years, 40 rolls of 1938-D Buffalo nickels had remained stored in Langworthy's collection, bank-sealed and uncirculated. Six months ago, the dealer decided to transfer them into coin tubes.

"'Just for the fun of it, I decided to check them," Langworthy said. "I took a look at the first coin on top, and there it was! A D mintmark over an S!"

Excitedly, the Jamestown collector-dealer scanned the remainder of his coins. One more of the variety emerged.

"I nearly went blind, looking at them," Langworthy grinned. Later he found a third coin with the D/S mintmark.

Langworthy took his good friend, Bob Kerr, into his confidence and showed him the find.

Kerr began a search quietly and emerged with a fourth specimen.

"We were afraid to say anything," admitted Kerr. "There are so many varieties and oddities; I guess we thought we might appear ridiculous.

"But I had it on my mind all the time. I spent hours with my eyes glued on a 10 power glass, looking . .

"When I found my D over S, I thought, 'Man, that sure looks like an S!' And it was!"

The two men have been friends for a long time; they began their friendship across the counter of Langworthy's shop.

Kerr is married and a World War II veteran. He has been interested in coins since boyhood. He served in the European theater of war, but there was little time for coin collecting, he said. He was with the infantry.

Langworthy has owned and operated the Jamestown Coin Supply, 25 North Main Street, for the past 10 years. Prior to this time he drove a bus.

Unmarried, and unaffiliated with any formal numismatic organizations, Langworthy meets his fellow collectors on the convention-show circuit. He attends as many of these as he can. He is planning to attend the Youngs-
(Continued on Page 2)

Bowers Agrees To Check Coins

Coin World readers who discover specimens of the 1938-D/S in their collections or stock are invited to send them to:

**Q. David Bowers
O'Neil Building
Binghamton, New York**

Bowers has agreed to authenticate all specimens sent to him free of charge. Names of the owners will be published in Coin World; a list of all conditions will also be published.

Coins must be sent insured; and postage for return shipment is to be included.

Don Sherer Gets Formal Appointment To ANA Post

Don Sherer, of Phoenix, Ariz., today is officially the 16th general secretary of the American Numismatic Association.

Formal appointment of Sherer to the key post of the world's biggest numismatic organization came over the March 2-4 weekend in Chicago.

Here the A.N.A. officers and board of governors met in special session at the Oak Park Arms Hotel to formalize Sherer's appointment.

Sherer has been acting general secretary since the death of Lewis M. Reagan December 29 in Wichita. Reagan had served as general secretary of the organization for 17 years.

Transition of duties to Sherer, assistant to Reagan since 1959, was achieved without disruption of the complete affairs of the A.N.A. thanks to a foresighted set of officials.

They created the assistant's post in 1959 as insurance against any emergencies; Sherer has been completely informed of A.N.A. affairs since that time.

Headquarters for the A.N.A. will be moved to Phoenix within the near future from Wichita. Correspondence, however, should continue to go to Wichita until all details of the move are completed.

Mrs. Ada Winex, of the A.N.A. staff of Wichita, will go to Phoenix temporarily to aid in the establishment of the new headquarters, and to assist in training new personnel.

The entire group of A.N.A. officials assembled in Chicago for the session with C. C. Shroyer, of Fremont, Ohio, presiding.

Secretary Sherer is no stranger to his fellow numismatists—he has traveled from coast to coast during his years of devoted service to the A.N.A.

A past National Coin Week chairman, and former A.N.A. board of governor member, Sherer is a past president of the Phoenix Coin Club.

A former executive in the Folger Coffee Company and the Goodyear Corp., Sherer was affiliated with the Phoenix Valley Bank before he established his own firm, Don Sherer and Associates, Real Estate Investments, in Phoenix.

Secretary Sherer joins illustrious company as he officially takes over his duties. Former secretaries and general secretaries of the A.N.A. include the following:

1891—Charles T. Tatman, Worcester, Mass.
1892-94—O. W. Page, Waltham, Mass.
1895—George W. Rice, Detroit.
1896—Dr. George F. Heath, Monroe, Mich.
1904-07—Howland Wood, Brookline, Mass.
1908-09—Frank G. Duffield, Baltimore.
1910—George L. Tilden, Worcester, Mass.
1911-15—Waldo C. Moore, Lewisburg, Ohio.
1916-18—John M. Oliver, Springfield, Mass.
1919-20—H. H. Yawger, Rochester, N. Y.
1921—Aldren Scott Boyer, Chicago.
1922—J. M. Swanson, Newark, N. J.
1923-38—Harry T. Wilson, Chicago, Ill.
1938-44—M. Vernon Sheldon, Chicago.
1944-1961—Lewis M. Reagan, Wichita, Kansas.

TOTAL PAID SUBSCRIPTIONS

THIS ISSUE 87,160

ONE YEAR AGO 45,449

TOTAL DISTRIBUTION

THIS ISSUE 95,638

NOTE: IF THE NUMBER OPPOSITE YOUR ADDRESS IS **102** IT'S TIME TO RENEW!
See Index For Subscription Blank

First revealed to the collecting fraternity in the March 16, 1962 issue of "Coin World," the 1938-D/S "overmintmark" nickel was labeled the "find of the century." Although overdate (one date numeral punched over another) coins were known for many instances, never before had an overmintmark come to light. "Coin World" called upon Q. David Bowers to verify and authenticate the variety. In weeks and months that followed, hundreds of additional specimens came to light. To illustrate that significant numismatic discoveries can still be made in today's era, in the years since 1962 a number of other overmintmarks have come to light in the nickel series and elsewhere. Perhaps even more remain to be discovered by some lucky finder.

How was the 1938-D/S buffalo nickel created? I can only surmise. In that year, the last year buffalo nickels were coined, no pieces were struck at Philadelphia and none at San Francisco. Coinage was slated only for the Denver Mint. This was in contrast to the previous year, 1937, when buffalo nickels had been struck at all three coining locations.

Each year dies, including those designated for Denver and San Francisco, were prepared at Philadelphia. My theory is that late in 1937 or early in 1938, at least two dies (for there are two slightly different varieties of the 1938-D/S known today) were made in Philadelphia with S mintmarks on the reverse, designated for shipment to San Francisco. Also, dies were made with D mintmarks for shipment to Denver. It then developed that no coins were to be produced in San Francisco that year. There was no reason to save the S-mintmarked dies for the following year, for this was to be the last year of the buffalo nickel, so the dies would be useless. As an economy measure the two (at least) S-mintmarked dies were overpunched with a D mintmark and sent to Denver for use in regular coinage.

When I saw my first 1938-D/S nickel I considered it to be a rarity, perhaps a fantastic rarity. Were there just a few specimens known? Or would dozens or hundreds turn up? Perhaps it was as rare as the 1913 Liberty head nickel. I didn't know.

Following the publication of the initial announcement in *Coin World* I received letters and telephone calls from all parts of the United States. In following weeks and months many 1938-D/S nickels turned up, a few at first, then several dozen, and within a year or two, several hundred. Investors and hoarders with rolls of 1938-D buffalo nickels looked through them in the hopes of finding the coveted D/S variety. At least two Kansas City collectors struck a bonanza and found several rolls. My firm started an active business in the variety, and thousands of dollars in checks were sent to these two fortunate collectors. Today I suspect that there are several thousand 1938-D/S nickels known. The variety is still much scarcer than the 1938-D nickel without the overmintmark feature, but it is hardly a great rarity. The point of all this is to show that new things can be discovered in modern times.

1938 marked the last year of the Indian/buffalo design. A national competition was announced whereby all American sculptors were invited to submit designs for a new nickel. The prize of $1,000 was awarded to Felix Schlag, a German-born Chicago resident. Schlag's obverse portraying Thomas Jefferson was kept intact as he submitted it. The reverse, originally designed with an angular view of Jefferson's home, Monticello, was redesigned to a full-front vista.

With the series containing several interesting and scarce varieties interspersed among dozens of regular issues from three mints, the numismatist today can look upon a long line of Jefferson nickels dating back to the first year of issue, 1938.

While stories of nickels themselves make fascinating reading, stories of how these coins were used in commerce can be equally interesting. To me this is a great part of the lure of numismatics. Hold a worn coin in your hand, perhaps a Liberty nickel of the year 1900, think of its background—the places it has been, the things that it has seen, the things that it has done—and magically you are away from today's rush-rush age of computers, jet planes, microwave ovens, shopping centers, and the like.

> *Tell me nickel where you've been*
> *The things you've done, the things you've seen*
> *If you could speak, what would you say*
> *About the glories of yesterday?*

Around the turn of the century a pocketful of nickels could open up a wonderland of experiences.

By the 1890s a popular novelty for entertainment in the home was the motion picture. No, not the full-screen movie films of today, but small devices, often designed for parlor use, which projected or displayed series of acrobats who tossed balls and stood on their heads, horses which jumped over barriers, and other animated scenes. All were produced by means of spinning discs, hand-cranked moving glass slides, and other gadgets. Such curiously-named devices as the *Zoetrope*, the *Praxinoscope-Theatre*, the *Phenakistascope*, the *Viviscope*, and, in contrast, the simply-named *Wheel of Life*, entertained those who could afford them.

Thomas Edison, the wizard of Menlo Park, began experimenting with pictures in motion in 1888. In 1889 his laboratory devised a crude projector which used celluloid film. This device, which was approximately synchronized with an early Edison spring-wound cylinder phonograph, was designated as the *Kinetophonograph*. The screen images were poor at best, so Edison scrapped the idea in preference to a peep-show type of machine which permitted one customer at a time to view a smaller but sharper picture through a glass lens. As he did with the phonograph (which he considered to be a business device primarily and an entertainment device a distant second), Edison doubted that film projection on a screen would have much popular appeal. Thus, he patented his device only in the United States and ignored the rest of the world. This miscalculation was to cost him millions of dollars in profits in years to come!

In 1891 the *Kinetoscope*, a peep-show device which used a continuous 50-foot loop of film, was patented. This gadget achieved immediate popularity, and within a

A CURIOUS ADAPTATION OF THE PRAXINOSCOPE.

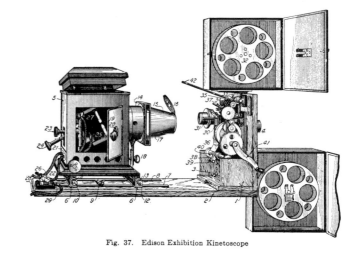

Fig. 37. Edison Exhibition Kinetoscope

At the upper left is shown a very early projector, an adaptation of the Praxinoscope, a popular parlor entertainment device. At the upper right is an Edison Exhibition Kinetoscope, a motion picture projector from the 1910 era. Below is shown an advertisement for films and projection devices. Photographers from Edison and other filmmakers would roam the world in search of interesting subjects, as these varied Hawaiian films illustrate.

few years arcades lined with coin-operated cylinder phonographs and Kinetoscopes were a common sight in larger cities, often operating under the *Edisonia* name.

Meanwhile, other experimenters, primarily in Europe, took up where Edison left off and made many improvements to the full-screen projector. By 1896 several competitors were in the field. In that year Edison produced the *Vitascope*, a full-screen silent projector. Historians generally agree that the first "movie" shown to a paying audience was that projected in Koster and Bial's Music Hall on April 23, 1896, in New York City. The next day the *New York Times* wrote that "an unusually bright light fell upon the screen. Then came into view two precious blond persons of the variety stage, in pink and blue dresses, doing the umbrella dance with commendable celerity. Their motions were all clearly defined."

Within two months the Lumiere brothers, who had built a large firm in France which manufactured projectors, cameras, and also shot films, introduced a competitor, the *Cinematographe*, to America. Thousands flocked to Keith's Theatre in New York's Union Square to view the spectacles. A few months later, in October 1896, the American Mutoscope Company, a manufacturer of hand-cranked peep-show machines which used a series of photographic cards flipped and viewed in rapid succession, introduced the *Biograph* at Hammerstein's Olympia Music Hall in the same city.

By the end of 1896 theatres were drawing crowds all over the United States. In St. Louis the *Chronicle* reported that at the Century Theatre audiences were treated to realistic views including "the Empire State Express coming toward the audience at the rate of 60 miles an hour."

The New Haven *News* reported on November 23rd that Poli's Wonderland Theatre was to begin an exhibition of the Biograph: "Interest in this great American invention for the display of moving photographs has reached a high degree, and there is certain to be a crush at the popular theatre all this week. . . One of the most popular in the collection shows President-elect McKinley strolling around on his lawn and reading congratulatory telegrams brought to him by his secretary. So natural and lifelike is this view that it seems to the spectator as if Major McKinley himself were there instead of his picture. Other immensely popular views are Niagara Falls, the Empire State Express, a Republican parade at Canton, Joe Jefferson in the drinking scene as 'Rip Van Winkle,' and little Billee and Trilby. It is a display that will cause astonishment and delight."

By 1902 the re-named American Mutoscope and Biograph Company offered film, mainly of 25-foot and 50-foot length, featuring dozens of different subjects.

How'd You Like to be the Ice Man? featured a drama in which "the ice man enters the house and is finely entertained." Possibly in the same category was *The New Maid*, in which "the wife finds her husband making love to the maid and punishes him." These early screen pictorials were hardly pornographic; indeed, a kiss was considered risque.

Other early Biograph topics included *Aunt Jane's Experience with Tabasco Sauce* (old lady puts plenty of sauce on her oysters, gets badly burned), *How Nora Entertained Officer Duffy* (youngster puts firecrackers in a pan of flour, and a policeman is covered with white), *Five Minutes to Train Time* (baby is packed in a trunk and comes out completely flattened), *A Patient Sufferer* (boys throw a dead cat in the doctor's hall; doctor assaults his patient, mistaking him for the boys), *Champion Beer Drinker* (fat Dutchman drinks about 30 glasses of beer and then turns into a keg), and *A Non-Union Paper Hanger* (man affixing wallpaper, pail of paste flies in air, and man is covered with the contents).

1902 documentary subjects included *Pole Vaulting at Columbia University, Eeling Through the Ice* (fisherman chops a hole in the ice and spears for eels), *Skating in Central Park, New York City, Yale Football Squad of 1901, Ladies' Day at the Public Baths, Sailors of the Atlantic Fleet,* and *Starting a Skyscraper,* the latter a view of "the immense excavation for the foundation of the new Macy Building in New York City." The new Macy Building, by the way, was built on the site of Koster and Bial's Theatre, the place where it all started.

Before 1902, projected motion pictures were shown in opera houses and vaudeville theatres, often as part of an extensive program which featured live entertainment as well. In that year the Electric Theatre was opened in Los Angeles by Thomas L. Tally and became the first specially-constructed permanent motion picture theatre in America. Three years later the first nickelodeon theatre opened. Located in Pittsburgh, it showed one- and two-reel subjects for the admission price of a nickel. The term *nickelodeon* was thus derived: *nickel* for the price of admission and *odeon,* the Greek word for *theatre.* By 1910 there were close to 10,000 nickelodeons in the United States and thousands more overseas.

Typically such a theatre was a Coney Island of electrical gimmickry. On the front were often hundreds of flashing bulbs and bright lights to draw the passerby, often with a sign such as *Bijou Dream 5c,* or *5c/Dreamland/5c.* On Locust Street, near 7th, in Des Moines, Iowa, a large lighted electric sign proclaimed that *Nickeldom* offered moving pictures and illustrated songs to anyone caring to part with a five-cent piece.

By the 1910-1914 years nickelodeons were big business. In the motion picture industry the nickel was king!

Above: Two Vitagraph films were available at 12c per foot in 1907. It would be fun today to see "The Bad Man" which was described as "a vividly dramatic production, replete with thrilling situations, ending in a hair-raising climax," or the other film "Fun in a Fotograf Gallery," which was noted as being "too funny to describe."

The hapless victim tied to railroad tracks, pictured at the lower left above, was a cliche in early thrillers.

Right: The Canton Metal Ceiling Company in 1911 offered prefabricated theatre fronts "made up in many artistic designs to suit individual taste, location, or purse." Most such installations were made by altering store fronts. The theatre inside usually had a flat floor. Patrons sat on movable wooden chairs and looked at the flickering screen in the front of the room.

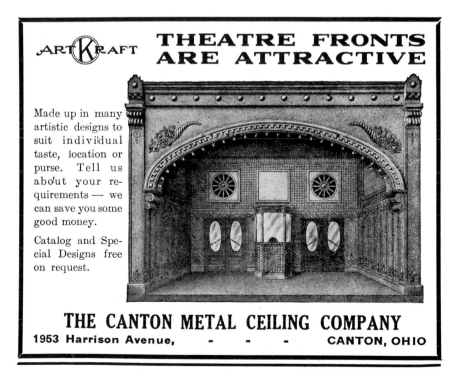
FOR MUTUAL BENEFIT, MENTION THE BILLBOARD WHEN WRITING ADVERTISERS.

S.L. Baxter, who opened the magnificent Isis Theatre at 1724 Curtis Street, Denver, in 1913, started business with a small nickelodeon theatre in 1906. His first effort consisted of a rented storefront with electrical signs out front and, inside, rows of kitchen chairs on which the patrons sat to watch the one- and two-reel adventures. The Isis, Baxter's crowning achievement, had a seating capacity of 2,000 and was billed as "one of the finest theatres in the country, drawing an ultra high-class patronage." Music was supplied by a tremendous Wurlitzer theatre pipe organ, "the largest instrument ever installed in any theatre in the world," which set the owner back $50,000.

Further along Curtis Street in Denver, at no. 1751, was located the Paris Theatre, a huge structure which was described as: "Unquestionably the largest theatre in the United States giving a high-grade program for 5c. Seats 2,200. Represents a capitalization of $250,000, paid up. The front of the theatre is of such exceptionally artistic and elaborate treatment that it has been copied many times. The Paris Theatre also is noted for having the greatest amount of electricity used in any theatre front."

The finances of the Paris Theatre are amazing to contemplate today. With a five-cent admission charge the establishment took in just $110 totally when all 2,200 seats were filled! One wonders whether the "capitalization of $250,000, paid up" was ever recouped by the shareholders!

The Cyclopedia of Motion Pictures, a work published in 1911, gives detailed instructions how to set up a nickelodeon theatre. Illustrated is a financial program for a country theatre in a town of 1,100 people. Expenses to operate the theatre for one week were: rent, $3.50; rental charges for eight reels of film, $12; electricity, $3; ticket seller's salary, $1; pianist, $2.50; coal (an expense only during the winter), $2; tickets, carbons for the projector, and miscellaneous, $1; and newspaper advertising, 50c, for a total expenditure of $25.50. Against this, were average weekly receipts of $45.00, representing a profit of nearly $20.00 a week for the owner-operator. On the other end of the financial spectrum were huge theatres such as the aforementioned Isis and Paris which accommodated thousands. Still, by today's standards receipts were small.

While the omnipresent nickel paid the bills and furnished profits, an occasional pitch was made for the dime:

"Double price. A 5c theatre may run on Saturday night at a 10-cent admission fee. This not only increases the gross receipts for Saturday evenings but acts as an advertising feature for the theatre. A better show should be given, to justify the double price, in order that the patrons may not think the double price is being charged merely because a manager can get it on Saturday. The program, however, should not require double time, or there will be no gain by the double price. It may be slightly longer in time, and may have advertisable differences in quality if desired."

Theatres became larger and more ornate. Costs rose. Theatre pipe organs such as those made by the Rudolph Wurlitzer Company in North Tonawanda, New York, and the competing products of the Robert-Morton Company in California, became a necessity, often at $10,000 to $50,000 per unit. Gone were the 25-foot and 50-foot reel movie scenarios of the turn-of-the-century style and in their place were more elaborate productions lasting over an hour. In the early days almost any type of action on the screen was sufficient to attract an audience. No mention was made of individuals or stars in the movie. *Keystone Comedy,* or *New Biograph Show,* or *Latest Essanay Film* on the marquee was sufficient to draw a crowd. That began to change as Charlie Chaplin, Mack Sennett, Buster Keaton, and others attracted followings. The star system was born.

All of this naturally increased the expense of operating a theatre. As a result, by the advent of World War I the nickel theatre was an anachronism. The Miles Theatre on Griswold Street in Detroit featured vaudeville acts and projected movies with an electric sign out front proclaiming admission charges of 10c, 20c, and 30c. 25c to 50c for adults and 10c to 25c for children became commonplace.

In the 1920s the "golden age of the motion picture palace" emerged with such fantastic edifices as New York's Roxy Theatre, Hollywood's Pantages and Grauman's Chinese theatres, and others costing hundreds of thousands if not a million dollars or more to build. Indeed, so proud was movie entrepreneur Sid Grauman of one of his Los Angeles houses that he named it the Million Dollar Theatre. The nickel disappeared, at least as the admission price. Still there was use for it in the theatre lobby where a nickel would buy a candy bar, a box of popcorn, a cigar, or a pack of gum. Curiously, the nickel pack of gum survived until the 1960s.

Speaking of nickels, the oft-quoted comment, "what this country needs is a good five-cent cigar" comes to mind. We haven't had a good five-cent cigar in a long time, and undoubtedly there are connoisseurs among us who argue that today we don't even have good fifty-cent or one-dollar cigars. However, around the turn of the century one could pass by a carved wooden cigar store Indian, go into a tobacco shop, and for a handful of Liberty nickels get in return several fine imported cigars. No longer.

Then there was nickel beer on draft. All during the 1890s and early 1900s a nickel would buy a large mug of beer at virtually any drinking establishment in America.

Wurlitzer Hope-Jones Unit Orchestra Installed in Isis Theatre, Denver

SEATING capacity, 2,000. One of the finest theatres in the country, drawing an ultra high-class patronage. A $50,000 Wurlitzer Unit Orchestra, the largest instrument ever installed in any theatre in the world, now supplies the music for this theatre. Mr. Samuel L. Baxter, Proprietor, states that he has gained an astonishing volume of new patronage, and that the first month after the installation of the Wurlitzer Hope-Jones Unit Orchestra was the biggest attendance month in ten years. Upon the opposite page we reproduce Mr. Baxter's letter, which tells interestingly, an exhibitor's actual experience with THREE kinds of music, and why he thinks that the Wurlitzer Hope-Jones Unit Orchestra provides the only logical music for the accompaniment of motion pictures.

The ornate Isis Theatre in Denver, circa 1913.

BUTTERFLY THEATRE, Milwaukee, Wis.
Most Luxurious, Exclusive, Refined
Photo-Play House in America.
Absolutely Fireproof—Perfect Ventilation.
Change of Program Daily.
Complete Change of Air Every 3 Minutes.

NIGHT ILLUMINATION, SAXE'S ORPHEUM THEATRE
5TH AND EDMOND STREETS, ST. JOSEPH, MO.

Around 1910 thousands of nickelodeon theatres dotted the American landscape. Admission was usually just a nickel or sometimes ten or fifteen cents for an especially long or interesting feature. As theatre owners scrambled to outdo each other, the fronts often resembled scenes from Arabian Nights. The Butterfly Theatre, shown above left, in Milwaukee, Wisconsin, featured a larger-than-life goddess in the form of a brilliantly illuminated butterfly. What a thrill it would be to see today!

To the left, the Arcade Theatre notes that any seat costs a nickel. "Come in and laugh," the placards beckoned.

MR. HURRY-UP

The Biograph's Latest Whirlwind of Comedy.

LENGTH, - - 620 FEET.

"Mr. Hurry-Up"

The well-known character of New York, on one of his strenuous days, made the more so by an aggravating toothache. This production shows him a veritable cyclone of energy. First enjoying (?) his hurried breakfast then rushing off to the office, where he is seized with a toothache. A wild dash for the dentist's, and the tooth is out, but the pain drives him to a neighboring cafe, where he overindulges in alcoholic delusion. Arriving home he is seized with a bounding, tossing, whirling delirium, which furnishes a fitting climax to the most laughable film ever produced

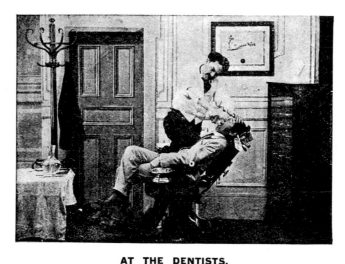

AT THE DENTISTS.

AT THE MONKEY HOUSE,

LENGTH, - - 247 FEET.

This is a real novelty—up-to-date and extremely funny. It shows a trip among the animals at Central Park, New York, ending with a visit to the monkey house, where the much-talked-of-incident of the flirtation of a famous tenor with a lady spectator is enacted.

AMERICAN MUTOSCOPE & BIOGRAPH CO.

11 E. 14th Street, NEW YORK CITY.

KLEINE OPTICAL CO., Chicago,
SPECIAL SELLING AGENTS.

PACIFIC COAST BRANCH:
116 N. BROADWAY, Los Angeles, Cal.

Above: This 1907 Biograph film was the "latest whirlwind of comedy." Many early films, once widely shown and advertised, are unknown today for the cellulose nitrate film base of which these were made has long since deteriorated.

Right: The Colonial Theatre in Bloomington, Illinois, circa 1908, offered many attractions for a nickel. Note that this was before the "star system" was born. Instead, the names of the film manufacturers, Biograph and Selig are given. Soon the system would change, and with it the nickel theater would be obsolete.

Then, too, there was the nickel lunch. How far removed from reality in today's world!

Until well into the 20th century a patron with a handful of nickels could have a veritable feast at any one of the Horn & Hardart Automats in New York City. Behind rows of metal-framed glass windows, looking like dozens of post office boxes, one could see tempting slices of pie, sandwiches, snacks, cookies, bread, and other things. The first Horn & Hardart Automat devices were made in Germany and imported to the United States shortly before 1890. Indeed, the term *automat* in German means *coin-operated*. Now, alas, the nickel automat is a thing of history. Visitors to the restaurant in the basement of the Smithsonian Institution's Museum of Science and Technology will see a Horn & Hardart Automat exhibited, not dispensing slices of lemon pie for a nickel, unfortunately, but just for historical purposes to remind us of the years of long ago.

Close to my own heart are coin-operated pianos and orchestrions of the 'teens and 'twenties. The nickel was king, too, in the field of automatic music. Drop a nickel into the beckoning slot of a large Style H Seeburg orchestrion and you would be rewarded with *Way Down Yonder in New Orleans, Barney Google,* or *Alexander's Ragtime Band,* played by a piano accompanied by two ranks of pipes, a chirpy xylophone, bass drum, snare drum, cymbal, triangle, and castanets—"equal to a seven-man orchestra," according to an original Seeburg advertisement.

Think of all the nickels that were spent in Woolworth's! Indeed, the term "five-and-ten-cent store" originated there. Inspired by this, the Link Piano Company of Binghamton, New York, produced an advertisement which read:

"If dollars are hard to get, go after profitable nickels with a Link piano. You'll find they soon amount to *dollars* of profit. A Link gathers the nickels that are 99% profit, yet amply repays its customers with the latest popular music, excellently played to perfect dance time. It's little nickels, largely profit, that count toward dividend dollars. Woolworth first proved the possibilities of profitable nickel sales. . . ."

The Electrova Company of New York City published a catalogue showing a cascade of Liberty nickels flowing into an open money bag. "In the lobby of a hotel in New York City the receipts in the cash box of an Electrova piano showed a record of $126.85 during the month of October 1911. This should look good to you if you are the proprietor of a hotel. And billiard parlors prove a fertile field in which to garner the nickels—20 of them make a dollar, you know. If you conduct a billiard parlor, it should not tax your credulity to believe that an Electrova, playing as it does, lively and inspiring music, would prove a large source of revenue from your patrons. And, let us remind you that this is extra money and you do not have to work for it."

Prohibition, which came to America in 1920 and which forced the closing of bars and saloons, was given a profitable aspect by the Operators Piano Company, manufacturer of *Coinola* pianos and orchestrions: "In dry territories everybody now has more money to spend legitimately. Therefore the nickels are flowing into Coinolas in most respectable places."

The Wurlitzer *Automatic Harp*, first marketed in 1905, featured a large harp played by tiny mechanical fingers which plucked the strings whenever a nickel was dropped in the slot. Approximately 1,500 of these were sold to buyers who were enticed by such advertising as "operated by a nickel-in-the-slot arrangement, it is not only a great attraction, but a money maker of no small proportion." For some reason the Cincinnati Zoo bought two! Perhaps one harp was for the monkeys!

Around the turn of the century the American Automusic Company of New York and its New England affiliate, the Auto-Manufacturing Company, marketed the *Encore*, a self-playing automatic banjo. Operated by a nickel, these devices were sold by the hundreds to restaurants, hotels, seaside resorts, saloons, and other public places. For a nickel one was rewarded with 90 seconds worth of banjo music; tunes such as *Swanee River* and *My Old Kentucky Home,* to mention two favorites.

John Keyes, proprietor of the Hotel Windsor in Altoona, Pennsylvania, apparently had an automatic banjo "on location" in nearby Johnstown, for he reported:

"For the six months that I have had the Encore it has never been out of order, which is something extraordinary for a slot machine. My machine in Johnstown has netted me as high as $50 in one week. It is not only a money earner but has also increased my business."

The Chicago *Chronicle* was so enamored of this device that it reported "this nickel-in-the-slot machine will call forth soul-stirring melodies. Returns are expected to exceed the yield of the Klondike region."

An *Encore* was shown at the Paris Exposition of 1900, a large world's fair, and received favorable mention from the awards jury.

Still there were some problems. Not everybody experienced a deluge of nickels. The Iola Cafe in Brockton, Massachusetts, had some problems with its banjo and wrote to F.R. Pendleton, president of the Auto-Manufacturing Company, who subsequently replied:

"We have been notified that your machine does not get enough patronage with the nickel slot, so we inform you that we think the Encore will pay better with a penny slot. Business has been so pressing here in Boston, and we have been putting out so many machines, that we are

"Money grows on trees," so implies this 1908 advertisement of the Rudolph Wurlitzer Company. Shown are all sorts of ways to spend a nickel: at the upper left patrons are literally standing in line to drop nickels in the slot of a huge PianOrchestra orchestrion. These immense instruments, made in Germany and marketed by Wurlitzer in the United States, sold at the time for $1,200 to $5,000 each. Many customers were able to recoup their investment via nickels in the coin slot within a few years. More modestly priced were such nickel grabbers as the Mandolin Quartette (which sounded like a group of mandolin players), the graceful Automatic Harp, and the tiny 44-note Pianino, the latter described as "the best 44-note nickel-in-the-slot piano on the market. A little gold mine for saloons and cafes."

all out of penny slots at this time. However, we expect to get more soon, and we will make the changeover for you.''

There were other problems as well. The same Pendleton had to write to W.E. Lyon, a collection agent, in Boston: ''You will remember that in the past we have given you small items for collection. We now have an item we would like to get settled and wish your services in the matter. We enclose an itemized bill for the amount, and give you the man's address. This bill was incurred by Mr. Babcock's having thrown a cut glass bowl through the front of our machine while in the store of Mr. M.C. Page, 124 Broad Street. He is liable for the amount and has promised payment, but has not done so. We hope you can collect this account and send us your check for $8 soon.''

On the other hand, there was always the prospect of new business, as this solicitation to the Dominion Atlantic Railway Company of Kentville, Nova Scotia, operator of trains and steamships, shows:

''We are aggressively introducing as a novel attraction to passengers upon public steamships, etc., as well as stationary locations and cities, the Encore, an automatic banjo operated as a nickel-in-the-slot device. These are unusually attractive and give entire satisfaction whenever introduced.

''We propose to introduce these instruments on your line of steamers operating between Boston and Yarmouth and other locations. We will pay you 20% of the receipts.

''We can confidently assure you that these instruments will not only furnish a high standard of entertainment to your passengers on the steamers, but also that the receipts will unquestionably be an important revenue to your company.''

All over America, nickel-by-nickel, coin pianos yielded tremendous profits. A few of these nickels came from the hand of young George Gershwin, considered today to be among the greatest of all American composers. He first became interested in piano music when he listened to a nickel-operated instrument in a neighborhood store!

The J.B. Seeburg Piano Company, which with the Rudolph Wurlitzer Co. led the coin-operated music business in America, sold thousands of instruments with such inducements as:

''To prove beyond quibble the statement that Seeburg instruments pay big profits, actual records of instruments are given. Among the instances cited are: 'a Seeburg Style E in a chili parlor in Kansas City earned $1,200 in one year; a Style A in a cafe in Atlanta earned in one week $162.50; a Style H in a dance pavilion in the little city of Wausau, Wisconsin, earned $40 in three days; a Style K in a soft drink parlor in Chicago earned $103 in five days. A Seeburg instrument installed in your place of business will pay astonishing profits.' ''

Although it is a little late, I can add one more testimonial to the Seeburg list: at the 1975 American Numismatic Association convention held in Los Angeles I exhibited from my personal collection a large Seeburg Style G orchestrion with a colorful art glass front. During the course of the week-long show hundreds of nickels, mostly of the Jefferson type (unfortunately!), were dropped into its slot. The proceeds were subsequently given to the Young Numismatists group of the American Numismatic Association.

Nickel music stayed on for a long, long time—well into the jukebox and electric phonograph era. As late as the 1950s and early 1960s the nickel would still buy a phonograph tune. Alas, that too is gone.

Before I leave the subject of nickels I must mention the Mills Novelty Company. Here indeed was an empire built on nickels. Founded by Herbert S. Mills before the turn of the century, the Mills Novelty Company grew to become America's largest manufacturer of coin-operated amusement devices. Included were automatic punching bags, weighing scales, strength testers, vending machines, horoscope dispensers, gambling machines, and even a violin-playing device, all operated via a nickel or a penny in the slot. When it came to advertising, the Mills Novelty Company was not about to take a back seat to anyone. Under the clever direction of James Mangan, who was a numismatist, by the way, and who decades later in 1959 and 1960 advertised gold *celeston* fantasy coins from the ''Nation of Celestial Space,'' Mills printed many statements which, to say the least, make entertaining reading today.

The Mills *Violano-Virtuoso*, nickel-operated, consisted of a real violin played mechanically by means of rosined rotating celluloid bows, with the accompaniment of an abbreviated 44-note piano. While the performance of a finely-tuned, finely-regulated Mills *Violano-Virtuoso* was fairly decent in musical terms, in practice most instruments were more apt to sound ''like a cat scratching on a screen door,'' in the words of one observer. Be that as it may, Mills Novelty Company presented the *Violano-Virtuoso* to be the greatest gift ever to music lovers and others:

''To the hostess the Violano-Virtuoso gives a delightful, unfailing source of entertainment for her guests. She can arrange a musical program suitable for any occasion and know that it will please the most critical of the company. How could an evening or dinner party be made more enjoyable than by the works of the master composers of the latest opera selections, rendered with all the skill of the most noted concert artists? The

"THE MECCA," 431 Walnut St., CINCINNATI.

Above: the Mecca, a saloon located at 431 Walnut Street in Cincinnati, Ohio, was the first commercial establishment to install a Wurlitzer Automatic Harp. Manufactured by the J.W. Whitlock Company, of Rising Sun, Indiana, the nickel-in-the-slot Automatic Harp, first made its appearance in 1905. By 1906 several hundred had been sold in the Cincinnati area, including two to the Cincinnati Zoo! Wurlitzer, who obtained distribution rights from Whitlock, marketed the device until the World War I era. Close to 2,000 were made.

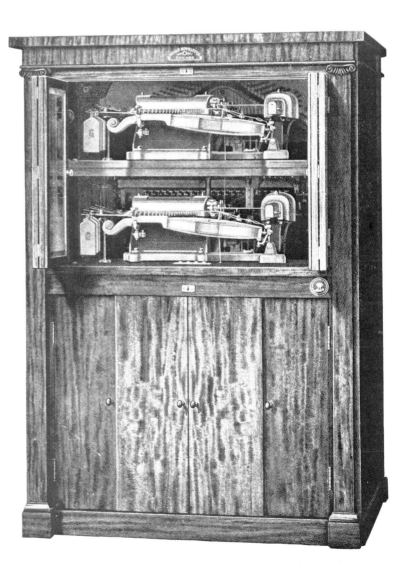

Right: the Mills Violano-Virtuoso violin-playing machine featured a 44-note piano accompanied by one or two real violins. The example shown to the right is the two-violin model. Each violin was equipped with four strings and was played by tiny rosined celluloid discs which rotated at varying speeds. The result was quite charming, provided the instrument was properly tuned and maintained. Equipped with a nickel slot, these instruments would often recoup their cost within two or three years. Close to 5,000 were made, mostly of the one-violin model, from about 1909 to 1930. Examples are fairly plentiful today, and several hundred survive.

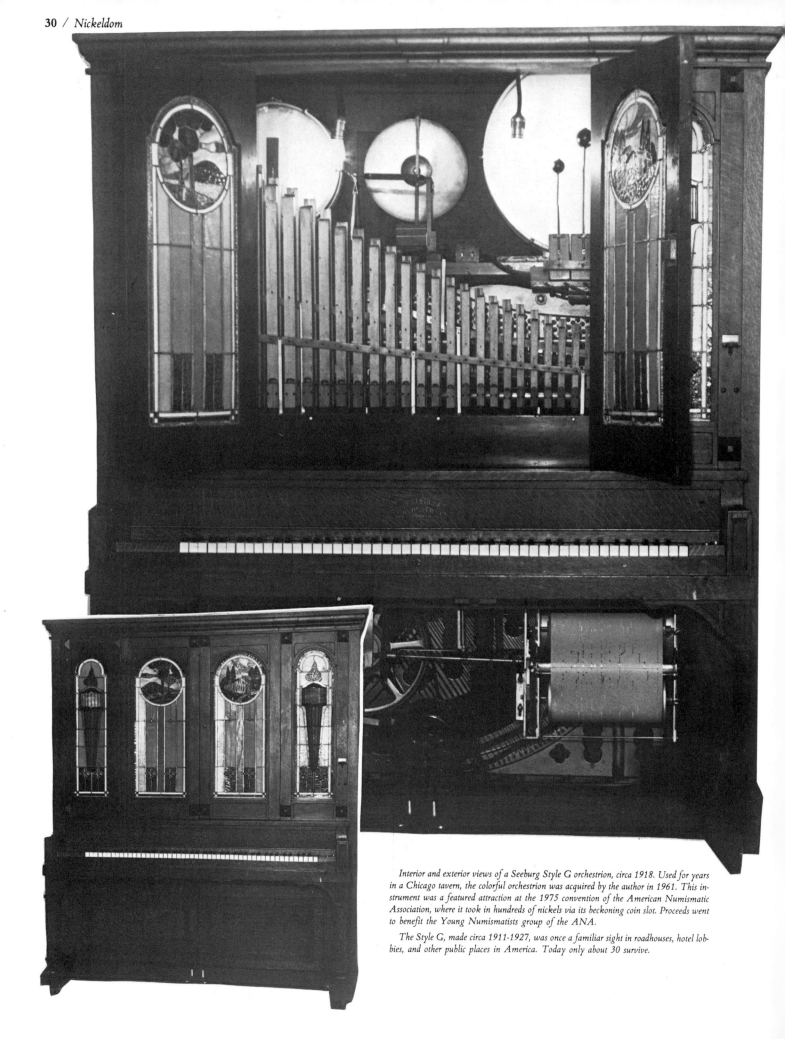

Interior and exterior views of a Seeburg Style G orchestrion, circa 1918. Used for years in a Chicago tavern, the colorful orchestrion was acquired by the author in 1961. This instrument was a featured attraction at the 1975 convention of the American Numismatic Association, where it took in hundreds of nickels via its beckoning coin slot. Proceeds went to benefit the Young Numismatists group of the ANA.

The Style G, made circa 1911-1927, was once a familiar sight in roadhouses, hotel lobbies, and other public places in America. Today only about 30 survive.

STYLE "H"—"Solo Orchestrion"

Piano; xylophone; 68 pipes, giving violin, piccolo, flute, and clarinet effects; mandolin attachment; bass drum; snare drum; tympani; cymbal; triangle, and castanets.

"MASKED MARVEL." Equal to seven man orchestra. Equipped with patented soft drum control, enabling instrument to render wonderful solo effects.

Double veneered hardwood case finished in mission oak (silver grey finish by special order); adorned with two hand carved wood Caryatids, representing "Strength and Beauty," typical of this combination of excellence in case design.

Tempo regulator; automatic loud and soft controls; uses special Style "H", 88-note, ten-selection music roll with famous SEEBURG automatic rewind system.

Height: 7 feet, 3 inches; Width, 6 feet, 4 inches; Depth, 2 feet, 10½ inches. Weight, boxed for shipment: 1800 lbs.

J. P. SEEBURG PIANO CO.   MANUFACTURERS, CHICAGO

The Seeburg Style H solo orchestrion, "equal to a seven man orchestra," provided a veritable jazz concert each time a nickel was dropped into its slot. With its carved statues, brightly lighted colorful art glass front, and interior instruments consisting of a piano, xylophone, pipes (giving the effects of violin, piccolo, flute, and clarinet), mandolin attachment, bass drum, snare drum, tympani, cymbal, triangle, and castanets, it was a tremendous attraction. Although hundreds of these were made circa 1911-1927, only about three dozen exist today. Like other instruments of this genre, the music is programmed on perforated paper rolls, usually ten tunes per roll. Drop a nickel in the slot and such melodies as "Way Down Yonder in New Orleans," "Alexander's Ragtime Band," "In the Good Old Summertime," and "If you Knew Susie" will delight the ear.

Violano-Virtuoso is always ready to give you a greater variety of selections than any other music can offer..''

The violin player was a boon to the country's social problems as well:

'''The reason that boys and girls leave home,' once said a keen observer, 'is that so few homes are made interesting for young people. The natural craving for amusement very often overcomes personal attachment.' If you have sought for means to make your home attractive and have failed to solve the problem, why not get a Violano-Virtuoso? With it you can provide a source of constant interest and entertainment. You can buy a piano or violin, but consider that it will be years before a child can play either of them well, and then only if practice has been made a daily duty performed constantly. Why should you spend money for music lessons, and why should the satisfaction of enjoying the best playing of the best compositions be deferred when you can have a Violano-Virtuoso now? If you, as a child, had to sacrifice the advantages given by the Violano-Virtuoso, see that your children have them.''

Mills went on to say that the nickel-operated *Violano-Virtuoso* would perform marvels in all sorts of locations ranging from the hotel lobby to the restaurant, from the dance hall to the ocean liner passenger lounge, and even in church. Concerning the latter, ''one of the most perplexing problems of the church today is to obtain attendance. Empty pews where even the most scholarly preachers preside give evidence of something needed which will add to the interest offered by good sermons. But you will notice that the churches which provide the best music are the ones which as a rule are more nearly filled. Here then is the solution of the matter. Make the church more attractive by giving the public the oppor-

tunity to hear musical programs such as are seldom offered except by highly paid artists—and this can be done through the meeting with the Violano-Virtuoso.''

Far more interesting to donate to the First Presbyterian Church via a coin slot than in the collection plate!

My favorite I have kept till last:

''For the merchant, announcements of Violano-Virtuoso concerts to be given in the store on certain days are sure to bring hundreds of people who ordinarily would not come and many of whom will buy before they leave. In fact, so popular can such events be made that admittance by ticket may be required to prevent overcrowding!''

The exclamation point added was mine; Mills originally presented it with a straight face.

Consider again the lowly nickel, a worn Liberty nickel of the year 1900 with little numismatic value. Where has it been, what has it seen? To gain admittance through the brilliantly lighted dazzling electrical front of Denver's Isis Theatre in 1913? To receive a ticket saying ''good fortune and a lover will come to you next month'' in a coin-operated Mills Novelty Company fortune-telling machine? To hear *In the Good Old Summertime* played by a Seeburg orchestrion with its piano, pipes, drums, and a colorful art glass front that would make Tiffany envious? To buy a glass of beer in Johnny Bernat's Crystal Palace Hotel bar in Leadville, Colorado, or in New York City's Atlantic Garden? To buy a ham sandwich in a Horn & Hardart Automat? To buy a pair of shoelaces or perhaps a pet turtle in the wonderland of treasures offered by F.W. Woolworth's five-and-ten-cent store? We'll never know. But, thinking about it is a lot of fun!

Craig-y-nos Castle.

I have much pleasure in saying how greatly I appreciate the marvelous Orchestrion you made for me, which has been the admiration of all the royal personages and celebrities who have listened to this perfection of mechanism and melody under my roof.

Adelina Patti-Nicolini.

H. M. THE SULTAN OF TURQUEY
Constantinople.

H. H. SULTAN OF DELI
Sumatra.

DAVID SALOMONS, BARONET
Broomhill, England,

BARON DE L'ESPEE
Paris.

Exc. TITO HEKEKYAN PASHA
Alexandria, Egypt.

ATLANTIC-GARDEN
New York
etc.

No. 9 Concert-Orchestrion

contains all the striking devices, Castanet, Carillon, two small drums.
Height 13 ft. 1 inches.
Width 11 ft. 1 inches.
Depth 5 ft. 3 inches.
Price, including 12 music rolls . . $ **7000.—**
Extra music rolls, each . . $ **20.—**

For the public and private places that could afford them, the orchestrion or self-playing automatic orchestra, was a great attraction. Equipped with a coin slot, a mammoth orchestrion such as the Welte shown on this page could provide a veritable symphony for the patrons of a restaurant. Often the management would let patrons play the instrument via a coin slot during busy hours. At less busy times the instrument would be played free to attract customers. The Atlantic Garden, mentioned above in the Welte advertisement, issued a Civil War token which noted that the establishment provided "free concerts." The concerts were on a Welte orchestrion.

Prime among users of large orchestrions were members of the "Upper 400" social register. In Pittsburgh the prominent families of that city, the Mellons, Snyders, and Fricks, each entertained their guests with orchestrion music. Likewise, Newport, Rhode Island, the summer retreat of millionaires around the turn of the century, had many instruments in its mansions. Adelina Patti, the famous opera singer who lived in a castle during the 1890s, considered her Welte orchestrion to be her finest possession. Likewise, such personalities as circus showman P.T. Barnum, the Vanderbilts (a member of the Vanderbilt family had one orchestrion in his New York home, another in his Newport home, and a third aboard his yacht!), and others gave glowing testimonials.

A magnificent Welte, Hupfeld, Wurlitzer, or Seeburg orchestrion was undoubtedly the ultimate nickel-operated machine.

Orchestrion in the Castle of Adelina Patti

No. 10 Concert-Orchestrion

contains all the striking devices, Castanet, Carillon, two small drums.
Height 14 ft. 5 inches. — Width 16 ft. 8 inches. — Depth 9 ft. 9 inches.
Price, including 12 music rolls . . $ **10000.—**
Extra music rolls, each . . . . . $ **20.—**

Larger Orchestrions built to order.

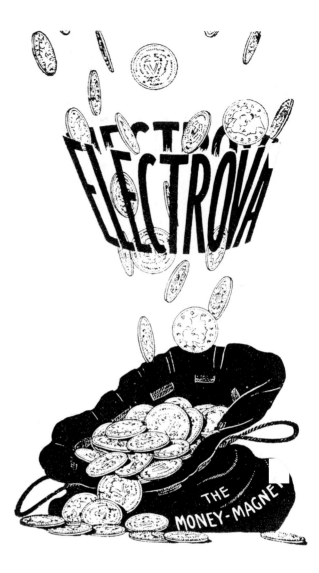

This colorful Electrova nickel-operated piano, circa 1912, features on the front five colorful art glass panels plus two lamps on the corner posts. As the illustration to the right indicates, such a device was literally a "money magnet" for nickels of the era!

In 1898 Roth & Engelhardt, a St. Johnsville, New York, piano manufacturer, marketed the Style D *Peerless* nickel-operated coin piano, the first such device to be made in America. The following year, 1899, the Rudolph Wurlitzer Company introduced the *Tonophone*, a nickel piano produced in North Tonawanda, New York. From these beginnings came an industry which eventually spawned a multitude of firms, including the J.P. Seeburg Piano Company (founded in 1907), the Link Piano Company, the Operators Piano Company (manufacturer of *Coinola* pianos and orchestrions), the Western Electric Piano Company, the Marquette Piano Company (manufacturer of *Cremona* instruments) and many more. In Europe such firms as Hupfeld, Welte, and Weber made a wide variety of coin-operated pianos and orchestrions, many of which were sold in the United States.

By 1910 nickel-operated devices were to be seen in virtually every place of public accommodation, including amusement parks, cafes, hotels, restaurants, billiard parlors, and, as a Rudolph Wurlitzer Company ad suggested, even newsstands! Prominent among customers for coin-operated pianos were bordellos. As historian Harvey Roehl has written, nothing would stimulate fast turnover of trade in a bordello better than a series of snappy two-minute tunes played in the lobby on a nickel piano! Roehl tells the story of a ''madam'' in Baltimore, Maryland, who installed a new coin piano. A few days later she was hopping mad because it wouldn't work. A call by a service man revealed the problem: it was literally stuffed with nickels, hundreds more than the coin box could accommodate!

Millions and millions of nickels flowed into the slots of these devices. Chances are that any worn shield, Liberty, or early buffalo nickel in existence today has been through coin piano slots at least several times! Such instruments are avidly collected today, together with music boxes and other automatic musical instruments of the 19th and 20th centuries. Organizations such as the Musical Box Society International and the Automatic Musical Instrument Collectors Association (AMICA) number several thousand members.

The Operator's Bell De Luxe

Like the "Famous Future Play" but Minus the Indicating Arrangement
Just the Machine for Places that are not Entirely "Closed"

The Bell De Luxe vender has the following improvements.

Positive Coin Top.
Check and Nickel Separator.
Reloading Device.
Percentage Regulator allowing a change from 25 to 50% in profits.
Steel strips on reels which are indestructible.
Non-Beating Attachment.
Everlasting clock works.
Gum Container holding 65 packages.
Anti-Clogging System.
Removable Mechanism.
All metal construction.
Nickel-Plated Case.

How to operate the Bell De Luxe Vender.

Player puts nickel in slot, pushes plunger at coin top, pulls down handle and receives package of gum. Reels revolve and stopping show certain combinations which if on the reward card are good for a dividend or premium. This is paid out in brass checks, from 2 to 20, each good for 5 cents in trade.

Liberty Fruit Gum.

As used in this machine is of the very best quality and is neatly put up five sticks to the package.

Dimensions: Width, 17 in.   Depth, 11 in.   Height, 22 in.   Weight, 82 lbs.

The Operator's Bell Deluxe slot machine, circa 1912, was billed as "just the machine for places that are not entirely closed." In an attempt to circumvent gambling laws the device did not pay out coins but, rather, paid out gum (which on its own was indicated to be worth the nickel deposited) and, important to numismatists, "brass checks, from two to twenty, each good for 5c in trade."

Checks bore varying imprints, often with the name of the establishment owner. In many instances in which the proprietor had a nickelodeon or orchestrion, perhaps one similar to the attractive Peerless shown to the right, the tokens were inscribed "Good for One Tune." Thus a law enforcement official raiding the establishment would find not a "gambling machine" but, rather, a device which ostensibly did nothing of the sort; all it did was dispense nickel gum while at the same time providing tokens good for music—certainly a desirable situation! Such machines were thus allowed to be run in areas in which they would have otherwise been shut down. Several hundred different varieties of "GOOD FOR ONE TUNE" and related nickel-size tokens are known today. These formed the subject of a monograph, "A Tune for a Token," written by the author in 1975.

"MECHANICAL devices for the playing of music coming from the factories of the Peerless Piano Player Company are among the best known in the world to-day and have received the Highest Awards for excellence in four World's Expositions. The Peerless Coin Operated Piano was the first successful instrument of that character to be placed before the public and still retains its supremacy for many distinctive points of merit. It is made in twelve different styles and embodying features not found in any other similar instrument."

The New Style "A" Peerless-Orchestrion
Design IX
Made Wholly in America
This is one of the many new designed Peerless Automatic pianos for use in Clubs, Cafes and Restaurants.

Also the HARMONIST Player-Piano made only in one type—straight 88 note and in three styles. It presents fresh ideas. It gives the dealer new talking arguments. The best proposition yet offered to the dealer for the money. Write for catalogue and territory.

Caille

The Caille Brothers Company

COIN-CONTROLLED MACHINES

The Caille Brothers Company of Detroit, Michigan, produced a wide variety of coin-operated machines during the early 20th century. Many of these, such as the ornate Caille *Centaur* slot machine shown at the upper left, used nickels. Drop a nickel in the slot, push a lever, and the front disc would spin around and around like a roulette wheel. If it stopped in the right place you would be rewarded with a shower of nickels deposited in the bottom cup. "These machines appeal to the known spirit of speculation, so strong in every man. They interest and gratify that element in him at small cost to himself, and they give him a fair show and a 'good run for his money' against slight odds," noted a catalog. "The merchant who is anxious to increase his business can do so by means of these machines. They are made expressly for the purpose of stimulating trade in a manner equally satisfying to merchant and customer. The machines listed therein will increase the business of any merchant and are particularly adapted to liquor dealers, druggists, cigar stores, billiard rooms, etc. Experience has demonstrated that they will positively increase trade 50% to 100% if a square deal is given. An investigation would surely prove profitable and interesting to you. We have ample evidence to offer and can refer you to numerous customers who know by pleasant experience that Caille trade stimulators do stimulate trade."

Colorful names such as *Liberty Bell, Silver Cup, Big Star Six, Check Boy, Special Tiger, Eclipse, Ben Hur, Detroit, Puck, Lone Star, Owl, Bull Frog, Yankee,* and *Black Cat* were given to these gambling devices. A particularly impressive model, shown below, was the *Eclipse Triplet* which featured three instruments in one and which took in a constant stream of nickels, half dollars, and quarters.

Caille

Mills Dewey

Earns From $50 to $100 Per Week

Measures		Weighs
67x28x17 inches	....	215 lbs.
172x72x44 centimeters	....	98 kgs.

Packed for shipment:

65x33x23 inches	....	474 lbs.
166x84x59 centimeters	....	215 kgs.

The Mills Dewey, usually nickel-operated, was manufactured from the late 1890s through the 1920s and was the most popular cabinet-style gambling machine ever devised.

Mills World Horoscope

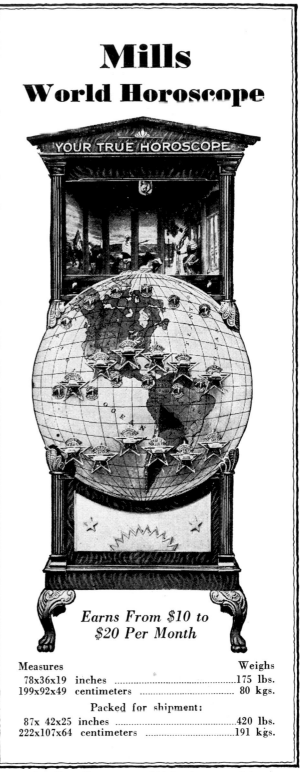

Earns From $10 to $20 Per Month

Measures		Weighs
78x36x19 inches	....	175 lbs.
199x92x49 centimeters	....	80 kgs.

Packed for shipment:

87x 42x25 inches	....	420 lbs.
222x107x64 centimeters	....	191 kgs.

The Mills World Horoscope, available for either cent or nickel operation, told the fortune of anyone caring to part with a coin.

The Mills Novelty Company of Chicago was the foremost manufacturer of coin-operated arcade and gambling machines during the early 20th century. Founded circa 1890, the firm quickly expanded to market a wide variety of coin-operated slot machines, strength-testers, fortune-telling machines, peep shows, and other devices. In the musical line Mills made the *Violano-Virtuoso*, a nickel-operated violin player. Mills noted that "Pages of description could not do justice to this truly magnificent instrument which the U.S. Government has signally honored and designated as one of the greatest scientific inventions of the age. The *Violano-Virtuoso* combines in itself two of the world's most beautiful instruments—the violin and piano. Together their tones blend in sweetest harmony giving practically all the effects of a splendid stringed orchestra. Musicians rave over its music, which is indeed rendered with the wonderful inflection, technique, and dramatic force of the greatest maestros."

New England Notes

2

In today's era of high numismatic values in many areas it is refreshing to know that often a modest budget will build a superb specialized collection.

"What do you collect?" is a question often asked of me. My interests are varied and range from old picture postcards to coin-in-the-slot nickelodeon pianos from the Roaring Twenties to cast-iron kitchen implements and antique food preparation machines.

In the field of numismatics I have collected many different things over the years, often building a collection to gain knowledge and then selling it. When I first began my interest in coins in 1953 I, like so many other collectors of the time, started by searching for coins in circulation. At that time it was theoretically possible to obtain a complete set of Lincoln cents in pocket change with some patience. In practice, the 1909-S V.D.B. cent, 1914-D, and 1931-S, to mention three key dates, remained elusive and had to be bought from a coin dealer. Then I went on to Proof Indian cents, then to Proof Barber half dollars, then to United States commemorative coins. Prices weren't very high in those days. A typical Proof Indian cent cost all of a few dollars. I remember paying Urban C. Thobe, a dealer, $3.50 apiece for a whole string of Proof Indian cents in the 1880s. Barber half dollars weren't very expensive either. Typically a date from 1892 through 1912 cost $7 to $10. It was a big purchase for me when in 1954 I visited New York City and bought from Harvey Stack an example of the rare 1913 for $25.

Then the copper coins of Connecticut minted from 1785 through 1788 attracted my interest. I found particularly fascinating the information, mainly obtained from reading the writings of numismatic scholar Eric P. Newman and conversations with Ken Bressett, that many of these coins weren't made in Connecticut at all but, rather, were issued as counterfeits by Captain Thomas Machin who operated a secret mint on the shores of Orange Pond near present day Newburgh, New York. Also, I found that the crude die work of these pieces gave each an individual character. Condi-

tion, too, was a challenge. Hitherto I was tuned into the grades of Uncirculated and Proof, a reasonable expectation for a set of modern coins. Now in the Connecticut series I found that Fine might be a high condition for a particular variety, and that for other varieties the best known example scarcely graded Good!

A student at the Pennsylvania State University at the time, I went to the library and read all I could on the subject of Connecticut history. Seeking to find out more about the mysterious Thomas Machin (Eric P. Newman wrote to me and said that Machin's personal notes and papers, known to be in an old desk as of the 1850s, had since disappeared), I also read avidly about Upstate New York.

I remember one amusing incident in which I endeavored to take out a reference book and was told that it was an "overnight book." Due to the fact that it might be needed for someone else's research it could only be borrowed for 24 hours; not for the customary two weeks. As the dusty old volume was a hefty one I pleaded for an extension, but "one can't fight city hall" and my protestations were in vain. Then I looked at the library slip on the inside cover of the book and found out that the book had not been checked out for over 80 years; the last date stamped on it was 1879!

A few years ago I became fascinated with nickel-size brass tokens which were once used in electric pianos and slot machines. By looking through boxes of numismatic odds and ends and by writing to token collectors I was able to assemble over 100 different examples. The average cost? Many were 25c to 50c each, and even an "expensive" one was apt to cost no more than $5. In 1975 I wrote a monograph on the subject, *A Tune for a Token*, which was published by the Token and Medal Society. I was surprised and delighted when at an awards ceremony the same organization presented me with its Sandra Rae Mishler Gold Medal Award for the outstanding reference book in the token field published that year.

CLARK'S TRADING POST, located near Lincoln, New Hampshire, offers the visitor a trip backward in time to "the good old days" of years ago. On view to be seen, enjoyed, and experienced are all sorts of exhibits ranging from old advertising to huge steam locomotives. Operated by Murray Clark and his family, the Trading Post has been a favorite vacation stop for the author for many years. Murray Clark, a numismatist with a special interest in currency, first introduced the author to the rich history and lore surrounding early American obsolete paper money.

Above: The 1880-style train station at Clark's Trading Post serves as dispatch point for several trips on the White Mountain Central Railroad each day. Visitors are treated to a two-mile trip along the Pemigewasset River and the adjoining woods. Part of the route goes over an authentic 1904 covered wooden railroad bridge moved piece-by-piece from the neighboring state, Vermont.

Above: Outfitted in the old-time style, this popcorn wagon does a land office business during the hot summer months. Whereas a nickel would buy a bag of popcorn around the turn of the century, today the price is 35¢. With inflation being what it is, probably tomorrow it will be higher!

Above: The Pemigewasset Hook & Ladder Company building, an 1884-style firehouse complete with a wonderland of fire-fighting memorabilia within. To the left in the same picture is the Americana Museum and to the extreme left is another Victorian-style building under construction.

Right: Two Amoskeag horse-drawn pumpers from the turn of the century. Items such as these, now rare and highly desired by collectors, were once common in communities throughout the United States.

Often a client will ask why I don't collect United States rarities. Probably the main answer to this is that in the course of dealing in coins and buying many collections over a period of years I have bought and sold nearly all of the famous rarities in the book, and for me the cataloging and describing of these for sale is as enjoyable as owning them for a protracted period.

As I look back I marvel at my own diversity of numismatic interests. I am not alone in this regard. It has been my experience that most numismatists tend to form many different collections over a period of time.

My good friend, the late Oscar G. Schilke, who lived in Connecticut, was a numismatist—and appreciated coins for the many *pleasures* they offered. As I related in my *High Profits from Rare Coin Investment* book, Oscar combined collecting with investment and, as a result, built a financial treasure over the years.

At the same time, Oscar was always seeking the byways, the little-traveled roads, of numismatics. To be sure, he had a type set of United States coins by designs, a superb one. A collection of 1793-1857 large cents by dates and varieties was outstanding. And then there was a superb display of quarter eagles from 1796 to 1929, including many Proofs. Then, too, there was a magnificent collection of United States and colonial paper money. California small denomination gold coins provided still another interest.

For Oscar there were other things too, pieces which were not as valuable but which were equally fascinating from a numismatic viewpoint. He had a collection of rolled-out coins issued by penny arcades and as souvenirs at expositions. You are probably familiar with the type of rolled-out Lincoln cent with the Lord's Prayer on one side. Well, Oscar had dozens of different types—including pieces dating back to the 19th century; rolled-out coins from the 1893 Columbian Exposition, for example. Seeking to make an "original" contribution to his collection of rolled-out coins, Oscar visited the 1939 World's Fair in New York with two 20-cent pieces from the 1870s in his pocket. He picked two pieces in Extremely Fine grade with fairly heavy toning. His theory was that an Uncirculated coin would be too bright and when rolled out would lose its design detail. He went up to a concessionaire and watched as each of his two 20-cent pieces was rolled out. Presto! He had what probably remain to this day the only rolled-out 20-cent pieces from this 1939 event! Silly? Perhaps. But to Oscar and to a collector of rolled-out coins, such items were fascinating.

A few years ago, following the American Numismatic Association convention held at the Americana Hotel in New York City, I was joined by my two sons, Wynn and Lee, and two friends from Boulder, Colorado,

Beverly and John Rives, and drove in a rented Hertz car to North Woodstock, New Hampshire. This town, located at the entrance to Franconia Notch (known for the "Old Man of the Mountains" or "Great Stone Face" rock outcropping), has as its best-known attraction Clark's Trading Post. Managed by Murray Clark and his family, Clark's Trading Post does a land-office business with vacationing tourists visiting the White Mountains.

On view to be seen and enjoyed at the Clark enterprise are such fascinating items as a standard-gauge steam locomotive and passenger cars (which depart regularly from the ornate 1880-style railroad station once located in New York City's now-defunct Freedomland Park and since relocated piece-by-piece at Clark's), an arena and show featuring trained black bears, a very nice exhibit of coin-operated nickelodeons and orchestrions, an old fire station with some really ingenious equipment (including two wonderfully complex-looking old Amoskeag horse-drawn pumpers), the Americana Museum (a large structure with a wide array of exhibits, including old radio and telegraph equipment, probably the world's largest collection of memorabilia relating to Moxie soft drinks from the turn of the century, children's toys, old steam engines, and many other things), some old cars and trucks (including one with a MOXIE license plate), a roll-operated Tangley circus calliope with 43 gleaming metal pipes, and a well-stocked gift shop.

For the curious passerby who wishes to part with a nickel in its slot the *Yankee Wisecracker*, a clever coin-operated "talking" scale will give forth, when stepped on, such messages as "I'm a scale, not a freight elevator!" and "You've been eating too much!" On the more serene side of things, there are two nicely marked nature walks through the New Hampshire hills.

During my stay there I enjoyed the different facilities of Clark's Trading Post and visited surrounding areas as well, including a nice afternoon spent going up the Mount Washington Cog Railway, managed at the time by Murray Clark's brother Ed. This railroad actually features original authentic equipment first put in use in the 1860s and 1870s, and is almost like stepping back in time over a century ago!

One evening Murray Clark and I were discussing numismatics. Murray has been a numismatist for many years. In his gift shop he features a small numismatic-souvenir section which enjoys a brisk trade during the summer months selling tokens of various kinds, modern Proof sets, silver dollars, old bank notes, and other pieces —mainly priced from a few dollars up to $10 or so. On the personal side of things, however, Murray goes into it quite a bit deeper and is forming a nice collection of currency, including United States issues, obsolete bank notes, and currency of Canada. Particularly interesting

Above: The author and his wife Christie pose in 1890-style costumes for photographers Maureen Clark and Jay Bartlett in Kilburn's Photo Parlor (see above right photograph) at Clark's Trading Post. Named after the Kilburn Brothers, well known stereographers of nearby Littleton, New Hampshire, during the turn of the century, the Photo Parlor today features exhibits of antique photographic apparatus as well as a studio where pictures can be taken in the old style.

Above: Climax standard gauge steam engine at Clark's Trading Post, one of several pieces of authentic operating steam equipment in use on the White Mountain Central Railroad.

Left: Murray Clark and Christie Bowers admire an old time photograph. Murray is a "collector's collector," and has an interest in just about everything. Bank notes, coins, typewriters, firearms, steam equipment, posters, radios, lightbulbs, nickelodeons, antique cars, old tins and containers, memorabilia concerning old hotels and resorts, children's games, fire-fighting equipment—you name it and Murray and his family collect it!

to him are early paper money issues of his own state, New Hampshire.

Murray showed me many obsolete pieces of paper money issued by New Hampshire merchants during the Civil War era when coins disappeared from circulation and notes were privately issued as an emergency measure. Then came an array of notes from New Hampshire banks of the 1830s, 1840s, and 1850s. What impressed me was not the value of the pieces, for most cost Murray all of $5 to $10 or so, and some cost just a dollar or two, but their beauty and historical significance. Within an hour I became absolutely fascinated with the collection!

My interest concentrated on his obsolete currency issues. Being a director and owner of one of America's largest numismatic firms I have handled large quantities of obsolete currency—sheets, bulk lots, and so on. However, these have all come and gone through the firm—with scarcely any time taken by me personally to *appreciate* them in depth, apart from the time needed for proper cataloging. So, here at Clark's Trading Post I was in effect seeing obsolete currency and its true significance for the first time in my life.

Murray had one reference book on the subject, *North American Currency*, by Grover C. Criswell. We spent 15 minutes leafing through it, with Murray guiding the "tour." He pointed out that obsolete currency bills, or *broken bank notes* as they are often called, were issued in many really unusual denominations. The People's Bank of Paterson, New Jersey, for example, produced such esoteric values as $7, $8, and $9! Other banks issued such denominations as 87½c, $1.25, $1.75, and $14!

I was not a complete stranger to this, for in 1975 I had purchased two collections of $3 bills. One of these was subsequently given by me as a gift to the American Numismatic Association Museum in Colorado Springs, Colorado. The second was put into a bank vault where it remained ever since the day of purchase—for it was something that I thought might be interesting if I ever had the chance some day to look into it. In the meantime it had been all but forgotten. The thought of it did cross my mind briefly a few months before my visit to Clark's —and I asked the person from whom I bought it if he would like to buy it back! His answer was negative; his collecting interests had turned elsewhere. So, you see my interest in $3 notes was just about as low as it could be!

As Murray kept talking about obsolete currency I resolved that one of the first things I would do upon my return to the office in California would be to go to the bank and dig out the collection of $3 notes and look through it carefully for the first time!

"How do I begin a collection of obsolete currency? Where are some places to buy from? How much should I expect to pay?" I asked questions like this of Murray, just as I have heard similar questions in other numismatic areas asked of me for many years.

Murray related that he made purchases from a number of different sources, but that Roland Hill, a Massachusetts dealer in currency, was his most steady supplier and sent him frequent shipments. He gave me Mr. Hill's address. I said I would write to him as soon as I returned.

All too soon the visit ended, and my sons and I were aboard an American Airlines Boeing 747 en route from Boston back to Los Angeles.

The first chance I had on my return I took the collection of $3 notes from the bank vault to my office and spent a number of hours studying it carefully. I decided that my main area of interest was New England, so I separated the collection into two parts—$3 notes of New England (of which there were nearly 200) and $3 notes of other states (of which there were about 500). The notes from other states went back to the bank vault with the idea in mind of selling them as a lot or trading them someday. The New England $3 notes were carefully sorted and put into individual holders.

So I had an "instant collection" of New England obsolete currency—all of the $3 denomination. Now I wanted to add to the group. Looking through the classified and display sections of *Coin World* and *Numismatic News*, through the periodical publication of the Society of Paper Money Collectors, and through the monthly publication, *The Bank Note Reporter*, I came up with about 25 names of dealers who specialized in broken bank notes. To that list I added Murray's friend, Roland Hill, and a few others I knew from previous business transactions.

Out to many different areas of the United States went a letter stating that I was beginning a collection of New England obsolete currency and welcomed price quotations, approvals, and correspondence pertaining to the subject. Within a matter of a week or two shipments from Richard Hoober (accompanied by some very interesting historical commentary), Rarcoa, Don Embury, the Brandywine Company, Roland Hill, Bob Medlar, Bryon Cook, Commercial Coin Company, Currency Times Past, Ed Leventhal, Bebee's, and others were on my desk. I sorted through these with care and picked out a couple hundred additional notes. Most were priced in the range of about $5 and $10, although some were higher and a few were lower. In the weeks that followed additional sellers responded. Some sent me several shipments.

Julian Leidman, the well known dealer from Silver Spring, Maryland, who often deals in obsolete currency, told me I should get in touch with John Ferreri of Connecticut. John, Julian said, was really enthusiastic about

New England currency and had specialized in it for quite some time. Subsequent correspondence revealed that John, whom I was later to meet at a convention in New York City, is a really likable person—full of interest, enthusiasm, and spirit concerning his specialty. Over a period of years he had assembled approximately 1,500 different notes from the six New England states—Connecticut, Maine, Massachusetts, Vermont, New Hampshire, and Rhode Island. His advanced interest paralleled my beginning interest, so I was able to learn quite a bit by correspondence from him.

I have always been oriented toward study and research, so an early goal was to read as much as possible on the subject. I quickly found that most of the area of obsolete New England bank notes was uncharted. Grover C. Criswell's *North American Currency* gives an overview of the subject, but it does not go into comprehensive detail. For example, among obsolete currency of New Hampshire only 91 different notes are listed. This is not a deficiency in the book, for the author did not envision it to be the final word on the subject. In fact, the author's foreword states: "This work is by no means complete, nor is it intended to be . . . I set about compiling a book which would list the more common varieties . . ."

From Quarterman Publications in Massachusetts I obtained a copy of *The Obsolete Bank Notes of New England*, by David C. Wismer. This publication, which sold for $25, is a condensation of a series of articles originally published serially in *The Numismatist*, journal of the American Numismatic Association, from 1922 through 1936. To Mr. Wismer's writings of years ago has been added an interesting modern introduction by George W. Wait. This reads in part:

"In our daily activities we spend paper money and seldom look at it, except to notice the denomination . . . The Treasury Department emphasizes that all of our $1 bills contain the portrait of Washington, all of our $5, Lincoln, all of our $10, Hamilton, and so on. Such was not the case in 1860. A buyer might pay for his purchase with any one of many kinds of bank notes or a combination of them. These bank notes were issued by state-chartered institutions with varying degrees of solvency. A famous token dated 1857 bore the words 'never keep a paper dollar in your pocket till tomorrow.' Not only were there many banks of questionable integrity, but a large proportion of the floating supply of paper money was counterfeit . . .

"Obsolete bank notes provide a most interesting field for collecting, not only for the bank note collector but for the historian, art lover, and student of engraving. Those interested in the process of engraving may trace a simple early design from black and white to the very elaborate color notes of the 1850s and 1860s. Bank presidents tried to outdo each other in picking the best of thousands of designs, including depictions of lavish scenes and beautiful women. And, of course, the fancier the note, the more difficult it was to counterfeit. Because a great many banks went broke, the term *broken bank notes* has been commonly applied to all early bank notes, whether or not they were good. This is really a misnomer, since most genuine bills were redeemed and in a few instances will still be redeemed by banks still in business or their successors. The collecting of these obsolete notes is probably one of the most interesting, educational, and rewarding of all branches of numismatics, although it was not recognized as such until quite recently . . ."

The Wismer book vastly expanded my horizons. Whereas the Criswell reference listed 91 different notes from New Hampshire, Wismer listed 528! By making a rough tally of the Wismer listings I noticed that the volume listed 683 notes of Connecticut, 754 of Maine, 2,419 of Massachusetts, 528 of New Hampshire (which was to prove to be the most difficult state to collect), 1,215 of Rhode Island, and 579 of Vermont. This meant a grand total of 6,178 different types of New England currency listed.

I quickly found that perhaps 50% of the notes I was receiving in the mail were not listed in the Wismer reference. By simple mathematics this would mean that about 12,000 different varieties had been issued totally in New England. But, considering that the notes I received were only a portion of those available throughout numismatics, I am sure that even this estimate is conservative. Perhaps the number of notes originally issued was far greater—15,000 to 20,000 or more designs! And, New England broken bank notes are considered to be scarcer than those of certain other areas such as New York and Georgia—so what the total population of broken bank note varieties issued from all different places in the United States was, is anyone's guess!

From Julian Leidman as a surprise gift one day came another reference on the subject, a red clothbound book entitled *Vermont Obsolete Notes and Scrip*, by Mayre B. Coulter, published by the Society of Paper Money Collectors in 1972. This book, a fairly comprehensive dissertation on the subject of paper money from the Green Mountain State gives rarity ratings and approximate values for many different issues. Even so, I learned that there were numerous varieties which weren't listed and, best of all, my beginning collection had some of them!

I soon realized that there was no definitive volume on the subject and that I had to "fly by the seat of my pants." Collecting obsolete currency is like sailing in uncharted waters. Complicating this is the situation of price.

The diversity of the dollar is illustrated by this montage of $1 notes, mostly dating from the early 19th century. Literally thousands of different variations and designs were produced.

Within a couple of days I received in the mail from two different sellers the same variety of $4 note from a bank in Portland, Maine. One note was priced at $18, the other at $90! Was the $90 vastly overpriced? Probably not, for there are few price guidelines to go by. I have found that Seller A can price a note at $20 and Seller B can price the same note at $10. In the next shipment another variety of note will be priced by Seller A at $10 and Seller B at $20! So, there really aren't any rules. I have always paid what I think a note is worth to me. If I pay $15 for a given note today and then next week the same note is quoted to me for $10, all I can do is shed a secret tear. On the other hand, if the same note is later quoted to me for $25 a smile crosses my face!

I soon found that rather than being a problem this uncertainty was part of the fun. It is interesting to obtain a note for, say, $20 and find that it is unlisted in any of the standard reference books.

For all I know it might be the only such note in existence! Or, perhaps it is quite common and I just don't know it. To me this contributes to the "thrill of the hunt" and is more interesting than following a standard price list and simply ticking off pieces mechanically as I acquire them.

Two months after I started collecting I sent John Ferreri in Connecticut, who by that time was a good mail-order friend, a listing of some of my duplicate notes. I was delighted to learn that he, an advanced collector with many years of experience, was able to find seven different pieces which he didn't already have!

A number of interesting facts soon became evident. The Wismer book, which lists over 6,000 varieties of New England notes which were once printed, is in no way representative of notes which exist today. The reason for this is that Wismer used old banking guides, counterfeit detection manuals, and other references from the 1830-1860 period to compile his list. Many of the notes therein were issued only in limited quantities and have all been redeemed since or in some instances may never have been issued at all but were merely contemplated. As his references mainly date from 1830 onward, nearly completely absent are the thousands of issues from the 1790-1830 period, even very common notes. Also absent are the scrip or private fractional currency issues from the 1860s.

I have learned that particularly rare are high denomination New England broken bank notes. While Wismer lists numerous $500 and $1,000 notes, the only one I was able to acquire for my collection was a single proof $500 note. John Ferreri reports having found only one $1,000 note in his many years of collecting. Another friend-by-mail, Leonard Finn, reports that he owns but one each of the $500 and $1,000 denominations, both notes being from the Franklin Bank of Boston. I would find it immensely interesting to own a $500 or $1,000 note which actually circulated. What tremendous sum of money this would have represented originally in an era which a *year's* salary for a working man was on the order of just $200 to $400!

While $3 notes are unheard of today and, in fact, the expression "queer as a $3 bill" suggests something that isn't logical or desirable (witness Maria Muldaur's song of a few years ago, *You're Just a Three-Dollar Bill*), at one time $3 notes were very common in America. Actually, $3 notes from the early 19th century were no more unusual than, for example, $2 notes, $10 notes, or $20 notes. In fact, $10 notes and $20 notes were scarcer!

When the United States government commenced issuing its own currency in 1861 it was decided to issue $3 notes as part of the series. Preparations were made for doing this. When currency was actually issued, the lower denominations were made only in the values of $1, $2, and $5. The $3 denomination was forgotten. Somewhat related to $3 bills are such coins as $3 gold pieces (minted 1854-1889) and 3-cent pieces (made in silver 1851-1873 and in nickel 1865-1889).

I learned that counterfeit notes are avidly collected, and that in many instances they sell for as much or even more than originals!

I was able to obtain a $3 note which purports to have been issued from "The Hamilton Bank" of Boston in 1857. Across the note is an old counterstamp which reads COUNTERFEIT. Examination of the piece reveals that the word "HAMILTON" is fuzzy-appearing and is slightly different in shade from the rest of the features.

Looking through my collection of notes I found another $3 bill, a genuine issue from the Lafayette Bank of Boston. I noticed that it was quite similar in appearance to the note I had from "The Hamilton Bank." Putting the notes side-by-side I noticed that the "Hamilton" note had the same ink signatures of bank officials as did the Lafayette note! So, the "Hamilton" note had been produced years ago by rubbing out or otherwise obliterating the word "LAFAYETTE" and carefully hand-inking "HAMILTON" in its place!

What probably happened is that the Lafayette Bank failed or its notes became worthless. Someone in the 1860s found himself possessing a Lafayette Bank note which could not be redeemed. In those days $3 was a lot of money and represented the best part of a week's salary. At the same time the Hamilton Bank of Boston was a going concern and its notes were accepted. So, presto-chango, with a few hours' work the worthless Lafayette note become a valuable "Hamilton" note! To me such a situation contributes very much to the joys of collecting. The cost involved? The counterfeit note cost me $20 and the genuine set me back $11. It is my guess

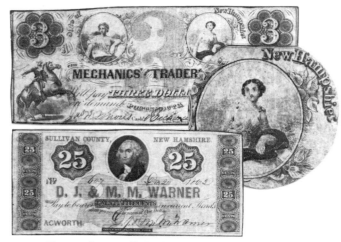

True or false? Actually, some of both! The above note, with the erroneous "New Hampshier" spelling is a forgery. The bottom note with the state erroneously spelled still another way, "New Hamshire," is, believe it or not, authentic.

An interesting case of a switcheroo: a worthless $3 note of the Lafayette Bank of Boston, similar to that illustrated at the bottom, had the word "LAFAYETTE" erased and the designation "HAMILTON" put in its place, thereby giving it the appearance of being an authentic $3 bill from the Hamilton Bank, a going financial concern. Such alterations are very common among early American bank notes. Sometimes worthless notes were purchased by the hundreds or thousands and altered en masse.

Often a note will have an interesting story behind it. The above note, in the unusual denomination of $1.75, was issued by the Vermont Glass Factory of Salisbury in 1814. Various denominations were produced including $1.00, $1.25, $1.50, $1.75, $2.00, $3.00, and $5.00. The notes have various views of the glass works as well as such slogans as "By Manufactures We Thrive."

The December 1813 issue of "The Literary and Philosophical Repertory," of Middlebury, Vermont, noted the following concerning this establishment:

"The Glass-Factory is situated in the town of Salisbury, on the north shore of Lake Dunmore. . . A large portion of the lake, and the land adjoining it, formerly belonged to Mr. Epaphras Jones, who suggested the idea of its being a favorable spot for the manufacture of glass, and who had the honor of being the principal instrument in the formation of a company for that purpose. The Legislature of the State, on petition, cheerfully granted to Mr. Jones and his associates an active incorporation, to which very liberal privileges were attached. Mr. Jones now resides in the neighborhood of the Factory and is the company's general agent for the erection of the buildings and the inspection of the works.

"The company owns about 2,000 acres of land which lie, chiefly, around a large bay of the lake and command its only outlet. On this outlet stands a sawmill, in the vicinity of which exists a sufficient quantity of good timber to keep it in operation for many years to come. Their land also commands the main stream, which supplies the lake, and on which a head and fall may be made to carry any mechanical works which the company may hereafter deem it profitable to erect.

"It is believed that no establishment of this kind in the northern states enjoys more numerous or greater advantages from its local situation than the Vermont Glass Factory. At least this is the opinion of the ingenious and persevering superintendent of the Factory, Mr. Henry R. Schoolcraft . . .

"From the unusual success which has attended these works since their commencement, the many advantages which they hold, and the variety of materials with which the place abounds for making all kinds of glass, we are led to believe that they will become one of the first establishments in the union.

"Respecting this present state of the Vermont Glass Factory, it is necessary to add but few words. It is sufficient to state that the works are now in full and complete operation. The first glass was blown in them about the middle of last September. It is now exhibited for sale in the stores of this village and is beginning to circulate through a large section of the country . . ."

Despite the glowing expectations, there were clouds on the horizon. Within a year of its September 1813 opening, finances of the firm apparently reached a crisis. The bank notes were no longer being redeemed. Then fire struck, and the business was terminated.

It would be interesting to locate some examples of the Vermont Glass Factory's products today. Probably most, if not all, items were unsigned. Early advertisements of the firm reveal that a main product was window glass, but apparently other items were made as well. Fortunately for collectors, Vermont Glass Factory notes are fairly plentiful. Today they serve as an interesting numismatic reminder of an anticipated glorious enterprise that might have been but which never materialized the way its founders hoped.

$3 note issued by the Kirtland Safety Society Bank, operated in Kirtland, Ohio, a suburb of Cleveland, by the Mormons. From Ohio the Mormons moved westward to Nauvoo, Illinois, and then to Great Salt Lake. Many interesting currency issues are linked with Mormon history.

This $3 note of the Phenix Bank of New York is unsigned and represents a "remainder" note never issued. The phenix (usually spelled "phoenix") bird occurs in many places throughout American numismatics, including several varieties of Hard Times Tokens issued during the 1833-1844 era.

The notes of the West River Bank of Jamaica, Vermont, quite plentiful today, feature cupids cavorting with Liberty seated silver dollars. Often early obsolete notes are of stunning beauty. Literally thousands of different design combinations exist.

that if I were to take these two notes and arrange them in a display case at a convention, surround them with a picture of the Lafayette Bank and the Hamilton Bank (if I could find these in a book of old engravings), and tell the interesting story of how they were made it would be of great interest to numismatists. And, who knows, perhaps it would even be awarded a prize of some sort. And, yet, here is an exhibit which would cost me just $31—the price I paid for the two notes—certainly a nominal sum in monetary value, but still possessing untold numismatic and historical significance.

Not all counterfeits were made by altering notes. There were other types. Sometimes the corner designs of a $10 bill would be pasted on a $1 note to raise its denomination. Other times—quite often—counterfeiters would make up false plates and print the notes they needed. Usually the workmanship was not up to the standards of the New England Bank Note Company, the Graphic Company, and other earlier issuers, but other times the quality was indeed quite good. Occasionally a ludicrous error was made, as in the case of a phony note which had the state name spelled as "New Hampshier." But not all mistakes were counterfeits. Other notes from the same state, absolutely genuine, had the state spelled as "New Hamshire" in at least two instances!

I learned in a subsequent conversation with my friend Murray Clark that certain notes which were stamped "COUNTERFEIT" were really genuine notes which had been redeemed.

They were marked thusly so that they would no longer circulate. This is particularly true of notes called in by two early-date clearinghouses, the Bank of Mutual Redemption and the Suffolk Bank, both of Boston. Of course, in most instances those marked "COUNTER-FEIT" really were. The more usual way of marking genuine notes when they were redeemed was to cancel them with one or more small punch holes—or, as in the case of the State Bank and the South Royalton Bank, both of Vermont, to cancel them with huge holes.

During the first year of my collecting New England obsolete currency some nice surprises came my way. Ed Leventhal, genial proprietor of Boston's J.J. Teaparty Company, learned of my interest and asked me if I would like to purchase his specialized collection of obsolete Massachusetts currency which he had been forming over a period of years. I asked for more information, acquired same, found the price to be reasonable, and added his group to my own holdings. Grover Criswell sold me a nice collection of proof notes (notes which were not actually issued but which represent trial designs and impressions on special paper), including pieces once owned by author D.C. Wismer. Dr. John Musculus and Jess Peters furnished substantial numbers of interesting pieces. So, note by note, group by group, the collection grew.

The motifs featured on the notes are interesting. A girl feeding chickens, a sailor in a crow's nest high on a mast, railroad trains (of all sizes, shapes, and varieties), pigs in a farmyard, an Indian raid, stately bank buildings resembling Grecian temples, steamboats, whales, figures of Liberty and Justice (seated, standing, and even flying), factories, pioneer scenes, trees, George Washington (seated, standing, wearing a uniform, wearing a toga, and on horseback), boy and girl lovers . . . these are just a few.

A common set of notes from the West River Bank of Jamaica, Vermont, features a series of illustrations or *vignettes*, as they are called, of cupids playing with United States silver dollars. As George Wait has expressed, it is almost as if early bank presidents were playing oneupmanship with each other in the area of elaborate designs.

Condition of the notes is sometimes paradoxical with regard to their numismatic value. Often Uncirculated, or *New*, as they are referred to by collectors, notes are the least valuable and really wretched-looking ones are the most valuable! Why? The reason for this is rather simple. When a bank failed often it had on hand vast quantities of unissued notes. These notes, in New condition, have found their way into numismatic channels and in many instances are extremely common today. John J. Ford, Jr., a well-known enthusiast in the field, told me that during the 1950s he once had an eight-inch-high stack of uncut sheets of West River Bank (Jamaica, Vermont) notes and was doing a brisk business selling them for 60c each! On another occasion he bought from a New Orleans seller 14,000 sheets of obsolete Louisiana bank notes!

As is true of most other numismatic fields, the values of broken bank notes have appreciated in value attractively over the years. Notes that were once available for under $1 each are apt to sell for $20 or more today.

In the field of New England issues, New notes from such institutions as the Stonington Bank (Stonington, Connecticut) and the Bank of New England (East Haddam, Connecticut) can be obtained very cheaply. These notes, never issued, are what are known as *remainders* today—as are the Jamaica, Vermont and Louisiana notes just mentioned.

On the other hand, notes which actually circulated are apt to show extensive signs of wear, tear, and soiling. In these instances the original notes were entirely dispersed into circulation. In the intervening years most were redeemed or lost. Thus the "finest known" of a certain issue might only be in Fair or Poor grade, perhaps with a corner missing!

One of the most interesting reference books I obtained on New England bank notes was a small green-covered pamphlet entitled *Historical Account of Paper Currency and*

Banks, by Terrence G. Harper. The following account of strange doings in Vermont is largely quoted from that source.

But first, what if I were to tell that some of the most historical of all American paper money issues—notes with an absolutely fascinating and adventurous history—could be obtained for $10 to $20 each? Would you be skeptical? Well, after having read this commentary so far you probably wouldn't be—but if I had mentioned it to you in any other situation you probably would have pooh-poohed the idea.

I spent a nice evening at home reading Terrence G. Harper's 48-page monograph. I was fascinated with the three-page account of the history of the Franklin County Bank of St. Albans, Vermont. After reading the article I was eager to return to the office and get from the bank my Vermont notes. Lo and behold, I found I had several different varieties from the Franklin County Bank! The cost? Not much more than $10 per item. Now I'll tell you of Mr. Harper's account and you can judge for yourself whether or not these relatively inexpensive items are among the most fascinating pieces of numismatic Americana one could own.

The Franklin County Bank of St. Albans was chartered in 1849 with a capital of $100,000. Bills were issued of the denominations of $1, $2, $5, $10, and $20. From 1849 to 1865 the president was O.A. Burton. Cashiers were Edward W. Parker from 1849 through 1858 and Marcus W. Beardsley from 1858 through 1865.

Immediately after the great St. Albans Raid the Franklin County Bank was liquidated. It paid all of its debts but refused to redeem its bills unless a satisfactory account of proper possession could be proved. The story of the Raid is fascinating. This bank, along with the St. Albans Bank (notes of which are also common and inexpensive, by the way), was involved in one of the most daring robberies in Vermont history.

This incredible adventure of October 19, 1864, roused not only local but national excitement. Thousands of words have been written about this affair, some true and some highly romanticized. No history of the state of Vermont could be complete without mentioning it.

A group of armed desperadoes, representing the Confederate States of America, succeeded by well-laid plans in robbing these banks in broad daylight and escaping with their loot across the border to Canada.

That a robbery so bold and daring could be accomplished by just a few people in a village of the population of St. Albans might seem to be quite improbable. It was necessary to make it a complete surprise to carry it out effectively.

The citizens of St. Albans, like those of surrounding villages, were quite busy that October 1864 day with their own affairs in various shops, stores, and offices—with no suspicion of danger and with no readied weapons of defense. The Civil War conflict raging at the time had never been even remotely close to Vermont, and the northernmost holdings of the Confederate States of America lay hundreds of miles to the south!

The rebel plan was indeed a bold one and, as it turned out, very skillfully executed. Bennett H. Young, who led the raid, accompanied by two others, came into town from the city of St. Johns in Canada on October 10th and lodged at the Tremont House. Two accomplices on the same day stopped at the American Hotel. On the next day three others arrived. These men spent the next week in and around St. Albans and learned the habits of the people, the location of the banks and their safes, and the places where horses could be obtained when they were ready to leave. The desperate men attracted no more attention than did other strangers who arrived on nearly every train into this village and customarily stayed at the same hotels.

On October 18th, the day before the great raid, two more men arrived for breakfast at the Tremont House and were later joined by four additional plotters at dinner. On the 19th, the day of the event, five came to dinner at the American Hotel and six at the St. Albans House. It was subsequently learned that two of these late arrivals came in a carriage from Burlington, Vermont, and that the others came from Montreal on the train at noon.

The adventurers learned that Tuesday, being market day, would not be good for their purpose. The next day, however, would be the dullest of the week and few people would be in the streets. It happened by coincidence that on this particular Wednesday nearly 40 of the leading citizens and active men of the town were in Montpelier attending the sessions of the Legislature and in Burlington awaiting the disposition of important Supreme Court cases.

The names of the raiders, as far as can be learned, were Bennett H. Young, Squire Turner Treavis, Alamanda Pope Bruce, Samuel Eugene Lackey, Marcus Spurr, Charles Moore Swager, George Scott, Caleb McDowal Wallace, James Alexander Doty, Joseph McGrorty, Samuel Simpson Gregg, Dudley Moore, Thomas Bronson Collins, and William H. Hutchinson. They were mostly young men from 20 to 36 years, except McGrorty who was 38.

The afternoon of Wednesday, October 19th, 1864, was cloudy with threatening rain, and the streets were very quiet. By prearrangement, immediately after the town clock struck the hour of 3:00, the banks were

Main Street, St. Albans, Vermont, in the late 19th century. This view toward the north shows the escape road toward Canada taken by the marauders.

Early view of Main Street, St. Albans, Vermont, showing the Franklin County Bank and other structures.

$10 note of the Franklin County Bank signed by Beardsley and Burton. Dated June 10, 1864, this note could very well have been one of those carried off in the famous Confederate raid!

Hotel in St. Albans where some of the raiders stayed prior to the famous escapade.

Dutcher's store in St. Albans. During the raid one citizen was seriously wounded and subsequently died. Following the attack he was carried into this drugstore for emergency treatment.

Main Street, St. Albans, looking south. The Tremont House (right side of photograph) is where Bennett Young, leader of the raid, stayed.

entered simultaneously by men with revolvers which had been concealed.

Hutchinson and four aides were assigned to rifle the coffers of the Franklin County Bank. Marcus W. Beardsley, cashier, sat by the stove conversing with James Saxe. A woodsawer, Jackson Clark, also was present in the room. Hutchinson came in shortly after 3:00, and Mr. Beardsley arose to go behind the counter to see what was wanted. Hutchinson wished to know what the price of gold was. Beardsley replied that the bank did not deal in it. J.R. Armington then came in with money to deposit, and Hutchinson was referred to him. While Beardsley was counting the money left by Armington, Hutchinson sold the latter two gold pieces in exchange for greenbacks. Saxe and Armington then went out, leaving Hutchinson standing at the counter, keeping up a conversation with Beardsley.

Immediately after this, four others came in and stood in the corner of the room a few moments. Then one of them advanced a few steps, put his hand deep into his side pocket and drew out a heavy navy revolver—which he then pointed directly at Beardsley, looking him straight in the eye, but without saying a word.

Beardsley thought he must be an insane man and at first was inclined to run—but he did not, and stood returning his gaze. Two others stepped forward, drew their revolvers, and pointed them like the first, without a word from either. Hutchinson, who had kept his place at the counter, then said in a low but very firm tone, "We are Confederate soldiers. There are one hundred of us. We have come to rob your banks and burn your town."

Clark, a bank employee, made a dash for the door but was ordered back with the threat of instant death if he moved. Hutchinson said, "We want all your greenbacks, bills, and property of every description." They came behind the counter and into the vault, taking everything they found of value.

When they had secured their booty and were ready to leave, Hutchinson told Beardsley that he must go to the vault, where Clark had already been placed. Beardsley protested an act so inhuman, told him the vault was airtight and that no man could live long in it, and that if they were left outside of the vault they would raise no alarm.

This didn't impress Hutchinson a bit. He grabbed his prisoner by the arm, led him into the vault, and closed the door. Beardsley supposed that they would carry into reality their threat to incinerate the town and had vivid images of the horrid prospect of being burned alive.

Hearing voices in the room, he rattled the door of the tiny prison, and soon heard his name being called by Armington. He told him how the door could be opened.

He soon was free, his imprisonment having lasted about 20 minutes. When he emerged from the bank he saw the robbers galloping off to the north with Captain George P. Conger, home on leave from the Green Mountain Cavalry, in furious pursuit behind.

The daring adventurers succeeded in getting across the line into Canada, but 13 were arrested and held for trial. The money found on them amounted to $80,000. The prisoners were brought before Justice Coursol, and after a long and tedious examination at great expense to the government of the United States and the Franklin County Bank and other banks, the judge concluded that he possessed no jurisdiction in the matter, ordered the men to be discharged, and directed that the stolen money be returned to them. Having regained their ill-gotten funds, the raiders left immediately!

Four or five were later re-arrested, and another attempt was made to extradite them to the United States. They were brought before Justice Smith at Montreal, and after much more additional expense the judge ruled that transactions of the robbers in St. Albans were acts of war and were not liable to international extradition. The Canadian government, however, did not sympathize with the magistrates and their decisions. Parliament appropriated $50,000 in gold to be paid to the Franklin County Bank and others as partial compensation for the money successfully taken by the raiders. At that time $50,000 in gold was equal to $88,000 in currency.

The entire amount taken by the robbers was $208,000. The currency loss was therefore a net of $120,000. To this might be added a sum of not less than $20,000 which was expended in the arrests of the robbers and the attempt to secure their extradition.

The Vermont bank commissioner later reported that: "I visited the Franklin County Bank two days after the St. Albans Raid and have found by examination of their books that they suffered a loss of $72,443. I found by an examination of July 27th, 1865, that they had recovered $31,857 of the stolen funds, making $40,856 their actual loss; surplus on the day of the raid and unpaid interest then due reduces the deficit to $33,890.93. The act of Legislature relieving the bank from this liability to redeem its bills after June 1, 1865, leaves $54,031.00 not redeemed, of which $40,586 is in stolen funds, leaving $13,445 in honest circulation, which the directors are willing to redeem."

So, it is apparent that most of the currency of the Franklin County Bank still in existence—including hundreds of notes in collector's hands—has a good chance of having been among the treasure carried off on that long ago 1864 day by the raiders!

Time pressure, particularly related to my work at the time in cataloging the Fairfield Collection (the most valuable rare coin collection ever to be sold at

unrestricted public auction sale) forced me to spend less and less time with my New England notes. One day Julian Leidman, a close dealer friend, came by the office for a visit. We discussed the New England collection. Julian had helped me assemble a number of the issues earlier. He expressed an interest in buying it, and after some contemplation I offered to sell it for the price paid, my "profit" being a wealth of numismatic and historical experience gained along the way. The transaction was subsequently consummated, and over 2,200 notes found a new owner!

A few months later I had more time available, the first catalog of the Fairfield Collection having reached print, and I began to miss the notes! My thoughts again turned to currency, and I began a collection of $1 notes, not only of New England but of all of the United States, including obsolete issues, regular United States issues, and so on. During my formation of the specialized New England collection I learned of many interesting side roads, and it was frustrating not to be able to acquire, for example, a note of Colorado or Kentucky for it would not have fit in with my main collecting endeavor.

While New England notes certainly have their share of romance, as the St. Albans Raid vividly illustrates, other areas of the country are likewise fascinating.

For example, Clark, Gruber & Company, issuers of territorial gold pieces, some of which featured Pikes Peak as their motif, also issued bank notes in the 1860s. John J. Ford, Jr. told me he offered some of these a few years ago for about $600 each. Today the value is undoubtedly even higher. In the field of obsolete currency these are indeed expensive!

The Mormons, prior to their move to Nauvoo, Illinois, and, later, to what is now Salt Lake City, Utah, stayed for awhile in Kirtland, Ohio. At that time they had as their bank the Kirtland Safety Society, which issued bank notes, many of which were personally hand-signed by Joseph Smith, founder of the Mormon church, Later, in Salt Lake City, Brigham Young also signed many notes. I have in my collection a $1 note of the Deseret National Bank boldly signed by the well known Mormon leader.

The field of regular United States currency (that is, government issues rather than private bank note issues) is wonderfully varied and complex. Today the average numismatist will make a specialty within this field: one numismatist may aspire to own a specimen of each Federal Reserve note from $1 to $50, including signature and bank varieties. Another may aspire to own one each from as many different national banks as can be found in the states of Pennsylvania or New York.

In the past several great collections of currency have been formed. Colonel E.H.R. Green, son of Hetty Green (known as the "witch of Wall Street" and subject of the book, *The Day They Shook the Plum Tree*) amassed (perhaps "hoarded" would be a better word) a tremendous number of rare notes along with other numismatic delicacies such as all five known specimens of the rare 1913 Liberty head nickel. These were dispersed in 1942. Albert A. Grinnell, proprietor of a Detroit music store, diligently collected notes by varieties. His immense holdings were sold from 1944 through 1946.

Many years ago the noted Fort Worth, Texas dealer, B. Max Mehl, who died in the 1950's, tried to interest Amon Carter, a wealthy oil man and the co-founder of American Airlines, in rare coins. Both were members of the Fort Worth Rotary Club. Carter, however, showed little interest. One day Mehl asked Carter his birth date and learned it was 1879. At a subsequent Rotary meeting Mehl gave him as a gift a glittering United States $2½ gold piece of that date in a plush-lined presentation box. Carter was thrilled! The results were better than Mehl ever could have hoped for: Carter asked what other 1879 coins were available, and subsequently bought the extremely rare $4 gold stellas of that year. Soon, numismatics became a major interest and Amon Carter set about forming one of the greatest coin collections ever put together. Included were such rarities as the 1804 silver dollar, 1884 and 1885 trade dollars, and one of three known 1822 half eagles.

In an unusual instance of transferring interest from one generation to another, the family propensity for collecting was taken over by his son, Amon Carter, Jr. Amon's interest became even more intense and more cosmopolitan than that of his father. Of special interest was United States currency, and today Amon Carter, Jr. has the most outstanding collection in the United States. Included are many thrilling large-size high denomination $500 and $1,000 notes.

When I was beginning my interest in coins in the 1950s I met Amon Carter, Jr. for the first time at a convention. He apparently had heard of me and introduced himself. Then he asked, "Have you ever seen a $10,000 bill?"

I hadn't seen one and said so.

"Have you ever seen seven $10,000 bills?" My answer, of course, was no, whereupon he produced a dazzling display of seven crisp notes of that denomination!

Regular issue United States notes include some of the most beautiful engravings ever to be found on currency anywhere. Perhaps leading the popularity parade are the 1896 *educational* notes, silver certificates of the $1, $2, and $5 denominations. Illustrated are engraved scenes of History Instructing Youth, Science Presenting Steam and Electricity to Commerce and Manufacture, and on the largest denomination note of the series, the $5, Electricity as the Dominant Force in the World.

Legal Tender note, series 1862, bearing the signature of F.E. Spinner. When notes (of other denominations) were first issued by the government in 1861, dozens of clerks were employed to hand sign them. The waste of this was realized, and soon the signatures were affixed by the printing press.

Series of 1886 Silver Certificate bearing the portrait of Martha Washington. These scarce and beautiful notes are favorites with collectors today.

LARGE-SIZE $1 NOTES furnish a large selection of designs and variations for the collector. A wide variety of legislation gave rise to many different series of notes. Thus by the end of the 19th century several different major designs of dollar notes (and other denominations as well) were being issued concurrently, including Legal Tender issues, Silver Certificates (each note backed by "one silver dollar" held by the Treasury), Coin Notes (issued by the Treasury Department to pay for new silver bullion purchases), and, in circulation from earlier years, National Bank notes. Later to come (series of 1918) were Federal Reserve $1 notes.

The First Charter National Bank notes (see an example from California, Missouri illustrated below) are particularly interesting to the specialist. Produced circa 1865-1878 these were issued by banks in many different states. Those from certain western areas are quite rare: notes of Colorado, Utah, Montana, and particularly Wyoming being examples. On the other hand, certain populous eastern states such as New York, Pennsylvania, and Massachusetts are relatively common.

For years currency attracted a few thousand serious specialists. For the average numismatist currency was outside of the mainstream of interest. Beginning in the late 1970s this changed. In recent times there has been an increasing awareness of the beauty and history offered by various currency issues, federal issues such as illustrated on this page as well as the tens of thousands of varieties privately issued by earlier banks. The Society of Paper Money Collectors is one group specializing in the field.

Series of 1890 Coin or Treasury Note with "ONE" very bold on reverse. Made only in relatively limited numbers (about seven million notes in all, spread over three different signature combination varieties), these are considered to be rarities today.

Beautifully carved ornate First Charter National Bank $1 note from the Moniteau National Bank of California, a town in Missouri. On the back of each National Bank note of this era is a representation of each state's official seal.

Series 1891 Coin or Treasury Note. The face or obverse is the same as the 1890 series, but the reverse is quite different.

Also among silver certificates are to be found the beautiful 1886 notes with five silver dollars on the back (the *numismatic reverse* style) and the very popular 1899 series $5 featuring the portrait of Sioux Indian Chief Onepapa.

In recent years there has been a particular interest in National Bank notes. Unlike the earlier so-called broken bank notes, National Bank notes are official obligations of the United States government. First issued in 1863, production was continued through the 1920s. These are broken down into three main areas of different designs and different legislative backgrounds; the First Charter notes issued from 1863 through 1882, the Second Charter notes issued from 1882 through 1902, and the Third Charter notes issued from 1902 through 1929. Typically a National Bank note bears a standard design, the name of the United States of America, signatures of the register of the Treasury and the treasurer of the United States, the name of the individual bank issuing the note, and the signatures of that bank's cashier and president.

Notes were not issued by all states for each charter period. For example, among $1 notes (a denomination issued only during the First Charter period, later charter periods were limited to the values of $5 or more) no notes were issued by banks in Arizona Territory, California, Florida, Indian Territory, Mississippi, Nevada, North Dakota, and several other states and territories. Notes of Wyoming Territory are exceedingly rare, and just a solitary $1 specimen is known! On the other hand, $1 notes from Connecticut, Illinois, New York, Michigan, and certain other states are very plentiful.

Often a collector will specialize in notes from a particular state of interest. Hundreds of different varieties can be obtained from certain states, particularly populous eastern ones.

Still another field of interest is banks with interesting names, such as the Brotherhood of Railway Clerks National Bank of Cincinnati and the Brotherhood of Locomotive Engineers Co-Operative National Bank of Cleveland, both in Ohio. The state of Pennsylvania in particular is well known for its interesting town names, many of which are found on notes. Samples include Slippery Rock, Red Lion, Birdsboro, Mauch Chunk, Harmony, McKees Rocks, Glen Campbell, Confluence, Punxsutawney, Elk Lick, Pleasant Unity, Shingle House, Cherry Tree, Blue Ball, Leechburg, and Intercourse.

When I learned that my wife Christie's maternal grandfather, the late Fred C. Woodson, was cashier of the Placentia National Bank in Placentia, California 1925-1926 I sought to obtain several notes with his signature. Christie's mother related how Mr. Woodson enjoyed signing the notes and carrying one around as a souvenir to show people. Today her mother owns a $5 note from this period.

Thinking that finding a note for myself would be an easy task I contacted several currency dealers. I soon learned to my chagrin that this was not to be so. Specialist William K. Raymond informed me that to his knowledge just *one other note* was known on the Placentia National Bank, that being a $10 bill, and it was safely ensconced in the hands of a collector who didn't want to part with it!

There are many challenges to be found in the field of currency. Don Miller, the noted Pennsylvania numismatist, entered a new area of collecting a few years ago—the specialty of privately-issued fractional currency notes issued during the Civil War. Literally thousands of varieties were issued, and yet there is no comprehensive reference book available in the field. Therein lies the challenge for Don. Is a particular 3c note from Concord, New Hampshire, a 10c note from Indiana Furnace, Pennsylvania, or a 50c note from the Parker House Hotel in Boston common or rare? Years from now he will know—based on his personal collecting experience, not someone else's reference book. Such is the thrill of sailing in uncharted waters.

John Murbach of my staff, long interested in the numismatic history of Hawaii, once owned the only $500 note in existence from that island kingdom. Printed by the American Bank Note Company, the note was a proof and was never issued for circulation.

Another interesting Hawaiian currency issue is the set of card money printed by students at the Lahainaluna Seminary School on the island of Maui. Used at the company store, the notes were of six different denominations and designs. John Murbach relates that those notes were issued just to the extent of 228 sheets with a total face value of $448.59.

Lahainaluna Seminary was one of the earliest high schools in the Pacific area. Opened in 1831, it was situated two miles inland from the rowdy whaling port of Lahaina, Maui.

At first, both male and female students attended classes. However, it was soon learned that the boys and girls were spending more time seeing each other than studying. So, the religious directors of the seminary opened up a separate female seminary in Wailuku on the other side of a 5000-foot-high mountain! Today these early Hawaiian paper money issues are very rare.

Currency from the United States and other countries of the world indeed offers a rich field of numismatic history and romance. The collecting possibilities are virtually endless.

Many collectors consider the epitome of 19th century United States currency design to be the "Educational" notes. Officially designated as Silver Certificates, Series of 1896, these notes, issued in the denominations $1, $2, and $5, depict allegorical scenes done in classical style. $1 notes depict "History instructing youth." In the background is a view of Washington, D.C. Around the borders are names of prominent Americans. The $2 note illustrates "Science presenting steam and electricity to commerce and manufacture" in an age in which America was just beginning to feel its industrial might. The highest denomination of the series, the $5 note, shows "Electricity as the dominant force in the world." During this time electric railway systems were used in many large cities, many homes were converting from gas to electricity for lighting, and electric motors were supplanting steam and mechanical engines for power.

Front and back of an uncut sheet of First Charter National Bank notes of the Merchants Exchange National Bank of New York. Each sheet was printed with two different denominations: three $1 notes and one $2 note. The latter denomination, because of the large horizontal numeral, was known as the "Lazy Two" variety. In accordance with federal regulations, all United States currency illustrations in this book are shown reduced in size. In actuality, large-size U.S. currency notes are the approximate size of an IBM data processing card. (When IBM cards were first devised in the early 1920s it was decided to make them the size of a piece of U.S. currency so that people could easily adapt to handling them.)

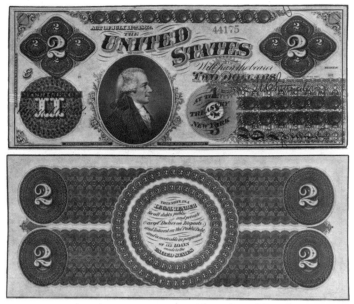

$2 Legal Tender note, series 1862. Issued during the Civil War, these were called "greenbacks" due to the distinctive color of the reverse. Interestingly, during one point of the war greenbacks sold for less than Confederate notes!

Souvenir sheet issued by the Department of the Treasury in conjunction with the American Numismatic Association convention in 1972. Pictured is the beautiful "Educational" motif used on the $2 note of 1896.

$2 Silver Certificate, series 1886. With signatures of Rosecrans and Hyatt. Many different signature combination varieties exist for this and other series.

$2 Silver Certificate, series of 1891. Portrayed is William Windom, Secretary of the Treasury 1881-1884 and 1889-1891.

$2 Coin or Treasury Note, series of 1890. The bold and beautiful back has made this a favorite with collectors.

$2 Federal Reserve Bank Note, series 1918, portraying a World War I battleship. Several dozen bank and signature combination varieties were issued.

$5 Legal Tender issue, Series of 1869. Depicted at the center is a pioneer family. To the left is the portrait of Andrew Jackson.

$5 Silver Certificate, Series of 1899, with Sioux Indian Chief Onepapa on the face.

$5, Series of 1923. The famous "porthole note" with Abraham Lincoln.

FIVE-DOLLAR NOTES offer many dazzlingly beautiful designs. On this page are shown several, including the famous 1886 Silver Certificate which displays on the reverse five Morgan silver dollars of the 1886 date. The Silver Certificate featuring Sioux Indian Chief Onepapa, shown at the upper right, has long been a favorite with collectors. Issued as the Series of 1899, eleven different signature combinations were produced. The Lincoln motif shown to the right has been dubbed the "porthole" note, due to the heavy frame around Lincoln's head. To the right is shown a representative example of one of the most interesting United States currency issues, a National Gold Bank note of California. These notes, issued in various denominations ($5 being the smallest), are printed on yellow-tinted paper and show on the reverse a cache of American gold coins. The notes were designed to replace heavy gold coins in the channels of commerce. Issued by various banks in San Francisco, Sacramento, Santa Barbara, Stockton, San Jose, Oakland, and Petaluma, these notes served their purposes well. Today, as currency authority Robert Friedberg has written, all issues are very rare in a state of preservation better than Very Good.

$5 Silver Certificate, Series of 1886, showing the famous "numismatic reverse" with five silver dollars.

$5 note issued by the First National Gold Bank of San Francisco, California.

High on the list of collectors' favorites is the "bison note" depicting a bison on the face with the explorers Lewis and Clark to the sides. Issued as the Series of 1901, these notes were produced in nine different signature combinations through the 1920s.

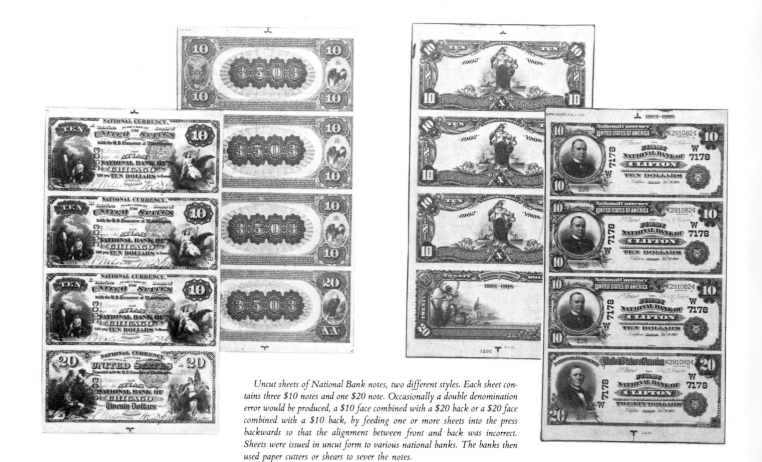

Uncut sheets of National Bank notes, two different styles. Each sheet contains three $10 notes and one $20 note. Occasionally a double denomination error would be produced, a $10 face combined with a $20 back or a $20 face combined with a $10 back, by feeding one or more sheets into the press backwards so that the alignment between front and back was incorrect. Sheets were issued in uncut form to various national banks. The banks then used paper cutters or shears to sever the notes.

A montage of National Bank notes from a wide variety of banks, towns, and states. Generally speaking, today notes of the $5, $10, and $20 denominations are most plentiful. $1 and $2 notes, issued only during the First Charter period, are quite elusive in all grades. Higher denominations such as $50, $100, and greater are likewise scarce, particularly among the earlier series. Collectors will often desire notes pertaining to their home state, or with an interesting historical association (such as a note bearing a facsimile signature of J.P. Morgan or a note issued in Baraboo, Wisconsin of circus fame), or with some other characteristic of significance. Literally thousands of different varieties exist. Unlike earlier broken bank notes, later National Bank notes were fully backed by the United States government and are redeemable even today (although no collector would want to do this!).

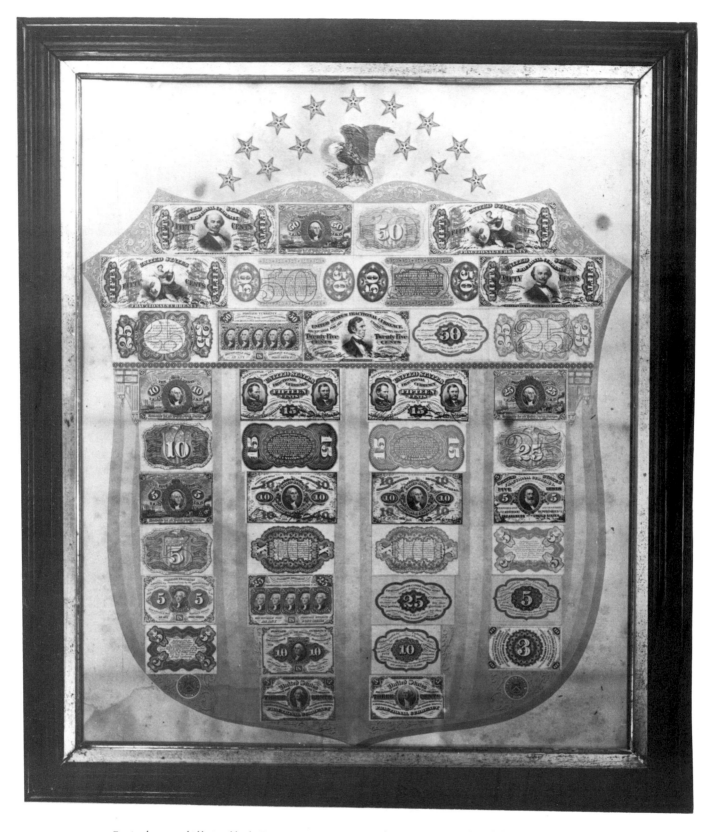

Fractional currency shields, issued by the Treasury Department in 1866 and 1867, measure 20 inches wide by 25 inches deep (outside frame measurement) and are framed in a gilt-lined wooden molding. Affixed to the front of a printed shield are 39 different fractional currency notes, each printed on one side. While most of the several hundred known shields have gray printed backgrounds, a few rare varieties have pink, green, or purple backgrounds. Prior to their shipment to various banks these shields were stored in a Treasury basement which became flooded. As a result, nearly all shields known today show evidence of staining, particularly along the lower border.

The purpose of the fractional currency shield was to assist in detecting counterfeits. A bank employee who suspected that a note was counterfeit could hold it up to the shield and compare the suspected with the genuine. Today fractional currency shields are highly prized by collectors.

During the early 19th century the Lahainaluna Seminary in Maui, Hawaii, was one of the pioneer high schools in the Pacific area. 228 sheets of currency were issued, having a total face value of $448.59. The six different denominations produced are shown above, each with a distinctive design. These particular notes, formerly in the collection of John Murbach, are exceedingly rare today. Throughout currency history many different enterprises issued notes. On the American mainland currency was issued by a wide variety of places, including schools, hotels, restaurants, railroads, and others. For example, Boston's Parker House Hotel, a popular stop with tourists today as it was over a century ago, issued fractional currency of different denominations during the Civil War.

The coins and tokens of Hawaii have afforded an interesting collecting specialty for many numismatists. The 1847 cent shown above is believed to have been produced on contract by a Massachusetts firm. Apparently many thousands were minted, for they exist today in several different die varieties. In 1883, with the backing of sugar king Claus Spreckels, the Kingdom of Hawaii issued a series of coins totaling $1,000,000 in face value. As part of this series 250,000 dimes, 500,000 quarters, 700,000 half dollars, and 500,000 silver dollars were struck at the San Francisco Mint, although they bear no mintmark. An example of the silver dollar is shown above. These pieces circulated widely in the Hawaiian islands and were used for many years. Today specimens of all denominations excepting the quarter dollar (which has come to light in several small hoards) are quite elusive in Uncirculated grade. A limited number of Proofs went to collectors, and these also are rare. Particularly elusive is a pattern issue, the 1883 eighth dollar or 12½-cent piece, which was produced in pattern form only. In later years Hawaiian coins piqued the imagination of inventive numismatists, and a number of fantasy and unofficial patterns were produced, including some beautiful pieces by Reginald Huth in the 1890s, and impressions in gold, some bearing the date 1884, produced in later years and sold to collectors, including King Farouk. The gold impressions lack the die quality and workmanship of the original 1883 issues.

Also popular with collectors are various tokens such as those issued by the Wailuku Plantation and dated 1871 and 1880, the Thomas Hobron token of 1879, the Grove Ranch Plantation tokens of 1886 and 1887, and the Waterhouse token of 1862.

Minting and Mischief

The United States Mint

3

The dollar, or one hundred cents, is the basic unit of United States coinage. Today silver dollars, or "cartwheels" as they are often called, are favorites with collectors.

Over the years dollars have been made in many forms. The 1776 Continental dollars, bearing the names of the original 13 colonies and legends attributed to Benjamin Franklin, were struck in pewter. From 1794 to 1935 the federal government produced silver one-dollar pieces. Following that, a descendant, the cupro-nickel composition Eisenhower dollar made its appearance. Trade dollars, made of silver and slightly heavier than the standard silver dollars, were made for trade in the Orient from 1873 through 1878. Tiny gold dollars were produced from 1849 through 1889.

Paper dollars were issued by the American government in many different varieties including Legal Tender issues, Silver Certificates, Federal Reserve notes, Treasury or Coin notes, and First Charter National Bank notes. In addition, literally thousands of different varieties of paper and metallic dollars have been produced over the years by private firms, banks, trading companies, and others.

In 1792, when the Philadelphia Mint opened its doors, coins in circulation were a diverse mixture of issues of other lands. French sous, British shillings, Spanish reales, and dozens of other denominations filled the channels of commerce. Although the dollar denomination had been adopted by Congress as the official monetary unit on July 6, 1785, no domestic coinage materialized. The aforementioned 1776 Continental dollar apparently was issued unofficially, for no coinage legislation providing for its production has ever been found. Even the engraver of the coins, the mysteriously-initialed "E.G.,"remains a mystery, although Eric P. Newman has suggested Elisha Gallaudet.

The obverse of this early American dollar, the 1776 Continental issue, depicts a sundial with the inscription, in Latin, FUGIO, meaning "I fly," referring to the rapid passage of time. Beneath the sundial is the admonition MIND YOUR BUSINESS.

When the United States Mint opened in 1792 the first issues produced were patterns. As Mint facilities were not ready for production until very late in the year, some of these early coins were produced elsewhere in Philadephia.

Prominent among 1792 patterns is a cent engraved by Birch and so identified by having the artist's name on the obverse. This piece, thought to be the work of young portrait painter Thomas Birch (information concerning Birch is conspicuously absent in numismatic literature), depicts on the obverse a young girl with flowing hair. Surrounding is the legend: LIBERTY PARENT OF SCIENCE & INDUSTRY.

Such a legend, containing as it did a bit of wisdom, was appropriate to the times. Earlier, paper Continental currency notes bore many similar axioms, usually inscribed in Latin, and accompanied by representative illustrations. Examples include a fighting heron and eagle with the motto: EXITUS IN DUBIOSEST ("The outcome is doubtful"), grain being threshed, with the inscription TRIBULATIO DITAT ("Affliction enriches"), and a beaver gnawing on a tree with the word PERSEVERANDO ("By perseverance").

The most famous 1792 pattern issue is the half disme. The *disme* spelling was soon changed to *dime*.

The 1792 half disme, or silver five-cent piece, is similar in concept to the Birch cent of that year and also bears the inscription, although slightly more abbreviated: LIB. PAR. OF SCIENCE & INDUSTRY. Apparently these early half dismes were struck outside of the mint building, as evidenced by an 1844 document, brought to light by Walter Breen, in which J.R. McClintock, a Treasury official, wrote:

"In conversation with Mr. Adam Eckfeldt [an early mint engraver, later superintendent] today at the Mint, he informed me that the half dismes were struck at the request of General Washington to the extent of $100, which sum he deposited in bullion or specie for that purpose. The Mint was not at the time fully ready for going into operation—the coining machinery was in the cellar

INTERIOR OF THE MINT, PHILADELPHIA. COINING ROOM.

CUTTING MACHINE.

The coining room of the Philadelphia Mint as it appeared during the mid-19th century. The large and heavy steam-powered presses shown were installed beginning in 1836. From that point onward manufacture became mechanized, production speed increased, and coins were of a more uniform quality. Then as now, the coining presses produced a terrific din.

To the left is shown a machine which cuts planchets or coining discs from metal strips. The leftover perforated strips are melted, cast in ingots, and then rolled again into still more strips for the same process. Today, planchet cutting is a highly mechanized process.

INTERIOR VIEW OF THE MINT, PHILADELPHIA. ADJUSTING ROOM.

Views of the Philadelphia Mint and accessories from the 19th century. The adjusting room in particular played an important part in early United States coinage. Legislation provided that silver and gold coinage be of full authorized weight. As it was impossible to add metal to a planchet or blank used to strike a coin, the planchets were often made slightly overweight and then filed down or "adjusted" to weigh the precise amount. Numismatists today are familiar with "adjustment marks," parallel striations which occur on many early United States coins of these metals.

Today the intrinsic value of coins bears little relation to the face value, so planchet weight, while observed within set limits, is not critical. The adjusting room is long gone.

DIES.

STEAM COINING PRESS.

of Mr. Harper, sawmaker at the corner of Cherry and Sixth streets, at which place these pieces were struck.''

In his fourth annual address, November 6, 1792, President George Washington referred to these tiny silver coins:

''In execution of the authority given by the legislature, measures have been taken for engaging some artists from abroad to aid in the establishment of our mint. Others have been employed at home. Provisions have been made for the requisite buildings, and these are now putting into proper condition for the purposes of the establishment. There has been a small beginning in the coinage of half dismes, the want of small coins in circulation calling the first attention to them.''

When full capacity was reached at the Mint in 1793 the only denominations produced for circulation were the copper cent and half cent. This was due to a complication which required Henry Voigt, the coiner, and Albion Cox, the assayer, to post substantial bonds of $10,000 each before handling gold and silver. Neither was able to secure a guarantee for the sum. In 1794 the amounts were reduced to $5,000 for Voigt and $1,000 for Cox. David Rittenhouse, Director of the Mint, furnished bond for Voigt, and Charles Gilchrist did the same for Cox. Once the financial hurdles were overcome, silver and gold coinage became a reality.

The Act of April 2, 1792, specified that silver dollars would weigh 416 grains, of which 89% was to be pure silver (371 grains) and the balance copper alloy for hardness. This standard was designed to compete with the Spanish milled dollar, the dollar-sized silver coin in most general circulation in the colonies. Indeed, earlier issues of Continental currency paper money were specifically payable in these Spanish issues.

The first year of silver coinage production, 1794, saw a paltry coinage of 1,758 pieces. As strange as it may seem, little public attention was given to these coins at the time of issue. There were only a few press notices, an attack on the design which appeared in the *New Hampshire Gazette* on December 2, 1794, being an example.

Coin collecting in the United States was virtually nonexistent at the time. It was not until several decades later that pioneer collectors such as Joseph J. Mickley began their cabinets and the United States Mint began collecting specimens of its own coinage.

Survival of 1794 dollars was a matter of chance. Among such random occurrences was the fortunate visit of an Englishman who came to America in 1795 as a tourist. Returning to Britain, he took with him about $10 face value in United States coinage, including two Uncirculated 1794 silver dollars. Considered no more than curiosities or souvenirs at the time, these were put away and forgotten in the traveler's country estate in Wakefield. Nearly 170 years later, in 1964, Lord St. Oswald, the pioneer traveler's descendant, put the two 1794 dollars and other coins on the auction block at Christies in London, through the British numismatic firm of A.H. Baldwin & Sons. When brought to Baldwin, the coins were carelessly loose in a pasteboard box!

Each of the two 1794 dollars, considered today to be the finest known specimens, sold for $11,400, a record price at the time. Today, of course, the value would be many multiples of that.

The 1794 silver dollar has been the subject of many studies over the years. The pieces are fairly easily traced in auction catalogs due to their high value and frequent illustration. It is estimated that approximately 100 different pieces of this date, mostly in well worn grades, survive in collections today. One numismatist, Jack Collins, has made a specialized study of these.

Silver dollars of the early years, 1794 to 1803, were made in several different styles, conforming in general design with other silver pieces of the same era. Typically, the obverse displays the head or bust of Ms. Liberty with the word LIBERTY above and the date below. The reverse depicts an eagle in one of several different styles. Curiously, the faces of the coin bear no evidence of value. To find this one has to examine the edge on which is lettered: HUNDRED CENTS ONE DOLLAR OR UNIT.

Even more curious is the fact that certain other early coins, the half dimes of the same era being examples, bear no mark of value whatsoever—on the faces or on the edge!

During this time in American history, despite the beginning coinage from the United States Mint, most transactions were conducted in foreign currency. Commercial ledgers, leases, and deeds, as well as most commercial transactions of the early 1800s were often figured in Spanish dollars or British pounds. A coin was usually taken in exchange at a value dependent upon its metal and weight. Thus, all manner of coins circulated at the value of one cent—including official United States cents made at the Philadelphia Mint as well as tokens portraying George Washington, copper coins of the states, and various foreign issues. The same was true of silver dollar-size pieces.

Close to 1½ million silver dollars were produced during the 1794-1803 years. Few were actually seen in circulation, however. Many of the coins when first minted were found to be worth slightly more in silver content than the popular Spanish milled dollars then in circulation. Vast quantities of the American-made coins were sent to the West Indies and exchanged at a slight advantage for a larger number of Spanish milled dollars. The

Spanish milled dollars were then brought back to exchange for American dollars at par!

All throughout the early history of United States coinage emphasis was on intrinsic or metallic value. Whenever a gold or silver coin became worth slightly more than its face value, due to the fluctuating silver and gold market, chances were good it would be exported or melted. This was a continuing problem for several decades at the Mint and accounted for the destruction of the majority of our early silver coins and nearly all of our early gold coins.

In 1804 the mintage of silver dollars and ten-dollar gold pieces was suspended in an effort to curb this practice.

In the early days it was the Mint's policy to keep dies on hand until they were used. Early in 1804 serviceable dies from 1802 and 1803 were still available. Coinage commenced early in 1804, and 19,570 pieces were struck, mostly dated 1803 but with some dated 1802, by the time the coinage suspension order arrived. No pieces actually *dated* 1804 were made.

In 1834 the Department of State desired to send specimen Proof sets of American coinage to the Sultan of Muscat and the King of Siam. Samuel Moore, director of the Mint, ordered that sets be prepared containing one each of the authorized denominations from the half cent through the ten-dollar gold piece. At the time, 1834, all denominations were currently being made except the silver dollar and the ten-dollar gold piece which had been suspended 30 years earlier (the actual coinage had been suspended, not the legislation authorizing the coinage). Desiring to include a specimen of the dollar, the largest silver coin, and the eagle, the largest gold coin, and realizing that neither was being currently produced at the Mint, Moore sought to determine the last date these were regularly minted.

Checking the coinage records he found that in 1804 19,570 silver dollars were struck. 3,757 ten-dollar gold pieces were minted in the same year. What Moore did not know was that while the 3,757 ten-dollar pieces were indeed dated 1804 at the time, the 19,570 silver dollars reported struck in 1804 actually bore the dates 1802 and 1803. There was no such thing as an 1804-dated silver dollar!

In 1834 it was the custom to keep on hand dies from earlier years. There was no official provision for the destruction of dies. Some were destroyed when they were broken, others were discarded when designs were changed, and still others were kept on hand. Searching through the supply of back-dated dies, no dollar or ten-dollar dies with the 1804 date could be found. So, Moore directed that new dies be made up with the 1804 date, thus officially completing the specimen set with the last-dated specimens of each denomination. Thus was born, 30 years after its date, the first 1804 silver dollar!

At the time coin collecting was beginning its first stirrings of popularity. A few years later during the 1840s William DuBois set about forming the Mint Cabinet, later to become the National Coin Collection (presently on display at the Smithsonian Institution). What better way to acquire needed coins than to exchange rarities for them? So went DuBois' reasoning. In 1843 a pioneer American collector, Matthew A. Stickney of Salem, Massachusetts, obtained an 1804 silver dollar from the Mint by exchanging for it an Immune Columbia "cent" struck in gold.

In 1867, Stickney, then the owner of one of the most impressive coin collections in America, wrote to Edward Cogan, a pioneer New York dealer, concerning his 1804 dollar:

"I was applied to by letter, July 4, 1866, by Mr. T.A. Andrews of Charlestown, Massachusetts, for the dollar of 1804, which he understood I had in my possession and wished to obtain by purchase, for a friend in California, or information where he could get another. In reply I stated, 'I have a genuine Proof dollar of the United States coinage of 1804. I do not dispose of my coins which are not duplicates, at any price. It is not likely that if I parted with this dollar I could ever obtain another, as I have been told by a gentleman (W. Elliot Woodward, Esq.), largely engaged in selling coins at auction, that he thought it might bring $1,000.'

"On the 18th of November, 1866, Mr. Andrews wrote to me again, offering in the name of his friend '$1,000 in currency or the value in gold coin,' saying: 'I merely make the offer as requested to do, being aware that you stated that you do not dispose of coins except duplicates.' I declined the offer on the 23rd of the same month.

"Of the genuineness of my United States dollar of 1804, I think there cannot be entertained a doubt, as it was handed to me directly from the Cabinet of the United States Mint in Philadelphia, on the 9th of May, 1843, by one of its officers (Mr. W.E. DuBois), who still holds the same situation there, and who can testify to it."

At least eight 1804 silver dollars were struck during the 1830s and 1840s. In the late 1850s and possibly the early 1860s at least seven more were made, the latter with a slightly differing reverse. Today 15 specimens are known to exist. In 1974 my firm purchased the Idler-Granberg-Atwater-Neil-Hydeman specimen, advertised it for sale for $165,000, and sold it to a Minnesota firm which reportedly resold it soon thereafter for $225,000.

Texas dealer B. Max Mehl, who glorified the 1913 Liberty head nickel and spent over $1,000,000 advertis-

The 1804 silver dollar has been one of the most controversial coins in American numismatics. Apparently no pieces bearing the date 1804 were struck prior to the mid-1830s, and most pieces were issued even later, circa 1858-1860. As most pieces were privately produced at the Mint for private gain, facts surrounding their issue were kept hidden. Obfuscating the issue were numerous pronouncements issued by various officials who stated that these pieces were indeed genuine Mint products struck in the year 1804. Scholars, studying the fabric of the coins, weights, and other characteristics, differed. Finally in 1962 Eric P. Newman and Kenneth E. Bressett wrote their landmark book on this singular coin, "The Fantastic 1804 Silver Dollar," and laid the matter to rest.

Time has increased the fame of the 1804 dollar, and despite its uncertain birth, the piece has remained today what dealer B. Max Mehl originally called it, "The King of American Coins." Whenever one appears on the market it is a cause for a flurry of excitement.

The above specimen, shown in enlarged illustration, is the Idler coin sold by the author's firm in 1974.

ing to buy specimens of that coin, also had a great fondness for the 1804 dollar. When the specimen I owned was offered earlier for sale by Mehl in 1947 as part of the Will W. Neil Collection he described it as follows. The exclamation points are those put in the description by Mr. Mehl himself:

"The celebrated 'King of American Coins'—the 1804 dollar! Lot number 31. 1804 United States silver dollar! The famous Idler specimen. The best known specimen of this great rarity . . ."

While other United States silver dollars, the 1870 San Francisco piece being an example, may be rarer than the 1804, no silver dollar has been accorded the publicity that the 1804 has garnered over the years. Indeed, the single coin issue was the subject of one of the most fascinating books ever written on an American numismatic subject, *The Fantastic 1804 Dollar*, by Eric P. Newman and Kenneth E. Bressett.

Adding a certain amount of whimsy and spice to the entire situation are numerous Mint declarations over the years, many of them in letter form, stating that the 1804 silver dollars were of course genuine Mint products actually made in the year 1804! At the same time, certain privileged officials at the Mint, including perhaps those who were writing the letters, were secretly profiting by filtering 1804 dollars and other "goodies" to favored dealers and other "friends of the Mint."

In his monumental work, *The U.S. Mint and Coinage*, Don Taxay devotes a chapter entitled "A Workshop for Their Gain" to the land office business the Mint did in 1804 silver dollars, pattern coins, and other products which were easy to make and still easier to sell.

In 1861 Theodore Eckfeldt, grandson of Adam Eckfeldt and a night watchman at the Mint, had a lively trade selling pattern coins to dealers in Philadelphia, New York, and other eastern locations. Each time a protest appeared, either in the numismatic press or, worse, in a public newspaper, the Mint would deny restriking and making rarities. Even so, the practice of midnight mischief, perhaps too tempting to resist, went on and on. Taxay writes that Henry R. Linderman (director of the mint intermittently from April 1867 to December 1878) was particularly pernicious in this regard and struck coins for his own personal gain. In contrast, earlier Mint officials such as Snowden and Pollock, while perhaps enriching themselves, used many of the coins to acquire specimens for the National Collection.

Despite the checkered background of the 1804 silver dollar it is considered today to be one of the most desirable of all United States rarities. Time seems to increase its fame.

In 1834, Robert M. Patterson, who became director of the Mint in July of that year, secured the service of Ti-

tian Peale, member of a distinguished American family of artists, and Thomas Sully to formulate new coin motifs. To this duo was added Christian Gobrecht to assist Mint Engraver William Kneass who was in failing health.

Gobrecht, born in Hanover in York County, Pennsylvania, on December 13, 1785, was apprenticed at an early age to a Manheim, Pennsylvania clockmaker. Following the clockmaker's death, Gobrecht, his apprenticeship incompleted, set out on his own and moved to Baltimore where he engaged in the engraving of designs on faces, dials, and cases of watches and clocks.

He then engaged in engraving for the graphics trade, cutting type faces and making illustrations. In 1810 he engraved a portrait, after a painting by B. Thott, of George Washington, for inclusion in J. Kingston's *New American Biographical Dictionary*, published in his own city. For *Delaplaine's Repository* he engraved portraits of David Rittenhouse, Benjamin Franklin, and Benjamin Rush.

In 1811 Christian Gobrecht moved to Philadelphia and set up trade as a portrait engraver, medal engraver, and die cutter. By 1816 he was employed by Murray, Draper, Fairman & Co. as an engraver of bank note vignettes and numerals. In 1825, following a design by Thomas Sully, Gobrecht engraved a medal for the Franklin Institute. Many other medals, some of which were struck by the Philadelphia Mint, were prepared during the late 1820s and early 1830s.

In autumn 1835 Gobrecht joined the Mint staff. His first task at the Mint was to prepare an obverse design of the figure of Liberty seated, based upon paintings and sketches by Titian Peale and Thomas Sully, following the request of Director Patterson and Engraver Kneass. The inspiration for this seems to have been rooted in the neoclassicism movement of the era. Gods, goddesses, and other allegorical figures were often portrayed in long flowing robes and with such accoutrements as birds, wreaths, shields, weapons, and other objects.

The reverse design portrayed a flying eagle, modeled after Peter, an eagle which in the early 1830s was a mascot at the Mint. During one unfortunate day he perched on a flywheel of a coining press and was killed. Through the art of taxidermy Peter was saved for posterity by being stuffed and mounted in a flying position. At the United States Mint exhibit at the World's Columbian Exposition in Chicago in 1893 Peter, in all his glory, sat atop a colorful banner overlooking selections from the National Coin Collection there on display.

In 1836 pattern silver dollars were struck. The obverse bore a seated representation of Liberty, the reverse a flying eagle.

Director Patterson, viewing initial impressions of the die, was so delighted with the new design that he directed Gobrecht to place his name on it. Gobrecht, following the signature used on certain of his medals, boldly signed it C. GOBRECHT F. (the F being for *fecit*, in Latin, *made it*) in the field above the date.

A contemporary newspaper article about the design called Gobrecht "conceited" for placing his name so prominently on the piece. The engraver's feelings were hurt, and, despite placations of Director Patterson, Gobrecht removed his name from the field and placed it inconspicuously on the base of Liberty.

According to Mint records, just 18 initial impressions were struck in silver with C. GOBRECHT F. in the field. However, this design was so historically important and so popular with collectors that in later years, especially 1858-1860, additional pieces were made for trading and resale. Today the coin still remains an extreme rarity, and it is doubtful if more than a few dozen are known to exist.

The engraver's signature controversy resolved, the Mint struck on December 31, 1836, 1,000 Gobrecht-designed silver dollars with the engraver's name in tiny letters on Liberty's base. These were struck on planchets or blanks weighing 412½ grains, the new standard which was subsequently adopted by law on January 18, 1837. As these pieces were struck prior to the official authorization (the authorized weight on December 31st, 1836, was the old standard of 416 grains), they have long been referred to as patterns by collectors. However, apparently nearly all of the 1,000 pieces, plus 600 additional of the same design (dated 1836) minted on March 31, 1837, were placed in circulation to serve the needs of commerce. Thus a good case can be made for their being regular issues.

Additional Gobrecht silver dollars, originals and restrikes, were struck bearing the dates 1838 and 1839. These differed from the earlier issues by the addition of stars around the obverse. Varieties were made with and without stars on the reverse and with reeded or plain edges.

Despite the success of Gobrecht's design, when silver dollar coinage in quantity was resumed in 1840 the flying eagle reverse design modeled after Peter was dropped. In its place a more conservative eagle perched on an olive branch and clutching three arrows was used. The same general motif had been used years earlier on many other silver denominations; the half dollars beginning in 1807 being an example.

Dollars of the new Liberty seated design were produced steadily from 1840 onward. In addition to those made for the channels of commerce, each year several dozen would be struck in Proof condition for use in presentation sets and for sale to collectors. There was an exception: apparently no Proof silver dollars were minted in 1853.

The years 1858-1860 were busy ones at the Mint. Coin collecting was beginning to achieve wide popularity. In 1858 the American Numismatic Society was founded. Collector groups met in several eastern cities. Other activities such as auction sales and numismatic publications likewise attracted interest. In the year 1858 Proof sets were made available for the first time to collectors. It is estimated that just 80 silver sets (containing coins from the three-cent silver piece through the silver dollar) and about 200 copper-nickel flying eagle cents (incorporating Gobrecht's earlier flying eagle design) were made.

A popular rarity at the time was the 1856 flying eagle cent. This popularity has extended to the present day. Actually, the 1856 flying eagle cent is a pattern coin, not a regular issue. The design was not officially adopted until February 21, 1857, a year after the 1856 pieces had been minted.

During the 1850s there had been agitation to abandon the old copper large-diameter cent. The rising cost of copper plus the bulkiness of the coin produced many complaints. Following much experimentation, the flying eagle design struck in copper-nickel alloy was decided upon in 1856. Pieces were struck, mostly as business strikes (with frost on the surfaces rather than the mirror-like fields of Proofs) for distribution to congressmen and newspaper editors who received them late in the 1856 year and early in 1857. About 600 original pieces were made.

By 1859 a specimen of the 1856 flying eagle cent was valued at $2.00, or, putting it in more dramatic terms, 200 times the original face value. This was too much for temptation to resist, and additional pieces were struck at the Mint, possibly by Theodore Eckfeldt who was making, among other things, 1804 silver dollars at the time.

The number of 1856 flying eagle cents restruck is not known. I estimate it to be on the order of 1,000 to 1,200 specimens, bringing the total mintage, including the 600 originals, close to the 2,000 mark. All of the restrikes, to my knowledge, are Proofs.

It is interesting to note that the idea of hoarding 1856 flying eagle cents has appealed to a number of collectors over the years. Today, hoarding them would be prohibitive due to cost, but in the years when 1856 flying eagle cents could be picked up for a few dollars each it was a different matter. The late John A. Beck, a Pittsburgh, Pennsylvania, numismatist, was able to acquire 531 pieces during his lifetime! This fabulous hoard was distributed during the mid-1970s by Abner

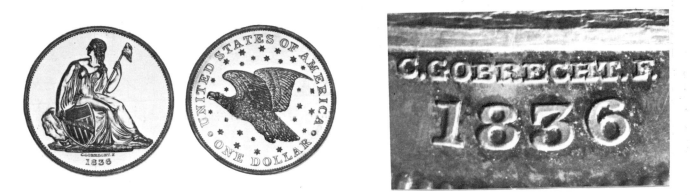

In 1836 the first Liberty seated pattern silver dollar made its appearance. Boldly signed C. GOBRECHT. F. (an abbreviation for "Christian Gobrecht made it") above the date and below the base, the coin invited criticism from several who saw it. It was considered a conceited action for the engraver to sign a coin so prominently. Offended, Gobrecht removed his signature and placed it in a less conspicuous spot. Eighteen specimens with the C. GOBRECHT. F. signature were originally struck in silver in 1836. In later decades, probably circa 1858-1860, additional pieces were struck. Today the piece remains quite rare and stands as a classic among coins of its denomination. Certainly it has one of the most interesting stories attached to any dollar.

Later Gobrecht dollars of 1836 had the engraver's name removed from the field (as shown above left) and placed inconspicuously on the base of Liberty. Note that the 1836 Gobrecht dollar has an obverse field without stars and a reverse field with an eagle flying upward amidst 26 stars, 13 small ones and 13 large ones. Certain varieties of later Gobrecht dollars, such as the 1838 shown above right, have stars on the obverse field and no stars on the reverse. Gobrecht dollars became a popular mint product during the 1858-1860 years (in particular), and numerous other varieties were made to tease and tantalize collectors; including issues in copper, pieces with reeded edges and plain edges, pieces with stars and without stars on the reverse, and so on.

To the right are shown two medals engraved by Gobrecht for the Massachusetts Charitable Mechanic Association. Each bears the distinctive and bold signature C. GOBRECHT. F. as used on Gobrecht's famous silver dollar of 1836. The illustrated medals were struck with a blank center reverse and then hand engraved as different awards were given; in this instance one award for cassimers and another for a life raft. By the time of the latter award, 1874, Gobrecht had been dead for 30 years.

Kreisberg and Jerry Cohen, dealers who handled the Beck Estate. Also included in the Beck Estate was a fabulous treasure trove of massive California 50-dollar gold slugs as well as other scarcities and rarities.

Amazing as the Beck hoard was, it pales when compared to the amazing group of 756 1856 flying eagle cents amassed by George W. Rice during the late 19th and early 20th centuries. Probably many of the Rice coins later passed to Beck. F.H. Stewart of Grand Rapids, Michigan, was another hoarder of 1856 flying eagle cents. In 1903 he offered some of them for sale at the following prices: Good $7.00, Very Good $7.50, Fine $8.00, Very Fine $8.50, AU $9.00, Uncirculated $10.00, and Brilliant Proof $11.00.

Indeed, the price structure of the 1856 flying eagle cent over the years is quite interesting. In 1859, as noted, a specimen was valued at $2.00. In 1881 in an auction by John W. Haseltine a piece brought $3.95. In the 1907 sale of the Stickney Collection by Henry Chapman $8 was the valuation. By 1916 the realization climbed to $13 when the Gregory Collection was sold by Henry's brother, S.H. Chapman.

On June 23rd, 1936, B. Max Mehl sold a specimen for $19.25. In 1941 at the W.F. Dunham sale the same dealer cataloged a piece which sold for $62.50. By 1946 Mehl realized $165 for the same issue at the W.C. Atwater sale. $175 was the price several years later at the 1950 Jubilee Sale by the same seller.

In 1954 the Anderson-Dupont sale by Stack's saw a realization of $310. At that time I was desirous of acquiring a specimen and telephoned Harvey Stack. "I'll have to charge you $300 for one. I know that's a lot, but one just sold for $310 in our sale," was his reply.

Prices continued to climb, and by the late 1970s a select Proof specimen sold for nearly ten times the 1954 valuation! As is the case with most other classic American rarities, the 1856 flying eagle cent has been a superb investment over the years.

The 1858-1860 period of restriking activity at the Mint, spurred on mainly by the 1856 flying eagle cent, furnished the opportunity to produce many earlier-dated silver dollars as well. In addition to 1804 silver dollars, Gobrecht dollars of 1836-1839 were restruck (including some in copper, a metal which was not used for pattern purposes during the original years). Additional Proof dollars were made bearing the dates 1851 and 1852, coins which in the meantime had become scarce. It apparently was realized that no original Proof silver dollars had been minted in 1853, so this oversight was made up for and 12 specimens were struck!

Even recent coins were the subject of restriking activity at the time. As mentioned, 80 silver dollars of 1858 were originally struck in that year as part of the Proof sets made available to collectors. It subsequently developed that no additional 1858 dollars were made for circulation, leaving the net mintage of silver dollars bearing that date at just 80 coins. Thus was created a rarity, a coin potentially far more valuable than the 1851 and 1852 silver dollars (with mintages of 1,300 and 1,100 business strikes respectively) which were recognized as being scarce. What to do? The obvious thing was to make more 1858 dollars, and apparently this was done in 1859 and 1860. How many more? No one knows, but based upon the frequency of surviving examples it is probable that about 100 to 200 extras were minted.

1860 Mint records show that 1,330 silver dollars were struck in Proof condition. In addition, slightly over 200,000 were minted for circulation. 1,330 Proofs is a remarkable figure for that year or any year close to it. In 1861, 1,000 pieces were made in Proof. The following year, 1862, during the middle of the Civil War which had split the nation, just 550 Proofs were issued. It was not until 1880 that the number of Proof dollars would exceed the record of 1,330 set in 1860. Even then the 1880 figure of 1,355 pieces represented a temporary high. Proof mintage was to slump from that point and to drop below 1,000 pieces for nearly every year until Proof silver dollar coinage was discontinued in 1904.

Most Liberty seated dollars from 1840 onward were struck at the Philadelphia Mint. There were, however, some exceptions. In 1846, 1850, 1859, and again in 1860, specimens were struck at the New Orleans Mint. The San Francisco Mint, which first produced coins of certain other denominations in 1854, minted silver dollars for the first time in 1859, during which year 20,000 pieces were struck.

On November 13, 1861, Reverend M.R. Watkinson of Ridleyville, Pennsylvania, wrote a letter to the secretary of the treasury to suggest that God be recognized on our coinage. The times were difficult, the Civil War was just beginning, and the thought found favor. The secretary of the treasury wrote to the Mint and said that "no nation could be strong except in the strength of God, or safe except in His defense," and that "the trust of our people in God should be declared on our national coins."

Various mottos were considered, including GOD OUR TRUST, GOD AND OUR COUNTRY, and OUR TRUST IS IN GOD. These were inspired by the verse in Francis Scott Key's *Star Spangled Banner* which suggests "And let this be our motto, In God Is Our Trust."

It was not until 1864 that IN GOD WE TRUST was adopted as the official motto. In that year it appeared for the first time on coins in circulation, the two-cent pieces.

Seventh Street front of buildings a few years before their destruction

An early 20th century view of the 1792 United States Mint as it appeared before its destruction. Frank Stewart, owner of a Philadelphia electric company, purchased the Mint property, tore it down, and then wrote a book about its history. What a shame it wasn't saved for posterity!

DIRECTORS AND SUPERINTENDENTS·OF THE UNITED STATES MINT, FROM 1853–1892.

Col. A. Loudon Snowden	James Pollock	Henry R. Linderman
	Col. O. C. Bosbyshell	
Adam Eckfeldt	Daniel M. Fox	J. Ross Snowden

A gallery of United States Mint officials from the years 1853 through 1892. These were the years of the greatest "hanky-panky" at the mint, and included above are pictures of some of those most closely involved. Henry R. Linderman in particular built a private collection, replete with many rare and one-of-a-kind patterns, die combinations, and other exotica.

COINING PRESS.

Mid-19th century view of a coining press in operation at the Philadelphia Mint. As each coin is struck it is ejected into a wooden drawer or hopper.

As years went by IN GOD WE TRUST was added to other coin denominations as well. In 1866 it made its appearance on the quarter, half dollar, silver dollar, and larger gold coins.

Since the late 19th century IN GOD WE TRUST has appeared on most of our coins. Among the exceptions are two caused by President Theodore Roosevelt who personally objected to the use of the Deity's name on money. In a letter dated November 11, 1907, he said:

"My own feeling in the matter is due to my very firm conviction that to put such a motto on coins, or to use it in any kindred manner, not only does no good but does positive harm and is in effect irreverence which comes dangerously close to sacrilege . . ."

During the same year, 1907, new designs were prepared by Augustus Saint-Gaudens, under Roosevelt's direction, for the $10 and $20 gold pieces. Following the President's wishes, IN GOD WE TRUST was omitted. In 1908 Congress intervened and restored the motto, which was continued from that time onward.

It is interesting to note that United States paper money carried no reference to God until 1955. In that year President Dwight D. Eisenhower signed a bill which provided that IN GOD WE TRUST appear on our currency. Matt Rothert, a prominent numismatist (later to become president of the American Numismatic Association; in 1973 I had the privilege of cataloging his superb collection for auction), first made the suggestion to the government in 1953. The idea came to him while attending church one Sunday morning. As the collection plate was passed, it occurred to him that only the *coins* in the plate had the IN GOD WE TRUST motto. He then thought that since our paper money has a much wider circulation abroad than our coins, a message about this country's faith in God could be easily carried throughout the world if it were on United States currency.

When the new silver dollars and other denominations with IN GOD WE TRUST made their appearance in 1866 they were immediately popular with collectors. Little leprechauns were again at work in the Mint, perhaps after hours, dreaming up things to sell to collectors. Wouldn't it be nice if there were some silver dollars, half dollars, and quarters dated 1863, 1864, and 1865 with IN GOD WE TRUST? Certainly that would be a good idea and would result in more than just a few dollars of private profit! Accordingly, specimens were struck in silver, copper, and aluminum to fill the demand which surely would occur.

However, the leprechauns did not cover their tracks completely. In 1977 when I was cataloging the Fairfield Collection for auction I described a most unusual coin: an 1865 pattern silver dollar with IN GOD WE TRUST on the reverse, boldly struck over a later-dated silver dollar, a piece dated 1866! Here for the first time was

graphic evidence that certain pieces dated 1865, and perhaps earlier issues as well, were produced during the 1866 year!

During the mid-19th century virtually no attention was given to collecting coins by mintmark variety. Collectors could care less whether or not 1850-O (New Orleans Mint) silver dollars were scarce or whether 1859-S (San Francisco Mint) dollars were hard to find. In fact, they didn't give a hoot whether or not they even existed! It was not until Augustus G. Heaton, a Philadelphia artist, published a pamphlet called *A Treatise on the Coinage of United States Branch Mints* in the early 1890s that any interest of note developed on the subject.

During this time most collectors desired one specimen of each silver dollar date. This demand was easily satisfied by ordering a Proof from the Philadelphia Mint. Few if any collectors saved Uncirculated examples of the coinage. It was reasoned that Proofs were *better* than Uncirculated pieces. Today the situation is viewed in a different light: Proofs, representing a different method of manufacture, are considered to be *different* (rather than better) from Uncirculated pieces. The result of this is ironic. Today Uncirculated dollars from this era are far, far rarer than Proofs.

At first glance this seems paradoxical. For example, in the year 1865 there were 500 Proof Liberty seated dollars struck plus 46,500 Uncirculated coins (pieces intended as business strikes for use in circulation). Of the 500 Proofs struck, presumably all went into the hands of collectors who paid a premium. Accounting for loss and damage over the years, it is safe to say that probably 300 Proof 1865 dollars still exist today.

On the other hand, all of the 46,500 business strikes of the same year went into the channels of commerce, most to be shipped overseas to be melted down for their bullion value. Collectors ignored them. After all, Proofs seemed to be a *better* condition than Uncirculated.

The survival of an Uncirculated coin today is strictly a matter of chance. Perhaps a few were acquired at the Mint or through banking channels by non-collectors who gave them as gifts. A few others were undoubtedly casually saved in drawers, desks, and other such happenstance places. The result is today that only *a few dozen* Uncirculated pieces are known. Proofs are at least ten times more common than Uncirculated pieces!

Early in 1850 a group of Mormons on their way to the California gold fields wintered in Nevada's Carson Valley for a few weeks, awaiting the melting of the snows before crossing the Sierra Nevada mountain range. Prospecting in the Carson River, these adventurers found traces of alluvial gold in a canyon on Mount Davidson's southern side.

1795 silver dollar with flowing hair design on obverse and small, delicate perched eagle on reverse. This style was made in 1794 and 1795 only. The 1794, of which just 1,758 were made, is a rarity today.

1870 Liberty seated silver dollar with IN GOD WE TRUST motto on reverse. This style, first adopted in 1866, was continued through 1873.

1796 draped bust silver dollar with small eagle reverse. This style was used from mid-1795 until 1798. On the reverse the eagle is smaller, differently shaped, and is perched on clouds.

1883-CC Morgan dollar. Designed by George T. Morgan, the Morgan dollar was produced from 1878 through 1904, and then again in 1921. Hundreds of millions were made.

1800 draped bust silver dollar. Reverse with heraldic eagle style as used from 1798 through 1804 inclusive. The "scratches" visible on the reverse clouds below the word "OF" are not scratches but, rather, are mint-caused adjustment marks; the result of filing away excess metal during the planchet preparation process.

1921 Peace dollar. This design, in sculptured high relief, was made only one year. The following year, 1922, saw a lowering of the relief to a more shallow format. In that style Peace dollars were made through 1935.

1844 Liberty seated silver dollar. This style was produced from 1840 through 1865 inclusive. Coinage was accomplished at the Philadelphia, New Orleans, and San Francisco mints.

1879 trade dollar. Trade dollars, weighing 420 grains and slightly heavier than standard dollars, were produced 1873-1878 for export to the Orient. From 1879 through 1885 Proofs were made for collectors.

SILVER DOLLARS were issued in many different forms over the years, a number of which are shown on this page. The silver dollar, with substantial silver content, was discontinued in 1935. Later "silver dollars," excepting certain specimens sold at a premium to collectors, are made of alloys, mostly copper and nickel. First coined in 1794, dollars were produced from that year through 1804, again for circulation 1840 to 1873, then 1878 through 1904, then 1921 through 1928, and again 1934 and 1935. While the earlier issues 1794-1873 saw fairly wide use in the channels of commerce, most later pieces were struck as the result of political influence exerted by western silver mining interests.

Naming their discovery Gold Canyon, the Mormons continued prospecting for several weeks, garnering as much as $5 per man per day. Spring came, and the travelers moved on to California, leaving their discovery behind.

Within a few months a group of Mexicans from Sonora moved in and began working the area. By 1851 they had been joined by various others, many of whom stopped on their way to California. At one time perhaps as many as 200 miners kept busy washing traces of gold from river bottom sand.

In 1853 the Grosch brothers, Ethan Allan and Josea Ballou, began prospecting the Gold Canyon area. Within a year or two they came to a startling conclusion: the "black sand" which earlier miners treated as an inconvenience was very high in silver content! Following a brief leave, they returned to the area in September 1856 and discovered two veins of silver ore. An assay indicated that it might be worth as much as $3,500 a ton! But success was not to attend the Grosch brothers. In August 1857 one incurred a gangrene infection which ultimately led to his death. A few months later the other died after a winter ordeal of freezing and hunger.

The discovery was not to remain dormant. By early 1859, Harry T.P. Comstock, James Fennimore, and others were busy prospecting. Reverting to earlier days, the main attraction sought by the miners was gold. $10 to $15 per day could be earned on a placer claim, a remarkable wage for the time. Little did the miners know, but the bluish-gray matter which kept impeding their gold mining efforts was silver ore far, far richer! The knowledge of the Grosch brothers' bonanza had not spread, and emphasis remained on gold.

Toward the end of June 1859 two Nevadans, B.A. Harrison and J.F. Stone, sent sacks of the bluish-gray ore to Melville Atwood, an assayer in Grass Valley, and J.J. Ott, who carried on the same trade in nearby Nevada City, both in California. Atwood was to later claim that the ore assayed at $3,500 per ton in silver and $876 in gold. While this may have been on the optimistic side, there was no doubt that a bonanza was in the offing.

The news spread like wildfire, and within the next several weeks speculators, miners, merchants, and others arrived, mostly from California. One of them was George Hearst, later to achieve fame as the owner of newspapers which emphasized sensational news happenings. It was Hearst's journalism, many believe, that incited the United States to fight the Spanish-American War.

By 1860 about 5,000 miners and others were concentrated in Virginia City and its surroundings, center of the bonanza which became known as the Comstock Lode. In the years from 1860 to 1863 over $22,000,000 worth of silver and gold came from Nevada's soil. 1864 saw a jump in production to close to $17,000,000 for this one year alone. Production stabilized, and as the richest veins were worked out, the bonanza diminished. By 1870 the yield of the area was slightly over $8,000,000 per year.

In the early years silver bullion was transported over land, mostly to California, to be converted into coin. The transportation costs were high, and the yield to silver producers was reduced proportionately.

On March 3, 1863, a legislative act was passed establishing a branch mint in Nevada. In 1866 a group of three citizens approved a Carson City site donated by Abe Curry, founder of that town. On September 18th of the same year the cornerstone of the new mint was laid.

Within a year and a half the building was essentially complete. The next two years, all of 1868 and most of 1869, were spent equipping the mint for its intended purposes; installing assaying and refining equipment, coining presses, and other devices. On January 8, 1870, the mint opened and received its first bullion.

Curiously, by this time Comstock Lode production had dwindled, and the outlook for the future was bleak. Many fortune-seekers left the city, buildings were deserted, and many businesses went into bankruptcy.

Then the tide turned. The Belcher and Crown Point Mine found a new vein which had excellent promise. Then in 1873 the Consolidated Virginia Mine tapped a vein described as "absolutely immense, and beyond all comparison, superior in every respect to anything ever before seen on the Comstock Lode," according to the *Mining and Scientific Press,* of San Francisco. In July 1870 shares in the Consolidated Virginia Mine cost $1 each. According to T.H. Watkins, a modern student of Virginia City lore, by 1875 the same shares fetched $700!

In the latter year Comstock Lode production zoomed to $26,000,000, then in 1877 it continued to an all-time peak of $37,000,000. From that point the trend was downward.

From 1859 through 1882, the latter year being the last great bonanza period, mines in the Comstock Lode produced close to $300,000,000 worth of metal, primarily silver.

The Carson City Mint opened with much promise. In 1870 coins of the higher silver denominations, dime through silver dollar, and the higher gold denominations, $5 through $20, were produced. Mintages were modest; 12,462 being the mintage for dollars. In 1871 the silver dollar mintage, each coin with a tiny identifying "CC" mintmark on the reverse, had dwindled to just 1,376 coins. 1872 saw the mintage of dollars at 3,150, then in 1873, the last year of Liberty seated coinage, just 2,300 were minted. These figures were

paltry compared to the millions of dollars worth of silver being extracted from the earth.

This seems paradoxical, and indeed it is. The explanation comes in several parts. First, politics reared its ugly head and a policy was set up whereby silver producers depositing bullion at Carson City had to pay a tax equivalent to the transportation that would have been charged if the bullion been shipped to San Francisco! In one fell swoop this negated any savings promised by the Carson City Mint!

Second, the Carson City Mint, located remotely from centers of commerce, paid silver producers in bank drafts rather than in cash. As cash was needed to pay miners and other expenses, bank drafts caused unwanted delays.

Third, studies indicated that the cost of producing coins at Carson City was nearly double that of producing coins at San Francisco and over five times what it cost to strike coins in Philadelphia! The high cost of labor, extreme cost of mint production, and limited facilities all contributed to inefficiency.

The result was that the Carson City Mint, intended to bring many benefits to local miners and merchants, was a failure from the very start.

A failure it might have been to commerce at the time, but not to numismatists today. The small trickle of coins which emanated from the Carson City Mint from the year of its opening, 1870, until its final closing in 1893 included some of America's most highly prized rarities.

In the early 1870s silver coinage at the San Francisco Mint was likewise nominal. Most Comstock Lode bullion was shipped to the East for coinage into silver dollars at Philadelphia. The bullion which did reach the San Francisco Mint was mainly coined into half dollars, silver dollars, and beginning in 1873, trade dollars.

Following an initial coinage of silver dollars in 1859, no coins of that denomination were struck at the San Francisco Mint until 1870. The number produced in the latter year was not recorded, but it must have been small. Fewer than two dozen specimens are known today, thus isolating the 1870-S as the rarest regular-issue American silver dollar. In 1872 9,000 silver dollars were struck at San Francisco. The following year, 1873, saw a mintage of just 700. Of the 1873-S dollars minted, not a single authentic specimen is known today. Here is one of the greatest unresolved mysteries of numismatics. Were indeed 700 pieces coined? Were they put into circulation, with the possibility that one may turn up someday? The answers are unknown.

In 1873 the mintage of silver dollars ceased. During that year silver was selling on the open market for $1.30 per ounce, a figure above what the government was paying, so little bullion flowed into the mints. The coinage law enacted in that year saw many changes, including an end to the unpopular two-cent and silver three-cent issues. No provision was made for further continuation of silver dollars, so coinage of that denomination ended.

For many years silver and gold had been emotional issues in American politics. The public was distrustful of paper currencies. (Early Continental Congress notes issued by the fledgling United States government had become so depreciated as to be worthless, and many privately issued bank notes were likewise of no value.) Intrinsic value was demanded in silver and gold coins.

Although the law did not specify this valuation, by the middle of the 19th century silver producers and others with motivation claimed that silver had a "true value" of $1.29 per ounce. From 1794 onward, silver dollars weighed 416 grains, including 371.25 grains of pure silver. Beginning with the coinage of 1836 Gobrecht dollars the total weight was lowered to 412½ grains by decreasing the amount of alloy. The value of silver remained the same. By dividing the number of grains of silver in an ounce, 480, by the number of grains in a silver dollar, 371.25, the figure of $1.2929 was derived.

Whenever the price of silver on the open market rose above $1.29, silver coins were exported or melted. Whenever the price dropped significantly below $1.29 there was a tremendous outcry, particularly from the western silver-producing states, demanding that the United States purchase silver bullion to make silver dollars, thereby providing a steady demand.

Following the Coinage Act of February 12, 1873, all was at peace on the silver market for a short time. Then the price of silver began to fall. Production in the Comstock Lode increased dramatically, adding to the supply in the depressed market.

At the same time a depression swept the United States, the Panic of 1873. Merchants, bankers, farmers, and others, primarily in the southern and western areas of the country, were hard hit. A cry rose for government support of silver. In this way prosperity would be restored to the West, it was reasoned. No matter that this would cause inflation. This was fine, for it meant that debts incurred earlier could be repaid later with dollars that were easier to earn.

Help came in the form of the Bland-Allison Act passed by Congress on February 28th, 1878, notwithstanding the veto of President Rutherford B. Hayes. This legislation required the government to purchase at the current market price each month $2,000,000 to $4,000,000 worth of silver and to coin it into dollars.

Why silver dollars? These achieved the maximum coinage efficiency. It was decided that millions of silver dollars would be easier to produce than twice the number of half dollars, ten times the number of dimes, and so on. Thus were sown the seeds of the greatest numismatic treasure hunt of all time . . .

THE GOULD & CURRY MILL—"DESILVERIZING" THE ORE BY THE PATIO PROCESS.

LOADING WAGONS WITH ORE TO BE TRANSPORTED TO THE MILL FOR GRINDING.

The Gould and Curry Mill was a gigantic enterprise. Ore was brought here from many different mining locations, pulverized, and reduced to extract the gleaming silver metal. Gould and Curry remained in business for many years. In reorganized form it was active until well into the present century, its shares being a popular speculation in the 1920s.

Today the collector with an eye for history will have no trouble assembling a nice collection of hundreds of different gold and silver mining stock certificates from the western areas of the United States, primarily Nevada and Colorado. Silver ingots produced by refiners such as Gould and Curry are occasionally encountered today. Most are stamped with their weight, fineness (percentage of pure silver), value, and, often, a serial number and the date of production.

INTERIOR OF A MINE—MINERS EXCAVATING SILVER ORE.

CARS LADEN WITH ORE COMING OUT OF THE MINE.

While the production of silver in Virginia City, Nevada makes romantic reading today, during the height of activity there in the 1860s and 1870s silver mining was very hard work, as these early engravings illustrate. Conditions were usually dangerous, damp, dark, and dusty. Pay was low, and accidents were common.

NEW SHAFT.
HOISTING WORKS OF THE YELLOW JACKET SILVER MINING CO., GOLD HILL, NEVADA.

"C & C" SHAFT.
JOINT SHAFT OF THE "CON. VIRGINIA" & "CALIFORNIA" MINING COMPANIES, VIRGINIA, NEVADA.

The Yellow Jacket Silver Mining Company, here shown in a view from the 1870s, was one of hundreds of different producers in Nevada's famous Comstock Lode. Mining enterprises ranged from large establishments such as this to tiny one-man operations which consisted of little more than a short tunnel, a pickaxe, shovel, and wheelbarrow. For over two decades the silver industry brought immense wealth to Nevada.

In 1870 the Carson City Mint opened, ostensibly as a convenience to the local mining industry. However, politics raised its ugly head once again, and various restrictions (see accompanying story) made it just as economical to ship the silver metal to distant San Francisco! Nevertheless, the Carson City Mint did produce a small but steady stream of silver and gold coinage from 1878 through 1885 and again from 1889 to 1893. The mint building stands today in Carson City and is the home of the Nevada State Museum. On the ground floor is one of the original coining presses, used today to strike souvenir medals, originally made in the Virginia & Truckee Railroad machine shops.

Virginia City today is an interesting place to visit. The main street, following a disastrous fire (virtually all mining towns in United States history have had one or more conflagrations), was rebuilt in 1876. The Bucket of Blood saloon, Piper's Opera House, and other early structures are of interest to the tourist today. While commercialism and tourism have converted most of the stores and shops to modern activities, still there is abundant Victorian-era architecture to be seen in its original form. Surrounding Virginia City are countless mine dumps, tailings, and other remnants of that city's days of glory.

"UNION SHAFT,"
JOINT SHAFT OF THE "SIERRA NEVADA," "UNION CON." & "MEXICAN" MINING COMPANIES.
VIRGINIA, NEVADA.

As the above illustration indicates, the Union Shaft tapped into the underground properties of several different mining companies. Each day hundreds of workers would come to the mill, descend by elevators deep into the earth, and chip away at the silver ore below. Silver was found in veins, called "stopes," many of which ran at unusual angles, therefore making access difficult.

At one time flooding was a serious hazard in many of the Virginia City area mines; so much so that production was curtailed in many areas. Adolph Sutro, a San Franciscan originally born in Germany, came to the rescue. With training in engineering and a great mechanical aptitude, he constructed the Sutro Tunnel which drained the unwanted liquid and permitted mining to continue at an increased pace. Sutro became a multimillionaire and moved back to San Francisco. There he established a mansion overlooking the Pacific at Seal Rocks. He dabbled in politics and ran for mayor and won. His final years were spent collecting early books, statuary, art, plants, and other artifacts. He is best remembered today for the huge French-chateau-style Cliff House which was built on the rocks overlooking Seal Beach in the late 1890s. Until it burned in 1907, this was one of the most prominent and imposing structures in western America.

GOLD AND SILVER.

Silver Dollar Treasure Hunt

4

Early in March 1878 the United States Mint was faced with a problem of immediately beginning to coin tons of silver dollars. The Liberty seated design, last used five years earlier in 1873, had been discontinued and was not in favor for readoption. Young and relatively inexperienced mint engraver George T. Morgan was given the assignment of producing a new silver dollar design as fast as possible.

Morgan, born in Birmingham, England, in 1845, attended the South Kensington Art School. Following that he became a student under Wyon at the Royal Mint in London.

In 1876, Director Henry R. Linderman brought Morgan to the United States and employed him as an assistant to William and Charles Barber. His initial appointment was for six months, but it later turned out that he stayed at the Mint for 48 years!

In 1877 mint engravers Anthony C. Paquet, William Barber, and George T. Morgan produced many different pattern half dollars. The issues were dazzling in appearance for the most part and included what today are known as some of the most outstanding designs in coinage history. In his book, *United States Pattern, Experimental, and Trial Pieces,* Dr. J. Hewitt Judd notes: "More patterns were made in 1877 than in any other year. Most numerous are the rare pattern half dollars which form one of the most beautiful and interesting series of all." In addition, several varieties of pattern dollars were made.

One of Morgan's pattern half dollar designs was selected to be the new silver dollar motif. The obverse depicted a young girl. Preparing for the series of 1877 patterns, Morgan enlisted the help of a friend, Thomas Eakins, a famous artist of the period. Eakins introduced him to Miss Anna Williams, a girl of 19, from the same city. In November of 1876, the same year the country was celebrating its centennial, Miss Williams and Morgan had several sittings.

It is interesting to note that the attractive young model sought no publicity at the time. In fact, her iden-

tity was kept secret and was discovered only by accident later in 1879 when a newspaper man found that the silver dollar was virtually a photographic likeness of her! From that time onward she rapidly achieved fame and became the recipient of thousands of letters and many visitors at her home and at the kindergarten where she taught school.

Within a few weeks after receiving his assignment in early 1878, Morgan had a design ready to go. It turned out to have quite a few problems such as the wrong number of tail feathers in the eagle and the wrong relief to the eagle's breast, but at least it was a design and could be used.

Early in the use of the Morgan motif a nit-picking observer noticed that there were only eight feathers in the tail of the eagle. Ornithological opinion at the time suggested that there should be one feather which is longest at the center, thus giving an odd number of feathers totally. So, the design was changed to seven feathers in the tail, a difference hardly noticeable even to the most careful observer today. In the haste to proceed with the massive coinage of dollars, many eight-tail-feather dollars were simply overpunched with hub dies with seven feathers, creating what collectors know today as the seven-over-eight tail feathers variety.

From the outset, Morgan's hurried 1878 design, at first called the Bland dollar after the originator of the enabling act which produced it, and later called the Morgan dollar, was criticized. It was hardly artistic, in fact it was quite ugly, its detractors said. Both the popular press and numismatic writers and editors condemned the production.

In July Director Linderman wrote to Morgan:

"Whilst the head on the obverse of the silver dollar is very good indeed, the eagle in the reverse looks a little as if it had been drawn from a model instead of from life, and it is evident that the artist has suffered from the necessity of crowding so much in a limited space.

"The wreath under the eagle rather unduly competes with the bird, and I think that the old English letters

The first Morgan dollar issued in 1878. By a minor technical oversight that only the most nit-picking observer would notice, the eagle's tail had eight feathers rather than an odd-numbered seven. Accordingly, the design was quickly modified. The 1878 dollar signaled the mintage of hundreds of millions of coins which were to bear Morgan's design.

The 1877 pattern half dollar, actually viewed today as a "miniature Morgan dollar," from which the 1878 dollar design was copied.

might have been omitted and modern letters used in their place.

"The changing of devices after a coin is once issued to any considerable extent is not good policy, and for that reason I think it is doubtful whether we should sanction any change of the devices of the silver dollar, unless there should be by law a change in the weight of the piece.

"With a view to get a good eagle for the gold coins less than the double eagle, as well as for the silver coins of less denomination than the dollar, I desire that you will make a new model of an eagle and cut therefrom a new reverse for the silver dollar, omitting the wreath, and substituting the modern letters now in use at the mint, for the old English letters. If you should succeed in getting an entirely satisfactory representation of an eagle, it is probable that we shall adopt it at some future time. The model must be regarded as an experiment and will be submitted to me for inspection."

Indeed, there was a good basis for the criticism of Linderman and others, one of whom referred to the eagle as a "turkey." Recently in United States coinage many beautiful designs had been produced. The attractive 1871 Indian princess issued by Longacre, why wasn't it used? Or, what about the stunningly beautiful 1872 Amazonian design by Barber? Then, too, there were many other designs of pattern half dollars and dollars to choose from in the 1870s, any one of which might have been more attractive.

George T. Morgan, perhaps feeling the criticism more sharply than anyone else, sought to produce a work of lasting beauty. The results were two of the most attractive patterns ever issued by the Mint. Made only in pattern form, these were the 1879 *Schoolgirl* design and the 1882 *Shield Earring* issue. Both of these feature a pleasing young girl's face with a happy countenance—done in an artistic and classical way.

Director Linderman took ill in autumn 1878 and died in January 1879. Undoubtedly his death plus general lethargy at the Mint was the reason the Morgan dollar design was not further changed. Two of America's most beautiful coins, the 1879 Schoolgirl and the 1882 Shield Earring dollars, were never seen by the general public.

In 1878 production of silver dollars began in full force. By year's end the Philadelphia Mint had produced over ten million of the new design, Carson City over two million, and San Francisco nearly ten million!

Coinage continued at record high levels. In 1879 the Philadelphia, Carson City, New Orleans, and San Francisco mints emitted 27,000,000 coins. The same figure was to be achieved 1880 through 1883. 1884 and 1885 saw an annual production of over 28,000,000 coins. Then came 31,000,000 in 1886 and 33,000,000 in 1887.

Beginning in the mid-1880s, silver fell in value to below 90 cents per ounce. As the Treasury made its purchases at the current market level, this meant that additional quantities of the white metal flowed into government vaults. In the year 1890 a peak production of 38,000,000 silver dollars was achieved!

On July 14, 1890, the Sherman Silver Purchase Act replaced the Bland-Allison Act and provided that 4,500,000 ounces of silver were to be purchased each month at a price not to exceed $1.00 for each 371.25 grains. These silver purchases were to be paid for by a special issue of paper money. Under the provisions of the earlier Bland-Allison Act 291,272,018.56 ounces of silver were purchased at a cost of $308,279,260.71 and converted into the staggering total of 378,166,793 silver dollars!

Under the Sherman Silver Purchase Act 168,674,682.53 ounces were purchased for an expenditure of $155,931,002.25. Most, but not all, of this bullion was converted to silver dollars, resulting in an additional 187,027,345 pieces being struck. Thus, over 565,000,000 silver dollars were produced because of those two pieces of legislation! In addition, about 5,000,000 silver dollars were struck from silver from other sources.

What was to be done with all of these dollars? Clearly, there was no need for them in commerce. Silver dollars had never been popular with the public. The only place they circulated to any extent was in the western states, and this was mostly as a result of a determined effort to make the public conscious of silver metal. Relatively few were needed for the channels of commerce. As a result, most dollars were minted, put in Treasury bags of 1,000 coins each, and shipped to Treasury vaults for long-term storage.

The Pittman Act of April 23, 1918 resulted in 270,232,722 silver dollars of earlier dates being melted down, slightly less than half the total minted earlier. This reminds me of the old army make-work chore of digging a hole and then filling it up again!

Another tremendous destruction of silver dollars resulted under the terms of the World War II Silver Act of December 18, 1942, which provided for the melting of approximately 50,000,000 silver dollars to obtain metal for wartime uses, including the Manhattan Project which eventually produced the atomic bomb.

George Morgan's design, first minted in 1878, was continued until 1904. During that time slightly over 570,000,000 Morgan dollars were struck. As noted, nearly half that number went to the melting pot under the provisions of the Pittman Act.

While careful mintage records were kept of Morgan dollars produced over the years at the Philadelphia, Car-

1870 pattern dollar featuring a new Liberty seated design by William Barber. The reverse employs the standard die of the time with IN GOD WE TRUST on a flowing ribbon above the eagle. Like most other patterns of this era, these dollars were made in a wide variety of styles, mainly to sell to numismatists.

James B. Longacre's Indian princess design, variety with stars around the obverse. Reverse is from the regular die. To tempt numismatists, specimens were made in silver with reeded edge, silver with plain edge, copper with reeded edge, copper with plain edge, aluminum with reeded edge, and aluminum with plain edge!

Pattern 1878 silver dollar by William Barber. Barber, Morgan's senior at the Mint, resented the selection of Morgan's design for the regular issue dollar. In 1878 and several following years, both Barber and Morgan produced many additional silver dollar patterns, some of outstanding artistic merit, but all were consigned to oblivion.

Above are shown three of the reverse variations, differing from each other slightly by the appearance of the eagle, position of IN GOD WE TRUST and other characteristics, which were combined with the regular 1879 obverse to create patterns.

This distinctive 1879 pattern silver dollar by William Barber featured a small head of Liberty on the obverse and a delicate eagle on the reverse. Like other patterns of the era, it was considered and then rejected. The Morgan dollar design, which found favor with very few people within the mint and without, continued in regular coinage use until 1921.

In 1878, 1879, and 1880 numerous experiments were made with metallic composition. One alloy proposed was "goloid," a metal in which the ratio of silver to gold was 16 to 1, a popular standard. Using this weight formula, two dollars struck in goloid metal would together contain $1 worth of gold and $1 worth of silver. It was a bright idea, but in practice it was rejected for neither mint officials nor the public would have been able to easily distinguish between a coin struck in regular silver alloy and one struck in goloid. To prove this point, Dr. Henry R. Linderman came before the Committee of Coinage, Weights, and Measures on January 17, 1878, and presented specimens struck in each metal. No one could tell them apart, for the only distinguishing difference was a secret mark which only Linderman knew. Various alloys were experimented with, but in the end all were rejected. To provide curiosities for collectors such nonsensical (from the viewpoint of their intended purpose) varieties as goloid metric dollars struck in aluminum were produced!

1871 Indian princess pattern silver dollar by James B. Longacre. The starless obverse gives this coin a particularly beautiful cameo-like appearance. Similar pieces, but with stars around the obverse border, were produced the preceding year, 1870. All were issued posthumously, for Longacre died on January 1, 1869. Today numismatists consider the Indian princess dollars to be among the finest of their era. Examples were struck in silver, copper, and aluminum.

William Barber's 1872 Amazonian design, produced in the denominations of $1 (shown above), 50c, and 25c, is a highlight of 19th century coinage. The obverse depicts Liberty seated in the form of an Amazonian woman. The design, considered beautiful by collectors today, was rejected at the time for its militaristic character: there were two eagles, two shields, and a sword—but no olive branch (representing peace) and no mention of the word LIBERTY.

The regular issue 1878 Morgan dollar (shown above) drew much criticism. Conceived in haste, the design was hardly a work of coinage art, its detractors said. And, when one reviews the illustrious pattern dollars of its era, one is tempted to agree.

High on the "most wanted" list of many numismatists is the 1879 "Schoolgirl" dollar designed by George T. Morgan. Morgan, reacting to the criticism of his standard design, produced this, one of the most beautiful patterns ever to emanate from the Philadelphia Mint. The reverse design was attractive in its own right and years later (1915) furnished the inspiration for the reverse of a commemorative $2½ gold piece.

If at first you don't succeed, then try, try again. And, this is what George T. Morgan did. Another one of his designs is the classic and beautiful "Shield Earring" pattern dollar of 1882. Like the Schoolgirl dollar before it, it was never adopted. What a shame!

United States pattern coins tell the story of what might have been, but wasn't. Nowhere is this more poignantly demonstrated than in the silver dollar series. Some of the most beautiful American silver dollars ever produced—and the 1872 Amazonian, 1879 Schoolgirl, and 1882 Shield Earring issues are candidates for this honor—never went beyond pattern form. While they are familiar to collectors today, the public never knew of them. What a loss to art and to numismatics!

son City, New Orleans, and San Francisco mints, no comparable records were kept of the date and mintmark varieties melted. As most issues had not been placed in circulation but, rather, had been bagged and sent to Treasury vaults, Morgan dollars in circulation were not proportional to their original mintages. For example, one of the commonest Morgan Dollars from a mintage viewpoint was the 1903-O of which 4,450,000 were struck. And yet, very few pieces were placed into circulation. Uncirculated 1903-O dollars were so scarce that when the first issue of *A Guide Book of United States Coins* appeared in 1946, the 1903-O was a rarity priced at $110. At the same time an Uncirculated 1893-S commanded a valuation of $100 and a Proof 1895 sold for $35, to mention just two other elusive issues.

Contrasting with the 1903-O is, for example, the 1897 Philadelphia Mint issue of which 2,822,000 were made for circulation. In 1946, this issue catalogued at $5. Twenty years later it still was valued at the same amount. Pieces were and still are common; apparently most of the original mintage was placed into circulation or was available via distribution through banks.

No one knew the story, but there were plenty of guesses. Some issues, 1895 Philadelphia Mint business strikes, for example, were presumed entirely melted. Others were thought to be partially melted. Still other issues may not have been melted at all. It was a guessing game and anybody's guess could be a winner!

There were some surprises now and then. In 1946 the 1885-CC silver dollar, a coin of which 228,000 were minted, was considered to be scarce and catalogued for $12.50. Then some were released through the Federal Reserve and the price plummeted to the point at which in 1957 Aubrey Bebee, who maintained an active market in dates and mintmarks of Morgan dollars from his Omaha, Nebraska office, was offering 1885 Carson City specimens for just $3.95 each. About the same time I purchased the Reverend Edward W.W. Lewis Collection in Norwich, Connecticut. Included were several hundred 1878-CC silver dollars for which we agreed upon a wholesale price of $2.00 per coin.

There was always the possibility of a bonanza. One day in the 1950s, I was notified by the Second National Bank of Wilkes-Barre, the financial institution in which I had my coin office at the time, that they had received a bag of 1,000 1903 silver dollars in Uncirculated condition. Did I want them for face value? I did, and shortly thereafter I realized a windfall profit by selling them at $7.50 per coin.

The big mystery remained concerning the 1895 Philadelphia Mint issue. In that year just 12,880 Morgan dollars were struck, the lowest recorded mintage of any dollar of the 1878-1904 years. Produced were 12,000 Uncirculated pieces destined for use in commerce and 880 Proofs. The Proofs, of course, went to collectors who paid a premium for them as part of their sets. Today, allowing for loss, damage, and destruction, probably 500 to 600 of these Proofs exist. In addition, some Proofs were invariably spent, either by intent or by accident, accounting for a few worn 1895 Philadelphia Mint dollars which have been authenticated and which are struck from the same dies.

What about the 12,000 pieces made for circulation? It is presumed that at the time of striking they were put into 12 canvas bags of 1,000 coins each and shipped to storage. Were there any put into circulation at all? So far as it is known, no. I have never seen nor heard of a single Uncirculated 1895 issue. All worn ones that I have seen have either been alterations (usually made by removing the mintmark from an 1895-O or 1895-S coin) or have been Proofs which have been circulated. None has shown the telltale mint frost which would indicate that it originally was produced as a business strike. So far as it is known, every one went to the melting pot! Thus, 1895 is isolated as the prime rarity among Morgan dollars today.

During the 1950s, when I was beginning my numismatic interest, I often would look through silver dollars at banks in the Wilkes-Barre, Pennsylvania area. The Forty Fort State Bank, the First National Bank in Kingston, the Miners National Bank in Wilkes-Barre, and the Second National Bank in the same city all kept on hand modest stocks of dollars. For certain occasions, particularly around Christmas time, there would be an increased demand to use these coins as gifts, and additional dollars would be on hand. Silver dollars were not and never had been a popular circulating coin in the East, so demand for use in the channels of commerce was negligible.

To obtain silver dollars the banks would place an order through the Federal Reserve System, in this instance to the Philadelphia Federal Reserve Bank. Back would come silver dollars in $1,000 bags. These would fall into two categories: mixed bags with circulated coins, and Uncirculated bags—the latter containing just one date or mintmark variety per bag.

More often than not the Uncirculated bags consisted of Philadelphia Mint coins. Issues from 1878 to the late 1880s were particularly common. At that time they were worth just face value, $1 each. Had I possessed the financial ability and desire I could have bought 5,000,000 silver dollars, 50,000,000 of them, or 200,000,000 of them—no one else wanted them or cared!

Searching through silver dollars would produce a scattering of dates and mintmarks. I remember finding a number of worn 1885 Carson City issues and saving them as duplicates for they were worth a small premium. 1892-S was slightly scarce, and some of those were saved

SALE 97

CATALOG

OF THE

CELEBRATED NUMISMATIC COLLECTION

FORMED BY

WILLIAM FORRESTER DUNHAM

CHICAGO, ILLINOIS

Complete Series of the United States Coinage

From Half-Cents to Twenty-Dollar Gold
From the First Coinage to 1936
Including the Most Famous of All Rarities

The "KING OF AMERICAN COINS"

The 1804 DOLLAR!

AND THE

"KING OF ALL RARITIES"

The 1822 HALF EAGLE!

Also: 1802 Half Dime; 1875 Three-Dollar Gold; 1852 Original Half Cent; Rare American Colonials including Virginia Shilling; The Largest Collection of Encased Postage Stamps Ever Formed; A Most Complete Collection of "Hard Times Tokens;" Extensive Collection of Canadian Coins and Tokens; Pioneer Gold Coins including a Brilliant Proof Kellogg & Co. $50.00; Rare U. S. Fractional Currency; Confederate Notes, over 2,500 Different Varieties.

Ancient Gold, Silver and Copper Coins; Rare Foreign Gold, Silver, Platinum and Copper Coins. Rare Medals, etc., etc.

TOTAL OF OVER FOUR THOUSAND LOTS!

TO BE SOLD AT

AUCTION

(ALL BIDS BY MAIL)

Tuesday, June 3rd, 1941

Cataloged and to be Sold by

B. MAX MEHL

Numismatist

Mehl Building   Fort Worth, Texas

On Tuesday, June 3, 1941, B. Max Mehl, the well known Texas dealer, offered the Dunham Collection by mail bid sale (interestingly enough, nearly all of Mehl's auctions were conducted as mail bid sales, without public floor bidding participation), spotlighted Lot 1179 as reproduced on this page to the right. Indeed, any catalog of the time would wax enthusiastic when an Uncirculated 1903-O dollar crossed the auction block. It didn't happen often.

U. S. SILVER DOLLARS, NEW ORLEANS and SAN FRANCISCO MINTS

Lot No.
1165 1859 Brilliant uncirculated; field slightly chafed, but with full brilliant luster.
1166 1860 Brilliant semi-proof. Equal to a perfect brilliant proof. Not a rare date, but certainly scarce so choice.
1167 1880 Uncirculated, with full mint luster. Very scarce so choice. Listed at $5.00.
1168 1883 Brilliant uncirculated.
1169 1884 Extremely fine with mint luster.
1170 1885 Bright uncirculated; sharp.
1171 1887 Uncirculated, with frosty mint surface; highest portions show slight cabinet friction. Scarce. Listed at $6.00.
1172 1889 Just a shade from uncirculated; mint luster. Very scarce.
1173 1890 Uncirculated. Very scarce. Listed at $6.00.
1174 1896 Uncirculated, with full original frosty mint surface. As scarce as last
1175 1897 Brilliant uncirculated. Rare so choice. Catalogs at $7.50.
1176 1899 **Plain edge.** Struck slightly off center. Very fine. Rare.
1177 1900 Uncirculated, with mint luster. Very scarce. Listed at $7.50.
1178 1901 Just a shade from uncirculated, but with considerable mint luster. Just as scarce as last.

Lot No. 1179

PERFECT UNCIRCULATED 1903 O MINT DOLLAR

1903 New Orleans Mint. Uncirculated, sharp, with full original mint luster. Just as perfect as the day it was minted. Excessively rare so choice. Listed at $35.00 and worth a great deal more in this remarkable condition.

1180 1904 Last year of issue. Just a shade from uncirculated; considerable luster.

SAN FRANCISCO MINT SILVER DOLLARS

Dollars were first coined at this mint in 1859. None were coined until 1870. 1871 was omitted. A small coinage was issued in 1872, and then none coined until 1878. Coinage was resumed in 1878.

1181 1859 Extremely fine with considerable luster. Very light scratch on reverse.
1182 1872 Practically uncirculated with mint luster. Rare. Listed at $25.00.
1183 1878 Uncirculated; cheek slightly rubbed, and with bright luster. Scarce. Listed at $5.00, as are all of the following when in uncirculated condition.
1184 1879 Brilliant semi-proof.
1185 1880 Brilliant uncirculated.
1186 1881 Brilliant uncirculated; almost equal to a proof.
1187 1882 Uncirculated; bright mint luster.
1188 1883 Brilliant semi-proof.
1189 1884 Just a shade from uncirculated, but with considerable mint luster. Rare. Listed up to $10.00.

also. I never did find an 1893-S. With the exception of the 1895, all dates 1878 through 1904 were available. I even found a couple of 1903-O dollars, but they were well worn.

1903-O dollars in Uncirculated grade were great rarities. In the late 1950s this issue was almost legendary. To be sure, circulated 1903-O dollars weren't that hard to find. As mentioned, I found a few in circulation myself. Aubrey Bebee in his 1957 catalog offered specimens of the 1903-O in Very Good grade at $14.50, Fine $19.00, Very Fine $33.50, and Extremely Fine at $47.50.

Uncirculated coins weren't priced at all. Instead there was the notation: "wanted."

I had never owned an Uncirculated 1903-O dollar and, indeed, prime collections which came on the market were apt to lack this particular issue. By 1962 the 1903-O dollar cataloged at $1,500 in Uncirculated grade in the 1963 (released in the summer of 1962) issue of *A Guide Book of U.S. Coins.*

Appropriate praise was given to an Uncirculated 1903-O on rare occasions when one surfaced in an auction catalog. For example, in November 1954 when Stack's sold the Anderson-Dupont Collection, Lot 2623 was described as: "1903-O. Uncirculated. Lightly toned, marred only by two tiny edge nicks at lower obverse. Hardly ever comes better than this. Probably the most famous date of the Morgans. Very rare." The coin sold for $175. In the same sale a Proof 1878 Morgan dollar with eight tail feathers fetched $28, an Uncirculated 1889-CC brought $30, and an Uncirculated 1892-S brought $52.50.

Going back a few years earlier in history the 1941 sale of the W.F. Dunham Collection, conducted by B. Max Mehl, featured Lot 1179, enclosed in a special frame on a page, and described as:

"PERFECT UNCIRCULATED 1903-O MINT DOLLAR. 1903 New Orleans Mint. Uncirculated, sharp, with full original mint luster. Just as perfect as the day it was minted. Excessively rare so choice. Listed at $35.00 and worth a great deal more in this remarkable condition."

The piece brought $24.50. In the same catalog a Proof 1895 dollar, Lot 1116, brought $7.35!

The same seller offered the Royal Sale in 1948. Lot 1837 was described as follows:

"1903-O. Dollar. Uncirculated. An even, beautiful, lustrous mint surface. Extremely rare in any condition, but especially so choice. A similar specimen in my sale of the Roe Collection, three years ago, brought $115. Probably not more than four or five known in this remarkably choice condition."

Amazing! The most prominent dealer in America at the time stated that no more than four or five were known!

The scene shifts to November 1962. At that time Morgan dollars were moderately popular with collectors. They offered many appeals then as they do today, primary being the appeal of obtaining a coin from the 1880s or 1890s in Uncirculated grade for less than one would have to pay for comparable coins of smaller denominations. Most Philadelphia Mint issues of the 1880s and 1890s were obtainable for about $2 to $3 per coin. They weren't rare; those prices simply reflected a dealer's handling cost.

To be sure there were some scarcities. The *Guide Book of U.S. Coins* at the time listed in Uncirculated grade the 1879-CC at $95, 1880-CC $25, 1881-CC $25, 1882-CC $12, 1889-CC $275, 1892-S $175, 1893-S a whopping $1,200, 1895-S $150, 1896-S $60, and 1901 Philadelphia $37.50. The rare Proof 1895 Philadelphia issue commanded $1,500.

High on the list of rarities were three more coins: the 1898-O at $300, the 1904-O at $350, and the famous 1903-O at $1,500. As noted, the 1903-O was one of the greatest rarities in American silver coinage in Uncirculated grade. Few would argue with B. Max Mehl's contention that just a few were known.

One nice November day in 1962 Jim Ruddy and I were quite excited. We had just received a telephone call from a gentleman who offered to sell us several rolls each of the 1898-O and 1904-O Uncirculated dollars for just over $100 per coin, just a fraction of the catalog value! And, if we purchased that group he would sell us a few, not just one but a few, Uncirculated 1903-O dollars, a coin which we had never seen in that grade!

In 1962 the purchase of silver dollars for $100 each was a big transaction. $2,000, the price of a roll of 20 coins, was not a figure to be sneezed at.

To lend perspective I recall that around then a Florida collector put his lifetime holdings on the market and solicited bids from dealers all over the country. Our offer of $14,000 won the collection. What a prize! Included were sets of Proof Liberty nickels, Barber dimes, collections of Liberty walking half dollars and Liberty standing quarters, and many other dazzling pieces. In today's market we would undoubtedly pay $250,000 or more for the same group!

The silver dollars represented big business. Not often did such a transaction take place. A year earlier we had announced that our firm had achieved a sales level of $1,000,000 per year, a previously unheard of figure. A well known New York coin dealer telephoned to express disbelief. But, the figures were indeed true.

17TH ANNUAL
BARGAIN PRICE LIST

UNITED STATES COINS
PAPER MONEY
COINS OF ALL COUNTRIES
NUMISMATIC ACCESSORIES

Price $1.00

4514 N. 30TH STREET
OMAHA 11, NEBRASKA

U. S. EARLY DOLLARS

We offer the following choice silver dollars, all conservatively graded and attributed by Bolender's Book, at real Bargain Prices:

Date	B. No.		Lists	Price	Date	B. No.		Lists	Price
1795	1	V.G.+	40.00 F	32.50	1799	8	Ex. Fine	80.00	59.50
1795	5	V. Fine	60.00	57.50	1799	11A	Fine	55.00	35.00
1795	5	Ex. Fine	100.00	95.00	1799	11A	Ex. Fine	100.00	75.00
1795	5	Ab. Unc.	175.00 U	125.00	1799	9	Ex. Fine	60.00	52.50
1795	14	Ex. Fine	100.00	90.00	1799	11	Ex. Fine	90.00	72.50
1796	2	V.F.+	125.00 E.F.	95.00	1799	12B	V.Fine	75.00	59.50
1796	4	V. Fine	75.00	72.50	1799	16B	V.F.+	100.00	80.00
1796	4	Ex. Fine	100.00	90.00	1799	18	V.F.+	100.00	80.00
1797	1	V. Fine	85.00	80.00	1799	21	V. Fine	75.00	57.50
1797	1A	Fine	75.00	65.00	1800	2	V.G.-Fine	60.00 F	32.50
1797	3	Fine	75.00	65.00	1800	10	Ex. F.	75.00	57.50
1797	3	V. Fine	100.00	90.00	1800	11	V. Fine	90.00	70.00
1797	3	Ex. Fine	150.00	135.00	1800	12	V. Fine	50.00	45.00
1797	1A	Ab. Unc.	140.00 U	100.00	1800	15	V. Fine	65.00	47.50
1798	2	Fine+	55.00	45.00	1800	19	Ex. Fine	75.00	62.50
1798	6	Fine	30.00	32.50	1800	19	Ab. Unc.	135.00 U	90.00
1798	6A	Ex. F.+	110.00	85.00	1801	2	Fine	40.00	40.00
1798	25	Fine+	40.00	35.00	1801	4	Ex. Fine	150.00	115.00
1799/98	2	V. Fine	55.00	49.50	1802	2	V. Fine	40.00	39.50
1799	1	Fine	55.00	35.00	1802	3	Fine	40.00	35.00
1799	5A	Ab. Unc.	110.00 U	85.00	1802	6	V. Fine	40.00	39.50
1799	6	F.-V.F.	55.00 F	39.50	1802/1	3	Ab. Unc.	150.00 U	95.00
1799	7	Ab. Unc.	150.00 U	90.00	1803	6	V. Fine	60.00	55.00

U. S. EARLY SILVER DOLLARS. The outstanding reference by Mr. M. H. Bolender is a "must" if you collect this popular series. Special price, including his 1956 Copyrighted List of Valuations................... 9.50

U. S. SILVER DOLLARS — BRILLIANT UNC.

Just as they were the day they left the Mints. All at Bargain Prices.

Philadelphia Mint

	Abt. Unc.	Brill. Unc.	Select, Br. Unc.		Abt. Unc.	Brill. Unc.	Select, Br. Unc.
1878 7 Fthrs.	...	1.50	1.95	2.95	1891	...	1.50	2.25	...
1878 8 Fthrs.	...	2.25	4.25	5.75	1892	...	3.75	4.85
1878 7/8 Fthrs.	...	7.50	9.75	1893	...	3.50	4.75
1879	...	2.15	2.95	1894	...Wanted
1880	1.45	1.05	...	1895	...Wanted
1881	...	1.95	2.75	1896	...	3.75	4.85
1882	...	1.95	2.75	1897	...	2.45	3.50
1883	...	1.95	2.75	1898	...	2.95	3.75
1884	...	1.45	1.95	2.75	1899	...Wanted
1885	...	1.95	2.75	1900	...	2.45	3.25
1886	...	2.25	2.95	1901	...Wanted
1887	...	2.85	3.75	1902	...Wanted
1888	...	2.45	3.50	1903	...	2.45	3.50
1889	...	2.45	3.50	1904	...	3.75	4.85
1890	...	1.95	2.75	1921	...	1.45	1.75

Carson City Mint

	Abt. Unc.	Brill. Unc.	Select, Br. Unc.		Abt. Unc.	Brill. Unc.	Select, Br. Unc.
1878-CC	1.95	2.45	3.75	1885-CC	...	3.95	5.25
1879-CC	...	4.25	5.50	1889-CC see below	...Wanted
1880-CC	...	4.95	6.50	1890-CC	...	2.45	3.50
1881-CC	...	4.50	5.95	1891-CC	...	2.45	3.50
1882-CC	...	3.25	4.50	1892-CC	2.25	3.45	...
1883-CC	...	3.25	4.50	1893-CC	...	13.50	17.50
1884-CC	...	3.25	3.95			

1889-CC V.G. $4.25; Fine $6.50; V. Fine $9.50. Brilliant Unc. Wanted.

Denver Mint

	Abt. Unc.	Brill. Unc.	Select, Br. Unc.
1921-D	...	1.45	1.75	...

Above left, above, and lower left: cover and two pages from Bebee's 1957 catalog. Offered for sale are silver dollars which by today's standards seem to be unbelievable bargains in virtually every instance.

CHOICE MORGAN DOLLARS — Continued

New Orleans Mint

	Abt. Unc.	Brill. Unc.	Select, Br. Unc.		Abt. Unc.	Brill. Unc.	Select, Br. Unc.
1879-O	...	3.45	4.75	1892-O	...Wanted
1880-O	1.75	3.45	4.75	1893-O	...	5.95	7.75
1881-O	1.95	3.25	4.65	1894-O	...Wanted
1882-O	1.95	3.25	4.65	1895-O	...Wanted
1883-O	1.95	3.45	4.75	1896-O	...	3.95	...
1884-O	1.95	3.45	4.75	1897-O	...	3.25	...Wanted
1885-O	1.95	3.25	4.65	1898-O	...Wanted
1886-O	...	3.75	1899-O	...Wanted
1887-O	...	3.45	Wanted	1900-O	...	1.95	3.25	...
1888-O	...	3.75	Wanted	1901-O	...Wanted
1889-O	...	3.25	Wanted	1902-O	...Wanted
1890-O	...	Wanted	1903-O see below.	...Wanted

1903-O V.G. $14.50; Fine $19.50; V.F. $33.50; Ex. Fine $47.50; Brill. Unc. Wanted.

San Francisco Mint

	Abt. Unc.	Brill. Unc.	Select, Br. Unc.		Abt. Unc.	Brill. Unc.	Select, Br. Unc.
1878-S	...	1.60	1.95	2.85	1892-S	...Wanted
1879-S	...	1.60	2.15	2.95	1893-S see below.	...Wanted
1880-S	...	1.50	1.95	2.75	1894-S	...	2.95	3.75
1881-S	...	1.95	2.85	1895-S	...Wanted
1882-S	...	1.65	1.95	1896-S	...	10.75	13.50
1883-S	...	1.95	1897-S	...	1.50	1.95	2.85
1884-S	...	Wanted	1898-S	...	2.45	3.25
1885-S	...	3.75	4.95	1899-S	...	3.45	4.75
1886-S	...	1.95	2.85	1900-S	...	2.45	3.50
1887-S	1.50	1.95	2.85	1901-S	...	0.75	3.60
1888-S	...	2.45	3.50	1902-S	...	2.50	3.45
1889-S	...	2.75	3.85	1903-S	...	31.50	36.50
1890-S	...	1.95	2.85	1904-S	...	2.95	3.75
1891-S	1.50	1.95	2.85	1921-S	...	1.35	1.75

1893-S V.G. $9.75; Fine $14.50; V. Fine $27.50; Ex. Fine $47.50; Abt. Unc. $85.00.

SILVER DOLLARS — PEACE TYPE

Philadelphia Mint

	Abt. Unc.	Brill. Unc.	Select, Br. Unc.		Abt. Unc.	Brill. Unc.	Select, Br. Unc.
1921	...	2.95	6.75	8.50	1926	...	1.95	2.95
1922	1.45	1.95	2.95	1927	...	1.65	2.95	...
1923	...	1.75	2.75	1928	Price on request
1924	...	1.85	2.95	1934	...	3.75	...
1925	1.95	2.50	3.75	1935	...	2.95	3.95

Denver Mint

	Abt. Unc.	Brill. Unc.	Select, Br. Unc.		Abt. Unc.	Brill. Unc.	Select, Br. Unc.
1922-D	...	2.75	3.95	1927-D	...	4.95	...
1923-D	1.75	3.45	4.95	1934-D	...Wanted
1926-D	...	3.95	4.95			

San Francisco Mint

	Abt. Unc.	Brill. Unc.	Select, Br. Unc.		Abt. Unc.	Brill. Unc.	Select, Br. Unc.
1922-S	1.45	1.95	3.25	1927-S	...	3.45	4.95
1923-S	1.45	1.95	3.25	1928-S	...	3.45	...
1924-S	...	3.75	4.95	1934-S	...17.50	...Wanted
1925-S	1.45	1.95	1935-S	...	8.50	...
1926-S	...	2.25	3.50			

You will marvel at our "Select, Brilliant Unc." dollars. However, we sell thousands of our "Brilliant Unc." dollars so they undoubtedly please the majority of collectors. When ordering please give a few second choice selections, on reverse of order blank (page 79).

A page from Bebee's 1957 catalog.

SILVER DOLLARS

	Quan. Minted	Ex. Fine	Unc.
1898	(735) 5,884,735	...	$4.50
1898O	4,440,000	$70.00	300.00
1898S	4,102,000	...	15.00
1899	(846) 330,846	3.50	10.00
1899O	12,290,000	3.00	10.00
1899S	2,562,000	...	15.00
1900	(912) 8,830,912	...	3.50
1900O	12,590,000	...	6.00
1900S	3,540,000	...	15.00
1901	(813) 6,962,813	7.50	37.50
1901O	13,320,000	2.50	7.50
1901S	2,284,000	...	22.50
1902	(777) 7,994,777	...	3.50
1902O	8,636,000	7.00	35.00
1902S	1,530,000	...	25.00
1903	(755) 4,652,755	...	3.00
1903O	4,450,000	400.00	1,500.00
1903S	1,241,000	7.50	75.00
1904	(650) 2,788,650	...	10.00
1904O	3,720,000	50.00	350.00
1904S	2,304,000	5.00	50.00

The 1963 edition of "A Guide Book of United States Coins," released in the summer of 1962, dramatically shows three rarities: the Uncirculated 1898-O silver dollar at $300, the ultra-rare Uncirculated 1903-O at $1,500, and the elusive 1904-O Uncirculated at $350. At the time the 1903-O Uncirculated dollar was so rare that most major collections lacked an example. Indeed, fewer than a half dozen were believed to exist in all of numismatics!

B. Max Mehl, who died in the 1950s, would have rubbed his head in amazement at the 1962 market. In 1941, when he sold the Dunham Collection, a group of coins which would probably bring close to $10,000,000 today, he announced:

"The grand total of the Dunham Sale is $83,364.08! This is the largest amount, by more than 35%, than ever before realized at a coin sale in America. The Jenks Sale, 1921, brought $61,279.46. The average per lot in the Dunham Sale was $20.00!"

So, the idea of purchasing a group of rare 1898-O dollars which cataloged at $300 per coin and the large group of 1904-O dollars which cataloged at $350 each was exciting. And, the prospect of owning several specimens of the exceedingly rare Uncirculated 1903-O dollar was thrilling, to say the least!

Being a bit cautious, I asked the dealer if I could think about it overnight. I didn't know him well and wanted to check his credentials. Could the coins have been stolen? Perhaps it was just a fantasy or a fraud of some sort. Still, there persisted the thought that the offer might be real and that a treasure of the "rarest of the rare" silver dollars would be in my hands soon!

The next day a telephone call came from Harry Forman, the Philadelphia dealer. Harry, who began his business in 1956, specialized in bulk groups and lots and was a dealer's dealer, so to speak. Harry, a good friend, called to tell us some startling news: in the annual Christmastime release of silver dollars at least several bags had turned up of 1898-O and 1904-O! 1903-O wasn't mentioned at the time; news of it was to come several days later.

Jim Ruddy and I were at once delighted and dismayed. We were pleased that we didn't nibble at the coins offered to us a day earlier but were disappointed that the seeming treasure trove might not be a treasure trove at all.

News of the find spread like wildfire, and before long the Federal Reserve System was inundated by requests for hundreds of thousands of silver dollars from all parts of the country. People who expressed little interest in silver dollars before now wanted to get a few dozen, a few bags, or a few dozen bags. The silver dollar treasure hunt was on!

Out of the Treasury vaults came bags which had not seen the light of day since the turn of the century. Soon thereafter, my firm bought 1,100 (a full bag plus 100 extra pieces) of 1903-O silver dollars at $17 per coin from a man who had obtained them through a Federal Reserve bank. Other bags came on the market, and thousands of coins changed hands. In the beginning this was like finding gold in the streets. Although the 1903-O dollar obviously was no longer worth $1,500, it still was exciting to have them by the hundreds and by the thousands. In fact, it was almost unbelievable! Throughout 1963 the demand increased. After all, what could one lose? Go to the bank, spend a thousand dollars for a bag of dollars, take it home—and if it contained worn issues of little value you still broke even. On the other hand, you might be surprised, as one San Francisco gentleman was, with a bag full of 1889 Carson City dollars!

It helped to have a friend in the Treasury Department. In 1963, as bags were pouring out of the Treasury by the thousands, more and more scarce dates came to light. One buyer befriended an employee who had access to the main storage vaults. Silver dollars were in sealed bags, so breaking the seal to examine the dates would have raised all sorts of complications—including having to recount the pieces. A simple procedure was devised whereby thousands of bags were "peeked" at by making a tiny hole in the bag, sometimes with a lighted tip of a cigarette, and then manipulating the cloth surface so that the date and mintmark of the coins could be ascertained by peeping through the hole. While the ethics of this practice certainly might be questioned, it did result in quite a few bags of rare dates being channeled directly into numismatics rather than to the general public.

While most Treasury finds were limited to Morgan dollars (mainly) and Peace dollars, a few earlier dollars were involved as well.

At least one bag each came to light of 1859-O and 1860-O Liberty seated dollars. In the intervening years since 1963 these have been widely dispersed among collectors. A bag of 1871 Uncirculated silver dollars came to light and was purchased intact by an investor who, as of this writing, still possesses it. A New York City coin dealer told John J. Ford, Jr. that his firm purchased and "put away" a bag of Uncirculated 1868 dollars.

At least several bags of worn, mixed Liberty seated dollars were found. Jim Ruddy and I purchased a quantity of these in 1963 through an agent who had obtained them in Detroit. Ohio dealer James F. Kelly, who later with Max Humbert, Michael V. DiSalle, Jim Ruddy, and myself, would form Paramount International Coin Corporation in 1965, obtained a large quantity of Liberty seated pieces from the Detroit Federal Reserve Bank.

We had a field day looking through these. It was almost like visiting Ali Baba's cave! Jim Ruddy and I set aside a large table area and marked on sheets of paper spaces for each of the Liberty seated dates: 1840, 1841, 1842, and so on, including branch mint issues. We were even optimistic and put in spaces for 1851, 1852, and 1858; three rarities! The coins ranged in condition from Fine to AU, with a few being less and a few being more. The average grade was Very Fine to Extremely Fine. Most pieces had a brownish-gray toning, the result o

The three stars, front and center, in the great Treasury release of 1962 were these former rarities: the 1898-O silver dollar (which cataloged $300), the 1903-O (which cataloged a lofty $1,500), and the 1904-O (which cataloged $350). Interesting stories abound from the initial days of their release. One entrepreneur with more silver dollars than ethics boarded a jet plane for London, hoping to unload these now-common coins on English dealers before they knew what was happening. Several bank and government employees thought they had their future fortunes made. Word of their treasure troves—of finding a bag of silver dollars worth hundreds of thousands of dollars—reached the press. Their hopes were dashed soon thereafter when it was learned that millions were released. Philadelphia dealer Harry Forman suspected what was going on from the outset and telephoned his colleagues to alert them, thereby short-circuiting many deceptions.

many years of bank storage. Presumably the coins had been taken from circulation by banks in the 1870s, following the discontinuance of the Liberty seated dollar in 1873, but before Morgan dollars were issued in 1878.

1851, 1852, 1858, 1870-S, 1871-CC, and 1873-CC were not represented, but, if memory serves, all other dates were. Particularly populous were issues of the 1840s, with 1846 and 1847 being the most common.

In those days it was uncertain how many more rare dates would be found. Would millions of Liberty seated dollars be found or was the present discovery the bottom of the barrel? No one knew. For that reason our firm was cautious. We would buy a group of dollars, sell them, and then buy another group from our agents. Jim Kelly reported that he did the same. Some very scarce dates did show up, although I was not among the fortunate discoverers. A number of 1871-CC and 1873-CC dollars came to light through other collectors and dealers.

Although my guess is just a guess and nothing more, I would estimate that perhaps 5,000 to 10,000 worn Liberty seated dollars came on the market during the great 1963 release. Spread over a wide number of dates, these coins found ready homes with collectors. It is safe to say that most have been dispersed by now.

I heard reports of a few scattered earlier dollars of the late 1790s and early 1800s coming to light, but if this was so I did not see them first hand.

Bags were found of such scarce dates as 1889-CC (I know of at least two which are still intact), 1895-S, 1896-S, 1903-S, and 1904-S. In addition, bags were found of most other dates. So far as I know, 1892-S, a coin which is very common in worn grades up to AU but which is fairly elusive in Uncirculated condition, never was discovered in bag quantities.

1893-S, scarce in all grades, remained elusive. A few scattered Uncirculated coins showed up, but not many. When all was said and done and the dust had settled, the order of things had changed. No longer was the 1903-O the King of Morgan dollars. In its place was the 1893-S, a coin which had been unaffected by the hoards.

Much to the dismay of observers, including me, no 1895 business strikes turned up. Apparently all 12,000 pieces from the Philadelphia Mint had been melted in 1918 under the terms of the Pittman Act.

Many dealers shared in the bonanza. Larry Goldberg, of the Superior Stamp and Coin Company of Los Angeles, sold many bags. Of the first year of issue of the Morgan dollar, 1878, he sold in recent years 15 bags of the 1878 7/8 tail feathers, over 15 bags of the 1878 8 tail feathers, and approximately 20 bags of the 1878-CC.

He related in correspondence to me that "when the Treasury Department was releasing quantities of silver dollars our downtown store was located several blocks away from the Federal Reserve Building where a large number of silver dollars were being held. Individuals working at the Federal Reserve would come in during their lunch hour and sell us large groups of Carson City coins, scarce San Francisco Mint issues, 1899 Philadelphia pieces, and at least five 1893-S coins per day. This went on for about six months. Most of these dollars were in circulated condition."

Larry further related the purchase and resale of two bags of 1899 Philadelphia dollars and a bag of 1889-O issues.

Aubrey Bebee related that he "had an opportunity to purchase numerous bags of silver dollars. Quite frequently we would receive calls from collectors who worked in banks in the East telling us they could supply us with bags of certain scarce dates. I purchased quite a few bags of Carson City Mint silver dollars. One time I was offered two bags of 1879-CC dollars and purchased them at $1,750 per bag. Having a number of this date in stock we resold one bag to our good friend, Norman Shultz, at our cost, plus shipping charges. The only Carson City dollars we were not able to purchase in bags were the 1889-CC and the 1893-CC. A collector in Montana, who was in the furniture business, located a bag of 1893-CC dollars, but we could buy only 500 pieces. Not being able to obtain a supply of this date previously, we agreed to his price of $6 per coin.

"Then there was a collector in San Francisco many years ago who located a bag of 1903-S dollars at the San Francisco Federal Reserve Bank. He sold us 100 pieces at $10 each. We wanted to buy more, but as he had other customers he allotted only 100 specimens to each of the nine other dealers he offered them to.

"Quite frequently we were offered rolls of scarcer dollars by a collector who worked in one of the casinos in Reno, Nevada. I recall buying five rolls of 1904-S dollars, many of which were prooflike, at $80 per roll. I thought that the price was quite high at the time, so I only took five of the ten rolls he offered us."

John J. Ford, Jr. recalled that during one day in the early 1950s, a decade before the great Treasury release, he and a friend, Ralph J. Lathrop, were detained in their travels by a parade featuring Dwight D. Eisenhower. Faced with a huge traffic jam, Ford and Lathrop parked and went into the nearby Federal Reserve Building to see what they would find by buying a bag of 1,000 silver dollars. They were rewarded with a sackful of rare 1893 Philadelphia pieces, each in perfect condition.

Harry J. Forman told me that during the period of the great Treasury release in the early 1960s, "I received a call from a good friend of mine who was then employed by the Provident Loan Society of New York. He was asking me for advice about making a loan on a bag each

of 1898-O and 1904-O silver dollars. As these coins at the time were listed in the *Guide Book* at several hundred dollars each, I advised him that I suspected that a release in quantity of these dollars was taking place.

"I made some inquiries and learned that a huge room at the Philadelphia Mint which had been joint sealed since the close of the New Orleans Assay Office in 1929 had been opened. This room contained over ten million silver dollars. A mass distribution of New Orleans silver dollars was then underway!

"To my knowledge almost every New Orleans issue except 1893-O, 1895-O, 1896-O, and 1897-O was released in quantities of at least one bag or more. I am often asked my opinion of how many bags of 1903-O silver dollars were released. I would say that a conservative estimate would be that approximately 30 bags came out at that time. In addition I really believe that even larger quantities of the 1889-O, 1890-O, 1891-O, and 1892-O bags became available. I was lucky enough at the time to acquire a bag of 1894-O silver dollars which I sold at the time for $40 to $50 per roll of 20 pieces. At the same time I purchased a bag of Liberty seated silver dollars containing nearly 700 Brilliant Uncirculated 1859-O and 1860-O dollars. There must have been at least ten bags of Liberty seated dollars released in all, containing many different dates in all grades."

Now, many years after the release, there are still a few mysteries. Rumors in the coin field abound, and the task of a researcher often is to sift fact from fantasy. After all, nothing makes a better story than tales of unverifiable treasures!

In this vein I remember a 1958 visit made by Kenneth Rendell and myself to a leading San Francisco coin dealer. Ken, who was a close boyhood friend and who later left coins to be prominent in the field of rare books and autographs (at one time he was president of the Antiquarian Booksellers Association of America and the Manuscript Society), and I were visiting dealers and making purchases. In Oakland, across the bay from San Francisco, we visited Leo Young and were amazed to see dozens of bags of 1955-S Lincoln cents, a popular sales item at the time, stored awaiting shipment. Leo, who during the 1950s was one of America's most active dealers (his son Gary carries on the tradition today), was also headquarters for rarities, and we were dazzled by the display he had. Then we went to San Francisco and visited a lady who was reputed to own the original coining dies for the 1855 Kellogg & Co. round $50 gold piece.

"Yes, I do own them," she said. "Quite a few dealers, including Earl Parker, have been trying to buy them for years, but they're not for sale." So, we left her small shop, an interesting place which had many antiques and fascinating artifacts.

We then went to another dealer who was especially social and talkative that August afternoon. I purchased from him, paying $50 for it, a silver ashtray which had been presented to pioneer San Francisco coiner Augustus Humbert by his friends. This relic later passed into the hands of John Rowe of Dallas, Texas. During the course of our visit the San Francisco dealer regaled Ken and me with tales of silver dollars.

"You think that 1934-S is rare, don't you?" he queried, referring to the scarcest issue among later Peace-design silver dollars. "Well, I have a surprise for you. Someday this will be very common. You know that over a million of them were minted, 1,011,000 to be exact," he said as he looked up the mintage figure in a nearby reference book.

"Well, I have been in the vaults of the Federal Reserve Bank here in San Francisco and have seen with my own eyes many bags of these coins; original sealed bags and marked as such," he stated.

I was dazzled by this information and wondered how soon it would be until these were released. For years afterwards I hesitated to buy 1934-S dollars except one or two at a time, fearing that the release of hundreds of thousands of them was just around the corner!

The great Treasury release of the 1960s came and went. When the Treasury Department was near the bottom of the barrel they called a halt to the project and inventoried what was left: some 3,000,000 silver dollars consisting mainly of Carson City Mint issues of the early 1880s. There were no 1934-S dollars! Nor, to my knowledge, had any bags of 1934-S dollars been released during the bonanza.

Fact or fiction? To this day I'm not sure about the tale of the pieces stored in San Francisco. My dealer friend, to my knowledge, was not the type given to making jokes of this nature or leading me on, and yet I still wonder.

Over the years silver dollars have been a really superb investment. The 1878-CC silver dollars I purchased from Rev. Edward W.W. Lewis in 1966 for $2 each have multiplied in value many times since then. 1889 Carson City dollars, despite their release, are worth several thousand dollars each now, up sharply from the $350 catalog value back in 1962. Likewise, nearly all silver dollars across the board have risen in price sharply.

This seems illogical, for now there are hundreds of millions of silver dollars in collectors' hands, far more than were known to collectors prior to 1962-1963. It seems logical that the prices should have dropped sharply.

The prices did drop on several examples, 1898-O, 1903-O, and 1904-O being three. 1903-O, the former great rarity of which perhaps just four to five Uncirculated pieces were once in collectors' hands, is now a

plentiful date. Apparently many thousands were released, with one person placing the estimate at over a million. The price fell sharply from $1,500, the *Guide Book* value then. A bad investment? Well, looking at it narrowly, yes. But, reality does not support this. Prior to November 1962 the 1903-O silver dollar was so rare in Uncirculated grade that most dealers had never seen one. Our firm, a major factor in the market, never had one in stock. Only when great collections came on the market would a single piece come to light. Most collectors considered themselves fortunate to even own a worn one.

So, the number of collectors who took a substantial loss when the price of Uncirculated 1903-O silver dollars dropped could be counted on the fingers of one hand. Even that assumption is unrealistic, for it assumes that the few people holding Uncirculated 1903-O dollars in November 1962 paid $1,500 each for them. Actually, probably most purchased them years earlier for several hundred dollars each. There was a small loss, but really insignificant compared to the rise in interest and prices in the rest of the market. Balancing the minute losses in the 1903-O situation were tremendous increases in dozens of other silver dollar issues.

What happened in November 1962 was one of the most beneficial things ever to befall numismatics. Because of the tremendous nationwide news coverage the number of collectors desiring early silver dollars multiplied many times. While no figures are known precisely, if 10,000 people casually or actively collected silver dollars prior to 1962, a few years later the number probably increased tenfold or twentyfold or even far more. True, there were more silver dollars in collectors' hands, but there were proportionately far more collectors desiring them. The result was a sharp upward price movement.

In May 1969 the government, through the General Services Administration, announced it would be disposing of the nearly 3,000,000 silver dollars which it belatedly held back from the general dispersal. A complex auction-sale arrangement was set up whereby collectors could bid for desired issues, mostly Carson City pieces. The GSA would then determine what the minimum acceptable bid would be, and all bidders at that amount or over would acquire them at the minimum acceptable figure.

By 1976, following a number of different auction presentations, approximately $55,000,000 was realized following an advertising expenditure of $7.8 million.

47,556 1878-CC dollars found new homes at $15 per coin. 270,949 mixed silver dollars of various mints, not including Carson City, were sold at $5 each. Large quantities of 1879-CC, 1882-CC, 1890-CC, and 1891-CC were sold. Still quite a few Carson City coins remained

on hand, including nearly 200,000 pieces of 1883-CC and more than 428,000 pieces of 1884-CC. Also remaining were hundreds of thousands of circulated Carson City pieces plus other mixed Carson City dates.

The disposition of coins by the GSA caused quite a controversy. Early in the game the GSA announced that these coins, souvenirs of the wild West, were "a good investment." Sparks flew in 1972 when the GSA brochure offering the coins was distributed. Anger centered around comments relating to what the GSA termed "a great silver sale." Beneath the headline was a statement from President Richard Nixon about these "most valued reminders." The brochure went on to say that the coins were "excellent for investments" and, later, "they are sound investments."

Leading coin dealers throughout the United States, many of whom had been very careful when using the term "investment" in advertisements, making sure to back it up with proven facts of price appreciation, rarity, or other numismatic information based on fact, were justifiably upset when the government violated its own rules in this regard.

In Sidney, Ohio, Margo Russell, editor of *Coin World*, maintained an ever-growing file as newspaper clippings came in from all over the United States reporting the reactions of dealers and others.

In Minneapolis, dealer Max Winters said, "It's a crummy deal when people buy these silver dollars for a minimum $30 price, thinking it's an investment."

In New York City, Dan Messer was particularly incensed, for the United States government ordered his firm to "cease and desist" for using similar terminology in 1960, despite the fact that the coins Messer was selling were far, far rarer and had a good numismatic investment history behind them.

In the same city Harvey Stack wrote to the chairman of the Securities and Exchange Commission and said, in part: "It seems to us that if this advertisement was circulated by a private firm you would start an immediate action for 'cease and desist.' This type of advertising is not proper and should be stopped at once." The Securities and Exchange Commission replied that it "did not want to become involved."

Chicago dealer Ed Milas minced no words and reported in the *Tribune* that the government ads were "a bunch of garbage," and that the whole sale is "actually fleecing people."

Walter Perschke, of Numisco Rare Coins, noted that "they are offering enough of these dates to go around for everybody who would want to collect them for the next 50 years."

And, the critics were right. Five years after the initial GSA announcement the most plentiful Carson City dates

U.S. GOVERNMENT SALE

- **collector's item**—the only coins with a double mint mark (CC). The now defunct Carson City U.S. Mint was the only one ever authorized to use more than one letter as its mint mark

- **uncirculated specimens**—these coins are an extraordinary value because they are exactly as found in the original sealed mint bags and were never in public circulation

- **the last of the 90% silver dollars**—today's U.S. coins have a maximum of 40% silver

- **mined from the Comstock Lode**—a true memento, these coins were made from the silver mined from the famous Comstock Lode

- **genuine 19th century coins**—these are not commemorative medals but rather real early American silver dollars

- **excellent for investments** or gifts—the value of these coins is high since demand is great and the group to be offered is the end of the Government's holdings of the 1882-83-84 uncirculated Carson City Silver Dollars

Bid now for these historic coins, genuine mementos of our American heritage. Be sure you take advantage of this unique opportunity to own a rare collector's item, packaged in an attractive presentation case including an historical account of the Comstock Lode's silver treasure. Prize these coins yourself or present them as gifts to friends and family.

Minted in Carson City, these Silver Dollars are the last true remembrances of the Great Silver Bonanza and the Old West. They are sound investments but most of all they are something you will be proud to own.

You may bid on only one coin of each year. The years to be offered are 1882, 1883, and 1884. The General Services Administration has established a minimum price for each coin, but you may bid above the price if you wish to improve your chances. If there are enough coins to go around, any amount bid over the minimum price ($30.00) will be refunded. However, if there are not enough to go around, coins will go to the highest bidders in descending order. Bids for The Great Silver Sale will be accepted until January 31, 1973. Complete the coupon below, include your check or money order and mail now before you miss this opportunity to own one of these famous Carson City Silver Dollars!

Offering its Carson City silver dollar hoard, the government was treading on thin ice when it proclaimed that the coins were "excellent for investments" and "they are sound investments." Responsible coin dealers, who recommended coins for investment only when they were of proven rarity and had a good investment track record, were appalled—and a furor ensued. The critics of the government proved to be right: virtually any other date of Uncirculated silver dollar purchased on the open market at that time would have increased in value more than the Carson City issues the government recommended for investment purposes!

Six-guns and overnight millionaires . . .

. . . were commonplace in the era of the Carson City Silver Dollars. These were the times when men toiled night and day taking silver and gold ore by the ton out of subterranean deposits discovered almost daily. When they came out of the mines, it was off to the 24-hour-a-day saloons and gambling halls for whiskey straight up, roulette, blackjack and five card stud where fortunes changed hands nightly. These were America's late-1800s in the Old West of Nevada, California and Colorado . . . the days of the Comstock Lode when shanty towns became shanty cities overnight. Magic names like Virginia City . . . Silver City . . . Cripple Creek, laden with silver, suddenly screamed riches and rowdyism.

Elsewhere, America was sanely trying to enter the 20th Century. Horse-drawn trains gave way to trolleys in the Nation's great cities . . . Sarah Bernhardt was making her first appearances on the American stage and the game of basketball was being invented. It was during these times that the Statue of Liberty was being erected . . . the first telephones were installed and Edison was developing the electric light.

These were some of the greatest and most memorable days in America's history. Days that will never be seen again!

It was in those wild days of the Old West that the Carson City Mint was organized to convert the precious metal of the Big Bonanza into the only coins in our history to carry the unique "CC" double-letter mint mark.

Mixed CC Dollars

These coins have never before been circulated by the U.S. Government. The years 1879 through 1885 plus 1890 and 1891 are included. These are the coins that have been culled out of the entire Government holding of CC dollars since they did not meet the numismatic standards for "uncirculated" classification.

Approximate number available: 517,569

Minimum Bid: $15.00

1882-CC
1st Major League Doubleheader
Total CC Silver Dollars Minted: 591,000
Total CC Silver Dollars Available: 35,700
Minimum Bid: $30.00

1883-CC
Northern Pacific Railroad completed.
Total CC Silver Dollars Minted: 1,204,000
Total CC Silver Dollars Available: 226,052
Minimum Bid: $30.00

1884-CC
Trolleys replace horse-drawn trains on East and West coasts.
Total CC Silver Dollars Minted: 1,136,000
Total CC Silver Dollars Available: 16C,620
Minimum Bid: $30.00

1880-CC
Sarah Bernhardt makes American acting debut.
Total CC Silver Dollars Minted: 591,000
Total CC Silver Dollars Available: 40,847
Minimum Bid: $60.00

1881-CC
Clara Barton organizes the American Red Cross.
Total CC Silver Dollars Minted: 296,000
Total CC Silver Dollars Available: 51,587
Minimum Bid: $60.00

1885-CC
Washington Monument dedicated.
Total CC Silver Dollars Minted: 228,000
Total CC Silver Dollars Available: 62,781
Minimum Bid: $60.00

Part of the government's enthusiastic multimillion dollar advertising campaign to divest itself of its immense Carson City silver dollar holdings.

SILVER DOLLARS poured forth by the millions from Treasury vaults beginning in autumn 1962. Discovered in that year's annual Christmas releases (nominal amounts were released each year to provide for Christmas gifts and the like) were such delicacies as Uncirculated 1898-O silver dollars which cataloged for $300 each, Uncirculated 1904-O dollars which fetched $350 and, best of all, Uncirculated 1903-O dollars, great rarities which cataloged $1,500 each! For Federal Reserve employees this was like finding money in the streets, and dozens reaped windfalls by taking individual coins, groups, and entire bags to coin dealers. Word of the bonanza spread, and the floodgates opened. Hundreds of millions of dollars came to light, including many other New Orleans, San Francisco, Carson City, and Philadelphia pieces which had been hidden away for many decades.

Finally, when the stock was nearly depleted, the government analyzed the situation and discovered it had on hand approximately three million early dollars, of which over two million were highly-prized issues from Carson City. Some of these quantities were immense in proportion to the numbers originally minted. For example, of 1,133,000 1882-CC dollars originally struck, the government found itself in the 1960s holding 470,000 Uncirculated pieces! Of 1883-CC and 1884-CC coins, pieces which originally had been struck to the extent of slightly more than 1,000,000 coins each issue, the government found it had 599,000 and 675,000 specimens respectively! And, of 1885-CC, a coin of which 228,000 were made, the government found it had about half of the mintage, or 122,000 pieces.

Silver dollars, long favorites with collectors, became the darlings of the numismatic world as more and more people started saving them. Countless thousands of citizens, lured by the government's widespread advertising (which extended to notices in post offices and banks as well as other locations), climbed aboard the collecting bandwagon. Still others were intrigued when they visited banks in 1962 and 1963 and purchased for $1 each sparkling new silver dollars minted nearly a century earlier. While the number of silver dollars in collectors' hands multiplied many times over, the interest increased even more than that, with the result being a sharp upward price movement.

Today silver dollars enjoy a strong popularity. The fact that, for example, an Uncirculated 1878 dollar, the first year of issue of the Morgan type, can be obtained for far less than an Uncirculated Indian cent of the same year contributes much to the appeal of dollar collecting, notwithstanding the fact that silver dollars are hundreds if not thousands of times commoner than Indian cents of the same period.

1903-O Dollars Hit News Again

The turbulent Morgan dollar pot was started boiling again, as news of the release of more 1903-O bags was reported from three different, widely-separated sections of the country.

"Doc" Fahrenberg, president of the Wisconsin Coin Dealers Association, purchased several from a member of the U.S. Air Force, at five dollars apiece, who had picked them up in Chicago. The owner of Doc's Coin Mart in Milwaukee said he knew definitely that three bags were in the city, and that they seemed generally quite plentiful.

Four more bags were reported to be in the Dallas, Texas, area by Charles "Shotgun" Slade III of Orlando, Fla. Unconfirmed information also indicates the presence of approximately five bags in the St. Louis, Mo. area.

Slade also mentioned, however, that bags of silver dollars which have been selling strongly for him were noticeably light on the 1903-O date.

None of these bags contain **any** later dates than 1904. The average bag contains anywhere from 10 to 20 Carson City dates and many San Francisco dates.

Just about all Philadelphia dates have shown up in the bags, with the exception of course of the 1895.

The Orlando, Fla., dealer recounts that out of 206,000 pieces recently sorted by a collector, only ten 1903-O pieces were found. It is his opinion that this is essentially still a scarce coin, and that the price will recover rapidly.

In autumn 1962 and early 1963 1903-O dollars, which cataloged $1,500 each at the time in the "Guide Book of United States Coins," furnished the ingredients for many news items, such as this April 12th article in "Coin World."

Among the U.S. Government's holdings of the 1880, 1881 and 1885 uncirculated Carson City Silver Dollars, being offered for the first time in this sale, are many variations of the standard silver dollar design.

According to coin experts, a majority of the 1880s are of an overdate variety. During inspection of the 1881 coins, experts discovered a previously unknown variety. This new variety has extra metal within the date. The only known die variety of the Carson City Silver Dollars minted in 1885 showed up in the GSA holdings.

For each of the three years offered, the number available for this sale constitutes approximately ½ of 1 percent of the total silver dollars struck in the United States during those years. In the case of the 1881 and 1885, there were less than 300,000 silver dollars minted at Carson City in each year.

U.S. Government Sale
Bids must be postmarked by October 31, 1973

$60
Per Coin Minimum Bid

SILVER DOLLAR COINAGE

YEAR	TOTAL UNITED STATES MINTAGE	TOTAL CARSON CITY MINTAGE	CC DOLLARS AS % OF TOTAL U.S. MINTAGE	NUMBER AVAILABLE IN THIS SALE	% OF TOTAL U.S. MINTAGE IN THIS SALE
1880	27,397,355	591,000	2%	114,982	0.4%
1881	27,927,975	296,000	1%	122,698	0.4%
1885	28,697,767	228,000	1%	130,807	0.5%

The above chart was prepared to provide the prospective bidder with an idea of the limited number of Carson City Silver Dollars minted in 1880, 1881 and 1885 and the number that are available in this sale. Every bidder is urged to consult numismatic publications for additional information.

United States government advertisement, 1973, for Uncirculated Carson City silver dollars of 1880, 1881, and 1885. What the government declines to point out to prospective purchasers is that among silver dollars, original mintages are not a guide to rarity. Some Morgan dollars of the 1878-1904 era with very small mintages are very common, simply because most coins were saved by the Treasury and subsequently became available to collectors. Other dollars with high mintages are rare because most were melted in 1918.

U.S. peddling silver dollars, at about $30

By JIM JONES
Minneapolis Star Staff Writer

The federal government is merchandising silver dollars in Minneapolis—at a minimum of $30 per coin.

Bankers with displays of dollars minted late last century in Carson City, Nev., are mostly amused, although it's a nuisance to protect the displays from shoplifters.

At Farmers & Mechanics Savings Bank, a display of 10 dollars is chained to a counter desk.

Coin dealers arent't amused.

"In fact, it's a crummy deal," says Max Winters, Minneapolis coin and stamp dealer, who thinks the government sale of nearly three million coins will "sour" the public on silver.

Minneapolis Star Photo by Jack Gillis

K. A. ALANGO, MARQUETTE NATIONAL BANK

Silver dollars are put in the vault each night

"They will buy the silver dollars for a minimum $30 bid price, thinking it's an investment."

"No way will they get that kind of money," he declared, "once the market is flooded."

The United States General Service Administration (GSA) began the public sale of the coins Nov. 1 through public bidding.

Stack's of New York City, a coin firm, has called on the Securities and Exchange Commission to investigate the GSA's use of the term "investment" in its brochure of the silver-dollar sale.

Dan Messer, another New York dealer, said his firm was ordered to "cease and desist" from using such words as "investment" in its own advertising in 1960.

According to Arthur F. Sampson, GSA head, the initial sale will consist of coins minted in 1882, 1883 and 1884 in the Carson City mint.

The 90-percent-silver coins were largely uncirculated. Each has a Liberty head on one side and an eagle and a wreath on the other.

"If the government sells 50 percent of the coins, it will knock the prices down," Winters claims. "The public will buy the coins and later beat our doors down thinking they have something of rare value."

"Any dealer with a number of them on hand is going to take a beating," Winters said. "coin magazines formerly advertising them for about $40 now are listing them for $33.

Under the GSA proposal the public is invited to bid a minimum of $30 per coin, on one coin of each year.

The Treasury Department has furnished nearly 60,000 banks, savings and loans organizations and credit unions with display materials.

According to its inventory there are 2,937,000 silver dollars in the collection.

The General Accounting Office discovered the coins, during an audit, in the vaults of the subbasement of the Treasury in Washington.

The coins, last of the government's holdings of 90-percent silver dollars, were thought to have been lost in the massive coin melts in the early 1900s to support national war efforts. They had been stored initially because the public preferred the new $1 bills.

Above: At "Coin World," in Sidney, Ohio, editor Margo Russell kept an ever-expanding file as clippings concerning silver dollars came in from all over America. Dollars first hit the news in 1962 with the spectacular releases of rare dates such as 1898-O, 1903-O, and 1904-O. After that time the government took a number of years to consider what would be done with the approximately three million pieces left over after the majority had been distributed to the public. The above article, which appeared in the Minneapolis Star, is typical of many which appeared in 1972-1973, ten years after the initial large releases.

Right: The April 13, 1977 issue of "Coin World" notes in an article by David L. Ganz that many thousands of Carson City silver dollars still remained unsold and that the General Services Administration was investigating ways to dispose of them.

Below: The inventory of Carson City dollars given below was furnished to "Coin World" by the Treasury Department in response to inquiries by the numismatic press. This group represents the most valuable treasure trove of coins ever to be made available to the American public from one source.

Coin World

THE WEEKLY NEWSPAPER OF THE ENTIRE NUMISMATIC FIELD
COMBINING WORLD COINS & NUMISMATIC SCRAPBOOK
Entire Contents Copyright 1977 By Amos Press Inc., Sidney, Ohio 45365
Volume 18 Issue 887 April 13, 1977 Single Copy U.S. 75¢

GSA seeks legislation to authorize sale of remnants of Carson City dollar hoard

By David L. Ganz
Special Correspondent

Carson City silver dollars held by the General Services Administration, portions of which were sold in nine different offerings over the period October 1972 through June 1974, are once again the subject of legislative controversy, as the GSA has renewed its attempt to persuade Congress to authorize their sale at prices substantially below the level of the previous "bid-sale" basis.

Draft legislation has been forwarded to Capitol Hill requesting Congress to enact a law which states that "After the silver dollars have been offered at least twice in accordance with (the bid-sale method), the (General Services Administration) is authorized to sell these coins by negotiation at such prices . . . in such manner, and upon such terms and conditions" as may be deemed proper by the GSA.

Additional terms of the proposed draft would permit the GSA to sell the coins at fixed prices, at additional auctions, or utilizing both methods in concert. Prospective purchasers could be limited to those individuals capable of making an offer on the entire remaining hoard of 977,589 silver dollars, or opened up to permit individuals to once again acquire what GSA once advertised as "The Coins Jesse James Never Got."

Transmittal of the draft bill "To Amend the Bank Holding Company Act Amendments of 1970" was made Jan. 19, the day prior to President Ford's departure from office. The proposal was suggested by Jack Eckerd, Administrator of the GSA, a Ford appointee whose tenure had been renewed by President Carter.

Eckerd resigned, however, following a tiff involving Speaker of the House Thomas P. O'Neill Jr., in which the chief member of the Democratic party on the House side of Capitol Hill was accused of trying to undermine the GSA head through control of lower-level staff appointees. Ironically, the Carson City dollar letter with the proposal was addressed from Eckerd to O'Neill.

In substance, the proposal made by GSA is identical to one made in July, 1976, and has become necessary because the silver dollars now in GSA hands are like an albatross.

Following discovery of hoards of silver dollars in the Treasury vaults in Washington, the Joint Commission on the Coinage decided on May 12, 1969 to dispose of the coins. There were, as Eckerd noted, three basic objectives.

First was to "insure the public a widespread opportunity to obtain the coins," second was "to obtain the maximum return on disposal for the Treasury," and finally, there was the aim of conducting the disposal operation within the government, rather than privately to assure profits remained with Uncle Sam.

The "bid-sale" idea was launched by Assistant Treasury Secretary Robert Wallace amid impressive fanfare, and the then-head of the GSA, Arthur Sampson, called an impressive press conference on Oct. 31, 1972 to explain what would become of the contents of the 2,850 bags of silver cartwheels.

Problems with the method of sale — which allowed for individuals to bid on a single coin up to a specified amount but to obtain the coin for the lowest "acceptable" price determined by the GSA — cropped up almost from the start.

First, the expected market never materialized. While the GSA ultimately spent $7.8 million in pursuit of receipts that have aggregated $55.3 million, a number of coins were deemed undesirable by collectors and other Americans at the minimum prices accepted by GSA.

Examples of the prices included $15 for the 1878-CC, which quickly sold out the 47,556 pieces on hand, and the mixed

★Please turn to page 18

Israel to issue new coin

A dove of peace and mountaintop city form Asaf Berg's "Brotherhood in Jerusalem" design for Israel's 29th Independence Day 25 pounds, a 34 millimeter, .500 silver crown to be struck in Uncirculated with Star of David Mint mark, Proof with tiny Hebrew letter "Mem." Ordering procedures for 1977 were described in the April 6 Coin World.

Rochette plans report on bourse table flap

Summaries of correspondence with most of the nine coin dealers denied bourse tables at this year's American Numismatic Association convention in Atlanta are being compiled for review by the association board of governors, according to Edward Rochette, ANA executive vice president.

The board, meeting in March, had voted not to allow 11 dealers bourse space this year. The action was taken because the dealers allegedly failed to maintain their tables at the 1976 New York convention through the Sunday closing day.

Though 11 dealers were named, two of those did not seek bourse tables for 1977, according to the ANA.

Several others, however, were vocal in protesting the board's action. A number of those maintained that they had in fact operated their tables on Sunday, or left the convention early because of what they thought were justifiable reasons.

Joining those dealers who previously told *Coin World* that their tables were manned on Sunday in New York was Mike Kliman of Numismatic Enterprises, South Laguna, Calif.

Kliman, in a letter to the ANA, a copy of which was forwarded to *Coin World*, denied that his table was left unmanned.

"My son, who has helped staff my table for the two previous conventions, remained an extra day in New York until the following

★Please turn to page 6

Amon Carter Jr. gets B'nai B'rith medal

Fort Worth *Star-Telegram* publisher and renowned numismatist Amon Carter Jr. was honored March 23 by the half-million member international B'nai B'rith organization for his generous and unselfish contributions to the community.

Carter received the organization's Gold Medallion Humanitarian Award from President David M. Blumberg during ceremonies attended by more than 350 persons at Ridglea Country Club.

"This is the nicest honor I've ever received, and I do mean that," the Texas numismatist said after Blumberg had placed the gold medallion around his neck.

Blumberg praised Carter's dedication to humanity, especially his devotion to youth, one of the main concerns of B'nai B'rith.

The Humanitarian Award is presented annually. Last year's recipient was then British Prime Minister Harold Wilson.

"A man's true wealth is measured by how he gives of himself to his family, his community and his friends," Blumberg noted, indicating that Carter has been generous to the community of Fort Worth and elsewhere.

Master of ceremonies for the occasion, Louis H. Barnett, read a telegram from House Majority leader Jim Wright praising Carter's "superb leadership and unselfish service" to the community. "He has earned the respect of all the nation," Wright said.

Co-chairman of the event, University of Texas regent Thomas Law, called Carter "a good friend and a true humanitarian. Besides being humane, he's also a very human person," Law remarked.

Witnessing the event was the only other Texan to receive the international honor, former Houston *Chronicle* publisher John T. Jones Jr.

A former classmate of Carter's at the University of Texas, both served in North Africa and spent several years in a prisoner of war camp together.

Released April 21, 1945, the pair went directly to the Ritz hotel in Paris, where Carter's father, Amon Carter Sr., had prepared a feast for them.

"We went from nothing to steak and cognac," Jones remarked. "I'd swap the tooth fairy for Amon any day," he quipped.

The junior Carter, an American Numismatic Association life member, is widely known in numismatic circles. Among his extensive holdings is the Adams' specimen of the 1804 dollar, which he purchased in 1950.

A 1960 member of the U.S. Assay Commission, he is also widely known as an avid syngraphist, most recently reporting the first $20 denomination inverted overprint among the current rash of such errors.

Amon Carter Jr. (L) receives the B'nai B'rith Gold Medallion Humanitarian Award from David M. Blumberg (R) as Mrs. Carter and past recipient John T. Jones look on.

Since the results of this examination of over 10 percent of this lot indicated that the contents of the bags were virtually as tagged, the very slow and costly examination of each individual coin was discontinued. The contents of the remaining 2,163 bags in this lot are tagged to indicate the following uncirculated Carson City dollars:

Year	Amount
1878	49000
1879	4000
1880	116000
1881	125000
1882	470000
1883	599000
1884	675000
1885	122000
1890	2000
1891	1000
Total	2163000

were not worth significantly more than the $30 people paid the government for them as an "investment" years earlier. On the other hand, nearly all of the other silver dollars, issues that weren't sold by the GSA but were released through the banks and the Federal Reserve System directly to dealers and collectors, went up in value sharply, many of them multiplying several times!

In addition to the GSA sales and Treasury releases, public interest in silver dollars has been spurred by many private sources. California dealer Joel Rettew placed advertisements offering a string of common dates of Morgan dollars for a nominal price. When orders were received he would send the coins in an album with many blank spaces for additional purchases to be made in the future. His interest whetted, a typical customer would then respond by ordering rarer dates from Joel to fill in the blanks. First Coinvestors and others ran nationwide advertisements offering silver dollars on credit terms and by monthly plans.

It is exciting to me today to hold an 1878 Carson City silver dollar, one of the most common dates, and to think that it was struck from Comstock Lode silver during the "wild West" days of the 19th century. Or, it is equally fascinating to hold, for example, an 1896-S silver dollar, a fairly expensive date but one of which 5,000,000 were minted (and of which presumably millions were melted), and speculate exactly how many were left after the melting occurred. 100,000? 200,000? A million? Perhaps just 10,000? The answer will never be known. Many have attempted to provide estimates.

Silver Dollar Fortune Telling, a book by Les Fox, gave estimates on the numbers known. John Kamin, publisher of *The Forecaster*, likewise estimated the population of many issues. Still, the number known of virtually every issue of Morgan and Peace dollars will forever remain a mystery. The unknown is always fascinating, and undoubtedly this provides a part of the romance of the series.

Although Morgan silver dollars minted from 1878 to 1904 provided most of the excitement during the great Treasury release, a number of Peace silver dollars were included as well.

While most Morgan dollars were made from 1878 through 1904, curiously enough an additional 86,000,000 were struck in 1921! Considering that following the Pittman Act of 1918 $270,000,000 worth of silver dollars were melted down, it seems curious that more of the same design would be made a few years later! I have no rational explanation for this, nor does anyone else. Perhaps the best commentary is given by noted silver dollar researchers Leroy C. Van Allen and A. George Mallis, who wrote in their book, *The Comprehensive Catalog and Encyclopedia of United States Morgan and Peace Dollars*:

"As is obvious, the Morgan and Peace silver dollars were made a political football throughout their unsettled existence like no other coins in American history!"

In 1920, Farran Zerbe, one of America's most prominent numismatists, proposed during the American Numismatic Association convention the design of a new silver dollar. On May 9, 1921, a bill was introduced in Congress to provide for a dollar "of an appropriate design commemorative of the termination of the war between the Imperial German government and the government and people of the United States."

A competition was held among leading artists and medalists, including Hermon MacNeil, Chester Beach, Victor D. Brenner, Adolph Weinman, John Flanagan, Robert Aitken, Henry Hering, Robert T. McKenzie, and Anthony DeFrancisci. Many of these notable sculptors had produced successful designs earlier, Brenner's 1909 Lincoln cent, Weinman's 1916 Mercury dime and 1916 Liberty walking half dollar, and MacNeil's 1916 Liberty standing quarter being prominent. Robert Aitken produced the massive 1915 Panama Pacific International Exposition commemorative $50 gold pieces.

Anthony DeFrancisci's proposals won. The obverse featured a young head of Ms. Liberty modeled after the Statue of Liberty in New York harbor. The features were derived from the artist's young wife, the former Teresa Cafarelli, who came to America from Italy at the age of five and who recalled with enthusiasm her first view of the famed statue lifting its lamp beside the golden door.

As quoted by Don Taxay, Mrs. DeFrancisci wrote to her brother shortly after the first Peace dollars bearing her portrait were made:

"You remember how I was always posing as Liberty, and how broken hearted I was when some other little girl was selected to play the role in the patriotic exercises in school? I thought of those days often while sitting as a model for Tony's design, and now seeing myself as Miss Liberty on the new coin, it seems like the realization of my finest childhood dream."

At the American Numismatic Association convention held in Boston in 1973, Mrs. DeFrancisci, by that time a widow, was a guest of honor. I had the pleasure of talking with "Miss Liberty," whose features I had earlier observed on thousands of silver dollars!

The first issue of Peace silver dollars, dated 1921, was produced in December of that year. 1,006,473 pieces were struck. The design was a very attractive one, appearing in high relief and giving an almost sculptured effect. There was trouble in paradise, however, for it was determined that the high relief design caused tremendous problems in striking the coins. It was exceedingly dif-

ficult, nearly impossible in fact, to bring up all of the design detail at the center of the coin, particularly the hair strands of Miss Liberty's head.

George T. Morgan, by then chief mint engraver (and designer of the Morgan dollar motif which the Peace dollar replaced), wrote to Anthony DeFrancisci on January 3, 1922:

"Today by American Express I send you 50 of the Peace dollars. I know you'll be disappointed, but the pressure necessary to bring up the work was so destructive to the dies that we got tired of putting new dies in. In changing the date to 1922 I took the opportunity of making a slight change in the curvature of the ground. I anticipate that at least 20 tons less pressure will be required to bring up the design. This could double the life of the die. I send you an early strike of the 1922."

The new design was changed to a very shallow relief. Although the design features remained the same, the sculptured effect was gone. DeFrancisci protested the abuse of his design and said that the changes were "small in mechanical gain but very damaging to artistic values." Most numismatists today would agree. The 1921 Peace dollars in high relief made during the closing days of that year are the only pieces true to the artist's original concept.

Peace silver dollars were made from 1921 through 1935, with an intermission 1929-1933. Quantities were immense. As was the case with Morgan dollars, many went straight to bank vaults where they would emerge in later years in the form of bags and isolated Uncirculated groupings to delight collectors.

1928 in particular, a coin with a mintage of 360,649 pieces, was elusive. In the early days the *Handbook of United States Coins*, Western Publishing Company's blue-covered companion to the *Guide Book of Coins*, noted tantalizingly that the 1928 Peace dollar was "struck for cornerstone purposes." When I first began looking through silver dollars in quantities in the 1950s I was delighted to find a 1928, believing that it had escaped from a "cornerstone" and had been carelessly spent. Then I found another, then another, then still more. Even so, the date remained scarce in comparison to others.

After 1928 there was a lapse in coinage for several years. Then in 1934 and 1935 over 7,000,000 additional dollars were minted as a result of Franklin D. Roosevelt's proclamation of December 21, 1933, which provided that new silver dollars would be coined to pay for recently purchased domestic silver. Why weren't

older silver dollars from the Treasury hoards used to pay for this bullion? Who knows? Again, the pieces did not circulate to any great extent. Most were bagged and sent to Treasury vaults.

The end of the Peace design came in 1935, or so it seemed at the time. Then on August 3, 1964, an act was passed which provided that 45,000,000 additional silver dollars be struck of the Peace design. On May 5th, 1965, President Lyndon B. Johnson ordered that they be struck. At the Denver Mint 316,076 pieces were made. These dollars were dated 1964.

At the same time the country was dropping silver coinage and switching to the new cupro-nickel standard. It was decided that only a few of the 316,076 Peace silver dollars dated 1964, if released, would reach the actual public. Most would be seized by collectors and speculators or would be otherwise hoarded. According to later Mint announcements, *all* of the 1964 Peace dollars were melted down. The legend persisted that some had been saved.

A letter from Denver dealer Dan Brown sheds some light on the subject and affords an interesting speculation:

"I was talking with Fern Miller a few years back when she was Director of the United States Mint here in Denver. She was telling me that when the order came in stating that the Denver Mint was to make the new Peace dollar everyone at the mint was elated. They set up the machinery for it, and at the proper time struck a large quantity. As has been the custom throughout the years, mint employees were each allowed to buy two of these new dollars. Quite a number of the mint employees took advantage of and bought two pieces each. Soon afterwards, word came in from Washington that they were not to strike any more dollars, and that if any had been given out they were to be taken back and held until further orders, which probably would be that the coins would be melted down at a future date.

"Mrs. Miller did mention the fact that she thought that everyone who had purchased the dollars in the morning they were first coined turned them in, but as no record was kept of purchasers, there was really no way of knowing for sure. So, as a result, there possibly are some of the dollars still in existence. These may show up in future years. Of course they would be great rarities. I don't think that the mint could declare them illegal under the circumstances and confiscate them, although this is a legal point."

So, perhaps the story of the silver dollar treasure hunt has not ended!

The Secret of the Sierra

Weighing Old Coin, One Million Dollars.
2383. in Gold in Sight, Philadelphia, Pa.

5

Gold! The very word awakens thoughts of romance and excitement! Pirate treasure, the California gold rush, sunken galleons, immense fortunes—these and many other visions are inspired by the precious yellow metal.

For over a hundred years, until gold coins were discontinued in 1933, minted yellow discs provided the backbone of American commerce. Indeed, many contracts and agreements specified payment in gold. At many points throughout American history, particularly prior to 1865, gold coins had a higher value than paper money of equivalent denominations. For example, in 1864 $100 in United States gold coins would buy over $170 worth of United States ''greenback'' notes!

The United States government produced gold coins from 1795 through 1933. Well after the first Mint coinage, until 1857 in fact, a wide mixture of foreign gold coins saw active circulation in America.

Particularly common in the channels of trade were Spanish pieces. To supply the needs of commerce these were minted in vast numbers.

During the early 1700s Spain controlled much of the New World. The Spanish flag flew over nearly all of Central and South America as well as Mexico and many islands. Each year the king of Spain would send two fleets of galleons to the New World to collect the royal share of gold and silver mined in the colonies there. After calling on various ports and loading up cargo holds the ships would meet each year in the harbor of Havana, Cuba, to form a flotilla for the long return trip home. Accompanying them would be lightly-laden ships armed with cannons and other weapons to ward off pirates, an extreme hazard in those times.

In the year 1715 the flotilla was delayed. It was not until late July, when the threat of hurricanes in the treacherous Straits of Florida became a hazard, that the fleet left.

By noon Tuesday, July 30th, six days after leaving the Port of Havana, 12 ships, 11 laden with treasure and one accompanying French vessel, *El Grifon*, had progressed up the coast of Florida to a point off the coast slightly north of the present day community of Vero Beach. The skies grew ominous, and within a few hours the heavens were nearly as black as night. The wind began to rise and the sea became rough and dangerous. Early the next morning, shortly after midnight, a hurricane struck with full force! Tremendous waves, much larger than the ships themselves, buffeted and tossed the vessels. One by one the ships were torn apart or smashed onto reefs. By the next morning only one, the French gunboat, was still afloat. On the bottom were 11 Spanish galleons, over 1,000 crew members, and a king's ransom in silver and gold bars, gold doubloons, and silver pieces of eight.

Within a few days word of the terrible fate reached Havana. Salvage operations began immediately, and many millions of dollars worth of treasure was recovered. From that time onward the stranded and sunken ships were an attraction for government and private vessels from different countries.

In 1716 Captain Henry Jennings, in command of five ships provisioned in Barbados, Jamaica, and other British islands, came and overpowered the Spanish treasure divers who were working the wreck. With a force of 300 men he easily vanquished the 60 Spanish soldiers and other officials and laid claim to about 350,000 pieces of eight and other artifacts and took them back to Jamaica.

Other recovery attempts over a period of years yielded additional amounts.

In 1774, nearly 60 years after the ships went to the bottom, Bernard Romans, a British map maker, visited the site and observed that some of the wooden masts of the Spanish vessels were still visible above the water line. Landing at a nearby beach he and his crew found many Spanish coins which had washed up on the shore.

By that time most of the treasure easily recoverable on the sea bottom had been taken by adventurers. The ships continued to disintegrate, and by several decades later the site had been all but forgotten.

During the 1950s, many generations later, the visitor to Florida could hear tales of buried treasure, but little factual information could be obtained. It was known

that occasional Spanish ships had been wrecked off the shores of that state, but where no one knew. Beach-combers would occasionally find assorted coins washed up on the shore.

During the late 1950s Kip Wagner, a carpenter, was walking along the beach near Sebastian Inlet north of Vero Beach. A particularly strong hurricane had just raked the area and had washed up on the shore massive amounts of sand and debris. Spying a bright gleam, Wagner reached down and picked up a Spanish silver coin dated 1715. Apparently he was the first person on the beach after the storm, for soon he found another piece, then another, and then more. Wagner, a coin collector, was struck by the odd fact that all of the pieces found were dated 1715 or shortly before. Apparently, so he reasoned, they must have come from a common source. Could there be a hidden treasure nearby?

Wagner, in a dazzling display of ingenuity, went to the Archives of the Indies in Seville, Spain, and found before him the original government records of the great 1715 disaster. Outlined on maps were the locations where each ship went to the bottom!

Returning to Florida, he spent many months exploring the area off Sebastian Inlet. At first he didn't know what to expect. Would he come across the intact hull of a galleon, still outfitted with rows of cannon? Would he find gold coins sprinkled all over the sand on the sea bottom? The truth was less romantic. Flying over the area Kip Wagner noticed an oblong dark area in the sandy sea bottom. Returning to the site by boat he dived and found ballast stones once carried in the ship's hull to stabilize the ship and maintain its upright position. Also found were 18 cannons, each heavily encrusted with marine life. The ship itself was long gone, the victim of shifting currents, marine animals, and other predators. Covering the entire site were tons of sand.

Seeking capital, Wagner formed the Real Eight Company, named after the Spanish eight real silver-dollar-size coin. In 1961, using a device which blew sand particles away from the wreck site, the seekers hit paydirt. Found were clumps of silver coins!

Encrusted by lime and coral, these globs resembled rocks more than numismatic specimens. However, after being subjected to gentle chemical treatment the matrix separated and individual coins were obtained. Most silver pieces had etched surfaces due to the corrosive action of the sea water.

Thousands of silver coins were obtained this way, but only a few gold coins came to light. Had they all been recovered two centuries earlier by divers on the wrecks? Wagner was beginning to be discouraged. At last during one day the blower swept away sand and revealed what he described as "a carpet of more than 1,000 golden doubloons." During another especially favorable day, a few years later in 1974, divers obtained one by one over a thousand additional gold doubloons and minor gold pieces!

In 1977 the Real Eight Company commissioned my firm to sell at auction gold and silver treasures from the fleet. What a thrill it was for our staff to catalogue these coins, gold pieces nearly as nice as the day they were minted (gold is comparatively unaffected by salt water) and silver coins in various states of preservation, and present them to numismatists!

Bids poured in from all over the world. The sale was a spectacular success.

What a queer twist of fortune this was. Had the great disaster of 1715 not occurred the coins would have been sent to Spain where they undoubtedly would have been melted down.

As it was, this act of nature preserved for numismatists tens of thousands of coins which now grace collections in all parts of the globe, each one being a reminder of the golden days of the Spanish Main.

I have always liked gold treasure stories, and from the first time I read Edgar Allan Poe's short story, "The Gold Bug," I have been fascinated with the lure of hidden coins.

Until comparatively recent decades there was a great distrust of banks. Money kept in banking institutions, even those which appeared to be very solid, was usually lost if the bank failed. Indeed, United States banking history is dotted with hundreds of bankruptcies and failures which have cost depositors untold fortunes. A safer alternative, so it seemed to many, was to bury gold coins or hide them where they could be reclaimed later when needed. This was fine unless something happened in the meantime. If the person making the cache was killed then it would be undetected, awaiting discovery by a future treasure seeker or, as probably happened most often, it would be lost forever.

A few years ago I catalogued for one of our auction sales an interesting hoard of gold coins unearthed on a plantation near Vicksburg, Mississippi, by treasure hunters using electronic detectors. In 1863 the plantation owner left to join the Confederate Army. Before doing so he buried for safekeeping a number of United States gold coins, primarily $5, $10, and $20 issues. Fate was not kind, and the plantation was burned to the ground shortly thereafter by advancing Union forces. The owner was killed in battle. All was forgotten until one day in the early 1970s when a "beep beep" was heard on the treasure detector loudspeaker. Frenzied digging then took place, and soon bright and gleaming gold coins of the 1840s, 1850s, and 1860s, including a number of rare dates, came to light! The treasure seekers were thousands of dollars richer.

Treasure Coins

Silver from the 1715 Spanish treasure fleet. 8-real presentation piece 1714. Irregularly-shaped planchet and with weak striking in areas due to the crude minting process of the time.

Group of several silver 8-real pieces, dates from 1711 to 1715, as rescued from the sea floor by the Real Eight Company.

1714 gold 4-escudo piece from the 1715 Spanish treasure fleet disaster. Minted in Mexico City and bearing a distinctive "Mo" mintmark.

Undated (but struck in 1713) gold 8-escudo piece struck in Mexico City. One of the finest-condition pieces salvaged from the 1715 Spanish treasure fleet wrecks.

Reduced-size illustration of a large gold bar weighing 5 pounds, 2¼ ounces, and measuring 7 inches long; the largest gold treasure bar salvaged from the 1715 Spanish treasure fleet by the Real Eight Company.

Property of the captain? Measuring slightly more than 2½ inches in length, this souvenir from the Spanish treasure fleet bears the inscription MIO AMOR, "My Love." Perhaps it was received as a gift from a sweetheart.

Cross of virtually pure gold was apparently intended as a gift for Philip V, king of Spain. Recovered from the cabin area of the fleet's commander, General Esteban de Ubilla. Appraised by the state of Florida for $50,000.

Hoards of double eagles, $20 gold pieces—America's largest regular-issue coin denomination—have always been particularly fascinating to me. Over the years a number of hoards involving these have passed through my hands or have been called to my attention. In the early 1970s my firm acquired quite a few dozen Uncirculated $20 gold pieces of 1855-S, 1856, and 1856-S. Each piece had a lightly etched surface, but with all design details sharp—the result of immersion in sea water for a protracted period of time. The story was that a government ship enroute from San Francisco to the eastern United States was sunk. Down to the sea floor went thousands of dollars in gold coins which were intended to pay the troops stationed at an eastern garrison. When I obtained the coins the double eagles themselves were real, but whether the story was or not I don't know. Treasure stories often have an element of spice and imagination to them. One reason is that finders of treasure often seek to evade local and government officials who might lay claim, rightly or wrongly, to some of the findings. The second is that stories of treasure usually grow in the telling, and nothing makes a more exciting tale than glittering gold pieces brought up from the depths of the sea or found in a trunk in someone's attic.

More recently, in 1977, a dealer told me of a hoard of 60 pieces of 1854-S $20 gold pieces. I had occasion to examine a handful of these. Each coin appeared to be Brilliant Uncirculated, very sharp in detail, with some light etching of the surface. The story goes that these were found between the wall studs when an old building in San Francisco was torn down.

The greatest hoards of double eagles, however, have come not from within the United States or from the depths of our coastal waters but, rather, from foreign countries. Years ago foreign banks, merchants, and governments often demanded payment in gold. The value of United States currency was often questionable, and gold remained a safer alternative. Even in recent times this philosophy has prevailed. For example, in 1945 and 1946 the government of Saudi Arabia demanded payment in gold coins in settlement for oil purchases. At the time the United States had no gold coins on hand nor was it minting any, so a special issue of gold discs was struck at the Philadelphia Mint.

As a result of an international preference for gold millions of United States gold coins were shipped overseas during the late 19th and early 20th centuries. When the American government ceased producing coins in 1933 and directed that all banks and private citizens (except for numismatists building collections) must turn their gold coins in at face value, foreign interests held onto their American gold coins more tightly than ever!

Decades later this was to have a very beneficial effect for numismatists. When high values began to be assigned to United States gold coins, commencing with the strong interest in collecting gold coins by dates which developed on a large scale after World War II, foreign bankers started looking through their stocks.

Dayton, Ohio dealer James Kelly obtained from a bank vault in Argentina hundreds of Carson City Liberty head double eagles minted from 1870 through 1893. He stated to his supplier that he was willing to pay a premium for any $20 gold pieces with a distinguishing "CC" mintmark on the reverse, and he was rewarded with many treasures.

Switzerland, the world's banking capital, proved to be the richest lode. When I visited a leading bank there in 1961 I had a discussion with one of its officers. I inquired about the extent of their double eagle holdings and the price desired for individual specimens as well as quantities. At the time common date Uncirculated 20th century double eagles of the Saint-Gaudens type were selling at about $42 per coin. I had in mind buying a few hundred or possibly a thousand pieces.

"Right now I can quote you a price which would be good for up to 100,000 pieces," he said, "but if you want more than that I'll have to check and get back to you." I have no idea what the total Swiss holdings were, but judging from the vast quantities which were imported into the United States during the 1960s and especially during a feverish market in gold coins which occurred during the 1973-1975 years, it must have been in the millions.

Switzerland was an especially fertile source for scarce mintmark issues of the 1920s. From there I have purchased quite a few pieces such as Denver and San Francisco issues dated 1924 to 1931. Sadly, most if not all large original hoards have been depleted. Many gold coins now offered for sale by European banks and antique dealers are clever forgeries.

Speaking of double eagles, Jim Ruddy and I were delighted in 1962 when Yale University decided to part with an unneeded specimen of the MCMVII Extremely High Relief double eagle, one of America's most famous rarities. We purchased the coin and subsequently sold it for about $20,000. As has been the case many times when we have handled rarities, the event received nationwide news coverage. A few weeks later I was approached by a gentleman who lived on the outskirts of Philadelphia. He showed me a small black leather case lined with purple silk and velvet. There on a cushion was another specimen as nice as the day it was minted! I was told that Theodore Roosevelt, president of the United States in 1907, had presented the coin to his father as a gift.

Like nearly all other United States coin rarities, the MCMVII Extremely High Relief double eagle has been a tremendous investment over the years. I have handled several of them, and each time the price has been higher. Today a specimen would sell for several hundred thousand dollars.

Over the years my firm has purchased thousands of collections, some large and some small. Most have come from established collectors who built them over a long period of time. There have been a number of exceptions, however. Occasionally a non-collector will come across a treasure trove in a safe deposit box, dresser drawer, or other location.

Oscar G. Schilke, the well-known Connecticut collector, told me of an 1842 United States Proof set, complete from the half cent through the ten dollar gold piece, which was found in a bureau drawer by the descendants of one of Connecticut's early governors. The set would be worth over $100,000 today! Oscar negotiated for its purchase and at the same time acquired from the governor's heirs a beautiful fractional currency shield. Made around 1867-1869, about 400 of these shields were produced for distribution to banks. Each shield consisted of a printed background in the form of a shield design on which were pasted 39 different specimens of fractional currency notes of denominations from three cents to fifteen cents. They were used at the time as counterfeit detectors. A banker desiring to verify the authenticity of a note could hold it up to the shield and compare the suspected note with the genuine.

For years Oscar Schilke kept this fractional currency shield, an especially fine one, on the wall of his library. When I acquired his collection in the late 1950s I purchased with it the shield. The story of its original acquisition was quite interesting, so I purchased it for my own. Today it hangs on my office wall.

In another instance a car dealer from upstate New York came into the office and showed me a glittering handful of coins: four Brilliant Uncirculated 1931 Denver Mint double eagles, a scarce date. I offered him several thousand dollars each, their value at the time, and he declined saying he didn't need the money. It would be interesting to speculate where the coins are now.

In the same vein I was pleasantly surprised one day by a Cleveland visitor. His grandfather, he said, collected coins years earlier and had left behind a large collection of Proof gold coins. Four of them were brought along for my inspection that day: coiled and flowing hair $4 pieces of 1879 and 1880, a complete set of one of America's most prized rarities!

On still another occasion I learned from a Buffalo, New York man of a family collection which had gold Proof sets beginning in 1858 and continuing through the mid-1880s, a group worth several million dollars today

and worth several hundred thousand dollars at the time I learned of it in 1961.

Since the earliest days of civilization gold has captured the fascination of mankind. Wars have been fought to secure this precious metal, and kingdoms have risen and fallen because of it.

Although there have been many gold discoveries in North America over the years, none has been more famous than the California Gold Rush.

While we hear such rhymes today as "The days of old, the days of gold, the days of '49," and while the Forty-Niners are well known, it is interesting to note that the first California gold discovery was several years earlier.

When gold metal is involved, history often becomes distorted. So it is with the first discovery of gold in California. In 1896 J.M. Guinn, writing an article entitled "The Gold Placers of Los Angeles," stated with some documentation that the first discovery was made in June 1841.

In his monumental American history series Hubert H. Bancroft wrote in the 1890s: "The mine at San Fernando, near Los Angeles, where work was begun in 1842, is about the only satisfactory instance on record of the knowledge of the existence of gold in Alta, California prior to the discovery by Marshall [in 1848]."

Another source, the *Historical Sketch of Los Angeles County*, places the discovery date at "sometime in the latter part of 1840, or the early part of 1841."

In any event, the approximate circumstances seem to be these: sometime around 1841 Don Andres Castillero, traveling from Los Angeles to Monterey slightly inland from the California coast, picked up some small pebbles which were a variety of iron pyrite. He soon showed those to a friend, Don Jose Antonio de la Guerra y Noriega, at whose home in Santa Barbara he was a guest. An excited discussion followed for it was believed that these pebbles, although they contained no gold themselves, were often found with gold in streams. Attending the discussion was Francisco Lopez, a farmer who lived at the Piru Rancho north of Los Angeles.

Shortly after this discussion, Lopez and another herdsman were searching for stray animals near the Piru Rancho. Lopez, seeking some greens for food, pulled a clump of wild onions up by the roots. Attached to the root system was a small gold nugget. Digging with a sheath knife he soon found more gold nuggets and flakes.

The news of this discovery spread like wildfire, and within a few weeks hundreds of people descended upon the gold site located on the San Francisco Rancho in the San Feliciano Canyon about 40 miles northwest of Los

CENTRAL CALIFORNIA IN 1848.

Central California as it was in 1848 before the Gold Rush. Sutter's Fort, located near the Sacramento River at the present-day location of the city of Sacramento, furnished a focal point for civilization in the Sierra foothills.

Angeles and about eight miles west of the town of Newhall.

In those days gold was extracted two ways. The first was by washing gold-bearing dirt in rapidly running water. After this the riffles or catch spots in the sluice or, in the instance of hand mining, the bottom of a prospector's pan would be examined, and tiny gold flakes could be seen. The second way was used by Mexican miners predominantly and consisted of "winnowing"—throwing gold bearing dust and dirt up into the air and catching the heavier particles, including bits of gold, as they fell to the earth first.

The Honorable Abel Stearns, a citizen of Los Angeles, sent on November 22, 1842, by Alfred Robinson, 20 ounces of California gold to the United States Mint at Philadelphia for assay. Writing in later years, Stearns gave still another date for the discovery:

"The placer mines from which this gold was taken were first discovered by Francisco Lopez, a native of California, in the month of March, 1842, at a place called San Franciscito, about 35 miles northwest from Los Angeles."

Upon receipt, the United States Mint weighed the gold and arrived at a figure of 18 34/100ths ounces which, after melting, yielded 18 1/100ths ounces of 92.6% purity. The value at the Mint was $344.75, with expenses of $4.02, leaving a net of $340.73 due the depositor.

The placer (pronounced "plasser") mines were worked from the early 1840s until late 1846 at which time the miners, predominantly Mexicans from Sonora, left to return to their homeland. It is believed that about $6,000 to $8,000 per year value of bullion was extracted.

In the brilliant light of later events the early Los Angeles County discovery has been almost forgotten.

The great California Gold Rush had its beginning with the inhabitants of Sutter's Fort. Founded in 1839 by John A. Sutter, a Swiss, the fort was a rough rectangle about 500 feet long by 150 feet wide enclosed with adobe walls. Within were various craftsmen, shops, stores, warehouses, parade grounds, and other facilities. Today the structure stands as a historical monument in Sacramento.

Sutter's Fort was the central focus for several thousand square miles of farming and ranching activity. Sutter himself in December 1847 reported owning 12,000 cattle, 2,000 horses and mules, nearly 15,000 sheep, and 1,000 hogs. Surrounding the fort were 60 houses, six mills, and one tannery. Several hundred people lived in and around the fortified enclosure.

Lumber was obtained from coastal areas where it was cut and sawed by hand and then transported by boat up the Sacramento River. Sutter dreamed of setting up a sawmill to the west in the mountain foothills where lumber was plentiful. Cattle fencing, houses, mills, and other construction projects necessitated a large quantity of structural timber. In addition, Sutter, being a businessman, envisioned supplying the small town of San Francisco with lumber from his mill.

James Wilson Marshall, born in 1812 in New Jersey, lived at Sutter's Fort and pursued his trade as a carpenter and wagon builder. His skill as a mechanic was considerable, and Sutter prized his abilities highly.

Sutter discussed with Marshall the establishment of a sawmill and suggested that Marshall find an appropriate site located near a suitable water supply for power. Several excursions were made until a site in the Sierra foothills about 40 miles above Sutter's Fort on the bank of the American River at a place called Columa (later called Coloma), or "Beautiful Valley," was found. In August 1847 Marshall and a group of helpers and assistants set out to begin construction. With tools and supplies on Mexican oxcarts and with an accompanying flock of sheep to provide food, it took a week to make the journey.

By New Year's Day 1848 three cabins had been constructed for housing and the main frame of the mill had been erected. Indians were engaged as laborers.

A mill channel or race was built by using an existing dry stream bed parallel to the American River and diverting water into it. To deepen the channel each day the larger stones were removed by hand, sometimes with the assistance of blasting. Then during the night the water would rush through and carry away dirt, sand, and smaller particles.

Early on the afternoon of Monday, January 24, 1848, Marshall was inspecting work in progress at the mill race. Heavy rains, which almost caused abandonment of the project through flooding, had washed away many rocks and much sediment. Among the pebbles on the bottom he noticed some gleaming yellow flakes. Could it be gold? He sent an Indian to fetch a metal plate. Marshall thought that he had found gold but wasn't sure. Many substances looked like gold, and he wanted to be certain.

"Boys, I believe I have found a gold mine," he said that evening. His companions were skeptical.

Early the next morning he again visited the mill race and saw gleaming about six inches below the surface of the water a small yellow nugget. If it were gold it would have been worth about a half dollar. Was it gold or was it some other substance? Again, Marshall was unsure. He took the nugget and pounded it between two stones and saw it flatten slightly. It must be gold! As historian Bancroft has written, "the mighty secret of the Sierra stood revealed!"

Marshall and his companions lost no time. All sloshed about in the mill race and within a short time had gathered three ounces of the yellow metal.

A few days later Marshall rode on horseback to Sutter and requested a private meeting with him. Following instructions in an encyclopedia, Marshall and Sutter performed an assay. The gold metal was subjected to acid, then to a specific gravity test, then to other scrutiny. Soon all doubts vanished.

Sutter returned with Marshall to the sawmill. Within a few days it was learned that gold existed all along the American River and in nearby ravines and tributary creeks.

Sutter at first was dismayed by the discovery. While the finding of several hundred dollars worth of gold was a blessing to the men involved, it was a distraction from the project at hand: to complete the sawmill and get it operating. After discussions he had the men at the mill promise to keep the matter a secret for six weeks, by which time it was hoped that the mill would be completed and the business would be in operation. The men cheerfully agreed, for the steady wages of mill construction were more attractive than the unknown possibilities of finding gold in very small quantities.

Sutter, a businessman, sought to control the gold area and to this end negotiated with the Columa Indians and surrounding natives. By trading merchandise he obtained a three-year lease of a tract ten to twelve miles square.

While Sutter urged secrecy by others, he himself could not resist the temptation to spread news of the bonanza.

Writing to an acquaintance on February 10, 1848, he said:

"I have made a discovery of a gold mine, which, according to experiments we have made, is extraordinarily rich."

While Sutter considered his lease from the Indians to give him prior claim to the property, he was still uncertain about its legality. Earlier, land in the area had been subject to Mexican land grants of uncertain validity. Marshall sought through Colonel R.B. Mason, chief representative of the United States government in California at the time, to secure better title. The envoy from Sutter was instructed not to mention gold but to acquire the land with water, mineral, and pasture privileges, the reason for mineral privileges to be the appearance of *lead* and *silver* in the soil! The messenger, however, was not equal to keeping it a secret, and with him in a leather pouch he took six ounces of the precious metal. At Pfister's store in the town of Benicia, near San Francisco, he told several listeners of the newfound treasure.

Upon reaching Colonel Mason in Monterey the messenger was not able to secure any promises with respect to Sutter's land on the American River. So, to bolster his own image, the gold samples were again shown.

Meanwhile back at Sutter's Mill on the American River, the workers spent much of their spare time searching for gold, keeping in mind their promise to keep silent for six weeks. All who searched were amply rewarded with the precious yellow metal. Marshall himself went three miles further up the American River, accompanied by James Gregson, and at a place in the river he named Live Oak Bar the two picked up with their fingers "a pint of gold," with some pieces being larger than a pea.

In the last week of February several Mormons who had heard of the discovery visited Marshall at the mill and requested permission to search for gold. Marshall complied with their request and the group set about searching in the mill race. The next morning one of the Mormons found a single nugget worth six dollars.

Word spread, and a number of other Mormons returned to the area and set up camp nearby on the river at a place they named the Mormon Diggings on Mormon Island.

Many Mormons had earlier come to California; some by the sea route and others overland via Santa Fe, in order to go from California to the new settlement at Great Salt Lake. Many of them had stopped at Sutter's Fort on the way to the desert area in order to await the passing of winter in the mountains. It was during this time that the gold discoveries were made.

Despite all of the distractions the sawmill began operation on March 11th, 1848. In the meantime many others had come to the American River. One day in March seven men found gold worth $250 at Mormon Island. This was at a time when a good day's salary was a dollar!

The Mormons continued to be active in gold mining, but still the lure of Great Salt Lake was before them. Despite their successes most Mormons had packed up and left by midsummer. ·

In the beginning gold was found by visually observing specks in the stream bed. Then washing gravel and water in a pan became the standard method. After a few minutes of sloshing the mixture all that would remain in the bottom would be black sand and gold particles. Then came the cradle which rocked the gravel and water mixture back and forth and which permitted greater quantities to be processed. Within a year or two the long tom became the main method. This latter device consisted of a long wooden box from ten to thirty feet in length, about 18 inches across at the upper end and wider at the lower. At the bottom end cross bars were placed to cause riffles to trap the gold. At the top end of the long tom several men shoveled dirt into the box which was filled

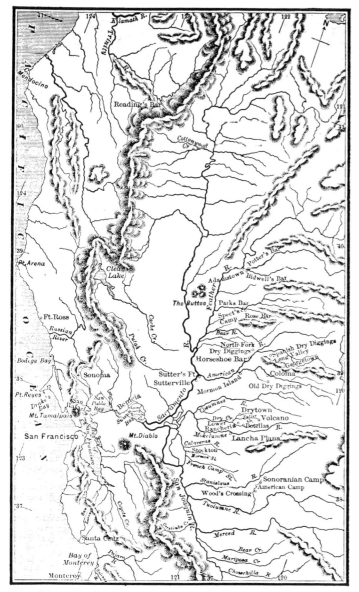

THE GOLD REGION IN 1848, FROM TUOLUMNE TO TRINITY.

SUTTER'S MILL.

One of several different 19th century views of what Sutter's Mill originally looked like.

Following the discovery of gold in January 1848, dozens of camps, some small and some large, were set up on the tributaries of the Sacramento River. Such sites as Potter's Bar, Bidwell's Bar, Spanish Dry Diggings, Volcano (which, due to its isolated condition, is essentially intact today to delight the tourist), Mormon Island, Horseshoe Bar, and others varied from a few tents to small towns with commercial buildings. Most are long gone, their period of activity having lasted just a few weeks or a few months.

Near Mt. Ophir today stand ruins which traditionally have been identified as an old mint. If this indeed is true, it is not known what coins were struck there.

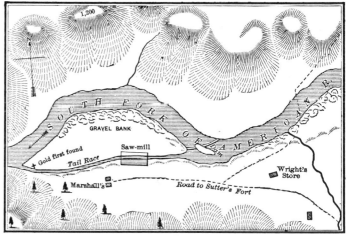

SCENE OF DISCOVERY.

Hubert Bancroft's map of the original gold discovery site. Today a park is in this location.

with a stream of running water. By use of the long tom yields of gold were multiplied many times over. One cousin of the long tom, the quicksilver machine, featured a riffle-box containing quicksilver or mercury to which the gold was attacted and formed an amalgam.

Still other miners used long sluices which channeled water into dirt banks and washed away the overburden. One particularly large sluice located at the settlement of Dutch Flat was over a mile long, cost $55,000, and took four years to build.

Placer mining referred to the finding of loose gold particles in stream beds and in soil. The supposition was that in primordial times these bits of gold had broken loose from outcroppings or veins further up the stream and had washed down. The search was made for the *Mother Lode,* or the vein from which all of the gold had originally come. While most gold was eventually found in placer locations, gold-bearing quartz veins were discovered beginning in 1849. These led to the production of large quartz mills which hammered quartz rock into small particles suitable for further separation and refining.

Meanwhile, up in the hills gold discoveries were spreading. Gold was found on the Feather River in a rich strike at a placer location which was given the name of Bidwell Bar. Additional riches were found at Clear Creek. It became evident that gold was to be found in streams for more than 100 miles along the foothills of the Sierras!

Back in more civilized parts of California it was hard to separate fact from fiction. News of gold discoveries had been spread before, and the reality of the present one was difficult to ascertain. True, some gold had been discovered—but was it really the bonanza which some had claimed or was it simply an overexaggerated situation? In San Francisco Captain J.L. Folsom called the first gold flakes he saw mica. Then being shown 20 ounces of similar heavy metallic material which the bearer said he gathered in only eight days Folsom said he didn't believe it. Bradley, one of Folsom's friends, in May visited Colonel Mason in Monterey where he was asked if there was any truth to rumors about gold being found on the American River. "I have heard of it," was Bradley's reply, "a few fools have hurried into the place, but you can be sure there is nothing in it." Around the same time another official, a man in Benicia, said, "I would give more for a good coal mine than for all the gold mines in the universe."

The first printed notice of the gold discovery appeared on Wednesday, March 15, 1848 in the *Californian,* one of two weekly newspapers then published in San Francisco:

"Gold mine found. In the newly made raceway of the saw mill recently erected by Captain Sutter on the American fork gold has been found in considerable quantities. One person brought $30 worth to New Helvetia [Sutter's Fort], gathered there in a short time. California is no doubt rich in mineral wealth; great chances here for scientific capitalists. Gold has been found in every part of the country."

Three days later the other San Francisco weekly paper, the *California Star,* printed a brief notice that gold had been found 40 miles above Sutter's Fort. The following week the same periodical reported that "so great is the quantity of gold taken from the mine recently found at New Helvetia that it has become an article of traffic in that vicinity."

During April small parties, usually two or three people, left San Francisco for the American River to seek their fortune. In the early part of May the Mormon leader Samuel Brannan, a merchant, visited San Francisco with a bottle of gold dust in one hand. Passing along the street he exclaimed, "Gold! Gold from the American River!" More notices appeared in the newspaper.

Soon the fever spread, and within a few weeks there were no longer disbelievers in the city. Many quit their jobs, put their affairs in order, shuttered their businesses, and otherwise made preparations to leave San Francisco and head for the gold areas.

During May 1848 it was estimated that 800 miners were working the streams and ravines for 30 miles to each side of the original discovery site of Coloma. By June the number was estimated by Consul T.O. Larkin at 2,000 miners, most of whom were foreigners. While perhaps 100 families came with tents, proper provisions, and teams, most had packed hurriedly with little thought for the future and came with little other than clothes and a few implements. Many, finding themselves short of provisions, returned to San Francisco to better equip themselves. Then they went back to the gold fields prepared for a longer stay. Early in July Colonel Mason, during his first inspection visit to the area, was given the estimate that 4,000 miners were busy. By the arrival of autumn in October it was estimated that 10,000 miners plus many Indian laborers were at work.

The most popular route was the closest—by water up San Francisco Bay to the Sacramento River, then by land from Sacramento to the gold fields. Passage was at a premium in commercial vessels so many miners bought small boats which they discarded upon arriving in Sacramento.

A census taken in San Francisco in March 1848 showed 812 people, of whom 177 were women and 60 children. In the same month it was estimated that 150 able bodied men had left for the gold fields. This figure represented about 35% of the male population leaving in that month alone!

PLACER MINING.

During 1848 and 1849 most individual miners used pans or devices such as the rocker to extract gold from stream beds. Gold, which in ancient times had washed down from higher deposits, was found mixed with gravel, magnetite (magnetic iron ore), and sand. Depending upon luck and location, a miner often would obtain one or several ounces of gold per day. Those fortunate enough to find a cache of gold flakes or gold nuggets in a pocket in the stream bed often would make far more, with returns of several dozen ounces per day being reported for fortunate individuals.

A miner would stake a claim on an exclusive area, usually along a stream bed, for water was necessary for most types of gold extraction. Sometimes, when rockers or long toms were used, several partners would assist. At night miners relaxed by gambling, playing cards, and drinking. Oysters were a popular delicacy, perhaps because they reminded so many miners of the earlier days back home in the East.

THE ROCKER.

By the middle of June an estimated three-quarters of the adult male population had gone to work the mines. Businesses stood vacant. The streets were largely empty of commerce.

On May 27th the *Star* reported that "Stores are closed and houses tenantless, various kinds of mechanical labor suspended or given up entirely, and nowhere the pleasant hum of industry salutes the ear as of late; but as if a curse had arrested our honored course of enterprise, everything wears a desolate and sombre look, everywhere all is dull, monotonous, dead."

The value of real estate had dropped to half its previous level with few takers on hand. Merchandise, except for provisions needed in mining, remained unsold. In the meantime the price of labor went up almost ten times as few were interested in carpentry, tending horses, and other mundane work when the golden bonanza beckoned.

The two weekly newspapers were suspended due to lack of readers and lack of people to produce them; the *Californian* on May 20, 1848 and the *Star* on June 14th.

In its final issue the *Californian* wrote:

"The whole country from San Francisco to Los Angeles and from the seashore to the base of the Sierra Nevada resounds to the sordid cry of gold! GOLD!! GOLD!!! While the field is left half planted, the house half built, and everything neglected but the manufacture of shovels and pick-axes, and the means of transportation to the spot where one man obtained $128 worth of real stuff in one day's washing, and the average for all concerned is $20 per diem."

Churches suspended services, the town council no longer met, ships remained at anchor in the harbor with no sailors to man them, and streets were virtually empty.

One of the first ships to be deserted in the San Francisco harbor belonged to the Hudson's Bay Company. The sailors departed for the gold fields, and the captain followed them, leaving the vessel in charge of his wife and daughter!

By summer's end the *Californian*, which had temporarily revived publication, reported that virtually every ship lost most of its crew within 48 hours of the time it arrived in San Francisco! The first steam powered ship, *The California*, which arrived on February 28th of the following year, 1849, was immediately deserted by her entire crew. Nowhere could substitute sailors be found at any price.

In the meantime discoveries continued to expand in the gold country. The Yuba River, a tributary of the Feather, was explored by Patrick McChristian, J.P. Leese, Jasper O'Farrell, William Leery, and Samuel Norris who arrived there in July 1848. In three months they made $75,000, an immense fortune.

Also on the Yuba River in other camps miners working under primitive conditions and with hand tools extracted $60 to $100 a day of the precious metal.

In June a group of Mormons left their claim on the American River and going to a tributary discovered placer deposits on what became known as Spanish Bar, 12 miles northeast of Coloma. This one spot alone produced more than a million dollars in gold.

At the site of present day Placerville a camp called Dry Diggings was established. Dry Diggings was a popular name, and Bancroft estimates that 50 places were called this at one time or another. Later the camp was known as Hangtown due to the administration of justice there. Still later it became Placerville. Men working there obtained from three ounces to five pounds of gold per day with the report given that "from the middle of June, through July and August, the 300 Hangtown men were the happiest in the universe."

At another location one fortunate Indian found a kidney-shaped gold nugget weighing 80½ ounces. The firm of Cross & Hobson of San Francisco paid $3,000 for it and sold it to the Bank of England where it was exhibited as a specimen from the new California gold fields. At the time unrefined gold was selling for $12 to $14 per ounce, and had the nugget been sold for its commercial value on that basis it would have brought just $966.

Other camps spread at Sullivan Bar, Jamestown, Don Pedro Bar, Murphy's Camp, Angels Camp, Chinese Camp, Wood Creek, and so on.

The story is told that Henry Bee of San Jose had ten Indian prisoners under his watch in jail, two of whom were charged with murder. He wanted to turn them over to the care of the mayor, but that dignitary had already left for the gold fields. Bee hit upon a novel solution: he took all ten prisoners to the gold fields with him and set them to work in the placers! At the time it was estimated that 90% of all the able bodied men in San Jose had left for the Sierras!

In June 1848 four Mormons stopped at Monterey on their way to Los Angeles and displayed 100 pounds of gold gathered in less than a month at Mormon Island on the American River. Within two weeks there was scarcely an adult male left in town. 1,000 citizens left within a week of the Mormons' visit! Likewise, the California military forces were rendered ineffective by desertions. The troops deserted first, then the officers obtained furloughs to join them.

1848 was a good year at the mines. Most miners and adventurers who came there expected to do honest work. The rewards of digging repaid them amply. It is reported that during the first year crime was at a minimum even though treasure lay around and most

SAN FRANCISCO IN 1849, FROM THE HEAD OF CLAY-STREET.

CALIFORNIA LODGING-ROOM.

INTERIOR OF THE EL DORADO.

In 1849 San Francisco was a quiet village of fewer than 1,000 inhabitants. As the Gold Rush fever spread, dozens of ships jammed the San Francisco harbor, abandoned, with their crews departed for the more interesting activity of treasure seeking. By the early 1850s there were many crude hotels and lodging facilities (including several located in abandoned ships). On the other side of the economic spectrum were glittering gambling establishments such as the El Dorado.

property was left unguarded. When an incident did arise the miners settled it with their own justice. In Dry Diggings, later named Hangtown, a horse thief was caught in the act and was promptly captured, convicted, and strung up from a tree. On the American River a Spaniard was found holding a bag of stolen gold dust and was accorded the same treatment.

Some miners were greedy. Dreams of the Mother Lode haunted them. Many miners making $100 to $200 dreamed of going upstream to the place where gold could be taken out by the shovelful and a million dollars could be made in a few days. Abandoning their claims in search of the elusive Mother Lode, they searched, found little or nothing, and then returned to find that their original claims had been taken over by others.

The exact remuneration of the average miner is difficult to determine. Bancroft reported that many miners made $100 per day and that $500 to $700 was not at all unusual.

Much of this was extracted by using a simple tin or sheet iron pan measuring 10'' to 14'' across and with sides four to six inches high extending outward at an angle. Gold-bearing dirt and gravel was taken from a stream bed or from a hillside location, mixed with water, sloshed about in a rotary manner, and then swirled until the lighter materials had been ejected.

It was officially recorded that $2,000,000 worth of gold left the mines in 1848, but this was just a fraction of what really was found. A better estimate would be $10,000,000 to $20,000,000.

The shipment of the first deposit in 1848 of California gold, carried by David Garter, arrived at the Philadelphia Mint on December 8th. Director Patterson reported that it assayed as being worth a few cents over $18 per ounce. Additional specimens were given to private assayers who produced similar results. Garter's deposit, a private one, was made on December 8th and consisted of 1,804.59 ounces.

Secretary of War W.L. Marcy wrote to Dr. R.M. Patterson, Director of the United States Mint in Philadelphia transmitting a sample of gold metal from the California fields. Arriving on December 9th, this official government deposit contained 228 ounces with a purity of .894. The letter read in part:

"If the metal is found to be pure gold, as I doubt not that it will be, I request you to reserve enough of it for two medals ordered by Congress and not yet completed, and the remainder, with the exception of one or two small bars, I wish to have coined and sent with the bars to this department. As many may wish to procure specimens made with California gold, by exchanging another coin for it, I would suggest that it be made into quarter eagles with a distinguishing mark on each."

In 1848 the smallest denomination gold coin was the quarter eagle as the gold dollar was not produced until the following year, 1849. Thus, these coins, each stamped with "CAL." above the eagle on the reverse, were the first United States Mint issues specifically designed to be commemoratives or special souvenirs. It is estimated that 1,389 pieces were produced. Perhaps 100 to 200 coins exist at the present time.

There were many tales of wealth in the gold fields in 1848. An Irish team driver, John Sullivan, extracted $26,000 from a placer digging on the Stanislaus River. A miner named Hudson gathered $20,000 in six weeks from a canyon near Coloma. A young boy named Davenport found near the same location 77 ounces of gold in one day and 90 additional ounces the next.

On the middle fork of the Yuba River one fortunate seeker found nearly 30 pounds of gold in 20 days of looking. Three Frenchmen, removing a stump obstructing a road leading from Dry Diggings to Coloma, discovered a gold location which within a week yielded $5,000. A miner named Amador, a partner, and 20 Indian laborers extracted seven to nine pounds of gold each day. One observer reported seeing miners at Dry Diggings extracting from 50 to 100 ounces daily.

The abundance of gold caused it to sell for depreciated prices as miners were eager to exchange it for silver coins, provisions, and other things of value. Particularly eager in this regard were Indians who were not accustomed to wealth and who would exchange gold dust and nuggets for virtually anything which caught their eye. An ounce of gold usually sold in the fields from four to ten dollars depending on the sharpness of the buyer and seller. In San Francisco the price was higher.

By the end of 1848 gold had become common in the mining area and supplies and provisions had become scarce. It was reported that a horse normally worth six dollars traded then for $300, eggs sold for $3 each, a doctor would charge $50 to $100 for a visit, flour sold for $8 per barrel, a wagon and team cost $50 per day to hire, and cooks commanded a wage of $25 a day. A Coloma storekeeper's bill of December 1848 included such items as one box of sardines for $16, one pound of hard bread for $2, one pound of butter for $16, one half pound of cheese for $3, two bottles of ale for $16, for a total of $43—a rather simple lunch for two people.

As winter approached in 1848 the rains came and the weather grew cold. Many returned with their fortunes to San Francisco and other coastal areas to wait out the season. Others decided to stay in the mountains, with 800 spending the winter of 1848-1849 at Dry Diggings, for example.

For John Sutter, whose mill started the gold rush, the bonanza was a disaster. Employees of Sutter's Fort demanded increasingly high wages to the point at which

he could not afford to pay them. The shops, mills, and other businesses became idle. By January 1849 Sutter's operation came to an end, and he retired from business. His cattle drifted across the ranges and became wild, and other things deteriorated.

San Francisco remained the main link between the gold fields and civilization. The town had been established as Yerba Buena in the summer of 1835. In 1836 the Hudson's Bay Company opened a branch there and engaged in trading. Although the area was on Mexican soil at the time it was predominantly settled by Americans. During 1848 San Francisco was strained to its limits. As noted, the gold rush took nearly all of the adult male population. The two newspapers suspended publication and did not reappear on a steady basis until November 18th, 1848, when they revived under the combined title *Star and California,* subsequently changed in January 1849 to the *Alta California.*

By the middle of 1849 San Francisco Bay was crowded with ships, most of them deserted. At one time 500 could be seen. Some ships rotted, others were dismantled for their lumber, and still others were turned into temporary hotels.

During the winter seasons of 1848-1849 and 1849-1850 many returned from the gold fields to escape the bitterness and snow. During those times many crews were reformed and ships sailed once again.

During 1849 and 1850 San Francisco regathered its strength and emerged as a commercial center. Many found that it was more profitable to operate businesses to sell goods and services to the miners than it was to actually engage in mining. By this time the lustre had worn off of the gold fields, most of the easily available surface gold had been taken, and miners were reduced to hard work, often having to dig several feet below the surface before new unprocessed earth was found.

In San Francisco Montgomery Street became the main business area. Auction houses offered a wide variety of merchandise to prospective bidders. Import companies presented many tempting goods for the purchaser. Telegraph Hill, overlooking San Francisco, had on its peak a signal house with a semaphore pole which by its position indicated what type of vessel was approaching the harbor. The arrival of a clipper ship or other vessel was often a cause for celebration as it brought friends and relatives, mail from home back East, and merchandise and provisions.

Entertainment prevailed in many forms. The first dramatic company in San Francisco was Rowe's Olympic Circus which opened on October 29, 1849 and featured Ethiopian natives. Catering to miners and sailors were many bordellos and dens where low life prevailed. On Portsmouth Square were many gambling halls, mostly in the form of tents and other temporary structures. One of the most famous in 1850 was the El Dorado. The Parker House, a hotel and gambling hall, was at one time located in the area as was the Jenny Lind Theatre.

Land and building prices recovered from their mid-1848 slump and skyrocketed upward. Buildings tended to be of a temporary nature often made of canvas and wood. Labor was too rare and too expensive to provide for many buildings of substance. It was estimated that at least 1,000 shanties and small houses were built in the last part of 1849 at a cost of approximately five times what similar structures would have cost on the East Coast at the time. One observer noted that wooden frame houses were often built within just 24 hours!

Several disastrous fires swept the city. The first came on Christmas Eve 1849, the second on May 4, 1850, and the third on June 14th of the same year. On September 17th, October 31st, and December 14th additional fires of varying sizes broke out and destroyed extensive property. Then there was a respite until May 3, 1851, when another conflagration erupted. All of these fires caused the city to adopt the emblem of a phoenix (a bird rising from the ashes) as its official seal—and this was in an era long before the great 1906 San Francisco earthquake and fire.

At first the news of the gold rush was confined to California. Beginning in April 1848 the excitement spread beyond. On June 24th of that year the *Polynesian,* printed in Honolulu, Hawaii, ran a half-column article telling of the California gold strike. Ships from California cities arrived in Hawaii and spread the news further. It was reported on October 21st in Honolulu that "27 vessels have left Honolulu since the gold discovery, carrying 300 Europeans besides many natives. The islands suffer in consequence."

In Oregon, immediately north of California, and extending upward to British Columbia, the word spread. One observer wrote that an estimated two-thirds of the white population of Oregon had left for the gold fields by the autumn of the year. From Sonora in Mexico came four or five thousand others eager to strike it rich.

The first official notice of the California gold discovery was sent by T.O. Larkin on June 1st and received at Washington in the middle of September. Scattered announcements appeared as a result. The first to generate excitement on a broad scale was an article in the Baltimore *Sun* dated September 20, 1848, after which other eastern editors competed with each other in an effort to make the news sound as spectacular as possible, complete with exaggerations, embellishments, and made-up tales of fortune. There were little facts to go on at the time. These accounts would often be printed, embellished more, reprinted, and then revised once again. On December 5, 1848 the president confirmed

to Congress that gold had been discovered in quantity and exhibited a box filled with gold dust which was placed on exhibition at the War Office.

The New York *Journal of Commerce* ran an article which read:

"At present the people are running over the country and picking it out of the earth here and there, just as 1,000 hogs, let loose in a forest, would root up ground nuts. Some get eight to ten ounces a day, and the least active get one or two ounces. They make the most who employ the wild Indians to hunt it for them. There was one man who had 60 Indians in his employ; his profits are $1 a minute."

Gold fever swept America. On the East Coast notices were posted of clipper ships and other vessels leaving for San Francisco. Some adventurers took the long route around Cape Horn at the tip of South America. Others took one ship to Panama, crossed the Isthmus of Panama by land (often at the peril of disease), and then boarded another ship for the final journey northward to San Francisco.

The Pacific Mail Steamship Company was incorporated on April 12, 1848 without knowledge of the gold discovery. The founders anticipated a lively trade with the West Coast ports, particularly with the fur trade in Oregon. The route was to be between Panama and Astoria, Oregon. Three sidewheel steamships were built. The first of these, the *California,* sailed from New York on October 6th, 1848, at a time when the gold discoveries of California were just scattered rumors in the East. There was little public interest in gold at the time, so no passengers boarded for California. On December 29th the ship reached Callao in Peru and encountered residents who had been infected with the gold fever. Although only 50 berths were available on the ship many more requests were received. As many were filled as possible, despite the fact that originally it was not intended to take aboard any passengers until a landing was made at Panama.

When the ship arrived at Panama it found waiting 1,500 people, some of whom had purchased tickets, waiting for passage! When all was said and done over 400 people were admitted on board to find spaces wherever they could to sleep and eat. Fares were hiked accordingly, with one passenger paying more to sleep on a coil of rope than an earlier passenger in Peru had paid for a stateroom! Minimum accommodations were sold for up to $1,000, it was said.

The second steamer of the Pacific Mail Steamship Line, the *Oregon,* arrived in Panama in the middle of March 1849. After a great struggle for tickets some 500 passengers were received. Then came the third vessel of the line, the *Panama,* which encountered a similar situation. A huge crowd sought to pay virtually any price to get any type of passage available.

When the first ship, the *California,* after stopping at Acupulco and several other places along the western coast, arrived in San Francisco on February 28, 1849, it was greeted with a big celebration. However, the crew left the ship almost as quickly as the passengers did. Within a few hours just one person, an engineer, was left to man the vessel! Consequently, the *California* was stranded and was unable to make the return trip.

The most popular route was overland, usually beginning with St. Joseph or Independence, Missouri as the jumping-off spot. In these cities adventurers—single individuals, families, groups and companies—gathered to form caravans. In contrast with the sea route which was expensive if passage could be found at all, the overland routes afforded the possibility of even the most impoverished person going west. Some came with scarcely more than the clothes on their backs and the shoes on their feet. Others were over-equipped and brought with them pets, extra household appliances, and unneeded equipment and gadgets. Others carried clothing, household accessories, and other merchandise for resale.

By early April 1849 about 20,000 people were at the frontier preparing to head westward as soon as spring came and there was sufficient grass to feed the horses, oxen, and cattle. Early in May the first group left, and for the next month the trail westward was one unbroken procession of people, cattle, and wagons streaming westward.

Each night the group would break up into separate camps with the wagons forming a semicircle near a stream bed, or a circle in open country, with a campfire in the middle. Spirits were high, there was the flush of excitement, and the whole atmosphere was one of anticipation and adventure. Early in the morning the march began again. Many preferred walking alongside the wagons to the bumpy, jolting ride inside. Wagons came in all shapes and forms. Some were little more than carts, others were huge Conestoga wagons with canvas tops and with the bodies caulked with pitch to permit floating across streams.

As time went on the romance faded. Torrential rains would sometimes alternate with blinding sandstorms. Oxen would weaken and sometimes die. To lighten the load things thought necessary at the beginning of the trip were often cast to the side of the trail. And, once the procession was well into the countryside Indians were a fear, although in the early years the wagon trains were more of a curiosity than a threat to the native tribes. A cholera epidemic swept through the procession and thousands of people died. The trail from Missouri through Fort Laramie became littered with fresh grave sites, sometimes with a crude headboard but more often

Westward Ho! With confidence teams of wagons and cattle set out from Missouri and other points, headed westward to the California gold fields. At the start of the journey everything was optimistic. Singing, revelry, and merriment characterized the stops each evening as wagon trains drew into protective circles. During the day the adventurers resumed their trek, often carrying pets, machinery, appliances, and other items.

As the trail proceeded westward, hardships set in. Grass and water for the cattle became scarce. Extreme heat in the summer and extreme cold in the winter caused many difficulties. Cattle died, wagons and goods were abandoned, and many continued the journey on foot. Some never made it.

LEAVING THE WEAK TO DIE.

Many never made it to California. All along the trails westward were many gravesites, usually molested by coyotes and other predators, which gave mute evidence to the ravages of cholera, fatigue, bad water, and other afflictions. Starkly visible, too, were the implements of civilization: disabled carts and wagons, fancy clothing (often torn apart so that succeeding travelers could not use it), bags of sugar and coffee (often scattered or else dampened with turpentine or other substances so that others who followed could not use it—a sad commentary on human nature), skeletons of cows and oxen, boxes and steamer trunks, and other items—even gold assaying, refining, and coining equipment.

Sailing from New York, south past the tip of South America, and up the western coast to San Francisco, were clipper ships such as this. With full rigging and favorable weather conditions a clipper could make the trip in 90 to 100 days. For those who could afford it this was the most luxurious way to travel. The overland journey with its many privations was difficult, and the shortcut across the Isthmus of Panama was disease-ridden. Particularly fast ships, called extreme clippers, were originally designed for the China trade.

marked by signs where coyotes and other predators had unearthed the remains.

The northern route followed the Platte River to Grand Island, hence along the north branch to Fort Laramie, which at that time was the westernmost outpost of the United States. At Green River in the present state of Wyoming the Pacific slope was encountered. From there the journey was to Fort Hall at the junction of the old Oregon Trail. As the Sierra Nevada Mountains approached the trip became more of a hardship. The territory was dry with very little vegetation. The days were warm, nights were cold, and pleasures were few. Faced with sickness, cattle in poor health, and other privations, many abandoned nearly all of their personal effects and continued on foot with just a few possessions. Some went to the Mormon community at Great Salt Lake to spend the winter. Others took side trails and became lost. Still others were attacked by Indians who often would prey upon individuals or small groups.

By late 1849 travel was difficult for much of the route as earlier caravans had consumed most of the grass, and by late summer many of the marshes and small streams had dried up. The native Indians became bolder and presented a greater problem. The western deserts and impending winter together took a terrible toll. It was estimated that only half the oxen who started the journey, not even a quarter of the horses, and most of the wagons never completed the trip. The trail was lined with abandoned vehicles, carcasses, and other signs of privation. Nine-tenths of the emigrants by this time were on foot with little food. Many had to spend the winter in the desert or at a camp. Many more perished.

The southern route was less popular for the way was more circuitous. This route went from Independence, Missouri, down to Santa Fe, New Mexico, and from there via several different routes to California.

Historian Bancroft estimated that in 1849 23,000 Americans and 16,000 foreigners arrived by sea. An additional 42,000 came by the overland route. Many others came northward from Mexico. Close to 100,000 people made the trip.

Life in the camp provided many excitements. The 1850 California census noted that less than eight percent of the population was female, and in the mining districts the proportion of men to women was 50 to 1. Calaveras County had only 267 women in the total population of 16,884. The same county had only 69 people over 60 years of age, for only the youthful could endure the rigors.

In the profusion of wealth money often lost its meaning. A half dollar was the smallest coin to be generally seen in commerce, and to offer a quarter as a tip would invite a sneer. Laborers' wages increased to $10 and craftsmen had no trouble earning $12 to $20 per day.

Citizens were trusting and trusted. As noted, there was an occasional misstep which resulted in a jailing or lynching, but by and large the kingdom was peaceful. In the mining camps tents and shanties were seldom locked, and gold was left untended. One San Francisco shop posted a sign which invited patrons to select items wanted and leave the money in a receptacle, for the owner was on other business elsewhere. It was related that a gold watch was found in one of the mining camps and hung on a tree with a notice. It remained there for nearly two weeks until the rightful owner claimed it.

By late 1849 emigrants were arriving in substantial numbers, and problems increased. People from Indiana and Missouri in particular were considered to be illiterate and undesirable. One authority stated that "after the Missourians began to come, insecurity increased. In 1850 things had reached such a pitch that mail agents were afraid to carry gold, lest they should be murdered."

Revolvers became a common sight. Arguments were often settled by dueling; a common arrangement being for the opponents to place themselves back-to-back, march five steps, and then turn and fire until all the revolver charges were expended or one party was incapacitated. In 1854 it was estimated that in the preceding five years there had been 4,200 murders, 1,400 suicides, and 10,000 other unfortunate deaths. The following year, 1855, compiled a record of 538 violent deaths from various causes.

Gambling flourished in the camps. In the city of San Francisco, which represented "civilization" to the miner, gambling was a big business. Many casinos prospered.

Describing one such establishment Bancroft writes: "The abode of fortune seeks naturally to eclipse all other saloons in splendor; and, indeed, the mirrors are larger, the paintings more costly, and the canvassed walls adorned with brighter figures. At one end is the indispensible drinking bar, at the other a gallery for the orchestra, from which loud if not harmonious music floats upon the mirthy atmosphere laden with fumes of smoke and foul breaths. These and other attractions are employed to excite the senses and break down all barriers before the strongest temptation, the piles of silver and gold in coin and dust and glittering lumps which border the leather-covered gaming tables, sometimes a dozen in number. From different directions is heard the cry, 'Make your bets, gentlemen!' midst the hum and chink of coins. 'The game is made,' and a hush of strained expectancy attends the rolling ball or the turning card; then a resumption of the murmur and the jingling, as the stakes are counted out or raked in by the croupier.''

As gold became harder to find in the mountains, incredible tales sprang up. In 1850 the "gold lake story" made the rounds of the mining camps. It told of a lake

ARRIVAL OF A STEAMSHIP.

NEW WORLD MARKET, CORNER OF COMMERCIAL AND LEIDSDORFF STREETS.

HANGING OF JENKINS ON THE PLAZA.

California in the 1850s saw many varied activities. The arrival of a steamship, bringing news and mail from the East, was always a cause for celebration. Markets and auction houses offered a wide variety of goods, usually newly-arrived on a clipper ship or steamer from the East, Hawaii, or the Orient. By the mid-1850s lynching was a popular sport; a quick way to dispatch a real or suspected criminal who had incurred the wrath of a crowd. Vigilante committees, which took the law into their own hands, were set up to protect the public.

near the beginning of the Feather River, the shores of which were sprinkled with gold nuggets. One writer related that a Mr. Greenwood once lived on the shores of this lake and his children amused themselves by playing with the golden nodules. Another tale told of a marvelous volcano that spurted molten silver from its innards.

Perhaps most famous in the category of fantasy was the Gold Bluff hoax. In 1850 the story was spread throughout San Francisco that millions of dollars worth of gold lay on an ocean beach just waiting to be picked up, all the mining work having been done by waves which for eons earlier had pounded the gold-studded cliffs overlooking the ocean. A company was formed to exploit this bonanza stating that a profit of $43,000,000 was anticipated for the shareholders. Despite this heavenly promise, for some reason the shareholders were quite willing to sell their ownership interest to San Franciscans caring to part with the money. Eight ships were scheduled to depart for the Gold Bluff, but before any got under way the hoax was exposed and the bubble burst. One account relates that samples of the Gold Bluff sand shown to prospective investors in San Francisco were nothing more than common ocean sand sprinkled with brass filings.

In the realm of reality the inland gold country continued to produce gold at an increasing rate, although with more difficulty. Sluices and ditches were made to carry water to dry places so that gold could be washed out from the earth. In El Dorado County alone by 1856 more than 600 miles of ditches had been built. Mining of quartz rock became increasingly important. By 1858 seven mills were in operation near Downieville crushing 12,500 tons of ore annually. Other gold was extracted by the hydraulic method whereby a high pressure stream from a hose nozzle was directed against a dirt embankment. Many hills were literally washed away by this process.

The amount of gold extracted will never be known for sure. One authority has estimated $270,000,000. Bancroft's estimates were higher: a total of $456,000,000 from 1848 to 1856 divided into $10,000,000 for the first year, 1848, $40,000,000 for the second year, $50,000,000 for the third, $60,000,000 each for 1851 and 1852, $65,000,000 for the peak year of 1853, $60,000,000 for 1854, $55,000,000 for 1855, and $56,000,000 for 1856. It was further estimated that $331,000,000 worth of gold was exported from California.

The record nugget was found in November 1854 in Calaveras County and weighed 161 pounds, including approximately 20 pounds for attached quartz rock. At $17.25 per ounce the approximate value was $38,916. The measurements were about 15 inches by 6 inches by 4 inches.

From the beginning of the rush there was a coin shortage. Transactions in the gold fields were apt to take place in the form of gold dust or gold nuggets which were measured by the pinch for small purchases or on a balance scale for larger purchases. There was some chicanery, with charges being brought that Indians and other people not familiar with the intricacies of finance were often cheated by the use of weights wrongly marked so that a greater amount of gold could be received in a given transaction.

In the summer of 1848 a crisis arose in San Francisco. There were few circulating coins in banking or commercial channels, and yet United States customs regulations provided that duties on imported items could only be paid in coins. Colonel R.B. Mason instructed the customs collector to accept gold dust at the rate of $16 per ounce, but soon realizing that this was illegal he came up with a compromise. Merchants importing goods could deposit gold dust at the customs house at the rate of $10 per ounce as a security with the provision that it be redeemed in coin within sixty days. Otherwise the gold dust would be sold at auction. The few speculators who were able to obtain coins to use in the auction were able to buy gold dust from $6 to $8 per ounce while the merchants stood by helplessly. Later this order was modified to place a base price of $10 per ounce so that the government would not lose money; any overage realized at auction would be paid to the merchants who made the deposits.

Colonel Mason was faced with a problem. He knew a large amount of gold dust would be received, perhaps $10,000 to $20,000 worth at a time. Should this gold dust be auctioned and bring less than $10 per ounce there would be a shortage on the government books and Mason would be considered an incompetent manager. He strongly recommended that a mint be established to convert gold dust into coins.

Another problem arose when Oriental merchants, a main source of supply to San Francisco, demanded silver bullion and coins in payment for their merchandise; gold was not in favor with them. The few silver coins which could be had were purchasable only by offering a premium in gold dust for them.

Hence, the miner or merchant possessing gold dust had great difficulty exchanging it for coin. And, when the exchange was made it was often by paying a large premium.

On September 9, 1848, a large public gathering was held during which the value of gold dust was established at $16 per ounce. There was much dissatisfaction with this decision for it was felt that much of the gold was of high purity and should command $18 or more.

To fill this gap various individuals, bankers, and others produced private gold coins. The first of these

TURNING A RIVER.

By the mid-1850s elaborate systems of sluices, dams, and other devices to tap the energy of water were installed throughout the gold country. Areas which had earlier been worked by hand using pans, rockers, and long toms now became sites for deep digging and intensive hydraulic mining using high-pressure water streams. Often an area would be worked, reworked, and then worked again, each time producing an additional amount of gold.

By the late 1850s millions of dollars had been spent to erect water works in the Mother Lode country. In the illustration above an entire river has been blocked so that its stream bed can be excavated and worked.

FLUTTER-WHEEL, ON THE TUOLUMNE.

This flutter-wheel on the Tuolumne River represented an elaborate way to lift water into a trough. Gold-bearing gravel was then put into the trough and washed. Gold flakes were trapped by mercury metal in a series of crossbars or riffles. Then gold was separated from the mercury and refined.

were $5 gold pieces produced by Norris, Grieg & Norris, a Benicia City firm with connections in San Francisco and Stockton. The inscriptions of these pieces read: FULL WEIGHT OF HALF EAGLE/CALIFORNIA GOLD WITHOUT ALLOY.

Edgar H. Adams, celebrated researcher on the California private coinage series, noted that the first mention of privately minted coins appeared in the *Alta California* issue of May 31, 1849:

"We have in our possession a five dollar gold coin, struck at Benicia City, although the imprint is San Francisco. In general it resembles the United States coin of the same value, but bears the private stamp of Norris, Grieg & Norris, and is in other particulars widely different."

Assays of three of these pieces revealed the intrinsic worth to be $4.83, $4.89, and $4.95½ respectively, with 2½c per coin added for the value of natural silver alloy included.

For years numismatists bought, sold, and traded these Norris, Grieg & Norris pieces. All known specimens had the inscription: 1849 SAN FRANCISCO at the center of the reverse. Then around 1960 San Francisco dealer Earl Parker came up with a hitherto unknown variety, one with STOCKTON below the date. Offered at $10,000, it found no buyers. I remember considering it at the time and thinking that it was an immense sum of money. Finally it was bought by James F. Kelly, of Dayton, who subsequently resold it.

Shortly after the issue of the Norris, Grieg & Norris pieces, Moffat & Company, assayers and gold brokers, issued rectangular ingots of gold of several denominations, predominantly of the $16 value, a figure which coincided with the value of one ounce of gold. Also at the same time, the summer of 1849, five and ten dollar gold pieces minted by the same firm appeared.

By the end of the year many other private coiners were into the act. Some of these were formed in the East by speculators who hoped to make a fortune when they arrived in the Golden State. The Massachusetts & California Company issued $5 pieces in gold as well as other metals. It is probable that most if not all of these were struck as patterns and were produced in the East and not from California metal.

On August 7, 1849, the firm of Wright & Company requested government permission to coin $5 and $10 gold pieces which would be receivable for customs duty. Permission was refused. Shortly thereafter the firm reorganized as a banking institution under the Miners' Bank name, housed in what Adams described as "a little wooden cottage for which a yearly rental of $75,000 was paid." While this figure may be exaggerated, crude buildings, often made of canvas, often rented for $10,000

to $30,000 per year in prime San Francisco locations at the time.

Ten-dollar gold pieces were issued, although without government sanction. The obverse portrayed the simple inscription: MINER'S BANK/SAN FRANCISCO. The reverse displayed an eagle. A government assay showed that the Miners' Bank eagle contained just $9.65 worth of gold. The light value was recognized, and for this reason the coins were rejected. A letter printed in *Alta California* on April 11th, 1850, related that: "the issue of the Miners' Bank is a drug on the market. Brokers refuse to touch it at less than a 20% discount." On January 14, 1850, the firm went out of business.

The *Alta California* issue of May 31, 1849, reported that "we learn that Mr. Theodore Dubosq, a jeweler from Philadelphia, who recently arrived on the *Gray Eagle* has brought with him the necessary machinery for striking private coins." Although pattern copper coins dated 1849 with the Dubosq imprint are known, no gold specimens exist today. A few $5 and $10 issues dated the following year, 1850, are known to numismatists.

Apparently many pieces minted in 1851 were dated 1850, for it was reported that during the first three months of 1851 $150,000 worth were struck. An assay revealed that the Dubosq $10 gold pieces had an intrinsic value of $9.93 and $5 pieces, $4.96.

Exceedingly rare today are the $5 and $10 gold issues of the Cincinnati Mining & Trading Company. Apparently the firm was formed in Ohio with a large number of stockholders to engage in the activity of California gold coinage. It is not known whether members of the company ever reached California. Extant gold coins appear to be made of California gold alloy, possibly struck by Broderick & Kohler.

In the summer of 1849 the firm of Ormsby & Company, composed of Dr. J.S. Ormsby, a Pennsylvanian, and Major William M. Ormsby, who 11 years later was killed in Nevada during an Indian battle, was set up on K Street in Sacramento. Dr. William W. Light, an Ohio dentist, was employed at a salary of $50 per day to supervise the mint. Tiring of the employment he soon resigned and went to the gold fields to seek a greater fortune. $5 and $10 gold pieces were struck from dies using a sledgehammer. The pieces were lightweight and were thus unpopular in the channels of commerce. An assay revealed that the 1849 Ormsby $10 gold piece had an intrinsic value of just $9.37. Dunbar & Company, Shultz & Company, Templeton Reid, Pacific Company, Baldwin & Company, Kellogg & Company, and others contributed to the coins in circulation.

Among the most impressive of the early California coins were the 50-dollar round gold "slugs" produced by Wass, Molitor & Company in 1855. This firm,

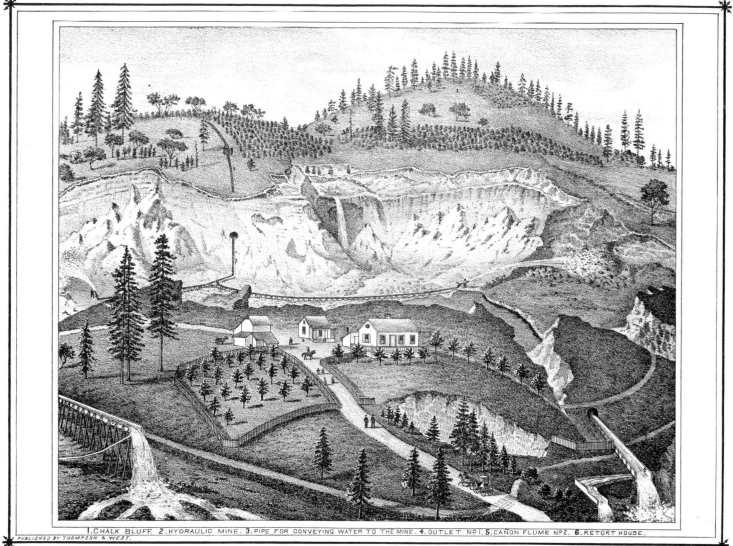

1.CHALK BLUFF. 2.HYDRAULIC MINE. 3.PIPE FOR CONVEYING WATER TO THE MINE. 4.OUTLET N°I. 5.CAÑON FLUME N°2. 6.RETORT HOUSE.

PUBLISHED BY THOMPSON & WEST.

RESIDENCE AND MINE OF **JOHN HUSSEY,** YOU BET. NEVADA C° CAL.

This illustration from the 1870s shows the private kingdom of John Hussey, complete with a nice home, forest preserve, and source of income: a hydraulic mine. By the mid-1850s most easily-accessible placer locations had been thoroughly worked by hand mining. Hydraulic mining, using high pressure hose nozzles called "monitors," became popular. Literally entire hillsides were washed away by this erosive process.

Today the tourist can visit Malakoff Diggins, a hydraulic mining site which retains its original nickname. Acres and acres of washed-out boulders and rocks greet the visitor.

Perhaps more romantic in appearance are such still extant towns as Angels' Camp, Mokelumne Hill, Placerville, Amador, Sutter Creek, and at the northern end of the Mother Lode country, Nevada City and Grass Valley, which have many original buildings standing. Typically, most structures are made of natural stone held together by mortar. Openings are covered by iron doors and shutters, originally as a precaution against illegal entry and, even more of a threat, fire.

The original site of Sutter's Mill at Coloma is now a state park. The mill has been reconstructed. Several other facilities in the area have been rebuilt or restored. In addition, a museum provides displays of interest.

Curiously enough, there has been little official government interest in preserving the many buildings and historical sites which dot the landscape near Route 49—the road which twists and curves through the gold fields. Each year some of the best-preserved structures decay and crumble more.

SACRAMENTO CITY.

In the 1850s Sacramento, reached by boat from San Francisco, was the jumping-off spot for the California gold fields. A thriving commercial center developed, replete within a decade or two with ornate Victorian buildings. In later years this area became a slum as activity in the city centered elsewhere. In the 1970s enlightened administrators undertook the restoration of what is now known as Sacramento Old Town. Today the tourist can see many building facades and interiors restored to the way they were in the 19th century.

which began business in 1851 and which produced coins dated 1852 and 1855, was one of the largest.

On November 25, 1851, Wass, Molitor & Company ran the following notice in the *San Francisco Herald*:

"Assay Office—Important Advantage—the subscribers are now ready to melt and assay gold-dust, and will pay to parties depositing the dust the net proceeds as soon as the dust is melted and assayed, less the usual percentage for melting and assaying. The advantage in this arrangement is that the depositor gets his money within 48 hours after depositing the dust." Shortly thereafter the first coinage materialized, the initial $5 gold piece apparently making its debut around January 8th.

The impressive $50 piece made its first appearance sometime early in 1855. The Sacramento *Daily Union* on April 30th of that year noted:

"Colonel Pardee of Wells, Fargo & Company's Express has exhibited to us a new $50 gold piece, which in a great measure is destined to supplant the old-fashioned octagon slug now in circulation. This coin is circular, almost entirely destitute of ornament, and plain as a maiden's countenance who has breathed the air of 50 summers. At the outer edge of one side are the words 'Wass, Molitor & Co, San Francisco,' enclosing on the centre of the coin the figures '900' and abbreviated word 'Thous.' with the figures '50' underneath and the word 'Dollars' below the latter figures. On the reverse of the coin is a homely head of Liberty and the figures '1855.' The coin certainly has no pretentions to beauty, nevertheless we would not like to refuse a few to break with our friends."

Apparently these were struck in very large numbers, for the newspaper *Alta California* on May 16, 1855, noted that "Wass, Molitor & Company have commenced issuing their $50 and $20 pieces at the rate of $38,000 per day. The coin is above the United States standard and is confidently received throughout the state."

In the same year the firm of Kellogg & Company produced a round $50 gold piece, the dies for which still exist today in northern California. The dozen or so specimens known today are all in Proof or impaired Proof condition. It is doubtful if any specimens ever reached actual circulation. Perhaps they were intended as patterns. Edgar H. Adams could locate no contemporary reference to them.

In July 1848 it was resolved by a meeting of San Francisco citizens that the state open an assay office to standardize the tests for gold being found in the nearby mountains. It was further suggested that the assayer convert gold dust and nuggets into ingots appropriately stamped with the fineness, weight, and value. On April 20, 1850 the office of State Assayer became a reality. Frederick D. Kohler, a private assayer, sold his business to Baldwin & Company and set up trade on behalf of the state. A May 24, 1850 announcement in *Alta California* read:

"The undersigned have opened an office in the building now occupied by Messrs. Baldwin & Company, south side of Portsmouth Square, and will be prepared to receive gold-dust for smelting and assaying on Monday the 13th, according with the provision of the law passed by the legislature, April 20, 1850. In making this announcement we beg leave to state that desiring to establish an office at the earliest practical moment our arrangements are necessarily less complete than they otherwise would have been; nevertheless, we trust that they will be found sufficient to meet the wants of the community."

On the first day nearly 5,000 ounces of gold were deposited. One gold bar received by Kohler had a value of $519 marked on it, and upon assay it was shown to be worth $570.54. However, most problems were in the other direction. During the first few days 40 fake gold nuggets weighing from a few ounces up to a pound each were brought in for assaying. Business became so intense that Kohler and his employees worked late into the night.

Ingots bearing Kohler's stamp were issued in many denominations, with such diverse values as $36.55, $37.31, $40.07, $41.68, $45.34, $50.00, and $54.09 being reported. Apparently at one time denominations up to $150 were produced. Most were made at San Francisco, however some were made at a branch in Sacramento.

The most important of the California private coiners was Moffat & Company. John L. Moffat, a New York assayer, went to California early in 1849 and opened an assaying and refining business in company with Joseph R. Curtis, P.H.W. Perry, and Samuel H. Ward.

In the same year Moffat began producing rectangular gold ingots of various values from $9.43 to $264, the most common being of the $16 denomination—equal to one ounce of gold. Albert Kuner, who arrived in San Francisco July 16th, was hired by Moffat to prepare dies for coins. The first piece to appear was a ten-dollar issue followed by pieces of the five-dollar denomination.

From the beginning these coins enjoyed a wide acceptance. A mixed group of Moffat & Company $10 coins bearing the dates 1849 and 1850 were shown to have an average value of $9.97 7/10ths.

Requests continued to be made by San Francisco merchants and citizens for the establishment of a government mint. While this was not acted upon favorably by Congress at the time, that legislative body authorized

1849 $5 gold by Norris, Grieg & Norris, with San Francisco imprint. This issue is believed to be the first California private gold coin.

$10 issue of the Miners' Bank. This issue, intrinsically worth considerably less than the indicated face value, was not accepted by merchants. On January 14, 1850 the firm went out of business.

$10 and $5 issues of the Cincinnati Mining & Trading Company, 1849. This firm, apparently formed in Ohio, intended to issue California gold coins. Although a few coinage specimens are known, it is uncertain whether the firm actually engaged in commercial operations in California. Today the pieces are exceedingly rare (photographs courtesy of the Smithsonian Institution as are all on this page).

Two ingots issued by F.D. Kohler in 1850. For a short time Kohler was the official California State Assayer. To the right is shown a $16 ingot issued by Moffat & Company. Moffat issued various denominations from $9.43 to $264.

1849 $10 by the Pacific Company. Little is known concerning the origins or operations of this firm. Only a very few pieces were struck.

1849 $10 and 1850 $5 issues of Moffat & Company. These issues, made in several varieties, were extremely popular and circulated widely throughout the Gold Rush area.

1850 $10 and $5 issued by Theodore Dubosq, a Philadelphian who came to San Francisco. Today these issues are exceedingly rare.

Two varieties of $50 octagonal gold "slugs" issued in 1851. These large and heavy pieces saw wide use in commerce.

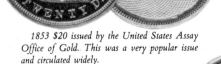

1853 $20 issued by the United States Assay Office of Gold. This was a very popular issue and circulated widely.

1850 $10 with horseman design issued by Baldwin & Co. of San Francisco.

1849 $5 by the Massachusetts & California Co., a firm organized in the former state. While patterns exist today in various metals (including gold), it is not known whether these pieces actively circulated in California.

Two issues of Kellogg & Co. of San Francisco. The $20 issue, shown to the left, was minted in large quantities as was a piece of comparable design dated 1855. The 1855 round-shaped $50 piece was apparently struck only in Proof condition. Little is known about this particular issue, and historian Edgar H. Adams was unable to locate any contemporary reference to the pieces. The dies still survive.

the secretary of the treasury in September 1850 to negotiate with the owner of an established assaying business in California to act as an agent of the United States and affix the United States government stamp to indicate the fineness and value of each piece. Moffat & Company received the contract. Augustus Humbert, a watchcase maker from New York, was appointed government assayer. Following the contract Moffat & Company ceased issuing private coins and moved to a larger establishment. On January 29, 1851, the *Daily Alta California* carried the following advertisement:

"UNITED STATES ASSAY OFFICE. We give notice that on or about the first of February ensuing we will be prepared to receive gold-dust for smelting and assaying, and forming the same into ingots and bars, in accordance with our recent contract with the secretary of the treasury, authorized by the act of Congress approved September 30, 1850, under the supervision of the United States Assayer, Augustus Humbert, Esq., who will cause the United States stamp to be affixed to the same. —Moffat & Company."

The first issues, $50 gold pieces of octagonal shape, were produced on January 30 or 31, 1851. Larger specimens of $100 and $200 denominations were made from the same dies and were similar except for the added thickness. Today only the $50 gold slugs are seen with frequency. In addition large ingots of $500 and $1,000 values were struck.

Although the $50 pieces were referred to as ingots by the Treasury, they soon became known as "slugs" by the public. Legend has it that a group of these massive coins, when wrapped in a handkerchief, were effective for "slugging" any adversary!

Despite the official United States sanction, and despite the fact that the $50 slugs of the United States Assay Office were received at face value in payment for customs duty, there was a divided opinion, even among government officials, whether or not they were legal tender in commerce.

When the director of the Mint in Philadelphia was queried as to his opinion about the $50 gold pieces struck in California, he said that they were a convenience for the owners of bullion but the stamp of the United States Assayer did not make them legal tender.

Nevertheless, the pieces did bring a stability to commerce. Most other types of private coins minted in 1849 and 1850 were brought to the U.S. Assay Office, received at varying discounts, and converted into gold. Included also were many private gold coins from other regions including the debased "Great Salt Lake City Pure Gold" pieces issued by the Mormons in Utah (a $10 Mormon piece had an intrinsic value of just slightly over $7), and $5 and $10 gold pieces of Oregon. Soon there were very few coins of smaller denominations in

circulation, a situation which created another problem. United States coins of lesser denominations minted at eastern mints still sold at a premium. At one time 3% was charged for changing a $50 piece into other coins. Again there was a cry for the establishment of a United States mint which would produce coins of many different denominations.

The situation continued to be acute, and the discount deepened, often equaling 4%, which made a U.S. Assay Office $50 gold piece worth just $48 in terms of other coins, not much of an improvement over the various minor privately-issued gold coins which the $50 pieces replaced. Finally on December 9, 1851, the United States Treasury authorized Moffat & Company to make $10 and $20 pieces. Subsequently these were produced. In the same year Moffat & Company was dissolved and a new firm comprised of the same partners but known as the United States Assay Office of Gold emerged. Coinage was continued through December 14, 1853.

Production of $50 gold pieces must have been tremendous. In 1851 it was estimated that output occasionally attained the figure of $100,000 value per day.

The $50 slugs and other issues were exported in large numbers, some from San Francisco and others indirectly from the East Coast. Early in 1853 the steamer *Asia* took $200,000 in $50 gold pieces from New York City to Liverpool. There were many other examples.

In late 1853 Curtis and Perry began the work which led to the building of the United States Mint. Certain of the old U.S. Assay Office of Gold machinery was used as well as the old facilities. The mint was extended along the street by an additional 20 feet to accommodate the expanded business.

The San Francisco Mint began producing official United States coins with an issue of $20 gold pieces on April 15th, 1854. Each coin bore a distinctive "S" mintmark. During the first year only gold coins were struck. In the following year silver pieces were added. It was not until 1908 that the first copper issues were struck at San Francisco and not until 1912 that the first nickel pieces were issued.

Following the opening of the mint there were still many proposals relating to coinage. Senator William W. Gwin advocated a coinage of larger issues, and James Guthrie, Secretary of the Treasury, on March 21st, 1854 seconded Mr. Gwin's proposal adding that: "I would recommend that the coinage be authorized for pieces of $100, $50, and $25 to be called the 'Union,' 'Half Union,' and 'Quarter Union,' but that the 'Half Union' only be struck for the present."

While the $25 and $100 pieces never materialized, in 1877 Senator Gwin's proposal for $50 coins was revived. At the Philadelphia Mint William Barber prepared two

*By May 16, 1854, San Francisco was a thriving commercial center with all sorts of amusement and business enterprises. On this page are
reproduced a few of the hundreds of classified advertisements which appeared in "The San Francisco Herald" on that day.*

obverse die designs (differing from each other only in minor details) and one reverse for a massive $50 coin measuring two inches in diameter. By that time the California Gold Rush was a thing of the past, and there was little need for coins of this denomination. Nevertheless a number of patterns were struck; at least one impression from each of the two die designs in gold and nearly a dozen impressions of each die in copper. No pieces were made for circulation. For several decades thereafter collectors admired the immense $50 *copper* patterns. It was presumed that the gold impressions had been destroyed. Then, as I noted in the first chapter of this book, in 1909 the numismatic world was shocked to learn that the 1877 $50 pieces in gold, one from each die, had been preserved. Sold by Philadelphia coin dealers Stephen K. Nagy and John W. Haseltine to industrialist William H. Woodin (later to be secretary of the treasury under Franklin D. Roosevelt), the pieces fetched the unheard of price of $10,000 each. An uproar followed, and it was alleged that the coins were rightfully the property of the United States Mint. The situation was resolved by trading a large quantity of other pattern coins to Woodin in exchange for the $50 gold issues.

The idea of a $50 coin lingered on. In 1915 the Panama Pacific International Exposition was held in San Francisco to celebrate the opening of the Panama Canal and to observe the rebirth of the Golden Gate city from the ashes of the April 1906 earthquake and fire. Robert Aitken, a well known sculptor, designed a $50 gold piece to commemorate the occasion. Bearing the helmeted head of Minerva on the obverse and a wise owl on the reverse, the massive gold issue was produced in round and octagonal shapes. At 11:00 in the morning of June 21, 1915, Superintendent T.W.H. Shanahan of the San Francisco Mint pulled a lever on a special hydraulic press, and 450 tons of pressure squeezed out the first $50 gold coin ever to be issued for public distribution by a United States minting institution.

It was hoped that at $100 each, twice face value, the coins would be eagerly sought by the public. 1,509 octagonal issues were made. Nine were set aside for assay, 646 were actually sold to the public, and, later, 854 unsold coins went to the melting pot. 1,510 round $50 gold pieces were made, including ten set aside for assay. Only 483 of these were sold. The vast majority, 1,017, were returned to bullion.

The most impressive group of United States coins ever issued to the public was the 1915 complete Panama Pacific set containing both shapes of $50 gold pieces, a commemorative quarter eagle, a specially-designed gold dollar, and a commemorative half dollar, all displayed on purple velvet with gold-lettered ribbons, housed in a hammered copper frame and offered at $200. Or, for twice the price, $400, a double set mounted in a similar frame could be obtained.

What is unwanted by one generation is often avidly desired by the next. 1915-S Panama Pacific International Exposition $50 gold pieces are no exception. By the late 1970s individual coins, the same types that were mostly unwanted by the public and were returned for melting in 1915, were commanding premiums in the $15,000 range each!

Today gold coins of all types are the specialty of many collectors. Most aspire to own a representative sampling of the different denominations or design types produced. Over the years several collectors have endeavored to assemble complete collections by date and mintmark. The late Louis Eliasberg of Baltimore, Maryland, formed a collection which included the only known specimen of the 1870-S $3 gold coin and one of three known 1822 $5 pieces (the other two are in the Smithsonian Institution). The late Josiah K. Lilly, whose collecting interests also extended to rare stamps, came close to Mr. Eliasberg's accomplishment. Upon his death the Lilly Collection lacked only a few pieces. In more recent times Harry Bass of Dallas, Texas, has assembled a nearly complete collection of United States gold coins from the dollar to the double eagle.

During the early 19th century gold was produced in commercial quantities in the southeastern United States. To convert dust and bullion to coins United States mints were established in 1838 at Dahlonega, Georgia, and Charlotte, North Carolina. Each operated until 1861 and produced gold coins only.

The United States $5 denomination is unusual in that it is the only value to be struck at all seven United States mints: Philadelphia, New Orleans, Charlotte, Dahlonega, San Francisco, Carson City, and Denver. At the same time the $5 series is remarkable for the number of rarities it contains. The aforementioned 1822 is one of America's most famous coins. Another major rarity is the 1841 New Orleans Mint issue. At one time this coin cataloged for just $50 in a standard reference book. Then a study revealed that only 50 specimens were struck, and of that number only one or two pieces could be traced to collectors. Should a specimen come on the market it would undoubtedly be valued at several hundred thousand dollars!

As is true of other collecting fields, numismatic discoveries are constantly being made. The 1849-C (Charlotte Mint) gold dollar was produced in two different varieties. On one variety, rather plentiful today, the reverse wreath is "closed" and ends near the numeral 1. On a much rarer variety the wreath is "open" and ends some distance from the number 1.

In 1956 when James Kelly sold a specimen of the 1849-C open wreath gold dollar at the American Numismatic Association convention sale for $6,000 the coin was believed to be unique; just one piece was

known. Shortly thereafter a Dallas, Texas, collector discovered a second. As luck would have it, a year or two later a third piece turned up, also in Dallas. In 1977 a Connecticut dealer located a fourth. In 1978 a fifth turned up! How many more remain to be found?

Sometimes coins can be rediscovered. Until 1978 it was believed that only one 1825 half eagle with the 5 in the date cut over an earlier 4 existed. The Louis Eliasberg specimen was the only piece definitely traced. Then in 1978 an almost-forgotten collection which had been stored for many decades in a Marquette, Michigan bank was sold at auction by Rarcoa. Among the prize gold coins which came to light was a second specimen of the 1825/4!

Of all United States coins one of the most unusual denominations is the $4 or "stella" piece, so-named because of the star design on the reverse. This coin, made only in pattern form, was suggested by Hon. John A. Kasson, United States minister to Austria, who earlier had been chairman of the Committee of Coinage, Weights, and Measures. He believed that a $4 United States gold coin would be useful in international commerce as it approximated the value of such popular European issues as the Spanish 20 peseta, the Dutch 8 florin, the Italian 20 lire, the Austria 8 florin, and the French 20 franc pieces. In 1879 Charles E. Barber prepared a design portraying Miss Liberty with long flowing hair. George T. Morgan at the same time engraved a competing design with Miss Liberty's hair tightly braided and coiled. Struck in 1879 and 1880, all stellas are rare today. The only issue which appears on the market with frequency is the 1879 flowing hair design of which 415 were made. Most of these were distributed to congressmen, coin collectors, and others who desired them at the time. Lee F. Hewitt, former publisher of the *Numismatic Scrapbook Magazine,* related that the reason many 1879 stellas show traces of handling and wear is that they were popular gifts from congressmen to "ladies of the night" in Washington, D.C., at the time of issue!

While production of United States gold coins officially ended in 1933, in recent years countless thousands of pieces have been produced by counterfeiters abroad. Often made of full gold weight, these counterfeits are customarily sold through banks, antique shops, and other outlets to unsuspecting tourists who believe that they are getting bargains. On a 1970 trip to Holland, France, and Germany I examined hundreds of coins offered by such sources and found that over 90% were clever counterfeits! Other clever counterfeits seen today include popular bullion-type issues. The only problem is that an assay will reveal that they contain only 60% to 80% of the gold they are supposed to! As most such bullion-type counterfeits are squirreled away by non-numismatists who do not assay or check them, these pieces are usually not detected.

In the United States the problem is not as acute, but it is still there. A few years ago John Kamin, the well known numismatist-economist, showed me a small type set of gold coins which one of his clients had purchased from an investment advisor. We were both appalled to see that the 11-piece display set contained two counterfeits: a false gold dollar of the 1854-1855 Type II design and a false $3 gold coin. The other nine coins were genuine. The two counterfeits represented nearly half the value of the collection!

So serious is the problem that the International Association of Professional Numismatists, the Professional Numismatists Guild, and the American Numismatic Association Certification Service (operated by John Hunter, Ed Fleischmann, and staff at the A.N.A. headquarters in Colorado Springs) have expended thousands of dollars and many hours combatting these forgeries. The main incentive for the counterfeiters probably will never be eliminated: the human desire to get a bargain.

For the collector gold coins offer a fascinating variety of possibilities. Cataloging a major collection of gold dollars, $3, or other specialized issues is always a thrill. And, to me there will always be something exciting about any gold coin, even a common one. I remember the first $20 gold piece I owned in my youth, an 1855-S. Not a rare date and not in particularly high condition, the massive and heavy coin made a deep impression. The sentiment has stayed with me.

1849 gold dollar, small diameter type minted 1849 to 1854.

1855 gold dollar. The Type II design with Indian headdress made from 1854 to 1856.

1881 gold dollar. The Type III style with modified obverse made from 1856 through 1889.

GOLD DOLLARS were first struck in 1849. From that year until 1854 the small-diameter style with a compact Liberty head (similar to that used on the $20 gold piece) was utilized. These are known as Type I dollars by collectors today. From 1854 through 1856 a new design, the Type II, appeared. The diameter was enlarged and the head of Liberty was changed to an Indian princess. Problems in striking up the design occurred, and most pieces showed weak areas on the reverse. In 1856 the design was again modified to the Type III style with a larger head on the obverse and some minor changes on the reverse. This motif was continued until the end of the series, 1889.

Gold dollars were struck at the Philadelphia, Charlotte, Dahlonega, New Orleans, and San Francisco mints. Rarities include the 1849-C with open wreath on reverse (fewer than a half dozen are known), the 1855-D (of which just 1,811 were struck), the 1856-D (total mintage just 1,460), 1860-D (mintage just 1,566), 1861-D (mintage unknown, but presumed to be on the order of about 1,000 pieces), and 1875 (400 made for circulation plus 20 Proofs for collectors). Most branch mint issues are very rare in Uncirculated grade.

1796 $2½ gold piece or quarter eagle. Type without stars on the obverse, struck only this year. Just 963 were minted.

1797 $2½. Capped bust to right with stars on the obverse. Heraldic eagle reverse. Minted from 1796 through 1807.

1808 quarter eagle. Capped bust to left, large diameter. This design was produced only in the year 1808, making it a prize scarcity today. 2,710 were minted.

1821 $2½. Capped head to left, style of 1821-1834. With E PLURIBUS UNUM motto on reverse.

1836 $2½. Classic head style, no reverse motto. Type issued from 1834 to 1839.

1866 $2½. Liberty head or coronet type minted 1840 to 1907, the longest continuation without change of a major U.S. coin design.

1911 $2½. Indian head style minted 1908-1929. The legends are incuse (rather than raised) on the coin.

QUARTER EAGLES were first minted in 1796. Production continued intermittently through 1929. As the above illustrations show, several interesting designs were produced, including the long-lived Liberty head style minted continuously from 1840 to 1907, the longest span of any United States coinage design. Rarities abound among quarter eagles. All issues from 1796 through the end of the capped head to left series in 1834 are very scarce. Among later quarter eagles a prime rarity is the 1841, struck only in Proof condition, and known today to the extent of only about a dozen pieces. Sometimes this is referred to as the *Little Princess* issue. 1848 with CAL. above the eagle is rare as is 1854-S. Of the latter issue just 246 were struck. 1863 is a Proof only issue; just 30 were minted. 1875 has an unusually low mintage of just 400 pieces for circulation plus 20 Proofs. Quarter eagles were struck at the Charlotte and Dahlonega mints from the late 1830s until just before the Civil War. All of these issues are elusive. Among Indian head quarter eagles the rarest date is 1911-D.

Three interesting Quarter Eagles: To the left is a specimen of the 1848 quarter eagle with CAL. on the reverse, struck from the first official government deposit of California gold. It has been estimated that just 1,389 were made. Above center and above right are two branch mint quarter eagles, a Charlotte Mint and a Dahlonega Mint issue, each distinguished by the presence of a tiny mintmark, "C" or "D," below the tail of the eagle on the reverse. As early quarter eagles circulated actively, Uncirculated specimens of issues prior to 1860 are exceedingly scarce.

1879 $3 gold. Made in one main style only, $3 gold coins were produced from 1854 through 1889. Never a popular coin, mintages were low in all instances. Prime rarities in the series include 1854-D (the only Dahlonega Mint issue of this denomination), 1870-S (a coin of which just two were struck), 1873, 1875, and 1876. In addition, most issues of the late 1870s and the 1880s are very elusive.

1879 $4 gold "stella." $4 gold coins were struck in pattern form only. The most often seen is the 1879 with flowing hair as illustrated here (regular size and enlarged). Just 415 were struck. Flowing hair pieces were also issued in 1880. In addition, a very small number of coiled hair $4 gold coins were struck in 1879 and 1880. Although all $4 gold coins were issued as patterns, numismatists often include them in type sets.

1795 $5 gold. Capped bust to right style with small eagle reverse as minted 1795 through 1798.

1806 $5 gold. Capped bust to right style, heraldic eagle reverse. Minted from 1795 to 1807.

1812 $5 gold. Capped draped bust to left style as minted from 1802 to 1812. Reverse with E PLURIBUS UNUM.

1813 $5 gold. Capped head to left style as minted 1813 through 1829. E PLURIBUS UNUM motto on reverse. Medium diameter.

1832 $5 gold. Capped head to left style, motto on reverse, small diameter. Minted from 1829 through 1834.

1834 $5 gold. Classic head type minted 1834-1838. No motto on reverse.

1849-C $5 gold. Liberty head or coronet type without motto on reverse. Minted from 1839 to 1866.

1885 $5. Liberty head or coronet type with IN GOD WE TRUST motto as minted from 1866 to 1908.

1908-S $5 gold. Indian head type with incuse legends (rather than raised) as minted from 1908 to 1929.

HALF EAGLES or $5 gold pieces were first minted in 1795. The first style depicted a capped bust of Liberty facing right, with a small eagle on the reverse. These were struck from 1795 through 1798. Next followed a similar obverse design but with the heraldic eagle reverse. Although this new reverse style was officially inaugurated in 1798, earlier-dated dies were on hand at the mint and specimens were struck of 1795 and 1797. This was not done to provide unusual varieties but, rather, was simply an instance of mint economy. During the very early years of mint operation unused dies were kept on hand until they could be utilized.

Many interesting varieties exist throughout the half eagle series, the 1803/2 overdate shown to the right being an example. Rare dates abound. All issues 1795-1798 are scarce. 1815 is a major rarity. All dates from 1821 through 1834 (with motto on reverse) are very elusive. 1822 in particular is exceedingly rare, with just three specimens known (two of which are in the Smithsonian Institution). Among later half eagles the 1841-O, a coin of which just 50 were made, is exceedingly rare, as is 1854-S, the first San Francisco Mint issue of this denomination. 1875 had an unusually low mintage of just 200 pieces for circulation and 20 Proofs for collectors. 1887 is likewise elusive, with the total mintage reported at just 87, all Proofs. The half eagle denomination is the only United States coin value struck at all seven mints: Philadelphia, Charlotte, Dahlonega, Denver, New Orleans, Carson City, and San Francisco.

1795 $10. Capped bust to right style with small eagle reverse as minted from 1795 through 1797. At the time the $10 piece was the largest value United States coin.

1803 $10 gold. Capped bust to right obverse, heraldic eagle reverse. This style was made from 1797 through 1804, after which coinage was suspended.

1865-S $10 gold. Liberty head or coronet type without motto on reverse. This style was produced from 1838 through 1866.

1879-CC $10 gold. Liberty head type with IN GOD WE TRUST motto on reverse as minted from 1866 through 1907.

1907 $10 gold. Type Indian obverse by Saint-Gaudens. Reverse without IN GOD WE TRUST. Style made 1907 and 1908.

1930-S $10 gold piece. Indian obverse. Reverse with IN GOD WE TRUST. Style made from 1908 to 1933.

EAGLES or $10 gold pieces were first minted in 1795. At the time of their introduction these pieces were the highest value circulating United States coins, a title retained until the double eagle made its appearance in 1850.

All eagles of the early years 1795-1804 are elusive. Then followed a hiatus during which no pieces were struck, due primarily to the fact that most early gold coins were being melted down or exported. In 1838 the Liberty head design made its appearance. Mintages from that time forward were fairly constant. Scarce or rare issues among Liberty head eagles include 1858, 1875, 1879-CC, 1879-O, and 1883-O.

In 1907 the Indian style by Augustus Saint-Gaudens made its appearance. Early issues, with periods before and after E PLURIBUS UNUM, were made to test the design and are rare today. When the standard type (without periods) was produced for circulation in 1907 it lacked the IN GOD WE TRUST motto, for President Theodore Roosevelt personally objected to the Deity's name on coinage. Mottoless pieces were made through early 1908. Then Congress restored the motto, and IN GOD WE TRUST appeared from that point through 1933. Later issues were stored in banks and circulated to very little extent. 1920-S of which 126,500 were minted and 1920-S of which 96,000 were minted are both great rarities today, primarily because most never were released and went to the melting pot following the discontinuation of the gold standard. 1933, a coin of which 312,500 were minted, is the rarest issue of the entire series. Apparently nearly all were melted. Just a few were released into circulation before the March 1933 order suspending gold payments was put into effect.

A rarity: 1907 $10 gold with tiny periods or dots before and after each word in E PLURIBUS UNUM. Wire rim. Just 500 of these were struck. In addition another rarity with periods, but with a rounded rim rather than a wire rim, was produced to the extent of just 42 coins. These experimental issues were made to test the new design by Augustus Saint-Gaudens, who was commissioned by President Theodore Roosevelt to improve the artistic appearance of American coinage.

Another rarity: the 1930-S $10 gold, a coin of which 96,000 were minted, is rare today for apparently most went to the melting pot following the discontinuation of the gold standard in 1933. Note that the coin has IN GOD WE TRUST on the reverse, as do other $10 issues minted from mid-1908 through the last year, 1933.

1851-O $20. Liberty head style without motto on reverse as minted for circulation from 1850 to 1866.

1875-CC $20. Liberty head style with IN GOD WE TRUST on reverse. Denomination spelled as TWENTY DOLLARS, as minted from 1877 to 1907.

1875-CC $20. Liberty head style. Reverse with denomination spelled TWENTY DOLLARS, as minted from 1877 to 1907.

MCMVII (1907) High Relief double eagle by Augustus Saint-Gaudens. Following Theodore Roosevelt's request, noted sculptor Augustus Saint-Gaudens produced new designs for the 1907 $10 and $20 gold coins. The double eagle featured the devices in high, almost sculptured-appearing, relief. The date was in Roman numerals. 11,250 were struck. The high relief caused many coining problems, with the result that each coin had to be struck three times in order to bring up the design properly. Accordingly, the high relief was discontinued soon thereafter and a new shallower format was instituted. The Roman numerals, which caused confusion to the public, were discontinued. Today numismatists consider this to be one of the most beautiful of all American coin designs produced for circulation.

1907 Saint-Gaudens $20 with date in Arabic numerals. Without IN GOD WE TRUST. Minted 1907 and 1908.

1922-S $20 gold. Saint-Gaudens design with IN GOD WE TRUST on reverse as minted from 1908 to 1933.

DOUBLE EAGLES or $20 gold pieces were first conceived in 1849, during which year several patterns were struck. Only one of these is known today, the specimen in the Smithsonian Institution. The following year, 1850, saw the first issues produced for circulation. These large and heavy coins were made in large quantities and served well in the channels of commerce during a time when public confidence in paper money was low. In 1907 the coinage was redesigned at the request of President Theodore Roosevelt. The illustrious MCMVII issues of Augustus Saint-Gaudens stand out as a highlight in American coinage. Later Saint-Gaudens issues used regular (in Arabic numerals) dates and were minted in large quantities through 1933. Most pieces made during the early 20th century were stored in banks or shipped to overseas banks and treasuries. Foreign nations preferred the security of gold to the uncertainty of American paper money. Many issues with high mintages, the Denver and San Francisco issues of 1924, 1925, 1926, 1927, 1930, and 1931 being examples, were shipped to storage and subsequently melted, for the most part. As a result many of these are extreme rarities today.

Other scarce issues in the series include 1870-CC (the first double eagle of the Carson City Mint), 1883 and 1884 (Philadelphia Mint issues struck only in Proof condition to the extent of just 92 pieces and 71 pieces respectively), 1887, 1907 MCMVII with Extremely High Relief (a pattern variety), and 1933. Although a substantial coinage of 1933 double eagles was effected, the government has held that no pieces were *officially* placed into circulation. The several specimens which have appeared on the market since that time have been seized by the Treasury. Numismatists have held that it is theoretically possible that anyone who desired to could have purchased a specimen from the Treasury prior to March 1933 simply by paying face value for it.

In 1861 Anthony Paquet, an engraver at the Mint, produced a new double eagle reverse design. Dies were shipped to the New Orleans and San Francisco mints. Coinage at Philadelphia revealed that the die, distinguished by tall letters on the reverse, produced striking problems, so withdrawal was ordered. At the time there was no telegraphic link to the San Francisco Mint west of St. Joseph, Missouri, so by the time the news reached San Francisco approximately 4,000 1861-S double eagles with the Paquet reverse had been struck. Today these are quite scarce.

The impressively large and heavy double eagle stands as the largest regular issue United States coin denomination ever made for circulation.

In 1877 the Philadelphia Mint produced two varieties of $50 gold coins, each differing slightly in obverse details. One specimen of each was struck in gold, and a dozen or so of each were produced in copper. Today the gold coins repose in the Smithsonian Institution.

Over the years a number of interesting pattern $10 pieces have been produced. Above are shown several. The 1862 with the experimental motto GOD OUR TRUST represents a motto that was never adopted. The 1868 pattern shows a Liberty head similar to that used on the contemporary nickel three-cent piece. The 1875 issue by William Barber depicts a compact head of Liberty with her hair tied back with a ribbon. The reverse eagle is somewhat similar to that used on the contemporary trade dollar. Two were struck in gold, several dozen in copper, a dozen or so in aluminum, and a few in white metal. The 1874 $10 gold piece represents an attempt at an international coinage. Suggested by Dana Bickford, this large-diameter coin gives on the reverse equivalent values in several different world currencies. This and numerous other attempts at universal coinage standards failed for many reasons, including the fact that currency valuations constantly changed in relation to each other.

PATTERN GOLD COINS were made in many different forms. With the exception of certain pattern gold dollars of 1836 (with the Liberty cap design), and certain varieties of the 1852 ''ring dollars,'' pattern gold coins actually struck in gold are extreme rarities. Typically, of a given pattern just one, two, or several impressions would be made in gold. A larger quantity would be made in copper or another lower-value metal to permit discussion and distribution of the design without incurring great cost. In addition, many strikings in copper, aluminum, and other metals were produced simply to create rarities for collectors. High on the list of such examples is the 1885 United States Proof set struck in aluminum, complete from the cent through the double eagle—to mention just one of many similar instances.

There are several famous pattern gold rarities. The 1877 $50 gold coins, the 1907 pattern pieces of Augustus Saint-Gaudens, and others have filled many columns in numismatic literature. Perhaps the most famous is the 1849 double eagle. Although several pieces were struck, only one 1849 double eagle is known today, the specimen in the Smithsonian Institution. Another was given to Secretary of the Treasury Meredith but is not presently accounted for. Should it be discovered it would probably break all price records for a United States numismatic item.

1868 pattern $5. This coin, of very large diameter (about the size of a $10 gold piece), is very thin, in order to maintain the correct weight. In 1860 the Treasury discovered that certain United States gold coins were being sawed in half, filled with platinum (which was much cheaper than gold at the time), and then rejoined. These deceptive coins, of the correct weight and appearance, caused great consternation. The thin piece illustrated above was one idea proposed. A coin of such thinness could not be divided and filled.

1852 pattern gold dollar. The "ring dollar." Around this time several different ring-shaped dollars were made in an effort to increase the diameter of the tiny gold dollar while at the same time maintaining the correct weight. The idea was never adopted.

The 1915 double Panama Pacific set illustrated above, originally sold for $400 in 1915, is mounted in a copper frame with gold-lettered purple ribbons and a blue velvet background. This set, containing two specimens each (to illustrate obverse and reverse) of the different coins issued for the 1915 Panama-Pacific International Exposition held in San Francisco, is the most impressive group of coins ever specifically sold as a set by the government.

As strange as it may seem today, only a few of the double sets, possibly not even a dozen, found buyers, and of the similarly-styled single sets (with one of each coin) sold for $200, fewer than 200 found purchasers. Today these sets are highly prized.

Pikes Peak Gold

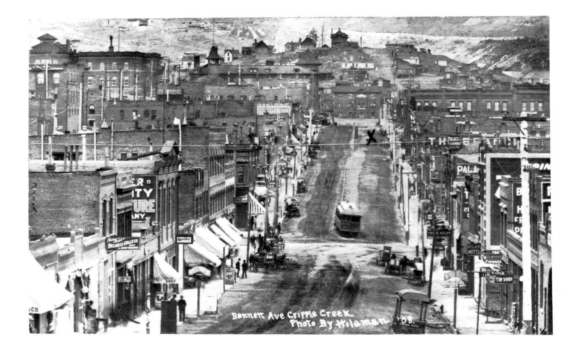

Bennett Ave Cripple Creek.
Photo By Hilaman '06

6

On a snowy February weekend I attended the American Numismatic Association midwinter convention held at the Broadmoor Hotel at the foot of Cheyenne Mountain on the western side of Colorado Springs.

In the 1890s the Broadmoor resort, the forerunner of the present day facility, was one of the West's most prominent spas.

In 1919 the Broadmoor Hotel as we know it today was completed on the same grounds. Financing was provided by Spencer Penrose who began his fortune as owner of the C.O.D. Mine during the Cripple Creek gold rush. In 1896 he had startled society in that mountain mining town near Colorado Springs when he and Grace Carlisle, an employee of the Old Homestead, one of the most prominent bordellos in Cripple Creek's red light district, mounted horses and rode into the saloon during the grand opening proceedings of the 150-room National Hotel, the largest ever built in that community.

Today the Broadmoor is a varied entertainment complex. In the center is the Broadmoor Hotel, a tall Mediterranean-style concrete structure nestled among pine trees on the shore of a small lake. The interior is reminiscent of a bygone era and is decorated with, among other things, an original oil painting by the celebrated artist, Maxfield Parrish.

During the 'teens and 'twenties Parrish was one of the best-known and best-loved American artists and illustrators. His crowning accomplishment from the standpoint of popularity was *Daybreak*, a print depicting two nymphlike girls on a portico overlooking a mountain lake, the whole scene lighted with luminous iridescence. Copies of *Daybreak* reached the market in 1923, and by the end of that year Parrish had earned nearly $25,000 in royalties. Two years later his yearly royalties for the same painting amounted to $75,000!

Maxfield Parrish has always been of personal interest to me. Some years ago I owned one of his paintings, *In The Mountains*, produced in 1933 and kept in his home as one of his wife's favorites.

Augustus Saint-Gaudens, the prominent sculptor who designed the 1907 $10 and $20 gold pieces, and Parrish, both residents of New Hampshire, were close friends. Some years ago I had the privilege of selling at auction a prized MCMVII High Relief 1907 double eagle which was consigned to me by Maxfield Parrish, Jr. His father had obtained it at the time of issue as a gift from the coin's designer.

On the same grounds as the main Broadmoor Hotel are several newer structures including the Broadmoor South, the Broadmoor West, and numerous outbuildings devoted to athletic pursuits and maintenance activities. Rounding out the facilities are a ski slope, golf and tennis facilities, a shrine honoring the late Will Rogers, and even a zoo.

The American Numismatic Association midwinter convention dealers' bourse was held in the Broadmoor Skating Rink, a large arena which has been the location for many ice skating and hockey events. The bourse was to have been held in the International Center, a large convention facility in front of the main Broadmoor Hotel. However, it was learned that an earlier reservation by a political group had been made for a dinner during one of the convention days, so that facility could not be used for numismatic purposes. Instead, the Skating Rink was adapted by covering the frozen floor with pads of insulating material. The result was a scene of buying and selling activity which, the first day, was held at temperatures near the freezing point. Complaints were vociferous, and a compromise was made whereby heat was turned on in the rink (with some danger of melting the ice as a result therefrom). Any dealer dissatisfied with the arrangements was given the option to leave early with a full refund of any fees paid. Actually, all worked out well in the end, and by the time the show was over three days later, most dealers and collectors had a really nice time.

Atop the Broadmoor South building is the Penrose Room, named after Spencer Penrose, a dining area with a panoramic view in three directions.

THE
BROADMOOR
COLORADO SPRINGS

THE ANTLERS.

The Broadmoor Hotel has been one of Colorado Springs' major attractions for many years. The top view shows the Broadmoor as painted by Maxfield Parrish, famous American illustrator, circa 1920, Parrish used artistic license and put the lake, which is behind the hotel in actuality, in front of it! Today the Broadmoor Hotel structure shown here has been supplemented by two other large buildings situated nearby.

At the center of the page is shown the earlier Broadmoor Hotel and Casino as it appeared in 1895. Dancing, riding, and various indoor and outdoor activities were enjoyed here by tourists and visitors.

To the right is shown the old Antlers Hotel, circa 1895. This structure was destroyed by fire in 1898, following a dynamite explosion in a nearby railroad car. A new elegant Antlers was built on the site and was famed as a luxury hotel until the last guest was registered in 1964. Today the site has been "improved" and contains a shopping center and modern hotel.

"This is a very nice restaurant. Are there any other places like this in the area?," I asked a friend of mine, a Colorado Springs resident.

"This is *the* place in Colorado socially," he replied. "There is nothing like it in Denver or anywhere else."

Founded in 1871, Colorado Springs enjoyed rapid growth from the beginning. By 1879 the population stood at 5,000. During the latter year it was estimated that 25,000 visitors stayed at its hotels and boarding houses to sample such local attractions as the mineral springs at Manitou five miles away and the scenic grandeur of Pikes Peak which overlooks the town. Today the population of Colorado Springs and vicinity approaches 200,000.

Following consideration of several sites, the American Numismatic Association established its Home and Headquarters on the campus of Colorado College on Cascade Avenue in Colorado Springs in the 1960s. Earlier the Association, founded in 1888 and chartered in 1891, had no permanent home but operated from the offices of various secretaries and other officials.

Today the spacious white edifice is a mecca for numismatists the world over. Within its confines, the ground floor and basement, are housed many activities, including a large numismatic library, an exhibit gallery, a theatre, and the facilities of the American Numismatic Association Certification Service which examines coins and determines their authenticity or lack of it. The whole arrangement is under the direction of Ed Rochette, the group's executive vice president.

The Association is fortunate to have two local members who have an intense interest in Colorado numismatic history. Adna G. Wilde, a member of the Board of Governors of the American Numismatic Association and a trustee of the Pioneer Museum in the same city, has done extensive research in several areas of Colorado numismatics, including the privately-minted Lesher "dollars" minted in 1900 and 1901. William C. Henderson, treasurer of the organization, is likewise a student of Colorado numismatic history and has written and lectured extensively on the subject.

The addition of the American Numismatic Association Headquarters notwithstanding, Colorado Springs has had a rich numismatic heritage of its own for many years. Beginning in the early 1890s it was the commercial center for the Cripple Creek District gold field, an immense treasure trove of gold ore spread over many square miles on the western slopes of Pikes Peak, today about a 90-minute drive by automobile.

Years ago the gold fields were more remote. Until the railroads were put through, travel was by stage, an arduous journey which took a day and a half. Cripple Creek historian Mabel Barbee Lee told of taking that journey as a young redhaired school girl.

In the middle of the night the stage in which she was riding with her mother and several other hardy travelers was accosted by a gang of bandits. Young Mabel took her prize possession, a shiny silver dollar, and hid it in her mouth as the bandits ordered the passengers outside, lined them up, and demanded that their money and valuables be dumped into an open satchel.

Approaching young Mabel, the leader said, "Git in line there, you young whippersnapper! This stick-up means you too!"

Her mother intervened and pleaded for her daughter's safety. Then, with a wink to another bandit, the chief pointed his pistol and said, "Don't it beat all how she was atryin' to cheat on us?"

"Guess we oughta learn her a lesson as a warnin'," his aide said.

Disaster seemed imminent, then the bandits broke out laughing as did the hostages. It seemed that young Mabel couldn't quite close her small mouth around the large silver dollar, and it was sticking out in plain sight! One of the bandits then took another silver dollar out of the satchel and slipped it in on top of the first one in Mabel's mouth.

"Next time, pug-nose, you'd better keep your little trap shut. Don't try no more funny tricks . . ."

After all was said and done and the bandits had departed with their ill-gotten loot, the driver congratulated his young passenger on doubling her assets during this harrowing event!

Today the drive from Colorado Springs to the gold district is an easy and pleasant one. Going from the Broadmoor, one takes Interstate 25 north. This modern route cuts through the western edge of Colorado Springs by the site of the old Antlers Hotel, torn down in the 1960s to make room for the "improved" Antlers Plaza Hotel and its surrounding shopping district. Today the visitor can only imagine what the old Antlers was like. A description from 1895 noted, "the Antlers Hotel is the foremost in Colorado and the Rocky Mountain region and has an enviable reputation throughout the land. Erected in 1882 at a cost of $200,000, it was several years ago practically doubled in size at a further expenditure of fully $75,000. It has a commanding situation at the head of Pikes Peak Avenue with an unobstructed view of the mountain range. It is a strikingly handsome structure of cut stone, thoroughly modern in construction and complete and elegant in all of its appointments. Its cuisine is of noted excellence, and thousands of visitors from all parts of the world have pronounced it one of the most delightful of hotels."

A popular early 20th century scenic postcard from Colorado Springs shows Pikes Peak Avenue in down-

town Colorado Springs with the old Antlers Hotel at the end, framing in the background Pikes Peak.

Headed for the gold fields, at Exit 60 I turned west on Route 24. One of the first sights on the left was the old Midland Terminal Railroad roundhouse on the corner of 21st Street. Built in 1887-1888, it was abandoned in 1949. Six years later it became the factory of the Van Briggle Art Pottery Company.

Founded in 1899 by Artus Van Briggle, an Ohioan who moved to Colorado Springs in the 1890s for reasons of health, the firm has one of the most illustrious backgrounds of any pottery in America.

Van Briggle's works were accepted for exhibition at the Paris Salon in 1903. The 24-piece showing attracted worldwide acclaim. One work, a vase entitled *Despondency*, was subsequently purchased in 1908 by Paris' Louvre Museum for $3,000, the largest amount ever paid to that date for a piece of pottery.

At the 1904 St. Louis World's Fair another Van Briggle exhibition attracted acclaim. *Siren of the Sea*, a bowl with a mermaid reclining on one edge, won an award.

Today in Colorado Springs one can still buy some of the original Van Briggle designs, including the prizewinning *Despondency* and *Siren of the Sea* as well as the popular *Lorelei*, a tall and slender vase incorporating a wistful wraithlike figure of a woman around the top opening.

Following a tour of the Van Briggle factory during an earlier visit I bought a couple of reference books about the firm and read them upon my return to California. Now during my subsequent visit I was equipped with the knowledge of the outfit's sentimental background and actually was a presold customer.

An avid reader of *The Antique Trader, Collector's News, Antiques Magazine,* and other publications in the field of antiques, I am quite aware of the countless hundreds of "limited edition" pottery and ceramic items being offered as collectors' pieces. Many of these have little or no true historical background apart from what was created a few weeks earlier by a press agent or advertising department. Not so with Van Briggle products. Here in front of me during my visit was a showroom full of interesting pieces with historical associations dating back to the end of the last century. Most remarkable of all, apart from a few brochures these items were not actively promoted or advertised. In fact, the son of the owner, with whom I spoke, made a point of telling me that Van Briggle ware is sold only at the factory location in Colorado Springs and is not available anywhere else in the world. Distribution by others is discouraged by the fact that no dealer's discounts, not even small ones, are granted.

Being a collector of many things and a new fan of Van Briggle products, I asked if the wares were dated so as to differentiate, for example, a *Lorelei* vase made currently from one of the same design made years earlier.

"No, we haven't put dates on them, just our company markings and in some instances the mark of the potter or finisher who worked on the particular piece. We have had others ask about dating, so maybe this is something we will do in the future," my host informed me.

After spending at least an hour looking around the premises under the guidance of Trudy, one of the most helpful salespeople I have ever encountered, I proposed an idea: how about making for me on special order some items with dates inscribed on the bottom? My suggestion was accepted, and an order for about two dozen pieces of various designs was subsequently placed. These subsequently arrived at my home in California in April. Upon unpacking them I was delighted to note on the bottom of each piece the dates of manufacture: February 27, 1978 and March 4, 1978.

Continuing westward toward the gold fields on Route 24 the turn-off for Colorado City comes up on the right. For a very short time this small community was the capital of the Colorado Territory. Today it is mainly a tourist area with numerous old buildings surviving from the last century. Then comes the exit for the Garden of the Gods, a fantastic park of huge red sandstone monoliths jutting into the air; relics of the primordial times when the Rocky Mountains were pushed up by the collision of the tectonic land masses composing what are now the eastern and western parts of the United States.

On past the Garden of the Gods and the exit for Manitou Springs and the Pikes Peak Cog Railway Route 24 climbs through the lower slopes of Pikes Peak. Markers along the road note the increasing altitude of the upward journey.

On the right soon appeared a red stone wall, and behind it, faintly visible through pine trees, an old house. In 1909 a young Irishman, Thomas Cusack, emigrated to America and settled in Illinois. Making his home in River Forest, he became a success in the field of outdoor advertising and billboards. Within a few years his trademark was a familiar one all over the Chicago area.

In the 1920s he moved to Colorado where he repeated his business success in the same field—billboards and signs painted on the sides of buildings. Today, according to his daughter-in-law, just one of these survives in Colorado, a faded sign for Wrigley's gum still visible on a brick wall in Cripple Creek.

Around 1920 a huge hydrogen-filled zeppelin caught fire over Chicago and plunged to the earth, crashing

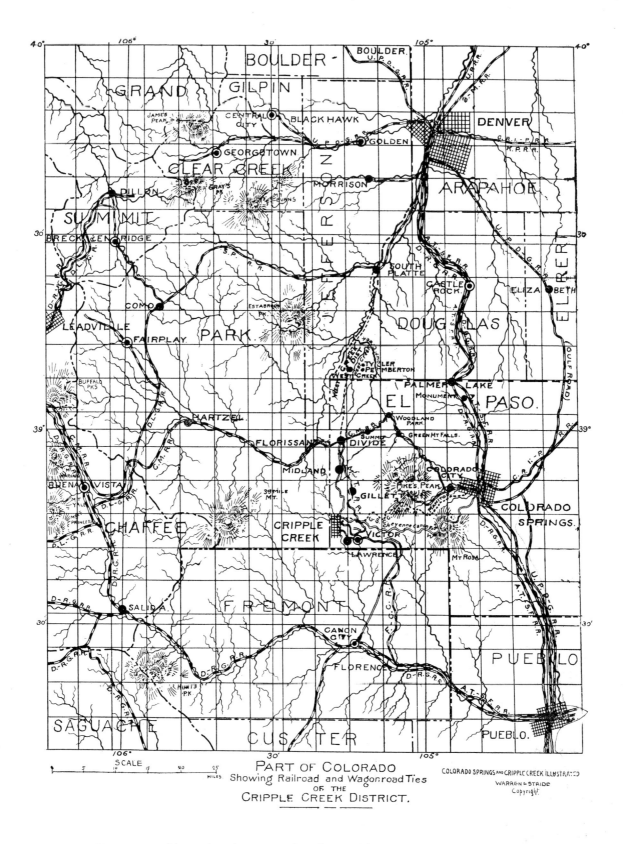

PART OF COLORADO
Showing Railroad and Wagonroad Ties
OF THE
CRIPPLE CREEK DISTRICT.

COLORADO SPRINGS AND CRIPPLE CREEK ILLUSTRATED
WARREN & STRIDE
Copyright

*Map, circa 1895, of the Cripple Creek District. Cripple Creek, separated from the commercial center of Colorado Springs
by Pikes Peak, was reached in the early days by horseback or by stage. Following the advent of the railroad, access became
easier and commerce flourished. Also seen on this map, toward the top, are the mining towns of Central City, Black Hawk,
and Georgetown, which during the 1850s and 1860s were sites for important silver discoveries.*

through the roof of the Continental Bank. Learning of the disaster, Thomas Cusack salvaged the bank's marble floor and other decorations composed of many shades of carefully cut stone. These were subsequently fitted into the flooring of Marigreen, the red brick mansion partly visible from Route 24 near Colorado Springs today.

The interior of Marigreen was furnished with oil paintings of rich character, some done by talented billboard artists on his staff who painted in imitation of classical masters. Adding to the atmosphere were tables, chairs, and other furniture, mostly of the ornate Victorian style with curved claw feet. Included was a Conover-Welte player grand piano in a marvelous carved case made in the early 1920s in Chicago to Mr. Cusack's special order. By means of specially perforated paper rolls the instrument reenacted the piano playing of great keyboard artists. A Colorado Springs friend, Art Reblitz, one of the nation's foremost experts in the field of piano technology, took me to see this piano and pronounced it one of the most marvelous Welte reproducing grands he had ever seen.

Further up the mountain the road went. At Woodland Park, a bustling community with its main street lined with modern stores and shops, Route 24 suddenly narrows. A few miles farther at the town of Divide, I turned left on Route 67 which led to Cripple Creek.

Continuing the drive on Route 67 past Divide, the next area of interest on the twisting, winding road, was a spot in which the pavement narrowed suddenly to one lane in width for a tunnel, which a marker noted was built by the Midland Terminal Railroad in 1893. The tracks are long gone.

A landmark, or what's left of it, on the way to Cripple Creek is the town of Gillett. In 1900 nearly 1,200 people lived there. It was called the Gateway City, for it was the first town encountered as one entered the Cripple Creek gold district. At one time the town had a flourishing bank, several saloons, and a newspaper called *The Forum.*

In the summer of 1895 Gillett attracted national attention when a widely promoted bullfight was held. On August 24th, 50,000 people, tourists from all parts of the United States and Mexico according to news coverage at the time, came to witness this unusual event, crowding the grandstands and nearby fields.

All did not happen quite as planned, for either just one bull was killed or perhaps several were killed after giving little or no resistance or challenge to the matadors. In any event, there was a protest about the cruelty of bullfighting, and the pageant came to a premature close, with the scheduled three-day celebration fizzling a few minutes after it started.

Today Gillett is marked by a couple of old buildings plus the gaunt stone skeleton of a former church, one of three which flourished in the town during its heyday. No signs marked the location of Gillett nor did I see any historical markers. Were not its location described in an old book I would not have known where it was.

Off in a large field to the left were many huge boulders, some the size of small houses, which looked like they had burst forth from a ravine after a frightening flood.

A short drive after that, I rounded a curve and saw a sign: Cripple Creek, City Limit, Elevation 9,494 feet. There before me in a wide natural bowl or caldera of an ancient volcano lay the present day city of Cripple Creek. On its descent into the town the road winds past countless mine shafts and mine dumps, including the Mollie Kathleen Mine, a present day tourist attraction.

The first structure encountered of significant size is the three-story green-roofed red brick and sandstone building which formerly housed the station of the Midland Terminal Railroad. Now converted to an historical museum it offers an excellent selection of artifacts from Cripple Creek's glorious past—including a model of a gold mine, numerous certificates and photographs, maps, miners' equipment, household accessories, and other memorabilia. Turning right, I drove onto Bennett Avenue and parked. With me that day were my two sons, Wynn and Lee, my fiancee Christie Valentine (we were married a few weeks later) and Marge, Steve and Chad Cerinich from Boulder, Colorado.

Today Bennett Avenue is indeed a nostalgic place to behold. Lining both sides of the street are brick and stone buildings, mostly of two-story height, nearly all of which have the date 1896 molded into the top of the facades—vivid testimony to the fire and rebuilding of that same year. Scanning the fronts of the buildings, mostly of red color, is like reading a business directory from the turn of the century: J.S. Neall & Company, T.R. Lorimer, Turf Club Room, Tutt Building, Piggott Block, Jamison Block, H. Schradsky, A & K Block, Parr Building, and Bell Bros., to mention a few.

The Gold Mining Stock Exchange building of cut red stone, now occupied by BPOE Lodge 316, is particularly impressive with its front in nearly mint condition.

Gone are the dozens of saloons, gambling palaces, bordellos, photography shops, and the like from years gone by. Replacing them are souvenir and novelty shops, open in the summer months, plus a handful of basic businesses: a real estate office, a barber shop, a few bars and restaurants, and further up Bennett Avenue, a new grocery store.

The Teller County Court House, built in 1904, is the most imposing building in the district. Standing several

In November 1891 Cripple Creek, shown above, was a collection of scattered tents and log structures. The main activity was ranching. Gold had been discovered, and adventurers were beginning to arrive in small numbers.

By December 1895 Cripple Creek had grown to be a medium-size city. Churches, hotels, and other trappings of civilization abounded. Still, the best growth years were yet to come.

Cripple Creek, located high in an ancient volcanic crater on the western slopes of Pikes Peak, is above the timberline. Trees were and still are few and far between.

floors high and resembling a large city high school, the building is testimony to the days when Cripple Creek consisted not of 450 people as it does today, but of over 25,000—with homes scattered throughout dozens of streets and avenues.

Myers Avenue, once the site of Cripple Creek's storied red light district, is a dirt strip with vacant fields to each side. Gone are the alluring girls and the parlors they occupied; all that remain are stories and legends.

In the summer months one can pay a dollar and gain admission to the only surviving bordello building, the Old Homestead at 353 East Myers Avenue. Built in 1896, the structure was once the home of girls who in their Parisian gowns and leghorn hats were the "scorched toast of the town," according to a brochure.

Cripple Creek's history is rich with stories of wealth and adventure.

In the 1880's Bob Womack, son of the Kentuckian William W. Womack, who came to Colorado and settled on a ranch in the broad volcanic crater where Cripple Creek is now situated, began prospecting for gold. Despite the derisive comments of others and the nagging notion that gold in the area might just be a hoax (in early 1884 some unscrupulous people salted some nuggets on worthless land near Canon City and started a gold rush; word soon spread of the sham, and for years afterward any mention of gold on the west side of Pikes Peak was apt to bring nothing but laughs), Womack continued his efforts.

Prospecting the creeks in the district, Womack encountered loose rock, called "float," which had drifted downstream from outcroppings which were presumed to exist at higher levels. While traces of gold-bearing ore were found, the quantities did not indicate commercial feasibility. Earlier, in 1881, Theodore H. Lowe, a mining engineer, discovered a gold-bearing rocky outcrop. The gold content was not sufficiently high to attract commercial interest at the time.

Still Bob Womack continued his exploration. Following each several weeks of effort he would take samples of his findings to Colorado Springs to have them assayed. Few people were interested in his discovery.

His luck turned in December 1890 when he received the financial backing of F.F. Frisbie and E.M. De la Vergne, the latter a Colorado Springs merchant. Subsequently a 48-foot shaft was sunk in Poverty Gulch, and a rich strike of sylvanite gold ore was located.

Going to Colorado Springs to celebrate the occasion, he sold his claim, the El Paso, for $500 cash and went on a drunken spending spree.

Word spread, and soon the district was flooded with speculators and prospectors. The town of Cripple Creek, named for a small stream which meandered through the area, the site where a cow had crippled itself during a crossing years earlier, was laid out. At first the name Fremont was thought of, but the United States Post Office rejected it on the grounds that another town in Colorado already had that designation.

By the end of 1891, pioneering miners had extracted from the earth gold valued at approximately $200,000 at the then-current reckoning of $20.67 per ounce. Today, of course, the value would be many multiples of that figure.

An influx of major capital did not occur, for investors, frightened by the earlier hoax, stayed away. The district was mainly composed of individual miners to the extent of several thousand who were busily prospecting on small claims. Only as production increased did outside financing become available. By 1892 production soared to $600,000 worth of the precious yellow metal.

1893 saw continually increasing population and more exploration in the hills surrounding Cripple Creek with resultant additional discoveries and increased production. By year's end $2 million worth of gold had been extracted from the earth.

The year 1893 was economically unfortunate in the United States. The Panic of '93 resulted in a precipitous drop in the price of silver. Mines throughout the west, including many in the Denver area north of Colorado Springs, closed their shafts. Thousands of laborers were out of work. Many turned their faces toward the Cripple Creek district where yellow gold held its alluring promise. At the beginning of 1893 the population of the Cripple Creek district was estimated at 4,000. During that year alone an additional 10,000 people entered the area.

In the same year the district's second major city, Victor, which came to be known as "The City of Mines," was established five miles southeast of Cripple Creek. On Battle Mountain overlooking Victor the area's most productive mines came into being. In the early years Cripple Creek was often decried for its lack of culture and for its vices. A marshal in Colorado Springs commented that the crime rate in his city had dropped to an all-time low because all of the criminals had moved to Cripple Creek! Indeed, the long journey to Cripple Creek by stage and, later, partly by railroad with completion by stage, appealed only to the most rugged type of individual.

All of this changed on July 1, 1894 when the race to link Cripple Creek with civilization was won by the Florence and Cripple Creek Railroad, with the Midland Terminal Railroad coming in 18 months thereafter.

The July 1st celebration was of a size Cripple Creek had not seen before. The mayor decreed that July 4th celebrations would be moved up several days to coincide

with the event. The ending shortly before of a tumultuous labor strike compounded the celebration and revelry. Now with the advent of modern rail transportation Cripple Creek indeed could be civilized; she could become Colorado's finest city.

Such thoughts plus the prosperity of the gold mines led the mayor of Cripple Creek to write a year later about his town's future:

"Not one century nor five centuries will see the Cripple Creek mines exhausted. Our greatest, our richest and largest mines will be found in the granite, and the grandchildren of our children's children will not see the end of gold mining in the hills that belt the Cripple Creek district.

"A century from now will see Cripple Creek the metropolis of a great mining district, extending 25 miles north and south and 10 miles east and west, with blocks of magnificent brick and stone fronts lining its thoroughfares, with palatial and royally furnished residences dotting its suburbs, with splendid electric street car systems, with its gorgeous electric lights . . . with its lofty church spires lifting into the blue ether of our mountains—with its 500 mills grinding and pounding away upon the daily product of the mines, and finally with its quarter of a million of energetic, progressive, and law abiding people . . ."

Several other railroads followed on the heels of the first two. The Colorado Springs and Cripple Creek District Railroad, familiarly known as the "Cripple Creek Short Line," ran from Colorado Springs to the gold district. Opened on April 12, 1901, it was financed by mining interests to the extent of $5 million. The scenic beauty of this line became world famous. When Theodore Roosevelt visited the district in the year of the railroad's opening he was so taken with the scenic grandeur that he described the railroad as "bankrupting the English language." The line continued to serve tourists and others until 1920. Today a motor road follows the original right-of-way.

In addition to the railroads, two electric street car lines provided intermediate and local service. At one time the Cripple Creek district was so busy that trains came and went at an average interval of six minutes throughout the day!

As thousands of people poured into the district other towns sprung up. Like Cripple Creek and Victor, during the early days most were made of makeshift structures no more impressive than wooden shanties. Goldfield, near Victor, became the area's third largest city with 3,500 inhabitants at the turn of the century.

Cameron, a town with just 700 inhabitants, was a favorite gathering place during festive occasions. Its Pinnacle Park, an amusement park complete with athletic fields, dance pavilions, rides, a zoo, and restaurants, hosted over 9,000 people on Labor Day 1900. During the same year the census recorded that the town of Anaconda had 1,000 people, Altman had 1,500 people, and Independence had 1,500 inhabitants. Lawrence, Beaver Park, and Arequa attracted still others.

On April 25, 1896, Jennie Larue, a dance hall girl, quarreled with her lover in one of the buildings in the red light district on Myers Avenue, one block below the main business street, Bennett Avenue. In the fray a stove was accidentally upset, and following the example set by Mrs. O'Leary's legendary Chicago cow, the fire quickly spread to the surrounding area. Within minutes the central district of Cripple Creek was ashes. What few buildings remained were the scene of a second holocaust on April 29th when a fire broke out in the Portland Hotel on Myers Avenue. Some said it was arson, others said it was accidental. When all was said and done fewer than ten buildings were left standing in the main commercial area, and many homes were destroyed as well. Muriel S. Wolle, who spent nearly 50 years of her life visiting ghost towns and mining camps of Colorado, vividly tells of this and other events in her fascinating book, *Stampede to Timberline*, a chronicle of miners and legends.

After the fire, one man paid $20 so his wife could sleep in one of the few houses remaining. The silver mining camp of Leadville sent $200 in cash and 5,000 pounds of flour to aid the victims. Colorado Springs and Victor likewise helped.

Like a phoenix, the mythical bird of antiquity which was consumed by flames and then rose again from ashes, Cripple Creek soon was rebuilt. A new city of red brick and stone stood in place of the old one before a year had passed on the calendar. With such sturdy construction and with the bright economic outlook, these buildings would endure forever, so it seemed. Perhaps an exception would be the aptly-named Phoenix Block, one of the few new structures to be built of wood. With its nine upper windows and three store fronts below, the wooden Phoenix structure did survive the later ravages of time and was still standing during my visit. However, it had problems coping with economics; it was starkly vacant and for sale.

The mines continued to yield and prosper. In 1898 production was estimated at $13.5 million, in 1900 at $18 million. Few accurate records were kept, and upon consulting three or four history books on the district one can easily come up with three or four different estimates. All told it is believed that about 500 million dollars worth of precious metal have been taken from the Cripple Creek district since 1891. Some estimates have placed the total far higher. By today's gold prices it was in the billions. By comparison, one estimate noted that Califor-

In April 1896 two disastrous fires swept Cripple Creek. Above and below are views of the main street, Bennett Avenue, during and after the ordeal by fire.

VIEW OF CRIPPLE CREEK FROM GOLD HILL
OCT 26 1896
PHOTO BY YELL

MT. PISGAH

DENTISTS

Bennett Ave Cripple Creek

A. J. Harlan Phot

By October 26, 1896, date of the top view, Cripple Creek had been largely rebuilt. Now Bennett Avenue, the main thoroughfare, was lined with buildings, mostly of red brick or stone. Thousands of structures carpeted the metropolis, which was on its way to becoming one of the most important cities in the American West. Below is shown a turn of the century view of Bennett Avenue with new brick and stone buildings.

nia's Mother Lode yielded about $270 million, or half the Cripple Creek total.

Leland Feitz, a modern day historian, estimates that by the turn of the century more than 55,000 people lived in the gold district, with Cripple Creek alone boasting a population of 25,000. Coming in second was Victor, with a population of over 18,000. Today only about 600 live in both cities combined.

At one time Cripple Creek had eight newspapers and Victor had two. Cripple Creek had about 60 doctors, two dance schools, four department stores, four book shops, nine photographers, a hospital, two undertakers, 20 meat markets, 14 bakeries, 49 grocery stores, 11 laundries, 11 blacksmith shops, and five livery stables.

Such establishments as the New Yorker, the Merchants' Cafe, the Saddle Rock, and the Delmonico offered a good dinner for less than fifty cents.

For the imbiber there were 73 saloons in Cripple Creek alone, with 150 throughout the area totally. Gambling casinos included the Antlers Club, Johnny Nolon's, the Board of Trade, and the Branch.

Before prohibition, which came to Colorado in 1915, a drink in the mining towns usually cost 15c. If the bartender was generous the rate was two for a quarter. Offering a 25c piece for a single drink, a customer was apt to receive a token worth 12½c in change. Thus, the Beaumont Saloon located at Second and Bennett streets from 1897 through 1904 issued a 12½c token as did the Klondike, operated by J. Kopff at 111 Third Street. Tokens issued by the latter establishment noted that "the best is not too good for my customers," and "imported wines served in our private wine rooms."

A wide variety of such tokens awaits the numismatist today, providing a tangible link between modern times and the wilder era of the early 1900s. Likewise, the Monarch, Mint, Cascade, Brunswick, Antlers, Scandia, and other drinking establishments in nearby Victor issued tokens. Even Gillett, gone today but remembered for its 1895 bullfight as noted, saw the issuance of a 12½c token by Herman and Wright who operated a saloon there in 1899.

Likewise, the numismatist with an inclination toward paper money can search for a number of elusive issues from the Cripple Creek district. The First National Bank of Cripple Creek opened its doors in 1893. Issued were Second Charter brown back notes in the denominations of $10, $20, $50, and $100 to the extent of $137,500 total. Second Charter dated backs of the same denominations were subsequently issued to the face value of $83,850. Third Charter dated backs of $10 and $20 values were issued to the total of $75,000, and plain back notes of the same denominations were issued to the ex-

tent of $190,550. As of 1935 only $2,875 worth of these issues in total remained outstanding!

The First National Bank of Victor opened its doors in 1900. Shortly thereafter in 1903 it went into receivership because of "incompetent management." Issued by this institution were Second Charter brown back notes to the extent of $80,350 in the denominations of $10, $20, $50, and $100. As of a 1915 reckoning only $1,410 face value of notes was outstanding.

During the boom years of the 1890s the rosy lustre of the gold district brought fortune to many miners, investors, and speculators. Most of this activity centered around Victor, where it was found that the main ore bodies lay.

Some 30 millionaires emerged from the area, a staggering concentration of wealth. Cripple Creek wasn't an ideal residential area as it offered virtually none of the amenities of upper class social life. Instead most millionaires and others of means lived in Colorado Springs or Denver.

Just one house with any claim to being a grand mansion was ever built in Cripple Creek, *The Towers*, also known as *Finn's Folly*, completed shortly before Theodore Roosevelt's visit to Cripple Creek in 1901. Today only a few scattered foundation stones remain at the site.

Winfield Scott Stratton first arrived in Colorado in 1872. A carpenter by trade, he studied mineralogy and assaying to try his luck at mining. In 1891 he walked to Cripple Creek with two accompanying burros laden with mining supplies. Meeting Bob Womack, the discoverer of the first profitable Cripple Creek ore, he searched for awhile in the immediate district. Then he went to Battle Mountain, six miles away, and prospected some granite outcroppings. On July 4, 1891, he staked out the Independence and Martha Washington claims. Within a short period of time the rich lode made Stratton the area's first millionaire. In 1899, after having extracted $4 million worth of metal, he sold the Independence to a London firm for $11 million. During the first 25 years of its operation the Independence produced $23,621,728 worth of bullion.

The nearby Portland Mine, discovered by John Harnan, was staked in 1893. Ultimately this became the richest of all Cripple Creek district mines. During the next 50 years gold estimated to be worth between $60 million and $80 million came from its works on Battle Mountain. The 3,200-foot main shaft was the deepest in the district.

After the turn of the century the Cresson Mine, located between Cripple Creek and Victor, became the area's second largest producer. In 1914 Richard Roelofs, manager of the mine, made one of the most spectacular

Above: The National Hotel, the grandest and most imposing place of public accommodation in the Cripple Creek District, is shown here in a 1908 photograph. Banners welcome delegates from the I.O.O.F., the International Order of Odd Fellows, one of many fraternal organizations which flourished in the town. Scarcely more than a decade later, its usefulness gone, the National Hotel was torn down.

Right: The Continental Hotel, a clapboard structure, is where Mabel Barbee Lee and her mother stayed after their first trip to Cripple Creek by stage, following a robbery enroute, during the early 1890s (see accompanying text).

discoveries ever recorded. Prospecting in a deep shaft he opened a small cave at the 1,200-foot level. Before him was a vista of gold covering the walls and hanging from the ceiling in crystals, "gleaming like a jeweler's shop," the discoverer related. A million dollars worth of metal was taken from this single discovery! So exciting was this bonanza that a steel door was put in place to cover it. For a time, ore from the Cresson Mine was transported in locked boxcars accompanied by armed guards! Ultimately the Cresson Mine yielded $50 million.

The Gold Coin Mine, located in the heart of Victor, was the result of an accidental discovery made when blasting rock for the foundation of the Victor Hotel unearthed a rich vein of gold-bearing ore. The hotel was forgotten temporarily, and one of the largest of all mining structures in the district was erected on the site, one which was to become incredibly profitable and which by 1899 produced 30,000 tons of ore per year. Theodore Roosevelt during his 1901 visit to the district was treated to a tour of the Gold Coin Mine, descending the shaft to the 800-foot level.

Later the Gold Coin sported a beautiful brick shaft house with stained glass windows inspired by the Chartres Cathedral in France; the most elegant shaft house in history!

Historian Muriel S. Wolle relates that despite the distraction offered by the munificent outpourings of the Gold Coin Mine, the Hotel Victor was built and was formally opened on New Year's night in 1898. The Victor *Daily Record* in its January 2, 1898 edition reported that a grand ball and banquet was given by the Gold Coin Company and its employees:

"The entertainment really began in the shaft house of the Coin where the reading room was gracefully tendered to the men by Warren Woods, president of the company, and accepted on behalf of the miners.

"Over the engine room in the shaft house a bathroom and lockers for 125 men have been constructed, and in the adjoining room there are tables containing all the latest periodicals and best books, so that the employees on quitting work can bathe, change their clothing, and acquaint themselves with the latest thing in literature before leaving the mine.

"The presentation of the reading room was followed by a reception held by Mr. Woods in the parlors of the Hotel Victor, which was attended by fully 400 people, including all the Gold Coin employees.

"The hotel was a beautiful spectacle, being decorated throughout with green and yellow bunting, palms, potted plants, and leaves of lycopodium.

"At 11:30 the doors of the big dining room were opened and 350 guests were seated at once. No prince ever sat down to a banquet more delicious or served with more perfection."

In addition to the Victor Hotel, during the 1890s the mountain town boasted a $30,000 opera house which seated 1,200 patrons, a newly constructed city hall, and other amenities. Like Cripple Creek, Victor suffered an ordeal by fire. On August 21, 1899, the town was ravaged by a conflagration which began in the 999 Dance Hall. A few days later Victor, like Cripple Creek before it, began to rise again from the ashes.

Despite such benefits as those offered to the employees of the Gold Coin Mine, the district had many labor problems. Miners complained of bad working conditions and inequalities in pay. Mine owners and managers complained of high-grading, a practice whereby miners stole particularly high grade ore by hiding it in their lunch pails, in hollow pick handles, and on their persons. The Independence Mine claimed to have lost $1 million through this practice. As a result the mine required its employees to strip and change their clothes each night when leaving.

In 1893 forty mines in the district were working eight hours per day and paying $3. Nine others were also paying $3 but requiring a nine hour work day. Trouble began in January 1894 when a number of the eight-hour mines posted notices saying that from that time on just $2.50 would be paid for that amount of work. It was noted that profits and production could not support a higher wage, although wealth pouring from the mines belied this statement.

In February the miners voted to strike unless a uniform wage system of $3 for an eight hour day was instituted. The threat was ignored. In March a veritable war broke out and resulted in a confrontation between miners, who constructed a fort, and over 1,200 law enforcement officials. Governor Waite of Colorado intervened as mediator to represent the strikers with two others representing the owners. Agreed on was the eight hour day with $3 pay. Peace ensued for a number of years thereafter. In 1903 more problems arose, with the situation climaxing in 1904. In one ugly incident the railroad station at Independence was sabotaged, and 13 miners were killed in the explosion.

In 1895 a promotional book on the Cripple Creek district described a miner's life:

"So much is due the prospector that a few words of tribute will not be out of place. Among the men of no other calling or pursuit in life has the virtue of perseverance been exemplified in so high a degree. The word *fail* has no place in their vocabulary. With the genuine prospector, disappointment—utter present failure—is but a spur to renewed endeavor. His days are days of unvarying hardship; his nights are filled with the dream of the happiest realization of the hope which sus-

Victor, Colorado in April 1894. Within the next five years the city was to multiply in size many times over. The hills surrounding Victor were to become the location for many important mines.

Victor as seen in a later view, circa 1907. The city, a bustling metropolis shortly after the turn of the century in 1907, is just a fragment of its former self now. By 1970 the population had declined to just 250 inhabitants.

Victor scenes from the mid-1890s. Above is shown the July 4th, 1895 Independence Day celebration. To the right is the Bank of Victor, an institution which later failed because of inept management. Below is a street scene showing typical wooden buildings.

The Gold Coin Mine in Victor was the district's most famous. In this view part of the mining shaft structures can be seen, including a tall smokestack. So profitable was the Gold Coin Mine that the owners installed leaded glass windows modeled after those in the cathedral in Chartres, France, in one of the shaft houses!

The Gold Coin Mine located in the center of Victor.

The Gold Coin Mine Club House erected for the pleasure and benefit of miners.

Victor on fire, 1899. The entire business section, including much of the Gold Coin Mine facilities, burned to the ground.

tains him in his daily toil. His life is the life of exposure; his fare is of the rudest, by day he dines on salt pork, and by night revels at Delmonicos. He contends with his fellow man, as with nature, bravely, and if, perforce, he yields to the inevitable, he yields with cheeriness.

"Oftentimes his ambition for the sudden getting of money is that this may be as speedily dissipated in riotous living, in which event, the ease with which he turns from luxury to toil, is at least worthy of admiration. More often the object longed for and toiled for is the comfort and enjoyment of the family far away, or is the retrieving of a fortune lost, or the making of a fortune new. He may be the man of mature or advanced years looking back with regret at failure in some other pursuit; or another, looking ahead with the light of certain success shining from youthful eyes. In any event, and with a great majority, his intentions are of the best—his purpose wholesome. That which not infrequently comes from all this, is, poverty becomes wealth, and bankruptcy solvency. Without these incentives, whether good or bad, and without occasional realizations, there would be no seeking after hidden treasure, no trial of men's souls to their better tempering, by a war with nature for that which she so begrudgingly yields."

The miners' daily routine was difficult. The night life may have been a partial compensation. Highlighting cultural activities were operas and visiting vaudeville shows. Victor boasted a fine opera house, and Cripple Creek had two. After the turn of the century the nickelodeon theatre became an entertainment fixture as well. For 5c to 35c one could behold the latest songs and dances, minstrel shows, or flickering one-reel movie subjects.

Victor always played second fiddle to Cripple Creek, a situation which the townsfolk resented for Victor was the main site of gold production. When Cripple Creek was selected as the seat of Teller County it was over the protest and great competition mounted by the officials of Victor. Thus, when Victor could criticize Cripple Creek it lost no opportunity to do so.

July 4, 1897 fell on a Sunday. Some citizens of Cripple Creek suggested that the celebration be deferred to another day in honor of the Sabbath. The Victor *Daily Record* found this rather amusing:

"The goody-goody people of Cripple Creek mean to suppress all sorts of patriotic doings on the fourth, which falls on Sunday . . . Are not the gambling halls, bagnios (bordellos) and saloons of Cripple Creek running wide open on Sundays? Is it more of a desecration of the Sabbath to have a drilling match than to go on a Myers Avenue debauch? Is it worse to play baseball than faro or roulette? Oh, consistency thy keepers are not the divines of Cripple Creek."

On Myers Avenue, a block away from Cripple Creek's main business area, the red light district held forth with activity lasting 24 hours a day. Lining the street were such places as the Old Homestead (the best known; a tourist attraction today), the Red Light Dance Hall, the Mikado, the Royal Inn, Nell McClusky's, the Boston, and Laura Bell's. In addition to elegant establishments managed by madams, many operations were conducted by individual girls in rows of wooden shacks called cribs. Such names as Frankie, Eva, and Kitty were lettered on the front doors.

The presence of the red light district was tolerated by most residents. One of the most sentimental occasions in Cripple Creek's history was the funeral procession and parade which saw the body of Pearl De Vere, proprietor of the Old Homestead bordello, transported in 1897 to the Mount Pisgah Cemetery by the Elks Club Band, several mounted police officers, and a dozen or more carriages, many of which held well-known personalities from the Myers Avenue establishments.

Amongst the population women were scarce, and many Cripple Creek residents argued that the presence of the red light district made the surrounding streets safe for ordinary citizens.

In 1914, Julian Street, a popular writer of national acclaim, visited Cripple Creek to gather information for a travelogue. He was shown the city's economic accomplishments, the business district, the impressive mines, and other attractions and took copious notes. When the story reached print in *Collier's* magazine the good aspects of the district were nearly completely overlooked, and the Myers Avenue red light district formed the main subject. Incensed at being sold out by a journalist they considered to be a friend, the officials of Cripple Creek decided to change the name of Myers Avenue to Julian Street to "honor" their former visitor!

During this time the investor in gold shares had his choice of literally hundreds of mines to put his money in. Some such as the huge Portland Mine, the Gold Coin, the Anchoria Leland, the El Paso, and the Vindicator, to mention several outstanding examples, proved profitable, but hundreds of others were worthless holes or, as often happened, nothing but scraps of mining claim paper or printed stock certificates.

In 1895 the Cripple Creek district was the home of such interesting outfits as the Aetna Gold Mining Company, the Alice Gray Gold Mining Company, the Anaconda Gold Mining Company, the Atlantic and Pacific Gold Mining and Milling Company, the Bankers Gold Mining and Milling Company, the Ben Hur Gold Mining and Milling Company (named after Lew Wallace's novel, *Ben Hur*, which in the late 19th century was the literary sensation of America), the Black Wonder Gold Mining Company, the Bonanza Cripple

3230. ELKTON MINE, CRIPPLE CREEK, COLO.

The Elkton Mine, circa 1910.

THE ANCHORIA LELAND M & M Co.

The Anchoria Leland Mine was an active producer of gold ore for many years.

The immense Vindicator Mine littered the landscape with tons of mine tailings, as did other mines in the district.

Independence Mine on Battle Mountain, near Victor, was one of the leading producers during the great Cripple Creek District gold boom. Thousands of miners earned $3 per day in the shafts of the Independence and its competitors.

Theodore Roosevelt, wearing a dark jacket and standing in front of a post to the left of center above, is shown with his party deep in the Portland Mine at the 700-foot level. Roosevelt displayed a deep interest in Cripple Creek and Victor activities and visited there twice around the turn of the century.

Working conditions deep underground in the Cripple Creek District were often hazardous, as this illustration shows.

The El Paso Mine, one of the most profitable enterprises in the Cripple Creek District.

The Eagle Sampler shown in a view from the turn of the century.

Strong Mine during the early 1900s. The Cripple Creek District had over 500 mines at one time; several dozen large ones and hundreds of smaller enterprises.

Creek Gold Mining Company, the Bonanza King Gold Mining and Milling Company, the Bull Hill Gold Mining Company, and the C.O.D. Gold Mining Company (from which Spencer Penrose, later to build the Broadmoor Hotel, secured his fortune).

Or one could invest in the Columbine Gold Mining Company, the Dante Gold Mining Company, the Edwin Booth Gold Mining Company (named after one of America's most famous actors, who probably had no connection with it—a report at the time noted that "all efforts to obtain information are abortive and the office of the secretary seems to be abandoned"), the El Dorado Gold Mining and Milling Company, the Franklin Gold Mining Company, the Gilt Edge Mining, Leasing, and Bonding Company, the Gold Crater Mining Company, the Golden Age Gold Mining Company, the Golden Fleece Placer Mining Company (did *Fleece* refer to its treatment of investors?), the Golden Galleon Mining Company, the Gold Hill Bonanza Mining Company, the Gold Sovereign Mining and Tunnel Company, the Gold Standard Mining and Tunneling Company, the Good Hope Gold Mining Company, and the Harvard Gold Mining and Milling Company.

Then in the district there also were such attractions as the Home Run Gold Mining Company, the Iron Mask Gold Mining Company ("a recent incorporation of which but little is known," reads an 1895 report), the Jack Pot Mining Company (which proved to be a real bonanza; the Jack Pot vein of gold ore and the Doctor vein of gold ore were mined together, and in later years the mine became known as the Doctor-Jack Pot or, shortened, the Dr. Jackpot), and the Jenny Lind Mining and Milling Company (named for singer Jenny Lind, "the Swedish nightingale," who made her debut under the management of impresario P.T. Barnum in September 1850 at the Castle Garden in New York; the doors were opened at 5:00, and 5,000 persons filled the hall; gross receipts for the first concert were $17,864.05).

Or, how about the King Solomon Tunnel and Mining Company ("thus far no shares have been dealt on in this market, although several inquiries have come from the East in regard to the holdings of the company," an early news item read), the Lincoln Boy Mining and Tunnel Company, the Little Joan Mining and Milling Company ("exploration has proven the existence of at least two veins, though thus far no profit-yielding ore has been found"), the Magna Charta Mining and Milling Company, the Monarch Gold Mining and Milling Company, the Mutual Mining Milling Company ("it affords an attractive venture"), the Napoleon Gold Mining Company, the New Haven Gold Mining Company ("under its excellent management these shares represent an alluring proposition"), the New York Mining and Milling Company ("quite certain to be more pleasantly heard from in the future"), the Nipple Mountain Gold Mining Company, the Nugget Mining and Milling Company, and the Ophir Mining and Milling Company (named for the fabulous mountain of biblical fame).

Then there was the Pharmacist Mining Company which was founded by a druggist who desired to become a gold miner but didn't have the faintest inclination how to look for ore. He threw his hat into the air and started digging where it landed. He became a millionaire!

The Plymouth Rock Mining Company, the Poverty Gulch Gold Mining Company, the Star of the West Mining and Milling Company (about which it was noted that one million shares were available at $1 per each, but that the mine had thus far produced only $200 worth of metal!), the Wheel of Fortune Gold Mining Company, and the World Mining and Milling Company attracted other speculators.

While emphasis was on gold metal in Cripple Creek, Victor, and surrounding areas, silver provided an incidental situation of major numismatic interest. On November 13, 1900, the Victor *Daily Record* carried an article which told of the unique business enterprise of Joseph Lesher, a former silver miner who abandoned his holdings near Denver during the Panic of '93 and the resultant silver slump and moved to Victor at the advent of the gold rush. Fortunate investments in real estate resulted in his becoming a well-to-do businessman.

Believing that use of silver would revive the sluggish market for the metal, he had dies privately made in Denver, purchased silver bullion from a Colorado smelting firm, and proceeded to stamp out his own private "money;" octagonal tokens or ingots which he designated as *referendum souvenirs*, the term *referendum* meaning that it was up to the person offered such a piece to accept or refuse it.

With an issue price of $1.25, each piece, called a *Lesher dollar* by collectors today, represented a nice profit, for silver cost 65c per ounce at the time (a slump from the previous $1.29 value) and the minting cost was but 15c.

The November 13th article noted:

"The Lesher 'referendum' dollar represents an outlay of 80c. The manufacturer charges $1.25 for one of them . . . Although Mr. Lesher is convinced that the intrinsic value of an ounce of silver is 1.29, he does not insist that everyone shall accept his valuation and is prepared to guarantee the parity of his dollars by redeeming each coin in lawful money of the United States. He keeps cash at the Bank of Victor and expects to arrange with the cashier to cash the 'referendum' dollars in the same manner that checks are cashed . . . Each coin is numbered consecutively. Mr. Lesher believes that the merchants of Colorado could put his souvenirs into cir-

Gold Hill   Anaconda Mines and Tunnel   ANACONDA, DECEMBER, 1895   Blue Bell Mine   Hartzell Mill

Anaconda, in the Cripple Creek District, was one of several small communities which sprang up during the 1890s. It furnished the center for over a dozen mines, several of which are indicated above.

GILLETT

Gillett, which once had many homes and stores, and which was the scene in 1895 of a bullfight held in a specially-constructed arena, today is a ghost town. All of the original structures are gone, and just a few foundations remain. This view shows it in the 1890s.

culation by accepting them for goods and using them to pay clerks, rent, and local expenses. The silver mine owners could pay off their miners in referendum dollars and so open many idle properties. The mint has turned out 100 of the coins, but no effort has been made to put them into circulation. The manufacturer will first sell them as souvenirs and at the same time try to induce the businessmen to adopt his scheme. The money factory is located at the Lesher residence on West Victor Avenue. The proprietor is well known to Victor people, and all of them wish him success in his patriotic enterprise.''

The distressed silver area was not Victor or Cripple Creek, where silver was found only as a minor byproduct of gold, but, rather, was centered around Georgetown, Silver Plume, Idaho Springs, and other districts north near Denver which were idled when silver plummeted in value.

The November 13th newspaper article had a marvelous effect on Lesher's business, for the next day the Victor *Daily Record* reported:

"LESHER DOLLARS IN DEMAND - The publication of his silver scheme has caused a sensation and a rush for the souvenirs; merchants are anxious to use them. The account of Joseph Lesher's scheme to coin silver to private mint appearing in yesterday morning's newspaper has caused a sensation, not only in Victor and Colorado, but throughout the United States.

"It set businessmen, financiers, and mine owners to talking and thinking and brought novelty seekers in great numbers to Mr. Lesher's house. He and his wife had hardly begun breakfast in their little home when the rush began. It seemed that everyone in town was anxious to become the possessor of a 'referendum dollar.' One rap after another shook the front door and visitor after visitor was turned away with the assurance that there were not enough dollars on hand to go around.

"The most welcome visitor of the morning was A.B. Bumstead, proprietor of the grocery on North Street. Mr. Bumstead was welcome because he proposed to accept the souvenir as an exchange for groceries and give them out to anyone who wanted them in change.

"This took a load off Mr. Lesher's mind, because he did not relish the idea of having his peaceful home turned into a sub-treasury. He gave Mr. Bumstead all of the 'referendums' he had, about 100, and afterwards referred all comers to the dealer in groceries . . .''

It was further related that the first edition was completely sold out and that the next issue consisting of 500 pieces would be manufactured in Denver.

The idea spread in a modest way, and soon other area merchants joined A.B. Bumstead in the issuance of Lesher's novelties. J.M. Slusher, a Cripple Creek grocer at 165 Bennett Avenue; Sam Cohen, a jeweler in Victor;

D.W. Klein & Company, a liquor dealer in distant Pueblo; George Mullen of Victor, and one out-of-stater, J.E. Nelson & Company of Holdrege, Nebraska, were among those who had pieces made with their names stamped on them.

Adna G. Wilde, writing a brilliantly-researched article in *The Numismatist*, estimated that fewer than 1,900 Lesher dollars were made totally. Of this number he was able to trace the precise location of 384 individual pieces which have appeared in exhibitions, auction sales, and dealers' catalogs over the years, a task made easier by the fact that nearly all Lesher dollars were stamped with a distinctive serial number.

Lesher produced his pieces in 1900 and 1901, later discontinuing the venture in the face of combined government opposition and fading novelty of the idea. Within a few years the pieces became highly desired as collectors' items. In 1914, Farran Zerbe, who later operated the numismatic concession at the 1915 Panama Pacific International Exposition in San Francisco and who was at one time editor of *The Numismatist*, interviewed Lesher and obtained for posterity much of what is now known about his early coining operation.

Following the turn of the century the Cripple Creek area began to decline. The most readily accessible ores were exploited first. Later efforts had to be concentrated deep in the earth with greater expenses due to access, ventilation, and the ever-present problem of flooding.

By World War I only approximately 150 mines of the former 500 were still in operation. By 1920 the figure had dwindled to just 40, and by 1930 to even fewer.

In 1934 when President Franklin D. Roosevelt raised the price of gold to $35 an ounce a boom hit Cripple Creek once again. Many mines reopened, and by 1936 there were 135 busily extracting ore. From an annual production of $2.2 million in gold shipped in 1932, the lowest year, production rose to $5 million (at the new $35 per ounce valuation) in 1937. By 1949 production dwindled to under a half million dollars.

In 1951 the Carlton Mill was built near Victor. In that year a small boom occurred, and over $2 million worth of gold was produced. Slightly over a decade later gold mining had ceased to pay as a commercial venture, and nearly all mines were shuttered. Rising production costs and extraction difficulties made mining to yield gold valued at $35 per ounce impractical. In recent years the accelerated price of gold has brought renewed interest in the Cripple Creek area. The Golden Cycle Corporation, a publicly-traded company, has been active in this area as have been several others.

Today the Mollie Kathleen Mine is apt to be the most prominent to the visitors to the district, not because of the yellow metal it produces, but because of the many signs around town promoting it as a tourist attraction.

"Lesher dollars," privately issued by Joseph Lesher of Victor, Colorado, were distributed through several merchants, including J.M. Slusher of Cripple Creek, Boyd Park of Denver, and A.B. Bumstead of Victor.

Unlike the mining camp of Central City, Colorado, which is a tourist attraction year-round due to its proximity to Denver, Cripple Creek is far enough from civilization that many of the structures are in their original state of preservation, and few new buildings have been added. Tourism is there, but on a smaller scale.

Cripple Creek, true to its past, is still creating stories and legends, perhaps not on such a grand scale as earlier, but interesting nonetheless. A new tradition may be the towering fountain of ice, a frozen fountain some 30 or 40 feet high towering like a miniature Washington Monument. Upon asking about this at a local store and inquiring as to whether or not this was created each year, I was told that "the town did this for the first time this year —interesting, isn't it?"

Much of the gold from the Cripple Creek district was shipped to the Denver Assay Office. With the discovery of the Cripple Creek district lode agitation for a branch mint to strike coins at Denver was accelerated. On February 20, 1895, Congress provided a $500,000 appropriation to continue the assay office with the thought in mind of opening a mint when legal provisions could be complied with. In that same year $5,600,000 worth of gold and silver bullion was processed by the establishment. In 1906, when the Denver Mint, housed in a new Renaissance-style structure at West Colfax and Evans streets in downtown Denver, opened for business, much of the gold bullion came from the Cripple Creek district.

Many of the Philadelphia Mint gold coins of the 1890s and, logically, Denver gold coins after 1905 were produced from Cripple Creek gold.

Hold a gold coin from that era in your hand, and chances are good that it may have been made from bullion from what has been called "the world's greatest gold camp."

(Note: for a modern-day view of the Cripple Creek District see pages 289-294)

The Good Old Days

19th century elegance: San Francisco's Cliff House

7

A lot can be learned from history. The saying "Those who have not learned the lessons of history are condemned to repeat its mistakes" is one of my favorites. Conversely, the *successes* of history often provide interesting ideas and inspirations. In numismatics, history provides a fertile field for research. Indeed, it could be argued that numismatics and history are one and the same.

In 1957 I read Bernard Baruch's autobiography. He credited much of his investing success and profits to a particular book entitled *Extraordinary Popular Delusions and the Madness of Crowds,* a thick volume published in the early 19th century. Seeking a copy of this, I soon located a reprint and read it from cover to cover. Instead of finding the 19th century equivalent to data on how to follow the Dow-Jones Industrial Averages, how to benefit from reading *Forbes* or *Fortune* or *Business Week* magazines, I found stories about whimsical speculations of ancient times.

I was particularly enchanted by *tulipomania,* a speculative fever which swept Holland. Charles Mackay, author of the 1841 book, related:

"In 1634 the rage among the Dutch to possess tulips was so great that the ordinary industry of the country was neglected, and the population, even to its lowest dregs, embarked in the tulip trade. As the mania increased, prices augmented, until, in the year 1635, many persons were known to invest a fortune of 100,000 florins in the purchase of 40 roots. It then became necessary to sell them by their weight in *perits,* a small weight less than a grain. A tulip of the species called *Admiral Liefken,* weighing 400 perits, was worth 4,400 florins . . ."

It was further related that a speculator seeking to obtain one rare bulb offered to trade 12 acres of land for it, and that another investor offered for a single rare tulip bulb 4,600 florins, a new carriage, two gray horses, and other inducements.

"The demand for tulips of a rare species increased so much in the year 1636 that regular marts for their sale were established on the Stock Exchange of Amsterdam, in Rotterdam, Haarlem, Leyden, Alkmar, Hoorn, and other towns. Symptoms of gambling now became, for the first time, apparent. The stock-jobbers, ever on the alert for new speculation, dealt largely in tulips, making use of all the means they so well knew how to employ to cause fluctuations in prices. At first, as in all these gambling mania, confidence was at its height, and everybody gained. The tulip-jobbers speculated on the rise and fall of the tulip stocks and made large profits by buying when prices fell and selling out when they rose. Many individuals grew suddenly rich. A golden bait hung temptingly out before the people, and one after the other they rushed to the tulip marts, like flies around a honey pot.

"Everyone imagined that the passion for tulips would last forever and that the wealthy from every part of the world would send to Holland and pay whatever prices were asked for them. The riches of Europe would be concentrated on the shores of the Zuyder Zee, and poverty banished from the favored clime of Holland. Nobles, citizens, farmers, mechanics, seamen, footmen, maid-servants, even chimney-sweeps and old clotheswomen dabbled in tulips. People of all grades converted their property into cash and invested in flowers. Houses and lands were offered for sale at ruinously low prices, or assigned in payment of bargains made at the tulip mart. Foreigners became smitten with the same frenzy, and money poured into Holland from all directions."

Alas, this idyllic situation came to an end: "The more prudent began to see that this folly could not last forever. Rich people no longer bought the flowers to keep them in their gardens, but to sell them again at 100% profit. It was seen that somebody must lose fearfully in the end. As this conviction spread, prices fell and never rose again. Confidences were destroyed, and a universal panic seized upon the dealers."

What does all this have to do with rare coins? Actually, quite a bit. From the Mackay book I went to other economic references, including many read in conjunction

with my studies in finance at the Pennsylvania State University. I began to draw an analogy with coins. While coins have had a long trend of investment success, I soon resolved in my own mind that coins divided themselves into two main categories: first, traditional scarcities and rarities and, second, speculative issues.

About the same time in 1957-1958 the market in modern United States Proof sets was undergoing a rapid speculative phase. The 1936 Proof set, obtainable for $300 to $400 just a few months earlier, had zoomed in price almost overnight to $600. I had purchased a few months earlier ten 1936 Proof sets for $300 per set. The total investment of $3,000 was a substantial part of my business inventory. James F. Ruddy, attending a convention of the Central States Numismatic Society, telephoned me with the news that during this one convention alone the price of 1936 Proof sets had risen by nearly $100, and that Cincinnati dealer Sol Kaplan was bidding the unheard of high price of $600 per set. Alarmed at the unnatural situation, Jim thought I might want to sell my sets. With the just-read tulipomania in mind I authorized him to go to Sol Kaplan and make a commitment for the sale of my holdings, which he did. A short time later the price of 1936 Proof sets fell back sharply, not to regain the $600 level for a number of years thereafter. In one transaction my investment in *Extraordinary Popular Delusions and the Madness of Crowds* had paid for itself a hundred times over!

I was soon to discover that reference books were literally worth their weight in gold. Today I consider my library to be one of my most valuable possessions—valuable not in terms of resale value but of knowledge.

While many books provide lessons in economics, most deal with the recorded history of persons, places, and events. Although little of this is directly related to coins, I find it nonetheless fascinating. For example, I possess many volumes, some lavishly illustrated, about the 1893 World's Columbian Exposition, the world's fair that created a sensation in the twilight years of the nineteenth century. After spending an hour or two poring through these books even the most casual reader cannot help but see the 1893 Columbian half dollar, one of America's most common coins, in a new and fascinating light. Its history suddenly comes alive! Of course, many similar situations suggest themselves.

I once had a memorable excursion for a day back to the year 1876. No, I didn't have use of a time machine. I was sitting in my library with 10 or 15 books surrounding me. The subjects were varied: music, politics, exploration, and geography—to mention just a few. This was in 1976, 100 years later, the occasion of America's bicentennial.

Part of this interest had been prompted by several telephone calls from the Smithsonian Institution seeking help with historical data for their exhibit relating to the 1876 centennial.

The exhibit opened, and during the 1976 bicentennial year hundreds of thousands of visitors to the Smithsonian had a rare glimpse of life in 1876, one hundred years earlier. In fact the exhibit, originally scheduled for just one year, proved so popular that by the time I saw it for the first time in 1978 it still was drawing large crowds. On display were many different things ranging from an ornate Wooton desk with dozens of pigeonholes, secret compartments, and ornate decorations, to a huge Welte orchestrion or automatic orchestra on a balcony overlooking the display and rendering spine-tingling marches.

What was life like in 1876? Actually, from today's perspective it was wonderfully unhurried, wonderfully simple. Life was centered around the family at home. Condominiums were unheard of, vacation homes were something that royalty in Europe had but not the public, and a wonderful event would be taking the train for an excursion of a day or two along the seaside or perhaps staying at a lodge in the mountains.

Entertainment? Well-practiced tunes played on the Estey reed organ in the parlor provided a centerpiece for an evening's singing and merriment. Or, perhaps the organ was not an Estey but, rather, was made by Daniel Beatty, a competitor, from Washington, New Jersey. Beatty, a showman in the style of P.T. Barnum, sold thousands of ornately carved parlor reed organs by mail!

On Friday or Saturday night seeing a performance down at the local opera house would be the highlight of the week. Perhaps *East Lynne,* "The Greatest Heart Story Ever Told," would be playing. Or, perhaps the attraction would be *Blue Jeans* with its exciting sawmill scene with the hapless victim being pushed closer to the revolving blade by the villain. Adding a touch of excitement was a buzz-saw on a stand displayed in front of the opera house during the preceding week. Or, perhaps the night's entertainment was that old standby, *Uncle Tom's Cabin.*

Today we are apt to forget how simple life was then and that many things we have now were not in common use, were not invented, or for that matter in many instances were not even dreamed of in 1876.

Today if I want to acquire a coin for a customer here in California I can pick up the telephone and in a matter of seconds have a seller on the line in New York City or London. Not so a hundred years ago. The telephone was a novelty item which had just been patented (February 14, 1876) by Alexander Graham Bell. This useful device was generally unknown to the public and was hardly in popular use. In fact it was not until 1879 that two cities were connected telephonically—Lowell, Massachusetts and Boston.

1876, the year of the American centennial, saw hundreds of different coin designs being produced throughout the world. Here are shown just a few of them—including, at the bottom of the page, a rare 1876 pattern silver dollar (never adopted for official use) and an 1876 Assay Commission medal featuring the portrait of George Washington. Occasionally a numismatist will endeavor to collect as many different worldwide coins as possible from a given year. For example, Harry X Boosel and Roy Harte both independently assembled beautiful collections of the year 1873. Others have specialized in 1876, 1877, or, into the 20th century, their birth year. By this collecting method a wide panoply of interesting coinage designs can be observed.

Today if I want to take a picture of a friend I can grab a Polaroid camera, push a button, and a few seconds later have a dazzling color picture just as I want it—or if it isn't quite what I want I can try again and within a minute or two have several different poses in front of me. Or, I can take my Nikkormat, aim it at a rosebud, and the device will calculate the shutter speed and lens opening desired. After developing I can project a color slide of the flower as a brilliant picture ten feet wide on a screen. Not so in 1876. George Eastman had not even thought of the word *Kodak,* Edwin Land (inventor of the Polaroid camera) hadn't been born yet, and photography was something limited to studios with cumbersome apparatus taking pictures of people who maintained stiff poses for a period of several minutes or more so as not to blur the film. Color photography? Unheard of.

Today I can pick up a copy of *Scientific American* and read about the volcanic features of Mars, mysterious particles called *quarks,* the cataclysmic collapse of the ancient isle of Thera, the crystalline structure of rocks on the moon, or what marine life is like 30,000 feet deep in the Marianas Trench in the Pacific Ocean. A hundred years ago there were still portions of the United States which had not been explored, and the world was amazed by tales not of men returning from the moon but of explorations in the vastness of the Arctic.

Today I can go to the Los Angeles International Airport and board a Scandinavian Airlines System jet plane, take the polar route to Copenhagen, and in a few hours view out of the cabin window the vast Arctic Ocean which 100 years ago took many months and the lives of many people to reach, and even then the outcome was apt to be uncertain.

Los Angeles to Copenhagen in a few hours by jet plane—amazing! 100 years ago things were quite different. The latest way to get there would have been by combination train and ship. From Los Angeles I could have boarded a coal-burning, steam-puffing train headed eastward, the latest mode of transportation, considering that the transcontinental rail link had been completed at Ogden, Utah only seven years earlier in 1869 with the driving of the Golden Spike.

Arriving in Chicago I would switch trains for New York City. Then would come a steamship voyage (with auxiliary sails in case something went wrong with the "modern" propulsion system) to Liverpool, England. Then would come a transfer to another ship for Copenhagen. Total elapsed time? About ten days to two weeks or more depending upon the scheduling.

On the other hand, certain things haven't changed much in the intervening 100 or so years. Today we have our sex scandals in Congress. In 1876 one of the most talked about scandals was on the same subject and involved Henry Ward Beecher, America's most popular preacher. It seemed that Mr. Beecher had a dalliance with one of his parishioners, and the conduct did not involve things learned at the theological seminary!

Political scandals? In the 1970s we had Richard Nixon, Spiro Agnew, the Watergate mess, influence-peddling by Koreans, political contribution scandals by major corporations, and probably some more that we haven't heard about yet. Things haven't changed much in that regard either. The November 1876 election pitted Rutherford B. Hayes, who served in the Union Army during the Civil War and who was later a member of the House of Representatives and governor of Ohio from 1868 through 1872, against Samuel Jones Tilden, leader of a Democratic faction called the *Barnburners,* who was governor of New York in 1875 and 1876. More people voted for Tilden than voted for Hayes, but we don't read in history books today about President Tilden. The reason is that the contest, after a stormy debate, was decided by the Electoral Commission several months after the election, on February 27, 1877, in fact, in favor of Hayes—who actually received a smaller number of votes!

Also on people's minds at the time was one of the most famous political scandals our country has ever known—the Tammany Ring which controlled New York City and diverted vast sums to "Boss" Tweed and his political cronies. One of the most famous political cartoons in American history was by Thomas Nast and depicted the limp figure of Columbia, representing the American people, being mauled by the ferocious "Tammany tiger."

In 1979, as these words are being written, fortunately the United States of America is not at war. Of course, there is always a skirmish going on in one place or another—Israel, Africa, or wherever. In 1876 things were more or less peaceable in the United States as well. To be sure, however, the military wasn't sitting still. In 1874 gold was discovered in the Black Hills in the Dakota Territory. The only problem with this was that Dakota was the rightful property of the Sioux Indians. The secretary of war of the United States proclaimed that there would be a lot of problems if Congress didn't do something *legally* to acquire the Dakota Territory so that white gold miners from the East who wanted to go there and exploit the area would be able to do so without having to worry about what the rightful owners thought! This sparked the second war with the Sioux Indians. Of course, the Indians eventually lost.

But, in a way the Indians had the last word in 1876, the centennial year. General George A. Custer, who at the time was 36 years old and who had been a brigadier general since age 23 (in spite of the fact that he had graduated last in his class at West Point), and his five

RESIDENCE OF ALBERT GALLATIN, COR. 16TH AND H STREETS,
SACRAMENTO, CAL.

The residence of Albert Gallatin, shown in this view of the late 1870s, is a typical Victorian "palace." Virtually every "captain of industry," leader of commerce, or other successful entrepreneur would announce his success to the world by erecting a mansion. Some places, like many coal towns in Pennsylvania, had just one palatial edifice, home of the mine owner. Other locales such as San Francisco had dozens. Newport, Rhode Island, in particular was the home of many structures, erected as "summer cottages" by the Vanderbilt, Belmont, and other families, mainly of New York. The Breakers, built in the 1890s by the Vanderbilts, is open to Newport tourists today. Marble fireplaces, richly carved wood panels, French furniture, bathtubs with hot and cold running fresh water as well as salt water, and other trappings of elegance are interesting to see.

HERD OF BUFFALO STOPPING THE TRAIN.

companies in the U.S. 7th Cavalry were ambushed by Chief Sitting Bull's 3,500 Sioux and Cheyenne braves. The fierce three-hour battle saw Custer and his 266 enlisted men, officers, and others wiped out completely. In fact, the only survivor was a wounded horse.

Today I can sit in my living room, reach behind the sofa, and turn the dials on a Marantz quadraphonic receiver and hear sounds coming from all directions at once. Or, bored with the music of the Los Angeles Philharmonic Orchestra or Linda Ronstadt, I can turn on a television set and by a connecting cable see my choice of a dozen different shows, the latest stock market reports, the weather, a travelogue of Bali or Rhodes, the political news in Israel or Lebanon, the price of potatoes in Maine, and what is playing at the local movies.

Not so in 1876. Not only could I not listen to a quadraphonic receiver, I couldn't even listen to a phonograph! It wasn't until the following year, 1877, that the wizard of Menlo Park, Thomas Edison, invented this ingenious little device—a curious gadget which recorded on tinfoil and produced all sorts of screechy sounds. Perhaps I could go to the movies? No, it wasn't until the 1890s that the forerunner of the movies, Edison's *Kinetoscope,* and related devices became popular.

Today I can wander down Sunset Boulevard or Wilshire Boulevard here in Los Angeles and window shop for a snazzy little sports car from Germany or Japan, a functional station wagon ideal for a weekend trip to the Sierras, or one of dozens of different kinds of standard sedans. In 1876 such vehicles were unheard of (it was not until the 1880s that Daimler Benz in Germany invented the first gasoline-powered motor car, and it was not until a quarter century later that they achieved any element of popularity).

A hundred years ago I would have been content with that old standby, the horse. Even then, horse transportation was apt to be uncertain. While there weren't jam-ups on freeways and turnpikes with hay-powered equines, there were other disasters. Just a few years earlier in 1872 the Great Epizootic swept America and killed 4,000,000 horses before all was said and done; almost a quarter of the nation's supply! This disaster was precipitated by an unknown virus which attacked horses and which entered America through Canada. America's horsepower—in the literal sense of the word—was dealt a severe blow.

In Philadelphia and New York during the epidemic one saw the strange sight of men harnessed to carts and streetcars pulling them along thoroughfares! In countless hamlets, villages, and cities around the countries, homes and businesses went without heat for no horse-powered wagons were available to haul coal. Garbage piled up and stagnated. Much public transportation ground to a standstill.

There also was a happy element to the horse situation. On May 17, 1875, the first Kentucky Derby was run in Louisville, Kentucky. Earlier a group of far-seeing investors acquired a parcel of land nearby from the Churchill brothers. They laid out a track and constructed grandstands. In honor of the land owners it was called Churchill Downs. The first Kentucky Derby in 1875 saw 15 horses at the gate competing for a purse of $2,850.

In 1876 baseball, the sport popularized a few years earlier in Cooperstown, New York by Abner Doubleday, was elevated to professional status by the founding of the National League.

Football, the most popular spectator sport in America today from the standpoint of the number of people who watch games on television, was having its problems a century ago. In 1873 President Andrew White of Cornell University refused to let his football team travel to Cleveland to play a game against Michigan. His reason: "I will not permit 30 men to travel 400 miles to agitate a bag of wind."

Readers of James Michener's novel *Centennial* (the centennial in Michener's book refers to a mythical town in Colorado, not to the year 1876) are treated to a virtually first-person account of the vast herds of buffalo which once roamed America. In 1860 it was estimated that approximately 60,000,000 of these ponderous beasts, actually properly called *bisons* from a zoological viewpoint, roamed the West. Then in 1871 something happened. A tanner in Vermont developed a process of treating buffalo hide to make it commercially usable as leather. The following year, 1872, a vast slaughter began. In 1889 a survey was taken and just 551—that's right, just 551 individual animals—remained. In 1876, the year of our nation's centennial, a popular *sport* out West was to shoot helpless buffalo from a train window.

Indians raised their annoying heads and often objected to incursions of buffalo hunters on their territory. However, this usually was not a major problem. The ever-inventive United States government would send in the Army and destroy all of the Indians' possessions, either forcing them to abject surrender or else driving them off to another location without homes, food, implements, horses, or other necessities of life. There didn't seem to be a great deal of objection about the treatment of the Indians in 1876, for they were well-known "enemies."

In a lighter vein, P.T. Barnum, America's most fabulous showman, opened his circus a few years before 1876 in New York City and billed it as *The Greatest Show on Earth.* Earlier, Barnum had achieved fame with his American Museum in New York City, an exhibition of stuffed animals and oddities, prehistoric curiosities, and other marvels. Today the American Museum, which

THE KING OF DESKS.

Wooton's Patent
CABINET OFFICE SECRETARY.

COMPACT, NEAT AND USEFUL.

THE ABOVE CUT REPRESENTS DESK OPEN.

For Full Information, Catalogues, Testimonials, &c., call on or address

THE WOOTON DESK CO.,

DESIGNERS AND MANUFACTURERS,

INDIANAPOLIS, IND.

The Wooton Patent Secretary, first marketed on a large scale in 1876, was typical of the elegance and ornateness of the era.

was destroyed in a conflagration, is perhaps best remembered for a sign which is alleged to have read: "This way to the egress," *egress* meaning exit. People would follow the sign hoping to see some type of a rare animal and would, instead, be out on the sidewalks of New York City forced to pay another admission if they wanted to continue their tour!

Barnum, always with an eye for showmanship, brought Jenny Lind, a relatively unknown Swedish singer, to America and billed her as the most fabulous entertainer on earth. Hundreds of thousands of Americans flocked to see her. General Tom Thumb, the well-known midget, was another Barnum exploitation, as was Jumbo the elephant, who we remember today as the origin of a descriptive adjective noting large size.

Today one can go to a shopping center on Long Island, New York, and spend a week there without seeing all of the merchandise—or probably without seeing all of the individual stores, for that matter. The same is true, of course, in Boston, Denver, Cleveland, Miami, Portland, and dozens of other places.

In 1876 things were different. The shopping center was unheard of. Filling the bill were specialty stores—a department store which was usually known as a *dry goods* store for the things it sold were *dry*: cloth, hardware, and the like; the grocery store with its open barrels of cookies, crackers, and nuts; the blacksmith who would make to your order a pair of andirons if you could come back for them a week later; and, when shopping was finished, an old-fashioned soda parlor where with your favorite sweetheart you could share lemon-flavored water.

Shopping by mail was just beginning to be popular. You might have found the Montgomery Ward catalog interesting. This firm, four years old in 1876, enticed the public with a wide variety of interesting things illustrated by engravings in its "wishbook."

Today collectors often wonder about ordering coins through the mail. "You mean a great percentage of the rare coin business in America is actually conducted by mail?" is often the question of a beginning collector who does not realize that nearly all large transactions take place this way. In 1876 not only were coins ordered by mail, but quite a few other things were also. As noted, Daniel Beatty of Washington, New Jersey, built up a large mail order business by selling parlor reed organs—cumbersome Victorian devices which measured nearly seven feet high in many instances—by precisely this method! Sears, Roebuck & Company likewise did an active mail order trade in this area.

Then, too, there was a virtually endless variety of patent medicine to be obtained by mail or from your local druggist's shelves. During the late 19th century one could order all sorts of lotions and potions from Lydia Pinkham in Massachusetts. All sorts of ailments from losing hair to "female disorders" to general lethargy could be cured, so it was claimed.

From Lockport, New York, the Seven Sutherland Sisters advertised that "ladies should remember it's the hair, not the hat, that makes a woman attractive." Backing up this claim were the seven sisters in question, Sarah Sutherland with hair three feet long, Victoria whose locks measured seven feet, Isabella at six feet, Grace at five feet, Naomi at five-and-a-half feet, Dora at four-and-a-half feet, and Mary at six feet. To soothe the fears of skeptics who might hesitate to mail the appropriate amount to Lockport, Dr. J.B. Duff, former vice president of the Louisiana College of Pharmacy and Medicine, was featured in advertisements: "Having made a chemical analysis of the hair grower prepared by the seven long-haired sisters, I hereby certify that I found it free from all injurious substances, being entirely composed of vegetable preparations. It is beyond question the best preparation for the hair ever made—and I cheerfully endorse it."

In 1862 Dr. J.C. Ayer, patent medicine salesman extraordinaire of Lowell, Massachusetts, was one of the many customers for John Gault's encased postage stamps, the mica-fronted brass frames which housed three-cent, five-cent, and other stamps of the period and which served to fill the need for pocket change during the Civil War.

Particularly popular were Ayer's pills "to purify the blood," Ayer's cathartic pills ("an unfailing remedy for constipation, indigestion, dyspepsia, biliousness, heartburn, loss of appetite, foul stomach and breath, nausea, flatulency, dizziness, headache, numbness, loss of memory, jaundice, diarrhea, dysentery, and disorders of the liver"), Ayer's Ague Cure, Ayer's Cherry Pectoral, Ayer's Hair Vigor, and Ayer's Sarsaparilla.

To promote its various products each year the firm would issue *Ayer's American Almanac* which extolled the virtues of the various nostrums amidst helpful information relating to the phases of the moon, astrology, and "miscellaneous phenomena." Spicing up the text were jokes. Samples:

"Doctor, what is to be done? My daughter seems to be going blind, and she is just getting ready for her wedding!" "Let her go right on, if anything will open her eyes, marriage will."

Another: "Beautiful ladies are angry if gazed at, and indignant if not."

Another: Judge: "Prisoner, are you married?" Prisoner: "No, Your Honor, those scratches on my face came from stumbling over a barbed wire fence in the dark."

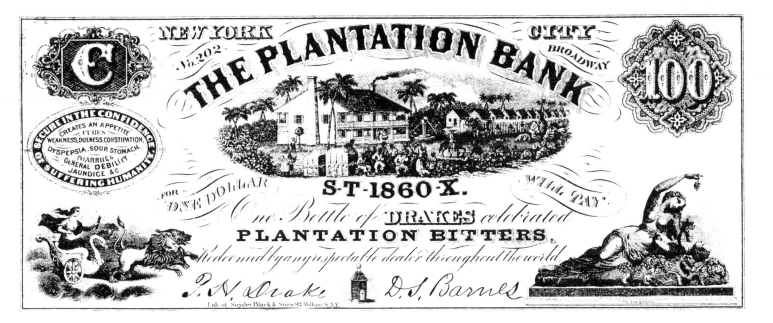

Ayer's Sarsaparilla.

AYER'S COMPOUND EXTRACT OF SARSAPARILLA is a skilfully-prepared combination of the best alterative medicines, classified in science as blood-purifiers.

It is composed of the Sarsaparilla root of the tropics, everywhere known as an alterative of great value, combined with Stillingia, Yellow Dock and Mandrake, all celebrated for curative qualities.

The medicinal principles of these vegetable ingredients are extracted in a manner which draws out and preserves their virtues entire and undiminished. Chemically united with the Iodides of Potassium and Iron, they form a medicine of unsurpassed power, being highly concentrated to the degree required for a powerful alterative, and combining blood-making, blood-cleansing, and health-restoring qualities in that nice proportion necessary to give each its full healing and curative influence. In the manufacture of AYER'S SARSAPARILLA, *quality is the paramount consideration.* By our processes perfect uniformity in its strength is secured, — all the vegetable ingredients contained in it being gathered for us at the precise period of their medicinal maturity, — and it is as rich in the virtues that compose it as it can be made.

Other preparations, made of cheaper materials, of little, if any, virtue, and put up in larger bottles, or sold for less price, only deceive and disappoint the sick. The concentrated power and curative virtues of AYER'S SARSAPARILLA are such that it is by far the best and most reliable, as well as cheapest, medicine, that can be used. When you are sick, the best medicine is poor enough.

Scrofula, or King's Evil, is a taint or infection in the blood, which vitiates the vital forces, weakens their power, and disorders or deranges their functions. It acts like a latent poison, reducing the vitality of the blood, and weakening and disabling the organs whose office is to secrete and expel the effete and unwholesome materials from the blood and body, thereby constantly adding to the foul corruptions, which dwell and gender in the blood, and rot out, as it were, the machinery of life.

Scrofula may be hereditary, or may be caused by impure vaccination, low living, unwholesome food, filth, impure air, exhausting habits and diseases, want of exercise, digestive derangements, especially in persons of sedentary habits, and life in localities that are deprived of fresh air and sunlight. Habitual intemperance may create it through the decline of vitality which it brings.

Scrofula predisposes to diseases of the lungs, liver, kidneys, digestive and uterine apparatus. When Scrofula is present in the system, one or more of the following manifestations may be found: a want of due bodily symmetry, small, weak, or crooked limbs; pale, inflated countenance, often fair, of transparent whiteness, sometimes with waxy yellowness about the mouth, or an agreeable redness of the cheeks, blue rings around the eyes, which are frequently large and of a pearly or bluish whiteness, especially where the disorder has attacked the lungs; when settled on the digestive apparatus, the vessels of the eyes may be noticeably injected with blood. The muscles commonly want firmness, and the whole system is deficient in stamina; the movements are sluggish, the habit of the body indolent, and the intellect dull. The eyelids are often swollen, inflamed and unclean; the nose is wide or swollen, and red or shining; the mouth and teeth are foul; the appetite is irregular, sometimes impaired, and sometimes voracious; the stomach is often sour, the breath fetid, and the bowels irregular; the limbs are wanting in firmness, and the joints weak, and general lassitude and debility are felt, with incapacity for physical or mental exertion. The latent virus of Scrofula induces not only ulcerous and tuberculous diseases, but also a variety of other disorders, such as **Ulcerations of the Liver, Stomach, Kidneys, Eruptions, and Eruptive Diseases of the Skin, St. Anthony's Fire, Rose or Erysipelas, Pimples, Face Grubs, Pustules, Blotches, Boils, Tumors, Tetter and Salt Rheum, Scaldhead, Ringworm, Ulcers and Sores, Rheumatism, Neuralgia, Pain in the Bones, Side, and Head, Female Weakness, Sterility, Leucorrhœa arising from internal ulceration and uterine disease, Dropsy, Dyspepsia, Emaciation, General Debility,** and, in many cases, **Consumption.**

Treatment. — Scrofula is so subtle, and so firmly engrafts itself on the system, that only the most searching and potent remedial agencies can remove it. To eradicate Scrofula from the system, commence taking AYER'S SARSAPARILLA in moderate doses, — for an adult, one teaspoonful three times a day, increasing gradually as it is found to agree with the stomach until it reaches nearly two teaspoonfuls. Continue this dose until some improvement is felt, and the disorder will gradually disappear.

BURNETT'S
Cooking Extracts.

LEMON, VANILLA, ALMOND, ROSE, NUTMEG, PEACH, CELERY, CINNAMON, CLOVES, NECTARINE, GINGER, and ORANGE, are the names of BURNETT'S STANDARD FLAVORING EXTRACTS.

Throat Diseases.

" Brown's Bronchial Troches, or Cough Lozenges. *From Rev. E. H. Pratt, East Woodstock, Conn.* I feel grateful to you, for placing within the reach of the suffering so valuable a remedy. I have used the Troches three years, with great benefit, not less to my general health than to my throat. I recommend them with great pleasure on every hand."

ADVERTISEMENTS.

Burnett's Cocoaine.

This is an article which we can heartily recommend, and that from knowing its great virtues. One particular case in our family of its efficacy we will mention. The person had suffered with a low fever, which was most tedious, and which left her with a terrible neuralgia in the head. The effect of these complaints was to cause much of the hair to fall off, and there seemed to be no power in the skin to give life to what remained. After she had tried some other preparations with no good results, we procured for her a bottle of *Cocoaine,* and the change which its use soon made was truly remarkable. The roots of the hair at once received new life, and before a bottle had been used the large spot upon the top of the head which appeared to be bald, was covered with what seemed a new growth of hair. And now she has as fine and healthy a head of hair as before her sickness. This Cocoaine is also a valuable article for children's hair, which is very apt to be dry. A very small quantity will keep their hair moist and their heads clean.

What we say of this article we say from our own actual knowledge, not for the sake of puffing the Cocoaine, but because we think others may be benefitted by our experience.
— *Boston Christian Freeman.*

Products such as Drake's Plantation Bitters, Ayer's Sarsaparilla, Burnett's Cooking Extracts, Burnett's Cocoaine, and Brown's Bronchial Troches, here shown in nineteenth century advertisements, were featured on encased postage stamps which circulated as currency during the Civil War.

ENCASED POSTAGE STAMPS, the invention of J. Gault, were patented in August, 1862. Each unit consisted of an official United States postage stamp of the denomination of 1, 2, 3, 5, 10, 12, 24, 30, or 90 cents, encased in a stamped brass frame with a protective clear mica cover.

At the time official government coins of all denominations were being hoarded. Encased postage stamps, which circulated at the value of the stamp therein, furnished a convenient unit for small transactions. Most pieces issued were of the 1, 3, and 5 cent denominations.

The back of each stamp bore the inscription of a merchant who purchased advertising space. Gault himself, through his firm, Kirkpatrick & Gault, 1 Park Place, New York City, advertised as did many others.

Dr. J.C. Ayer, a patent medicine promoter from Lowell, Massachusetts, used encased postage stamps to promote his Cathartic Pills and his Sarsaparilla. According to an encased postage stamp, Ayer's Sarsaparilla was ideal "to purify the blood." Another simply said "Take Ayer's Pills," presumably for anything that ailed you.

A prolific advertiser on encased postage stamps as well as magazines and periodicals of the period was Drake's Plantation Bitters, an alcoholic preparation which was marketed in amber bottles shaped like a log cabin. Proclaimed on the encased postage stamps was the mysterious Drake's trademark, "S.T. 1860. X." It was never stated what this meant, although one historian has proposed that it referred to the inception of the Drake business itself as: "Started Trade in 1860 with $10." A few years ago many crates of this substance were found on a river bottom, where they had lain since Civil War days when a paddlewheel steamer went to the bottom. An analysis revealed that the poison strychnine was one of the ingredients!

Other encased postage stamps proclaimed the services of the Tremont House, a Chicago hotel; the North America Life Insurance Company, of 63 William Street, New York; Brown's Bronchial Troches, which were recommended for coughs and colds; the Irving House, a New York hotel at Broadway and Twelfth Street, which featured the European plan; Mendum's Family Wine Emporium; Joseph L. Bates of Boston, Massachusetts, who offered "fancy goods" (including stereopticon viewers, although these are not specifically mentioned on the encased postage stamps); and White the Hatter of New York.

John Shillito & Company, the Cincinnati department store which is still in business today, advertised on encased postage stamps, as did Lord & Taylor. The latter firm, known today for its fashions, advertised in 1862 that it sold dry goods at three New York City locations, 461-467 Broadway, 255-261 Grand Street, and 47-49 Catherine Street in New York.

Most merchants appear on encased postage stamps of several different denominations. For example, the North America Life Insurance Company advertisement can be found on issues of the 1c, 3c, 5c, 10c, and 12c values. While two-cent encased postage stamps are listed in the references, collectors believe that these were experimental issues or else issues produced at a later date and were not made for actual circulation. Encased postage stamps of higher denominations such as 24, 30, and particularly 90 cent values are rarely seen.

It is believed that most encased postage stamps were produced by the Scovill Company, maker of brass, copper, and other metal goods in Waterbury, Connecticut. During the 1833-1844 years Scovill was a leading manufacturer of large-cent-size Hard Times tokens.

While some collectors endeavor to obtain an encased postage stamp of each variety and each denomination, most content themselves with a representative display of as many different individual merchants as possible, without regard to the stamp value.

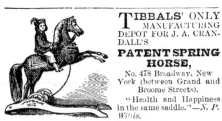

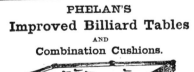

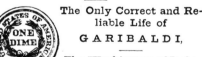

And, one more: "To what do you attribute your longevity?" asked an investigator of a centenarian. "To the fact that I never died," was the conclusive reply.

Speaking of jokes, around the same time H.C. Percy, cashier of the Home Savings Bank of Norfolk, Virginia, published *Our Cashier's Scrapbook; Being Bank Notes, New and Old, for General Circulation.* The red cloth-covered volume was a whimsical look at banking and contained such humor as:

"John, one of our wealthy customers, having occasion to leave town for a few days, left a dozen checks signed in blank for use of his better half, who proceeded, of course, to overdraw his account. On his return he protested, but to no avail, for the fair but sophisticated lady insisted that it couldn't possibly be, as there were three of the checks left now which hadn't been used at all!"

Buildings were very much in the public eye a hundred years ago. Citizens of a county would be justifiably proud of their new courthouse and would buy engraved pictures of it. Popular wall decorations in 1876 were *balloon views* (airplanes were to become popular years after the Wright Brothers escapade at Kitty Hawk in 1903) of one's town or city. Actually, these were not made from a balloon at all but, rather, were made in a lithographic studio by laying out a sketch of the city and drawing in different prominent buildings. Around the border of the view or map would be outstanding public structures, churches, and the homes of prominent citizens. Architecture varied, but many of the larger edifices were in the Victorian style—the more ornate the better! I, for one, think that 1876 was better than today in this regard. During the present time a *great* new building is apt to be a shapeless vertical rectangle with all of the artistic charm of an unpainted children's building block.

In recent years we have all enjoyed reading the financial adventures of Paul Getty, Howard Hughes, and Aristotle Onassis. Now that these colorful people have died the world has lost something.

In 1876 America had its financial heroes, or *captains of industry,* as they later became popularly known. In that year the H.J. Heinz Co., organized in Pittsburgh, Pennsylvania, was seven years old and was actively marketing the first selections in its famous *57 Varieties.* The first item sold? Horseradish.

Six years before the centennial, John D. Rockefeller founded in 1870 the Standard Oil Company of Ohio and capitalized it at $1,000,000. This laid the foundation for the family's multibillion dollar wealth we read of today.

In 1871, the same year that Mrs. O'Leary's historic and possibly mythical cow kicked over a lantern in Chicago and subsequently started a fire which destroyed $200,000,000 worth of property and left 90,000 people homeless, J.P. Morgan in New York City established Drexler, Morgan & Company, a banking firm. Later the name was simplified to the J.P. Morgan Company.

J.P. was a man of many talents. He had his fingers in banking, railroads, coal, shipping, utilities, steel, insurance, and probably a few other things as well. Later, shortly after the turn of the century, he founded the United States Steel Corporation, the world's first billion-dollar company. In doing this he purchased the assets of Andrew Carnegie. It is related that Carnegie made the deal with the Morgan interests while he was on a transatlantic steamer. The Morgan representative had an offer but did not reveal it to Carnegie, preferring instead to have Carnegie name his price. Carnegie did, and the deal was consummated. Later J.P. Morgan told Andrew Carnegie that he would have been willing to have paid $100,000,000 more if it had been necessary. Reportedly, this made Carnegie unhappy for the rest of his life!

Perhaps the most illustrious financial family in 1876 was the Vanderbilt clan. The following year, on January 4, 1877, Cornelius Vanderbilt passed away, leaving behind him a fortune estimated at $100,000,000. He started his career as a ferryboat captain; then he became involved in the steamboat business during Civil War. Later he got into railroads, the prime growth industry of the late 19th century, and was instrumental in the formation of the New York Central Railroad which commenced operations in 1873, and which established the first continuous train route between New York and Chicago.

A few years later, in 1879, a newspaper reporter demanded an interview with a relative, William H. Vanderbilt, then president of the New York Central Railroad. Vanderbilt was told that the public was eager to hear his views. "The public be damned!" was Vanderbilt's immortal reply.

In the same year, 1879, Frank W. Woolworth in Lancaster, Pennsylvania, succeeded in his second attempt to establish a store carrying merchandise mainly priced at five and ten cents. Soon bright red signs with golden letters proclaimed the merits of F.W. Woolworth all over America, and later, in Britain as well. This spawned a score of imitators including S.H. Kress, S.S. Kresge, and J.J. Newberry, to name just a few.

In 1876, the centennial year, there were about 45 million people in the United States, one-fifth of the population today. In 1874 construction was begun for the 1876 Centennial Exhibition to celebrate the 100th anniversary of American independence. Inspired by such events as the first world's fair held in London in 1851, the New York Exhibition of 1853, the Dublin Exhibition of the same year, the Paris Exhibition of 1855, the Great International Exhibition in London in 1862, the

WESTERN HOTEL.

ERECTED 1875.

Nọs 209 TO 219 K ST

Wᴹ LAND, PROPᴿ

SACRAMENTO, CAL.

THIS NEW AND ELEGANTLY FURNISHED HOTEL, BUT TWO BLOCKS FROM RAIL ROAD DEPOT AND STEAMBOAT LANDING, IS ONE OF THE FINEST HOUSES ON THE COAST. WITH BEAUTIFUL FRESCOED WALLS AND ALL MODERN IMPROVEMENTS, INCLUDING ELEVATOR, FIRE HYDRANT EXTINGUISHERS AND ESCAPES ON EACH FLOOR. BOARD AND LODGING $1. TO $2. PER DAY. **MEALS 25 CENTS.**
A COACH WILL BE AT ALL TRAINS AND BOATS TO CONVEY PASSENGERS AND SMALL BAGGAGE TO AND FROM THE HOUSE FREE OF CHARGE.

The Western Hotel, erected in Sacramento in 1875, is typical of a "grand hotel" of the late 19th century. While this edifice boasted "all modern improvements, including an elevator," a competitor a few years later was to advertise that "we don't have elevators or electricity, just comfortable beds and peaceful surroundings."

During the late 19th century elegant hotels were built in many locations throughout America, often at the terminus of a railroad track. To luxurious hotels in the White Mountains of New Hampshire went many excursion trains from New York and Boston. Others headed south to grand hotels along the New Jersey shore. For a time the Congress Hall Hotel in Cape May was used as "the summer White House" by the president.

On the West Coast San Francisco's Palace Hotel achieved renown as a center for high society and related functions. Near San Diego the Del Coronado, erected in the 1890s and still standing today as a cultural and historic landmark, attracted throngs of visitors who wanted to spend a week or two by the seaside.

INTERIOR VIEW OF A SCHOOL-HOUSE IN 1870.

In the 1870s reading, writing, and arithmetic were taught in schools as well as such virtues as respect for one's parents and belief in God. Have we progressed during the intervening years? A good question!

DEXTER SPRING CO.
HULTON, NEAR PITTSBURGH, PA.

Horsepower, in the most literal sense of the word, provided transportation during the 19th century. A small open carriage such as that shown above was ideal for short trips.

BANGS' SECTIONAL DRUG STORES

Patented Oct. 26, 1886.

The above represents the interior view of the new Opera House Pharmacy of Messrs. **Camp & Ellis,** Council Bluffs, Iowa. The manner in which it is spoken of by the Press of that city and Omaha and by the citizens and the traveling men shows very plainly how effectively fine stores advertise and advance generally the interests of the proprietors. Messrs. Camp & Ellis write:

MR. C. H. BANGS, Dear Sir:—We appreciate and thank you very much for the efforts made in getting us up a fine store and the many words of praise by our patrons and friends show that it is appreciated by them. All the *traveling men* are very much taken with it and pronounce it the finest store in the west. Yours truly, CAMP & ELLIS.

The following from the *Omaha Daily Bee* expresses the general sentiment: "**A Little Palace.** The new drug store of Camp & Ellis, in the Opera House block, is to be opened this morning. Last evening the *Bee* man had the privilege of looking in upon it, while the finishing touches were being put on, and by the brightness of the electric light it appeared like a little palace. It is not saying too much to pronounce it the finest fitted drug store in the west, Mr. Bangs, of Boston, an old druggist, who has of late years made a specialty of furnishings for drug stores in this line, and who has fitted up numerous ones in the east, gave this his personal attention. Every part is specially designed and most nearly all covered by patents. The finishings and furnishings are elegant The shelvings, counters, show cases, etc, are of solid cherry, ornamented with bronzes, and trimmed with dark green mottled marble. It has a parquette floor, hard wood inlaid. Choice bits of statuary, mirrors, China silk drapings and various other ornamentations are arranged with rare taste, making the store seem indeed palatial. Every possible convenience is provided for the display and handling of druggists' fancy sundries. It is the intention of these young men to confine their business to this line and prescriptions. They are both thoroughly experienced and educated, and with their extended acquaintance and popularity cannot but find their new venture a great success. The new store is a great credit to Council Bluffs, and is one in which all can take pride."

The more than flattering success of Messrs. Camp & Ellis since opening their new store is only another proof of the advantages secured by placing your business in the lead by showing your customers that you intend to occupy that position by the character of the place you fit up and ask them to patronize.

There are to-day hundreds of places and opportunities for stores of the highest class in modern fittings and appliances, with success assured from the start, where an inferior store would be a failure or only a moderate living. It is the latter class that feel soonest the pinch of dull trade or hard times, their customers being usually of the poorer class. In the fitting of a drug store much money may be expended without attaining the desired effect, viz., to impress upon your customer or the public the neatness and elegance of your store and stock, and to display the whole to the best advantage possible. To do this successfully requires either exceptional taste or experience, or both combined.

Many letters received from parties regarding fixtures would seem to indicate that they expect to buy by the yard or foot and that a yard of ash, cherry or walnut fixtures of a given make should govern the price of a yard of all makes regardless of results to be attained. To attain the best results careful arrangement with regard to effect must be considered as well as convenience in each and every department. To secure this the advertiser gives his customers the benefit of long experience in the drug business and the experience and taste acquired in the fitting of a large number of elegant stores. In addition to this you obtain the most practical style of fixture in the world in Bangs' Patent Sectional Druggists' Fixtures.

In Writing for Estimate send Floor Plan.

C. H. BANGS

111 Inman Street, Cambridgeport, Mass.   35 Murray Street, New York.

The Only Exclusive Manufacturer of Druggists' Furniture in the U. S.

An ornate drugstore interior from the 19th century.

Paris Exhibition of 1867, and the recent Vienna Exposition of 1873, America's leaders, particularly the prominent citizens of Philadelphia, wanted to show the world that America was a fully developed country with manufacturing and industry, art, science, and so on—and not just an insignificant former possession of England. The Centennial Exhibition would do the trick! And, indeed it did.

On July 4, 1874 the groundbreaking ceremony for the event took place in Philadelphia's Fairmount Park. Two years later some 294 buildings had been erected and 153 acres had been landscaped with grass, flowers, and shrubs.

Important structures included the Main Building which was 20 acres in size, the Art Gallery which checked in at an acre and a half, Machinery Hall with ten acres of space, Horticultural Hall with one and one quarter acre of space, and Agricultural Hall which comprised eight acres of enclosure. In addition there was an extensive zoological and botanical garden outside.

While it was officially called the Centennial *Exhibition*, the term *exposition* inevitably crept into popular but unofficial use. Likewise, even within the context of the official use of the exhibition word, some authorities referred to it as the 1876 *International* Exhibition and others to the 1876 *Centennial* Exhibition. Exhibition or exposition, international and centennial, it really didn't make much difference for it was the highlight of America at the time and everyone knew all about it!

The grand event opened on May 10, 1876. Accounts revealed that over 100,000 people thronged through the 106 admission gates.

Lending his fame to opening day was President Ulysses S. Grant and Dom Pedro, the latter being the Emperor of Brazil; the first major foreign head of state ever to visit America. Richard Wagner composed for the occasion the *Grand Centennial March*, which was played as the dignitaries mounted the grandstand. A chorus variously estimated at 800 to 1,000 voices sung John Greenleaf Whittier's *Centennial Hymn* and other selections.

Just as Dom Pedro was about to be presented to the audience Susan B. Anthony and four other women rushed to the grandstand and presented a Declaration of Women's Rights which threw the carefully planned proceedings into a grand turmoil!

There were other problems as well. On May 10th, opening day, it was reported that 504 children got lost and 161 arrests were made. Arrests for what? 160 for shoplifting and stealing and one for, believe it or not, fornication!

Over the years each world's fair has had a central attraction. The New York World's Fair in 1964 had its Unisphere, a steel representation of the globe with satellites around it, the 1962 Seattle World's Fair had its still-operating Space Needle with a restaurant on the top, the 1939 World's Fair had the Trylon and Perisphere, and so on. The most stunning sight to visitors at the 1876 Centennial Exhibition was the giant Corliss steam engine—a huge walking-beam steam-powered device with a mammoth 56-ton revolving flywheel. This was on exhibit in Machinery Hall and served to power many other devices by means of shafts, gears, and pulleys. A contemporary description notes that on opening day:

"The President of the United States [Grant], the Emperor of Brazil, and George H. Corliss [manufacturer of the awesome gadget] then ascended the platform of the mammoth motor. The President, having taken hold of the valve-lever of one engine and the Emperor of another valve-lever, both gave the turn simultaneously. Steam was on, the great walking beam began to ascend and descend, the engine was in motion, and eight miles of shafting and hundreds of machines of all descriptions were in operation and the International Exhibition of 1876 was at that instant thrown open to the world."

From fame to the junkyard: following the closing of the Exhibition the Corliss engine was taken to Corliss' factory in Providence, Rhode Island. In 1880 George M. Pullman (of railroad car fame) purchased the device and took it to Chicago where it did hard work powering his manufacturing facilities. Later, when Pullman's factory was converted to electricity, the Corliss engine which had once thrilled the world was dismantled, and in 1911 it was sold for scrap iron.

Many guide books to the 1876 International Exhibition were published. Some of these were pamphlets issued by railroads, hotels, and other financially-motivated parties. Others were hardbound books for sale to the public. Most were lavishly illustrated with engravings.

A wondrous array of products greeted the visitor to the Exhibition. Emphasis was on manufactured items, particularly machinery and mechanical devices. Electricity, while known at the time, was in its infancy, so most things were steam-powered or operated by springs or weights. Electricity was not completely overlooked, however. For example, a huge pipe organ in Horticultural Hall was played automatically by means of electrically-operated *fingers* or feelers which reached through holes in cardboard to touch a metal plate, thus actuating the proper notes to sound and symphonies to be played—an 1876 forerunner of today's data processing machines!

Among the various other items for the wonderment of the public were such diverse products as fire engines (horse-drawn, of course), many different plows, ore-handling equipment (mining in the West was an impor-

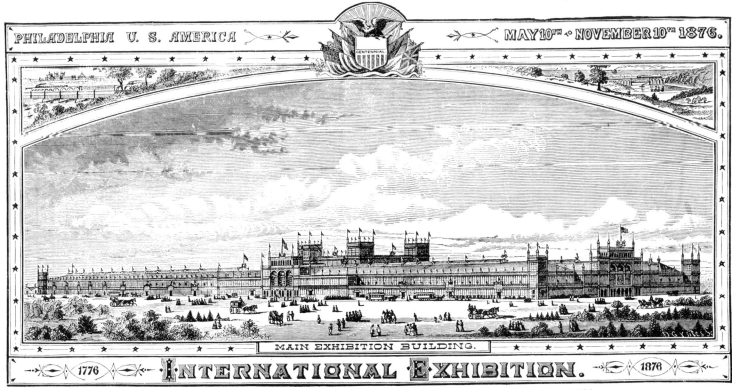

CENTENNIAL

MAIN EXHIBITION BUILDING.

1776 INTERNATIONAL EXHIBITION. 1876

MAIN BUILDING OF THE INTERNATIONAL CENTENNIAL EXHIBITION, PHILADELPHIA, 1876.

1880 feet in length and 464 feet in width.

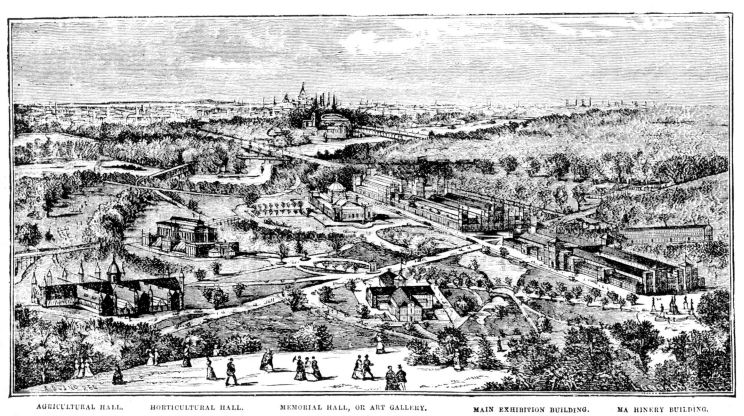

AGRICULTURAL HALL. HORTICULTURAL HALL. MEMORIAL HALL, OR ART GALLERY. MAIN EXHIBITION BUILDING. MA HINERY BUILDING.

BIRD'S-EYE VIEW OF THE CENTENNIAL BUILDINGS, FAIRMOUNT PARK, PHILADELPHIA.

Scenes from the 1876 International Exhibition held at Philadelphia to celebrate 100 years of American independence. This event was the first really great "world's fair" held in the United States.

GENERAL VIEW OF INTERIOR OF MACHINERY HALL, FROM GALLERY NEAR KRUPP'S GUNS.

HOE'S PRINTING-PRESS EXHIBIT.

CENTENNIAL MEDAL—OBVERSE.

Persons, places, and things from the 1876 Centennial Exhibition held in Philadelphia. Held in the middle of the Victorian era, emphasis of the fair was on beauty and ornateness.

CENTENNIAL BRONZE INK STAND.

CENTENNIAL MEDAL—REVERSE.

WHEELER & WILSON SEWING MACHINE CO.'S EXHIBIT.

VIEW OF THE INTERIOR OF THE MAIN BUILDING.

THE CORLISS ENGINE.

The gigantic Corliss Engine, steam-powered, was the central attraction of the Centennial Exhibition. This gigantic device provided the power to drive, via shafts, belts, and pulleys, many exhibits. In later years the mechanical monster was broken up and sold for scrap.

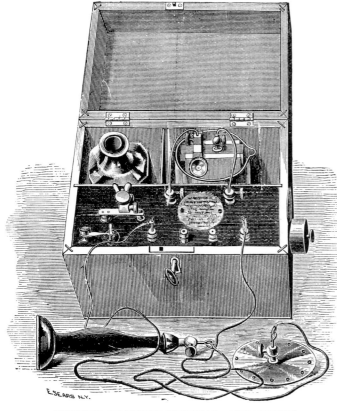

FAMILY ELECTRO-MEDICAL APPARATUS.

STILES' DOUBLE DESK AND BOOK CASE COMBINED.

PATENT WASHINGTON PRINTING PRESS.

Products shown at the Centennial Exhibition were varied and ranged from do-it-yourself medical kits to beds to desks to printing presses. Indeed, the fair was a showcase of American ingenuity.

PATENT FOLDING BED, EXHIBITED IN THE MAIN BUILDI

THE MINNEHAHA.

The "Minnehaha," an ornate soda fountain, was shown at the 1876 Centennial Exhibition. What a collectors' item it would make today!

AMOSKEAG FIRE-ENGINE.

The Amoskeag fire engine was the mainstay of hundreds of fire departments throughout America. This unit, a pumper, was kept hot by means of a connecting steam hose at the engine house. When an alarm sounded the hose was disconnected, a fire was ignited under the boiler, horses took their place in front of the vehicle, harnesses dropped automatically in place, firemen boarded, and the race was on! Arriving at the scene of the fire, the unit would be attached to a nearby water hydrant or would siphon water from a local stream or pond. By means of compression cylinders the water was pumped at high pressure through hoses, often with sufficient force to spray a distance of several hundred feet.

Amoskeag pumpers were originally made in Manchester, New Hampshire, at the immense Amoskeag Mills, a huge multistoried brick factory complex which extended for over a mile along the Merrimack River. The enterprise, which included a virtual city built for its workers (many of whom were European immigrants), produced a wide variety of cloth goods, printed items, and other manufactures. Today a substantial portion of the Amoskeag buildings remains, including the central tower which is dated 1844.

19th century Baldwin steam engine, typical of the motive force which spanned America. During the 1860-1890 years railroads exercised immense control over much of the United States, by virtue of land grants given to them earlier by the government as a reward for building trackage in sparsely populated areas. Often a community desiring rail service would have to erect a station and pay a substantial sum of money to induce a railroad to include it. Rates were unregulated, a situation which which caused many bankruptcies as well as many monopolistic situations. Frank Norris' novel, The Octopus,'' details some of this quite graphically.

'ELIA HALFORD'S GOOD WORK. — "SHE TORE THE NOTE ACROSS, AND THREW IT INTO THE BLAZE. 'OH! WHAT HAVE YOU DONE?'
AND HE GLANCED AT HER, IN AMAZE. 'GIVEN YOU YOUR FREEDOM.'"— SEE NEXT PAGE.

Some 19th century melodrama!

tant industry at the time), steam locomotives and railroad equipment, water wheels and hydraulic equipment, all manner of pumps, brick-making machines, marvelous printing presses (including the mammoth products of Robert Hoe which were the size of a locomotive!), typecasting and typesetting machines, paper-making devices, and so on.

Today the United States proudly displays its latest jet fighters at public exhibitions, and in Russia on May Day the latest Soviet rockets and space hardware are paraded through Red Square in Moscow. Likewise, a century ago in 1876 countries featured military arms as evidence of their "progress." The United States government exhibit included different types of gatling guns, breech-loading guns, a rifle-making machine (which was actually in operation during the event), various torpedoes, and other destructive things. On the more humanitarian side the government exhibit also showed such products as lighthouse signals, lanterns, geological survey charts, and other items, including an enveloping machine. Also shown were prehistoric fossils and relics unearthed during various government expeditions.

During this time the field of archeology was beginning to come into prominence. During the next several years O.C. Marsh and C.D. Cope would wage a battle at Yale College and elsewhere to establish priority of new discoveries and theories as dozens of crates of huge dinosaur bones arrived from Wyoming, Kansas, Colorado, and other western districts to startle the academic world. By 1883 Marsh assembled an awesome skeleton of a brontosaurus and noted: "A careful estimate of the size of brontosaurus, as here restored, showed than when living the animal must have weighed more than 20 tons."

In addition to man-made and natural relics shown by the United States government, there were virtually endless displays by many other principalities from around the world. Indeed, this was necessary in order to make the Exhibition *international* in keeping with its name. Great Britain showed steam apparatus of various kinds (that country was the world's foremost manufacturer of railway devices, steam manufacturing equipment, and the like), a coal-cutting machine, a new type of Jacquard loom, many types of sewing machines (apparently there were literally hundreds of different sewing machines on display in various areas of the Exhibition, so many that it was reported that the exhibits of this particular device became tedious after awhile), printing equipment and printed items, silverware, and carriages. Queen Victoria sent from her palace a loan exhibition of paintings from her personal collection. Apparently the United States was forgiven by England by the time 1876 came around, 100 years after the 1776 Declaration of Independence.

Second only in impressiveness to the Corliss engine as an eye-catching exhibit was a monster gun exhibited by Krupp, the famous German manufacturer of military hardware and heavy industrial equipment. Other items in the German display included pieces from the royal porcelain manufactory, different types of musical instruments, toys from Bavaria, clocks, samples of German printing quality including many fine books, and various engines and motors.

From Russia came an exhibit collection of Sazikoff, the court jeweler, plus precious gems and minerals, fur goods, church garments, military goods, scale models of warships, mechanical tools, educational and agricultural items, and art objects.

France contributed elegant art objects including porcelain vases, bronzes, Limoges ware, a $40,000 diamond necklace, various types of watches, enameled ware, rich velvets and silks, and a wild array of burgundy and champagne, not to overlook toilet soaps and perfumes.

From Central and South America came a mass of Mexican silver weighing 4,000 pounds, specimens of various minerals, mummies from Peru, items of manufacture from Chili and Argentina, and coffee from Venezuela.

Brazil, probably because of the presence of its emperor, Dom Pedro, had a particularly large exhibit which featured birds, insects, native gold and diamonds, rare woods, an extensive selection of cigars, agricultural goods, a display of silkmaking from cocoons, many different statues, and a gallery of paintings.

In a numismatic vein, two machines used in the Brazilian Mint were also shown. One was described as "the stamp for cutting out and making the coins" and the other "a machine for milling the edges."

The 1876 Centennial Exhibition had other numismatic aspects as well. Beginning in 1874 a committee on coins and currency was appointed in Philadelphia by the Exhibition authorities to collect specimens of American coins and paper money. Apparently no numismatist was represented on this committee (which seems to be typical of government actions at the time and perhaps even to the present day!), so it was concluded that the most brilliant way to assemble a collection for exhibition two years later at the 1876 Centennial Exhibition was to distribute circulars among national banks throughout the country asking them for their aid in sorting through coins from circulation and collecting specimens!

As you might expect, the response from banks was very poor, and little if anything came from that venture. Later, the more sensible suggestion was made that collectors could be consulted and that someone should consult the United States Mint to see what it could provide.

Henry R. Linderman, director of the Mint, turned down the request to set up an exhibit at the fair. He said that the Mint collection, called the Mint Cabinet at the time, would not be transported but "will remain at the Mint where it can be seen by anyone calling between the hours of 9:00 and 12:00 a.m. The United States Mint Cabinet numbers at present 6,443 pieces, of which total number of United States mintages is 813; the number of colonials is 712; the number of Washington medals 244; and of other medals 635; the balance of the collection consisting of fine Greek, Roman, and foreign gold, silver, and copper coins."

Linderman went on to say that: "The rarest American coins at the Mint are a Brasher doubloon in gold, the 1785 Immune Columbia cent in gold, and the 1804 silver dollar."

It was further related that the American series at the Mint were by no means complete, according to a reporter from the *Coin Collectors Journal,* the numismatic magazine founded in 1875 by J.W. Scott. It was stated that "the collection still lacks the greater part of colonial coins, of which but a feeble display is made, several of the rare small silver pieces, and many of the varieties of the early cents, some of the early gold issues, and other coins. After about 1830 full sets of all coins issued were kept at the Mint, some of which are unique. The state of the coins varies greatly, some being in exceedingly fine condition and others being very ordinary. Of 1793 cents, the Chain is Very Fine, the Wreath a beautiful Proof impression, and the Liberty Cap very ordinary, such a specimen, in fact, that it brings just about $10.00 at auction."

There were various numismatic activities—indeed many of them—on the Centennial Exhibition grounds. J.W. Scott, well known in the stamp field, offered coins for sale as well. The United States Treasury Department had at least one press which turned out medals of various sizes. In addition, literally dozens of different varieties of tokens and medals were produced by private sources. Also available were official centennial medals struck at the Philadelphia Mint in bronze and silver and offered for sale on the fair grounds.

Interest on the part of numismatists in 1876 centennial memorabilia began at a very early time. The February 1876 issue of the *American Journal of Numismatics,* the official publication of the American Numismatic Society, carried a description of 25 different varieties of medals issued by the government and private individuals. Correspondents were invited to submit additional descriptions of medals and tokens as they were issued or were learned of. Later the list grew to comprise many dozens of pieces.

In recent years there have been many complaints about the quality of United States coinage and the artistic merit or lack thereof relating to the products of the United States Mint. It is often lamented that despite the appearance of many elegant and beautiful designs in the past—the pattern Amazonian silver coins of 1872, the illustrious pattern half dollars of 1877, the beautiful Schoolgirl silver dollar of 1879, the elegant 1882 Shield Earring silver coins, the stunningly attractive MCMVII double eagle of 1907 and so on—many of our current coins resemble mere tokens rather than works of artistic merit.

In July 1876 the *Boston Transcript* took some potshots of the official centennial medals being produced at the United States Mint and said: "The Centennial folks are agitated because France has made a better medal than theirs and proposed selling it here. France always was a little ahead of us in the medal line, and it is hoped that she will continue to 'thrust her ware upon us' until we can do something creditable ourselves."

Coin collecting was in its infancy in 1876. There were several numismatic societies and perhaps a few thousand casual collectors, if indeed that many, around America. As transportation was primitive by today's standards and as telephone communication was non-existent, nearly all communication took place by mail. There was no such thing as a coin convention. The American Numismatic Association, founded in 1892, was not even a twinkle in the eye of its father, Dr. George Heath of Monroe, Michigan (who in 1888, 12 years after the centennial, first began publishing a private numismatic paper, *The Numismatist*).

There were regular monthly meetings of a few coin clubs. For example, on December 1, 1875, a month before the centennial year began, the Boston Numismatic Society secretary reported:

"A monthly meeting was held this day. The secretary read the report of the last meeting which was accepted. The president appointed Messrs. Green and Robinson to nominate officers for 1876, to report at the annual meeting in January. Also Mr. Davenport was nominated to examine the treasurer's account. The meeting was devoted to an exhibition of United States coins of 1795, but nothing was brought, except by Mr. Crosby, who showed two cents and two half-cents, and by the secretary who showed an eagle, three half eagles, three dollars, two half dollars, two dimes, six cents, and two half-cents. The Society adjourned shortly before 5:00 p.m."

Sylvester Crosby produced in that year one of the greatest numismatic books our country has ever seen: *Early Coins of America.* This mammoth volume gave background information concerning United States colonial coins and the circumstances under which they were struck. It is interesting to note that now in the late

THE
Early Coins of America;

AND THE

LAWS GOVERNING THEIR ISSUE.

COMPRISING ALSO DESCRIPTIONS OF

THE WASHINGTON PIECES, THE ANGLO-AMERICAN TOKENS,

MANY PIECES OF UNKNOWN ORIGIN,

OF THE SEVENTEENTH AND EIGHTEENTH CENTURIES,

AND THE

FIRST PATTERNS OF THE UNITED STATES MINT.

BY SYLVESTER S. CROSBY.

BOSTON:
PUBLISHED BY THE AUTHOR.
1875.

"The Early Coins of America," published by Sylvester S. Crosby in 1875, remains to this day the standard work covering colonial and related coinage. Containing original legislation data, historical information, die variety listings, and other knowledge, the book is a classic.

1776 Continental dollar struck in pewter. The obverse bears the word "Fugio," meaning "I Fly," referring to the rapid passage of time. The reverse records on interlocking rings the names of the original 13 states.

1652 pine tree shilling. This coin has been bent and then straightened. Legend has it that witches, once a hazard in early Massachusetts, could be warded off by use of such a bent coin!

COLONIAL COINS, a field which for the numismatist today encompasses coins of the states, pieces from the 1790s honoring George Washington, and related items, furnish a fascinating field of endeavor. Most issues were made from hand-engraved and punched dies, each die different from another. Several states, Vermont, New Jersey, Connecticut, Massachusetts, and New York prominent among them, issued their own copper coinage during the 1780s. Earlier, in the 17th century, Massachusetts produced a wide variety of willow tree, oak tree, and pine tree coins of various denominations from the twopence through the shilling, all in silver.

The Colonial Newsletter, a non-profit periodical directed to enthusiasts in the field, keeps collectors up to date on new discoveries. Did you know that certain New Jersey and Connecticut copper coins were unofficially made in New York? Did you know that many of the rarest Vermont pieces are actually counterfeits of the period (but have legitimate status with collectors today)? Did you know that the 1776 Continental dollar, one of the most impressive early coins, has its origin shrouded in mystery? Where was it made? Who made it? No one knows for sure.

These and many other intriguing aspects recommend colonials to the numismatist with an intellectual turn of mind. Within this wide field are many aspects of romance, history, and in a primitive sense, art.

1786 copper coin of Vermont. The obverse depicts a mountain scene and plow. The reverse Latin inscription refers to Vermont as the 14th state.

1787 Connecticut cent, one of over 300 different varieties of coppers issued by Connecticut from 1785 to 1788.

1787 Fugio cent. Struck privately for the federal government under contract.

1787 Nova Eborac (New York) copper. Like most colonial issues it was struck from relatively crude, handmade dies.

1773 halfpenny made in England for circulation in Virginia.

1787 New Jersey copper, one of many similar issues produced from 1786 through 1788.

1796 Myddelton token, considered by some authorities to be the most beautiful coin of its era. It was issued for a proposed British settlement in Kentucky.

Lord Baltimore silver shilling, circa 1660. One of several denominations produced for use in this colony.

20th century, over 100 years later, Crosby's book is still the standard authority on the subject!

In 1876 coins were sold in two main ways; the most prominent being through the auction houses. The auction houses then, unlike the situation today, were usually independent. Various private dealers cataloged sales for their clients and then had an unaffiliated auction house do the selling. The auction house itself usually was not involved in coins alone and was apt to sell a wide variety of other things as well—books, fossils, relics, antiquities, and the like. The second way of selling was directly from a dealer's stock, either by over-the-counter sales or by quotations via letter. Printed price lists describing dealers' offerings were few and far between.

An important dealer of the day was Ed Frossard of Irvington-on-Hudson, New York. Frossard had his own private business and also was editor of the *Coin Collectors Journal* published by J.W. Scott and Company. Scott was prominent in coins, although the firm was better known for stamps. There were two addresses—a main stamp facility at 75 Nassau Street in New York and the combined coin and stamp facility at 146 Fulton Street. At the time Scott offered to "pay the highest prices for large or small collections of any description." A modest catalog of American and foreign coins was available for 25c, and a separate catalog of silver coins was available for the same price.

Edward Cogan, who did business at 408 State Street, Brooklyn, New York, is generally regarded as the first professional numismatist in America. He once related how he became engaged in the business:

"Quite late in the year 1856 a friend of mine brought into my store in Philadelphia an electrotype Washington cent of 1792 and persuaded me to purchase it for 25c. Upon showing it, as a curiosity, to a gentleman he offered me 50c for it—and the curiosity was gone. My friend told me that a cent of 1815 would be worth at least $5.00, and that there was a desire springing up for United States cents. I immediately set about collecting an entire set from 1793, but had not the most distant idea at that time of ever making it a matter of business. I continued collecting from that time until the end of 1858, when finding the demand increasing and the supply quite equal to it, I commenced selling my duplicates. From that time I have followed the coin trade almost exclusively as a matter of business."

There were no cents struck in 1815—so it was a joke at the time that a cent of 1815 would have a high value! 1858, the year that Cogan started his professional dealership, was the first year that the United States Mint sold Proof coins directly to collectors.

S.K. Harzfeld of 1713 Park Avenue, Philadelphia, conducted his own business and also was the American representative of Adolph Hess of Frankfurt-am-Main, Germany. His advertisements noted that: "Rare and antique coins, medals, numismatic books, etc. are bought, sold, and exchanged. Coin cabinets are arranged and catalogued for public sale, are sold on commission in Philadelphia, New York, or Frankfurt-am-Main, Germany, with reasonable conditions. Every two months a catalog of rare coins and medals in stock will be issued and sent to those applying."

Other dealers in 1876 were William H. Strobridge, who catalogued coins and usually offered them for sale through Leavitt & Co., public auctioneers who held periodic sales at Clinton Hall in New York City; Henry Ahlborn on Cambridge Street in Boston; and John W. Haseltine.

Haseltine, who did business at 1343 Chestnut Street in Philadelphia, was one of the best known dealers of the time. He held auction sales in regular sequence and also was one of the first to do studies of die varieties, his work on American silver coins being particularly well known. At one time a leading numismatic publication commended him for his "correct and accurate descriptions of coins offered for sale and his omission of those grandiloquent descriptions that can in no way increase the value of a coin and should only be used, if at all, to describe really rare pieces."

Speaking of "grandiloquent descriptions," today, over 100 years later, it is generally considered that the more information the better—and auction catalogs which give a coin's history and other details, assuming that they are pertinent to the coin, are highly admired. However, in 1876 apparently certain catalogers had an abundance of time, printed catalogs were cheap, and a lot of irrelevant words were included. The following comment appeared in an 1876 issue of the *Coin Collectors Journal*:

"We cannot too much deprecate the fashion into which some coin dealers have fallen of giving minute descriptions of worthless coins that are filling page after page of their catalogs; pieces that ought to be thrown out or sold in large lots. The sale of David Proskey [another well known dealer at the time] at Bangs, Merwin & Co., on the 14th and 15th of last month would have made a good one-day sale, but as a two-day sale it was altogether uninteresting. During the first afternoon only about 30 pieces sold at over $1.00 each, and of these only two items sold for over $2.75 each."

The foregoing description is also remarkable for its description of generally low values at the time. Indeed, coins were worth minute fractions of today's prices.

Auctions were landmark events in the 1870s, just as they are today. In 1875 the Colonel M.I. Cohen Collection was sold at auction from November 25th through

CATALOGUE

OF THE

Numismatic Collection

FORMED BY

JOSEPH J. MICKLEY, ESQ.,

OF PHILADELPHIA;

NOW THE PROPERTY OF

W. Elliot Woodward,

OF ROXBURY, MASS.;

TO BE SOLD BY AUCTION,

BY

MESSRS. LEAVITT, STREBEIGH & CO.,

At the Book Trade Sale Rooms, Clinton Hall,

ASTOR PLACE AND EIGHTH STREET, NEW YORK CITY,

On Monday, October 28th, 1867,

And the five following Evenings,

Commencing each day at precisely half-past five o'clock.

————————

Orders for the sale will be faithfully executed by the Auctioneers,
EDWARD COGAN, Esq., 100 William Street, (P. O. Box 5768,)
New York City, or W. ELLIOT WOODWARD,
Roxbury, Mass.

————————

ROXBURY:

L. B. WESTON, PRINTER, GUILD ROW.

1867.

Title page of the Joseph J. Mickley Collection offering, owned by W. Elliott Woodward, a Massachusetts dealer, and sold at auction in 1867. Mickley was the most prominent early 19th century numismatist in America. Memorable among his accomplishments was the purchase at face value in 1827 of four Proof quarters from the Philadelphia Mint. Today each one is an extreme rarity.

DEATH OF JOSEPH J. MICKLEY.

THE INTERESTING CAREER OF A LINGUIST, ANTIQUARIAN AND MUSICIAN.

"MR. JOSEPH J. MICKLEY, who died suddenly on Friday evening, February 15, at the house of Dr. J. A. Meigs, on Spruce Street, above Broad, was well known both in this country and Europe for his antiquarian tastes. On the night of his death he had started out to visit Mr. Oliver Hopkinson, at 1424 Spruce Street, but feeling a sudden oppression he stopped at the house of Dr. Meigs, for many years his physician, where he expired half an hour afterward. The doctors declare fatty degeneration of the heart to have been the cause of his death.

"Mr. Mickley was born in Lehigh county, of "Pennsylvania Dutch" stock, on March 24, 1799. Sixty years ago he came to this city and learned piano-making. Later, he engaged in this business on his own account, and was so employed until 1869. Many years since he began collecting curious coins of all nations, and in time had the most valuable collection in the United States. In 1867 he was robbed of $16,000 worth of coins, and a short time afterward he sold the rest of his collection for a like sum. Two years later he went to Europe, whither his fame as an antiquarian had preceded him, and was warmly received there. He remained abroad three years, traveling through all parts of England and the Continent. While in Europe he perfected himself in the Swedish language, and became deeply interested in books and manuscripts bearing upon the early Swedish settlements in America. In addition to his collection of coins, Mr. Mickley possessed a large library of rare and curious books in many languages. He had a number of very old directories of Philadelphia and other cities, containing the names and residences of Washington, Jefferson, and other distinguished Revolutionary patriots. He had also many volumes relating to the history of Pennsylvania, and at the time of his death was translating a Swedish manuscript upon the same subject, in anticipation of publishing a work upon the early annals of the State. He was an acknowledged musical critic, and was said to be the best mender of musical instruments in the United States. Ole Bull was his intimate friend, and his house was for many years the resort of antiquarians, musicians and historians from all parts of the world. It was he who discovered that the violin which Ole Bull had bought for a Gaspar Desala was a counterfeit. Among his musical treasures was an autograph composition of Beethoven. Besides being extensively acquainted with European history and literature, Mr. Mickley could speak fluently French, German, and Swedish. He was very simple in his ways, and, while firm in his convictions and keen in his judgment of men, he was singularly gentle and lovable. Mr. Mickley was the first president of the Numismatic Society, and a well-known member both of the Franklin Institute and the Pennsylvania Historical Society. For some time past his books have been packed away. He was, however, making alterations in a house on Wood Street, near Franklin, where he could have his library about him, when death stepped in to cut short a life spent in quiet study and refined enjoyment."

The foregoing notice appeared in one of the Philadelphia papers, and (after a few corrections) is accurate and well informed. Allow me to add a few items, at random, without the formality of an Obituary or Eulogy. It is true he was "born of Pennsylvania Dutch Stock," but his language was the polished and correct German, not the *patois* of our neighbors. He came from a settlement of Moravians, to whom he belonged, and who have famous boarding schools at Bethlehem and Nazareth, about sixty miles north of this city. He was born at Catasauqua, now a noted place for iron manufacture, four miles from Bethlehem. Originally he was of French Huguenot stock, the name being Michelet; afterwards Germanized into Mueckli; finally Anglicised into Mickley. In October, 1863, the family had a centennial, and Mr. Mickley wrote and read a memoir, which was printed for their use in 1875. They had sore times among the Indians at the early settlement, without any fault of their own.

There is, in one of your magazines, an account of the beginning of his *numismatism*. He was about seventeen years old (say in 1816) when he formed a wish to own a cent, coined in the year of his nativity. He had hard work to find one, as you can readily understand. A good cent of 1799 now brings many dollars. This exercise only whetted him for further acquisitions in the same line. No doubt "the thing was in him," but that was what brought it to the surface; and probably it proved a great incentive to the study of languages, and history, and antiquities, as a diversion from the daily labor of making pianos and repairing violins. Here I may say, his linguistic appetite was remarkable. Besides the languages named in the obituary, he took pains to pick up a vocabulary in almost every country which he visited during three years' travel. I once asked him for the various renderings of *railroad*; he gave it to me in Italian, Spanish, Swedish, Russian, German, and modern Greek. (He could not answer for *ancient* Greek, although he was not without the classic touch.) He said he had trouble to keep his Italian and Spanish from running into each other. In the entertaining manuscript journal of his travels, to show how the Russians are given to the study of other languages than their own, he states that at Nishni-Novgorod, a town well on to the border of Siberia, he went into a restaurant, where were two young ladies, one of them smoking a cigarette. Supposing he might safely soliloquize in German, he said, "What a pity for such a nice girl to be smoking." Quickly she took out the cigar, and gave him to know that she understood women's rights, and German besides. With his usual *naivete*, he adds, "How careful we should be." He seemed bound to see everything in Europe, as well as the borders of Asia and Africa. He was almost stifled in the crypt of an Egyptian pyramid; needed his overcoat in Lapland, where he went in June, to see the sun go all round without making a dip; fell down the ancient well of Cicero at Rome, and was knocked down by a careless driver in Constantinople, and taken up for dead.

Your magazine has heretofore mentioned his acquaintance formed with the lady-engraver at the mint of Stockholm, Madame Leah Ahlborne.* Her father, M. Lundgren, the former engraver, had her educated in Paris in that profession, and she succeeded him. Her work is very superior,

---

The obituary of Joseph J. Mickley, published in "The American Journal of Numismatics," issue of April 1878, gives an interesting insight into the life of the most prominent American numismatist of the early 19th century.

and this makes it the more pleasant to mention, that at her express and repeated desire, he lately sat for his profile portrait, (photograph,) from which she is now engraving a medal of him. The legends will be in the Swedish tongue. Her aim is to have it ready for the Paris exposition. I need hardly say, that I forwarded to her a humble claim for one medal for the Mint Cabinet, and one for myself. She will be distressed to hear of his death, although at the age to which he attained, it could surprise no one.

The robbery of his numismatic cabinet, briefly mentioned in the obituary, was a prominent event, and a turning-point in his life. He was always ready, too ready, in the unsuspecting openness of his heart, to show his collection to friends or strangers. Sometimes (as he has told me) he would find a piece or two missing after such an opening of his drawers. Doubtless it was at some such visit as this that the robbery was planned. It took place on an evening, about eight o'clock, while Mr. Mickley was at work in his shop in the back building. The cabinet was kept in the third story front room of the main building. A slight noise induced him to go up there, not in time to encounter the burglar, one or more, but in time to see the devastation. How much was taken, cannot be definitely stated ; certainly as much as a man could carry away. A large part consisted of rare British coins, gold and silver ; but other countries were copiously represented, and many pieces were American duplicates. It is stated, that some time before he was offered thirty thousand dollars for the whole collection. The unstolen residue that went to auction in New York soon after, brought some fifteen thousand dollars. It is quite likely that the booty was worth an equal sum. I well remember when Mr. Mickley came into my office, with the painful intelligence. "Oh, I have been robbed—I have been robbed ! My coins taken ; I can't tell how many. But it was a mercy I did not encounter the man. No doubt he was prepared to blind and gag me, as such fellows generally are." It was a great shock to him ; probably he never fully recovered from it, even in the excitement of foreign travel. It never was certainly known what became of this treasure, but Mr. Mickley had good reasons for settling his suspicions upon a certain person. One day he said to me, "I believe I met the man that robbed me, just now in Chesnut Street." Years after, a few very fine gold pieces of England were offered for sale at the Mint Cabinet rooms. I was so well convinced that the labels were in his handwriting, that I sent for him to come and see them. He could not deny the likeness, but seemed reluctant to entertain the subject at all. They came from honest hands, through the few links of ownership that could be traced, but it was impossible to go backward for eight or nine years.

After that event, and the public sale of the remainder, his taste seemed to modulate from coins to coin-books, which shifting seems likely to occur with old collectors. One of his last dealings in this way, was to unite with me in importing two copies of a recent work of great merit, Henfrey's Numismata Cromwelliana.

In his house in Market Street near Tenth, where he lived longest, (twenty-seven years,) he had no front store. You had to pull the bell and go through a long entry, and up a dark stairway to reach his place of work and sale. How far the work was needful to him, I cannot say. It seemed rather to be kept up for the pleasure and healthfulness of employment. It is not easy to understand on other grounds, why a man who was constantly importing costly coins, and buying scarce books, should care for the compensation of tuning pianos and putting harps and violins in order. He was, however, the agent for the sale of a popular make of pianos, having a stock of them in his house.

Those students who know what it is to have an amateur workshop, (and methinks every brain-working man owes it to himself to have some such diversion,) can realize the pleasure that Mr. Mickley enjoyed amongst his tools and work-benches. And it was really amusing to see men of culture and refinement coming there to sit around his old stove, on three-legged stools, or anything that could be extemporised into a seat. They liked to chat with him, and he with them ; and once a week he held a quartette in a better room, taking one of the parts himself.

As a "mender of musical instruments," his crowning performance was one already stated in your magazine — restoring the violin which was owned by Washington. Not that it was in such great disorder, but that it had been played upon by so great a man. The charm of this piece of work was undoubtedly enhanced, when Ole Bull came in and took up the instrument. There was but one reserved seat that time, and Mr. Mickley formed the whole audience.

In fine, Mr. Mickley was an agreeable man to associate with, and an honorable man to deal with. He seemed superior to any meanness, and free from vulgar passions and habits ; from pride and vanity, from envy and jealousy, from evil speaking and harsh judging. He was eminently sincere, affable, kind, and gentle ; yet decided, and with a mind of his own. In the best sense of the word he was a gentleman ; not with artificial elegance of manners, yet with a good address, rendering him agreeable to refined society.

He was an Honorary Member of the Boston Numismatic Society, of the New York Numismatic and Archæological Society, and a member of various Historical Societies ; and it is understood that a Memoir of him is preparing, to be read to the Pennsylvania Society. Shortly before his death he received notice of his election as a member of the Societe Française de Numismatique et d'Archeologie, of Paris.

He was twice married, and leaves six children.

W. E. Du Bois, *U. S. Mint, Philadelphia.*

November 29th. The collection comprised 2,400 different lots and was described as being: "In some departments, particularly that of American coins, both colonial and mint issues, exceedingly full and complete." A contemporary reporter observed that the bidding was rather sluggish and that certain prices were not as high as to be expected. However, this was countered by the fact that "handsome prices for Fine and Very Fine pieces were realized by the auctioneer."

While "Fine" and "Very Fine" have specific meaning to collectors today, a century ago these terms were often used in a broad way to describe coins which today we might call Extremely Fine or even Uncirculated. Auction catalog descriptions tended to be fairly general in nature. The theory was that very little bidding would be done by mail and that anyone who wanted to bid by mail would send his commission to a dealer who would then attend the sale in person. Contemporary reports tell us that the same coin could be called Uncirculated by one cataloguer, Proof by another, and Very Fine by still another! This did not cause a problem at the time, for values in general were low and the ultimate decision was in the hands of the purchaser who could either accept or reject a coin. Today, of course, the situation is vastly different.

One ironic situation of the 1875 Cohen Sale was that a magnificent group of gold Proof sets of the years 1862 through 1875 inclusive, each including the $20, $10, $5, $3, $2.50, and $1 gold pieces and each originally costing about $55 per set at Mint, averaged $46.50 each—or less by $1.20 than the then-current value of gold! How sad. Today the 1875 gold Proof set alone is valued at several hundred thousand dollars. In 1977 I sold one coin from a set such as this, an 1875 Proof $3 gold piece, for $110,000! General lack of interest in such pieces 100 years ago is evidenced by the fact that only twenty 1875 gold Proof sets were struck at the Mint, and it is by no means certain that even this small number was sold in its entirety.

At the present time it is popular to complain about coinage designs. I myself have done so a number of times. In 1971 when the Eisenhower dollar was released I wrote that in my opinion it was neither a beautiful nor a magnificent coin, especially in comparison with some of the beautiful pattern American silver dollars of years ago and the examples of coinage art to be found among dollar-size coins of other countries.

In March 1876 a strong complaint was registered in one of the coin collecting publications about the design of Liberty seated coinage. Collectors today who enjoy Liberty seated coins, who bid high prices for them, and who consider them elegant compared to coins of the present time, probably would not agree. However, in 1876 Liberty seated coins were hardly a novelty to collectors and perhaps familiarity bred contempt. The diatribe said:

"Indeed, the further we advance in our theoretical knowledge of art, the less able do we appear of being able to carry out principles applying its rules. This applies particularly to Mint issues of the present day. Look at the uninteresting and lifeless Goddess of Liberty with its scared look and shapeless arm...and compare it with the striking and lifelike features of a 1793 wreath or chain cent and further comment will be unnecessary."

Collectors today might not agree. I, for one, think that a Liberty seated coin is more attractive in design than the rather plain obverse of a 1793 chain cent, but in 1876 a Liberty seated coin was common to a collector, something which would be tossed aside, whereas a chain cent was very valuable. Indeed, a chain cent in nice condition might bring all of $10 to $20 at auction!

Another early writer described Liberty seated as being a "young woman sitting on nothing in particular, wearing nothing to speak of, looking over her shoulder at nothing imaginable, and bearing in her left hand something that looks like a broomstick with a woolen nightcap on it. Such a figure has no proper place on a coin, it is without beauty and without meaning. Compare our silver coins with those of France, Germany, or Great Britain and see their inferiority in every respect. Why is it that we have the ugliest money of all civilized nations?"

As I said before, Liberty seated coin specialists would not agree today!

Grading standards, as noted, were quite relaxed in 1876 and varied widely from dealer to dealer and catalog to catalog. We had certain terms as Very Fair and Very Poor which are not seen today. On the other hand, the abbreviations AU and BU, so common today for Almost Uncirculated and Brilliant Uncirculated, were unknown in 1876. AU pieces years ago were described as *nearly Uncirculated*. In fact, the word *nearly* was in fairly popular use, and such descriptions as nearly Fine and nearly Proof (whatever that means!) were occasionally to be seen.

The term *Proof*, rigidly defined today, was loosely applied a century ago. Hence we have the editor of the *Coin Collectors Journal*, one of the two leading publications of the day (the other being the *American Journal of Numismatics*), describing a 1793 cent in the United States Mint collection as being in Proof condition. Often coins with what we would call today a prooflike surface were simply called Proofs back then. Machinery for making Proofs was not installed at the United States Mint until after the disastrous fire of 1816, so in theory no earlier United States Mint Proofs do or could exist. There are, however, many coins with prooflike surfaces, coins which were often called Proofs. Examples are certain 1796 silver coins.

Cleaning coins, a problem today, was likewise a matter of concern back then. Perhaps the simplest advice was

given in April 1876 by Ed Frossard who advised a correspondent that:

"The best way of cleaning rusted or worn coins in our opinion is to clean them out of your collection and replace them by such specimens as will not need cleaning."

A more serious comment was given by the same person in May 1876 when he wrote that:

"Few copper, brass, or bronze coins can be improved by cleaning. A gentle rubbing with soft flannel dipped in sweet oil sometimes improves the appearance of a coin by softly removing accumulated dirt, but the removal of rust and verdigris, which are formed by the decomposition of the metal itself, only exposes the corroded parts and disfigures the coin. We caution our readers against the use of oxalic and other acids, which eat into the metal and give it a very bad color. Cyanide of potassium, which we have heard recommended for this purpose, if properly applied, removes verdigris almost instantaneously, and leaves the copper in a better condition than sulfuric or other acids."

Fearing the death or permanent disablement of many of his readers, Ed Frossard went on in *The Coin Collectors Journal* to say that cyanide of potassium "must be used by skilled hands, and with the greatest caution, for its accidental introduction to the system, by coming in contact with any exposed blood vessels, decomposes the blood and causes immediate death."

Frossard continued by relating that: "Sweet oil, instead of removing verdigris from copper, only generates it, as the following analysis shows. Hence it is that a perfectly bright copper coin placed in a vessel containing sweet oil becomes tinged with green after a lapse of only one or two days and loses its brilliant polish. Silver coins can be cleaned by washing with castile soap and warm water and drying with a soft flannel."

Keeping company with the aforementioned *Ayer's American Almanac* and other publications, humor was also a part of the numismatic scene. A sample joke from the *Coin Collectors Journal*:

"Why are numismatists generally of a melancholy temperament?"

"Answer: Because they meet with so many reverses!"

Today if we look through our pocket change for Lincoln cents we would be indeed lucky to find a *rare* wheat-ear cent dated before 1959! Indeed, finding a *super rare* item such as a 1931-S Lincoln cent would be worthy of a front page article in *Numismatic News* or *Coin World*, and even then it probably would indicate that some child spent his father's coin collection! So, read this and weep:

In July 1876 it was reported to a young correspondent named Louis that: "You ought to find specimens of American copper cents from 1816 to 1857 in your neighborhood, but if you want them in Fine or Uncirculated condition, unless you have unusual facilities for inspecting large quantities of copper, you must apply to coin dealers or purchase at coin sales. Twenty years ago cents from 1793 to 1814 were frequently found in circulation, but at the present time most of them have found their way into the hands of collectors. Still, by looking over lots of old cents one sometimes finds even the rare ones."

In 1876 the hottest items on the market were Washington pieces—tokens and medals relating to the father of our country. The Mint Cabinet on display in Philadelphia featured these as its main attraction. In auctions of the day tokens and medals relating to George Washington were apt to bring far, far more than what we consider to be rarities today in the regular series. For example in the 1875 sale of the Colonel M.I. Cohen Collection a gold pocket piece allegedly carried by George Washington sold for $500, whereas, as noted, an 1875 gold Proof set sold for less than the gold bullion price, and an 1804 silver dollar, today valued at several hundred thousand dollars, sold for all of $325!

Very popular at the time were coins of Greece, Rome, medieval Europe, and other classic issues. It seems that these were more popular with scholars than with the average collector, for what appears to be a compliment and a mild protest at the same time appeared in one of the early issues of the *Coin Collectors Journal*. A Mr. A.B.J. of New York City, identified only by his initials, wrote and said:

"I am very pleased with the first number of your Journal and hope that you will be able to carry out your promise of popularizing the study of numismatics. Your paper promises to be exactly what is wanted by hundreds if not thousands of collectors desirous of becoming acquanted with the numismatic treasures of the world but who, alas, have not the means or access to heavy Latin and Greek publications, and if they did could not always understand what they were reading about

"What we want are not voluminous and learned dissertations on the position of the lobe of the left ear on a 1793 Liberty Cap cent, but plain statements in plain English on the coins of all nations with sufficient illustrations to make the matter intelligible to ordinary men, educated in the common schools of our country."

In 1876 mintmarks were not very popular, and auction catalog descriptions often omitted listing them. Indeed, there were no reference catalogs of any kind available listing United States coins. Occasionally a brief description would be given in a popular book or magazine, but there was no equivalent of the *Guide Book of United States Coins* that we know today.

For example, in December 1876 the *Coin Collectors Journal* published a list of known varieties of United

THE
MEDALLIC MEMORIALS
OF
WASHINGTON

in the MINT of the

UNITED STATES

BY

James Ross Snowden

PHILADELPHIA
J.B. LIPPINCOTT & C?
1861.

In the 1860s medals and coins of George Washington were among the most avidly sought after items by private collectors and by the Mint Cabinet (later to become the National Coin Collection). In 1861 James Ross Snowden produced a treatise on the subject, the title page of which is shown above.

Most medals featuring George Washington were of a complimentary nature. Examples are the Philadelphia Mint medal with the legend TIME INCREASES HIS FAME, the early 19th century medal with the inscription THE HERO OF FREEDOM, THE PRIDE OF HIS COUNTRY, AN ORNAMENT OF HUMAN NATURE, and the interestingly-inscribed medal which reads PROVIDENCE LEFT HIM CHILDLESS THAT THE NATION MIGHT CALL HIM FATHER.

There were, however, exceptions to this admiring spirit, and the famous Eccleston Medal, produced by Webb following a design by Daniel Eccleston, is such an instance.

Daniel Eccleston, of Lancaster, England, was a numismatist. In addition to the Eccleston Medal, issued by him in 1805, he produced in 1794 a halfpenny token with his own portrait. At one time Eccleston spent two or three years in America. W.S. Baker, historian of the Washington medal series, notes that during Eccleston's residence in Virginia he met Washington in Alexandria and was given an invitation to spend several days at Mount Vernon.

While Eccleston professed friendship with Washington, the medal belies any such sentiment. The obverse depicts Washington in a heavy suit of armor, "a singular conceit," as Baker has noted. The reverse inscription ostensibly honors Washington, but at the center a standing Indian, with head downcast, ruefully laments "The Land was Ours," hardly a happy note on which to end a tribute to the first president of the American nation situated on land formerly belonging to the Indian race.

The reverse inscription reads: HE LAID THE FOUNDATION OF AMERICAN LIBERTY IN THE XVIII CENTURY. INNUMERABLE MILLIONS YET UNBORN WILL VENERATE THE MEMORY OF THE MAN WHO OBTAINED THEIR COUNTRY'S FREEDOM. Then, as noted, an Indian appears at the center with the inscription surrounding: THE LAND WAS OURS.

Right: Title page of a typical auction catalog from the 1860s. Note that Washington pieces are among the items featured. Edward Cogan, who began business in the 1850s, was the first professional numismatist in America.

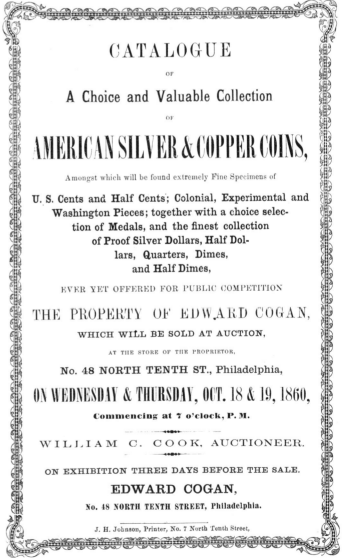

CATALOGUE

OF

A Choice and Valuable Collection

OF

AMERICAN SILVER & COPPER COINS,

Amongst which will be found extremely Fine Specimens of

U. S. Cents and Half Cents; Colonial, Experimental and Washington Pieces; together with a choice selection of Medals, and the finest collection of Proof Silver Dollars, Half Dollars, Quarters, Dimes, and Half Dimes,

EVER YET OFFERED FOR PUBLIC COMPETITION

THE PROPERTY OF EDWARD COGAN,

WHICH WILL BE SOLD AT AUCTION,

AT THE STORE OF THE PROPRIETOR,

No. 48 NORTH TENTH ST., Philadelphia,

ON WEDNESDAY & THURSDAY, OCT. 18 & 19, 1860,

Commencing at 7 o'clock, P. M.

WILLIAM C. COOK, AUCTIONEER.

ON EXHIBITION THREE DAYS BEFORE THE SALE.

EDWARD COGAN,

No. 48 NORTH TENTH STREET, Philadelphia.

J. H. Johnson, Printer, No. 7 North Tenth Street,

Over the years literally thousands of different coins, tokens, and medals have been produced with the portrait of President George Washington, "the Father of our Country." Most interesting to numismatists of yesteryear as well as to collectors today are the earlier issues, primarily those made prior to 1810.

At one time the Washington Cabinet of Medals was the numismatic centerpiece at the United States Mint in Philadelphia. At the top of the page is shown a special medal struck to commemorate the opening of this display. The 1819 cent shown directly above is counterstamped at the center with the portraits of George Washington and General Lafayette. In 1824 when Lafayette, French hero of the American Revolution, revisited the United States, many coins, notably large cents and half dollars, were counterstamped to provide a commemorative issue. Today these are exceedingly rare.

To the right are shown several different Washington pieces from the turn of the 19th century.

States coins from 1793 through 1857. However, mint-marks weren't mentioned in the list, for collecting by mintmarks was not popular at the time! All that was of concern was the date. It was recommended that readers desiring to know more about what coins were minted should subscribe to auction sales to get this information. Also, if they wanted to know about values they should acquire prices realized from auction sales for there was no other source of information.

In July 1876 W.S. Appleton, secretary of the Boston Numismatic Society, worked with William E. DuBois of the Mint in Philadelphia to compile a list of New Orleans Mint issues. It was stated in print that: "It may not be absolutely perfect, but it is thought to be very nearly so. If omissions are found I hope to be informed of them. I believe the same facts cannot be found elsewhere."

The list went on to give an incomplete and inaccurate chronology of New Orleans Mint issues. For example, it was stated that 1861-O silver dollars existed, whereas today we know that no pieces were minted in New Orleans that year. The list of New Orleans half dollars omitted the 1838-O, one of the most famous of all American rarities. There were other errors as well.

In October 1876 another correspondent wrote in to say that he had an 1862-O half dollar as well as some other coins. Today we know that no such thing exists, so the writer must have been describing a counterfeit. I mention this to point out the lack of general information available to the beginning collector at the time.

And yet branch mints sometimes did make the news. Often this news was rather humorous, at least from the viewpoint of numismatics today, over a century later.

For example, in June 1876 one of the San Francisco newspapers ran an article which said (and I paraphrase):

"Scandal at the Carson City Mint: It was reported by a special agency of the Treasury that the trade dollars coined at the Carson City Mint do not contain the amount of silver prescribed by law. The discrepancy is said to vary from one-half cent to two cents on all of the recent coinage. This most unexpected revelation explains some things in connection with the silver problem which were very puzzling. We now know why these coins were not as readily received in China as they were when they were first emitted. The Chinese are very expert on all matters relating to coins. When it was discovered that certain trade dollars were a fraud, the market for them was reduced.

"The excuse that is offered for this most outrageous and disgraceful situation is that the workmen at the Carson City Mint were not as skillful as they ought to be and hence caused devaluation in the intrinsic value of the coins. If they do work in that slovenly way at the Carson City Mint, the sooner that institution is shut up, the better it will be for the country and the commerce of the coast. The attempt to throw blame on the unskillfulness of the operator in this case is audacious. The fact is that somebody has been making $20,000 on every million of these coins struck. The reputation of the Carson City Mint will suffer for a long time."

Offhand, at this point if you are a numismatist interested in silver dollars and trade dollars you might say: "Aha! Here is an interesting aspect of trade dollar coinage which I was not aware of, a fascinating sidelight to numismatic history." Indeed, it is a fascinating sidelight, but not in quite the way you might expect.

In October 1876 the *American Journal of Numismatics* reported that the "scandal" at the Carson City Mint was something in the way of: "a idle tale invented by San Francisco newspaper reporters. The 'War of the Mints' rages between Carson City and San Francisco, and everything that one can say to disparage the other is poured out in venom in the issues of the respective daily newspapers. It is safe to assume that there never was a trade dollar that passed through the doors of the Carson City Mint whose weight was appreciably under the standard. This was confirmed by our correspondent, a broker in San Francisco, who weighed over 600 Carson City Mint trade dollars on coin scales and tested the integrity of each."

From 1861 through 1876 virtually no silver coins were in circulation in America. During the Civil War, fears about the outcome caused people to hoard silver and gold coins. Once the Civil War ended, this fear was still prevalent in many parts of America, and silver coins were not seen in the channels of commerce. In their place appeared paper fractional currency, tokens, and private bills.

This situation is dramatically related by a June 1876 article in the *Coin Collectors Journal* which reported that silver coins were being found in circulation once again as paper fractional currency was being redeemed:

"The reappearance of silver, so long hidden from our eyes that many young men of twenty years of age cannot remember having had a piece in their hand, has naturally attracted attention to the style, design, and workmanship of our coins, and it must be confessed that welcome and attractive as they are, their general look as well as their particular points, with one exception, is not satisfactory." Then followed a complaint about the Liberty seated coin design.

Newspapers all over America ran similar commentaries and educated the public on what the newly-appearing coins looked like.

Another article related:

"Silver coins are real money, which we have not seen in our daily transactions for 15 years, and its appearance has made a sensation. That sensation has caused a new hoarding of the pretty, fresh, white silver circles—and now it is almost as hard to get a dollar in change now as it was in 1861. We may all rejoice now at the return of the days when a dollar was a dollar, when the filthiness of lucre was not spread upon thin slivers and slips of paper, and when money could not be torn up and reduced by accidental wetting. The appearance of real money [silver coins] in circulation now will produce a change in manner in customs and speech. Pocketbooks will go out and purses will come in. People who like to handle their funds and who are attracted to the possession of precious metal may again jingle silver in the pouches of their undergarments. We will no longer call money 'stamps.' "

The return of silver coins was begun early in 1876 when the Sub-Treasury in New York City began redeeming paper fractional currency by paying out in exchange half dollars, quarters, and dimes of the dates 1874 through 1876.

While it is not stated in the numismatic journals, it is probably the case that the quantities of silver coins minted from 1861 to 1875, the pieces which were not put into circulation, were either stored by the Treasury and released in 1876 or were in many instances exported. It is known that many silver coins were shipped to the Orient for use in the China trade. This was particularly true of San Francisco half dimes and half dollars made during that period and, of course, trade dollars made during the 1870s, the latter being produced especially for that purpose.

Among collectors, paper money of the Confederate States of America, today highly prized, was viewed diffidently at the time. In 1875 it was reported that John Gill, a collector who lived in San Francisco "yesterday purchased from W.M. Duncan of Nashville, Tennessee, a bushel of Confederate paper money that contained $750,000 face value of paper money and $50,000 face value of Confederate bonds. Mr. Gill paid $50 in gold coins for them. The money and bonds were purchased by Mr. Duncan at the sale of the assets of the Tennessee Bank. Mr. Gill, a collector, has 5,000 specimens of Confederate money. He left last night for Atlanta where he undoubtedly will find millions more of the same."

Timekeeping in the good old days: the Sidney Advertising Clock, manufactured in Sidney, New York, circa 1886. This ingenious device, which tells the time and presents a panorama of changing advertisements, is a favorite with collectors today.

1876. THE COIN COLLECTOR'S JOURNAL. 193

An Essay on Coin Collecting.

During the last fifteen years the vein of collecting coins has greatly increased in the United States. Before that time there were collectors, men of note, perseverance and genius, like Dr. M. W. Dickeson, Edward Maris, J. J. Mickley, and a few others, whose opportunities for collecting the various issues of Colonial and old mint pieces have not since been equalled. Had it not been for the spirit of research of these gentlemen, at a time when old American coins were sent to the United States mint for recoinage by the thousand; many rare varieties of Colonial coins would have been utterly lost to us. The facilities extended those gentlemen by a liberal mint government enabled them to handle thousands of coppers, and to select from the mass such specimens as they considered worthy of preservation. The publication of Dr. Dickeson's "Manual of American Numismatics" drew the attention of American scholars to a subject which up to that time had been too much neglected by them. Americans versed in the subject of numismatics suddenly recognized the fact that the monetary history of the United States was at least as important to them as that of Rome or England, and that we had in our bakers' and grocers' till boxes, treasures which must prove the most valuable auxiliaries in our study of American history, and American development. Numismatic and archæological societies have been organized and established; the number of collectors has kept pace with the progress made in the knowledge of our coinage; works the most accurate and detailed have been published; and now, although there may still be some controversial points—and all has not yet been fully eliminated—we can be assured that the work of American numismatists during the two last decades has rescued the history of our Colonial and early mint coinage from oblivion.

In Europe, the collection of coins has for several centuries been the favorite pursuit of antiquarians. Entire sets of the coins of Roman Emperors and other ancient series, sometimes in the finest possible condition, as well as hoards of old national and modern coins, are frequently found. From these copious sources, collectors have been able to draw largely, and with the assistance of organized societies of antiquarians and the help of the various governments, to form those magnificent national collections, now the pride and ornament of the principal museums of European capitals. Of these various collections, that of the BIBLIOTHEQUE NATIONALE, in Paris, is beyond doubt the finest and largest. It is particularly rich in the specimens of Rome, Greece, Ancient Gaul, and of the French series, the latter so complete as to present specimens of the coinage of each ruler, in uninterrupted succession, from the time of Clovis (A. D. 510) to the present day. In England, the collection of the BRITISH MUSEUM is distinguished for its British coins, most of the coins illustrated in "Ruding's Annals" being found in the national collection, and as much money is spent yearly to secure the finest and rarest specimens of Greek and Roman coinage, the collection may in time equal that of Paris. The national collection at ST. PETERSBURG contains over 15,000 selected specimens; that at MADRID over 85,000 coins in all metals; VIENNA, in Austria, has a collection of 100,000 pieces, being the best and most complete collection of the coins of the German Empire, besides the usual Roman and Greek series. The PAPAL collection at the Vatican is rather small, but every coin in it is a gem; while at BERLIN a collection of modern formation is largely gaining every day, and receives the entire support of the scientific German numismatists.

In the United States, the only collection worthy of the name of a national collection is that at the UNITED STATES MINT, in Philadelphia. The collection numbers over 6,000 well-selected pieces, and contains the largest and finest number of Washington medals and tokens. This cabinet is unfortunately entirely deficient in that department, wherein it ought to excel, namely, the "Colonial Series." In time, no doubt, this will be remedied, and with a reasonable yearly appropriation for the purpose by Congress, many rare Colonial coins, now held by private individuals, must ultimately find their way into this cabinet.

Such collections as we have just enumerated may be termed complete cabinets; they include coins of all nations, both ancient and modern. They have a regularly recognized system of geographical, chronological and alphabetical classification; they are the result of the labors of many individuals, extending over prolonged periods. Their formation is necessarily reserved for scientific and learned institutions. Their care and preservation is intrusted to officers appointed by the State; they are the living repositories which link us to the past; they are made the means of distributing historical knowledge, and of contributing to our education and pleasure.

It is perhaps fortunate for amateur collectors that, failing to attain what is really beyond their reach, they remain satisfied with their more humble efforts, and do not throw numismatics to the dogs simply because, no matter what they collect, the most desirable specimens must always continue beyond their reach. Indeed, the enjoyment derived from the possession and contemplation of say twelve well selected coins, the result of one's first efforts, is probably as great as that ever afterward experienced by larger acquisitions, and that brings us to speak of the second and third kinds of cabinets, such as it is within the power of amateurs to form.

The second class or kind of cabinets consists simply of an assemblage of specimens, selected from the leading classes and embracing the principal types, without special regard to any particular arrangement, except that of placing the coins of each country together in chronological order. When the coins of any country become very numerous they may be classed according to their dimensions, in which case it will be found that the modern silver coins fall under three sizes: thus we have the penny, which for many ages constituted the sole coin; the groat, a coin of importance for a considerable period, and existing to this day; and lastly, the crown piece, from the commencement of the XVI. century. Such a miscellaneous collection forms really the most interesting and attractive cabinet, and its formation will amply repay any labor or outlay bestowed upon it.

In the third class, which is frequently an outgrowth of the second, the completion of one particular series is aimed at by the collector. If the miscellaneous cabinet is the most interesting to an amateur collector, a completed series of whatsoever country or age is the most valuable; and it is chiefly to the forming of such collections that experienced collectors devote their time and money. In making special collections of this class, the collector would do well to begin with some particular issue of his own country, chiefly because every collector ought to feel sufficient interest in his native land to make the collection of its coins a labor of love, and also because these are generally more accessible to him than those of any other country. It is a fact worthy of notice that many of the minor public collections of Europe contain only such coins as, in a historical point of view, belong particularly to the vicinity. We remember frequent visits, when a boy, to a very interesting little museum of local antiquities, situated at Avanches (Switzerland), the former site of the important Roman city of AVENTICUM, now reduced to a mere unimportant borough. In this museum, constructed entirely of material rescued from the neighboring ruins, is, among other antiquities, a collection of over 5,000 Roman coins—gold, silver and bronze—every one of which was found within a surrounding area of about five miles square. Such results can not, of course, be obtained in this country; but it would, no doubt, be gratifying to a Bostonian to know that the finest and most complete collection of the New England coinage, of the Massachusetts pine, oak and willow tree series, and of the Massachusetts cents and half cents, was in the possession of the Boston Numismatic Society; or to a New Yorker to feel assured that the majority of the "Confederatio," and other rare coins ascribed to his State, should remain in the undisturbed and continued possession of one of its institutions.

UNITED STATES COINS.

We take it for granted that most of our readers, being Americans, have devoted a considerable space in their cabinets to American coins. American coins are not particularly scarce or difficult to obtain, with the exception of certain *dates* of mint pieces and particular types of Colonial coins, of which so few specimens are known to exist that they are particularly remarkable on account of their absence from our cabinets. Fortunately, if in American dollars, for instance, the 1804 is unattainable, its omission means nothing more than a lack of the date, the *design* of the piece being the same as that of the preceding year, by no means a rare piece. The design of the 1796 half-cent, another rarity, is the same as that of the 1795, thin planchet; the 1799 cent, except in date, is the same as the 1800 (struck over 1799); the 1802 half dime has precisely the same design as the dime of the same year; and so it happens that leaving out certain dates, good collections of the various types of American mint issues can be made without any extraordinary outlay of money. The exceptions to these remarks are at least two types of the 1793 cent (the chain and wreath), the liberty cap of the date having its exact counterpart in a liberty cap of 1794, and the 1836 and 1838 flying-eagle dollars (really pattern pieces), neither of which are excessively rare.

The following table of comparative rarity of United States silver and copper coinage, from the year 1793 to 1857 inclusive, may be of some use to collectors. The greatest rarity is indicated by 6; N. C., signifies that none were coined; the asterisk denotes the introduction of a new design:

Yrs.	Dollars.	Half Dollars.	Quarter Dollars.	Dimes.	Half Dimes.	Cents.	Half Cents.
1793	N. C.	N. C.	N. C.	N. C.	N. C.	5	4
1794	5	3	N. C.	N. C.	4	2	3
1795	2	2	N. C.	N. C.	3	2	4
1796	3	5	4	4	4	3	6
1797	2	5	N. C.	5	3	2	3
1798	1	N. C.	N. C.	3	N. C.	1	N. C.
1799	1	N. C.	N. C.	N. C.	N. C.	5	N. C.
1800	2	N. C.	N. C.	4	3	3	3
1801	2	2	N. C.	3	3	3	N. C.
1802	2	2	N. C.	4	6	2	4
1803	1	1	N. C.	3	4	1	2
1804	6	6	3	5	N. C.	5	1
1805	N. C.	1	2	2	*4	2	2
1806	N. C.	1	2	N. C.	N. C.	3	2
1807	N. C.	1	2	2	N. C.	2	2
1808	N. C.	2	N. C.	N. C.	N. C.	3	1
1809	N. C.	2	N. C.	3	N. C.	1	3
1810	N. C.	2	N. C.	N. C.	N. C.	2	3
1811	N. C.	2	N. C.	3	N. C.	3	3
1812	N. C.	2	N. C.	N. C.	N. C.	2	N. C.
1813	N. C.	2	N. C.	N. C.	N. C.	3	N. C.

Numismatics in 1876: this article from "The Coin Collector's Journal" gives some basic collecting ideas. (continued on the following page)

Yrs.	Dollars.	Half Dollars.	Quarter Dollars.	Dimes.	Half Dimes.	Cents.	Half Cents.
1814	N. C.	2	N. C.	2	N. C.	2	N. C.
1815	N. C.	4	3	N. C.	N. C.	N. C.	N. C.
1816	N. C.	N. C.	N. C.	N. C.	N. C.	2	N. C.
1817	N. C.	2	N. C.	N. C.	N. C.	1	N. C.
1818	N. C.	2	2	N. C.	N. C.	1	N. C.
1819	N. C.	2	2	N. C.	N. C.	1	N. C.
1820	N. C.	2	2	2	N. C.	2	N. C.
1821	N. C.	2	2	2	N. C.	2	N. C.
1822	N. C.	1	2	4	N. C.	1	N. C.
1823	N. C.	1	5	2	N. C.	3	N. C.
1824	N. C.	1	3	3	N. C.	2	N. C.
1825	N. C.	1	2	2	N. C.	1	2
1826	N. C.	1	N. C.	N. C.	N. C.	1	2
1827	N. C.	1	6	2	N. C.	1	N. C.
1828	N. C.	1	2	3	N. C.	1	1
1829	N. C.	1	N. C.	2	2	1	1
1830	N. C.	1	N. C.	2	2	1	N. C.
1831	N. C.	1	1	2	1	1	4
1832	N. C.	1	1	2	1	1	1
1833	N. C.	1	1	2	1	1	1
1834	N. C.	1	1	2	1	1	1
1835	N. C.	1	1	2	1	1	1
1836	4	2	2	2	1	1	4
1837	N. C.	2	2	2	1	1	N. C.
1838	4	2	2	2	1	1	N. C.
1839	4	2	2	2	1	1	N. C.
1840	3	2	2	2	1	1	4
1841	2	1	2	2	1	1	4
1842	2	1	2	2	1	1	4
1843	2	1	2	2	1	1	4
1844	2	2	1	3	2	1	4
1845	2	1	1	1	2	1	4
1846	2	1	1	3	4	1	4
1847	2	1	1	1	2	1	4
1848	2	1	1	1	1	1	4
1849	2	1	1	1	1	1	2
1850	2	1	1	1	1	1	2
1851	4	2	1	1	1	1	2
1852	4	2	1	1	1	1	4
1853	2	1	1	1	1	1	1
1854	4	1	1	1	1	1	2
1855	3	1	1	1	1	1	2
1856	2	1	1	1	1	1	2
1857	2	1	1	1	1	2	2

Above: Continuation of an 1876 article on coin collecting. Notice that branch mints, numismatic issues of San Francisco and New Orleans, for example, are nowhere mentioned! The date and mintmark syndrome, so popular today, did not catch on until the early 20th century.

octagon, $7.00; G. Traecing, 5 cents, brass, 90c.; Taylor & Raymond, Louisville, Ky., brass, 35c.; Walton & Co., New Orleans, brass, 50c.; Weighell & Sons, head of John Bell, copper, $1.30; J. Ninkelmeyer, Union Brewery, white metal, 50c.; J. B. Wilson's, *rev.*, Bread, lead, 35c.; Weisenfield, & Co., St. Louis, rubber, 40c.

UNITED STATES COINS.

Dollars.—1794, everything distinct, $39.00; 1795, flowing hair, $2.13 do., fillet head $2.00; 1796, very fair, $2.50; another, $2.00; 1797, 7 stars facing, $3.25; do., 6 stars facing, $1.60; 1798, small eagle, 13 stars, $4.25; 1798, large eagle, $1.30; 1799, common type, $1.25; do., 5 stars facing, good, $4.25; 1800, fine, $1.75; 1802, fine, $1.75; 1803, good, $1.50; 1836, circulated, $3.70; 1838, brilliant proof, $27.00; 1838, brilliant proof, $37.00; 1852, brilliant proof, $28.00; 1853, fine, $2.25; 1854, fair, $2.00; 1855, good, $2.90; 1856, good, $2.90; 1857, fine, $2.60.

Half-Dollars.—1794, fair, $2.35; 1795, good, 90c.; do., variety, 65c.; 1796, 16 stars, good, $15.25; 1797, fair $4.50; 1801, 1802, 1803, poor, each, $1.00; 1805 over 1804, 80c.; 1805, 1806, 1807, fair, each 65c.; 1809, 70c.; 1810, 70c.; 1814, 65c.; 1815, $1.50.

Quarter-Dollars.—1796, very poor, 45c.; 1804, poor, 50c.; 1805, 40c.; 1806, 50c.; 1807, '15, '18, '19, '20, '21, '22, '24, '25, '28, poor to fair, each 36c.; 1831 to '39, each 31c.; 1857, O. mint, proof, 65c.

Dimes.—1796, fair, $1.25; 1797, poor, 50c.; 1798, poor and pierced, 50c.; 1800, poor, 50c.; 1801, poor, 25c.; 1802, fair, 25c.; 1803, fair, 35c.; 1804, very poor, 40c.; 1805, fair, 35c.; 1807, poor and pierced, 15c.; 1809, poor, 20c.; 1811, poor and pierced, 15c.; 1814, '20, '21, fair each, 15c.; 1822, good, 95c.; 1823, fair, 15c.; 1824, 20c.; 1825, '27, each 15c.; 1828, fair, 50c.; 1830, '39, each 10c.

Half-Dimes.—1794, fair, pierced, 35c.; 1795, fair, 15c.; 1797, poor, 25c.; 1800, good, 50c.; 1803, fair, 60c., 1805, pierced, $1.00; 1829 to '39, fair and good, each 6c.

Three cents.—1851 to 1862, fair to fine, 12 pieces, each 4c.

Cents.—1793, wreath, electrotype 40c.; 1795, fair, thick pl., $1.00; 1795, thin pl., fair, 45c.; 1796, fillet head, good, $1.25; 1797, fair, 20c.; 1798, fair, 10c.; 1799, electrotype, 50c.; 1802, good, 20c.; 1803, fine, 90c.; 1804, perfect die, tooled, $5.25; 1806, very good, $1.00; 1807, fair, 20c.; 1808, 12 stars, weak impression, $1.50; 1809, very poor, 30c.; 1811, very poor, 30c.

Half cents. 1794, fair only, 55c.; 1795, very poor, 25c.; 1800, fair, 15c.; 1803, fair, 15c.; 1804, good, 05c.; 1805, fine, 41c.; 1806, fair, 05c.; 1807, fair, 10c.; 1808, good, 20c.; 1809, fine, 10c.; 1810, good, 85c.; 1811, fair, 90c.; 1831, proof, original, $4.26; 1836, proof, original, $5.50; 1841, good, $4.00; 1852, proof, $3.50; 1857, uncirculated, 25c.; 1825 to 1857, all the common dates some duplicates, 30 pieces, each 06½c.

A random page from "The Coin Collector's Journal" in 1876. Described are recent auction results from an offering of United States coins.

COIN COLLECTING IN 1876 was much different from the situation today. Most collectors were students and were familiar not only with American issues but with coins of the world as well. *The American Journal of Numismatics, The Coin Collector's Journal,* and other publications carried long treatises concerning medals of England, crowns of Bavaria, coins of ancient Greece and Rome, and other topics which today would be in the realm of the specialist. Paper money, today collected avidly, was virtually ignored.

United States coins were collected by date sequence. Few, if indeed any, collectors cared whether or not silver and gold coins were being produced in Carson City, Nevada, in very limited numbers. Likewise, issues of Charlotte, Dahlonega, San Francisco, and New Orleans were ignored. Coins would be bought and sold without mention of a mintmark. Indeed, it was not known what mintmark varieties existed! Not until Augustus Heaton produced a treatise on the subject in the 1890s was there much of an interest, and even then the main thrust of activity had to await the 20th century.

High in popularity were coins, medals, and tokens pertaining to George Washington. The limited number of earlier pieces was supplemented by prolific outpourings of medalists such as Key, Merriam, Lovett, and others who produced individual pieces as well as sets for sale to collectors. Adding to the stream were many original and restrike medals available from the Philadelphia Mint. Coins of colonial times were likewise popular. The publication in 1875 of Sylvester S. Crosby's "Early Coins of America" lent impetus to this interest.

While a few dealers issued price lists, nearly all coin catalogs were devoted to auction sales. Values were determined by subscribing to as many auction sale catalogs as possible, for there were no regularly-issued priced reference books available. Grading was uncertain. What one seller would call Uncirculated another would call Very Fine. The Proof designation, so precisely defined today, was used very loosely and was often applied to Uncirculated coins or coins with light wear.

The average collector kept his coins at home in a series of wooden trays housed in a coin cabinet. Purchases were made by mail from various dealers, primarily in Philadelphia, New York, and Boston. Participation in auction sales was usually through a favorite dealer who, upon being paid a modest commission, would attend the sale in person and would verify the grading and other characteristics. By 1876 there were probably two or three thousand coin collectors in the United States, of which perhaps 1,000 belonged to numismatic organizations, subscribed to periodicals, and otherwise became involved in a serious way.

A Numismatic Adventure

8

From today's vantage point it would have been fun to have lived in the 1870s. Buying coins would have been like picking up diamonds in the street, at least in retrospect. Proof two-cent pieces minted from 1864 through 1873 cost about 25c each. Today each is worth hundreds of dollars. Proof Liberty seated dimes of the 1860s and 1870s, each valued at several hundred dollars today, cost all of 15c apiece! A rare 1858 Proof silver dollar, a coin worth many thousands of dollars today, cost $6, and most dates of Proof trade dollars could be obtained for $2 per coin.

A rarity a century ago was the 1796 quarter eagle with a Proof surface at $15. Today a bid of $25,000 might not capture it!

The days of the 1876 Centennial Exhibition and its surrounding numismatic activities are long gone, as is the 19th century way of life.

In 1978, while doing research for a 1953-1978 silver anniversary article about my rare coin firm, I was struck by the vast differences which took place during the quarter century involved. Today a numismatic view of 1953 seems almost, but not quite, as remote as one of 1876! The coin market was small in 1953, far ahead of 1876, to be sure, but just a shadow of the volume and valuation of the present time. Great rarities sold for fractions of today's valuations.

A Choice Uncirculated specimen of the famous 1909-S V.D.B. cent brought in the $15 to $20 range, an 1873 Proof two-cent piece $50, the rare 1877 Proof shield nickel $110, a Proof Liberty nickel in the 1900s $5, and an Uncirculated 1950-D nickel sold for 25c. A Proof common date Barber dime fetched $5, an Uncirculated 1875-S 20-cent piece brought $12, and an example of the rare 1796 quarter dollar in Uncirculated grade would set the buyer back all of $200.

Among Barber quarters, Proofs of most dates could be obtained for about $7 each. An Uncirculated 1901-S was a great rarity and sold for $375. The rare 1916 Liberty standing quarter in Uncirculated grade brought $125, much more than the $2 a common date such as 1926-D

sold for at the time. Indeed, it was a sensation when a roll of forty pieces of 1916 quarters turned up in Reading, Pennsylvania and sold for $4,000. In 1978 a choice *single coin* from that roll would have sold for nearly the same amount!

Proof Liberty seated half dollars in the 1880s cost $10 to $15 each. A 1921-S Uncirculated half dollar cost $90, and further along in the same denomination an Uncirculated 1938-D cost $7.

In the field of silver dollars if you wanted a Proof 1840 it would cost $125. The rare 1858 fetched the grandiose sum of $275, quite a bit more than the $20 one had to pay for Proof Liberty seated dollars dated in the early 1870s.

Uncirculated Morgan dollars in many instances could be obtained from banks at face value. True, there were some which were high priced. For example, an 1889-CC in Uncirculated grade cost $30 and the rare Proof 1895 cost $150.

An Uncirculated Indian head quarter eagle was apt to cost about $7 unless you wanted a rare 1911-D in which instance $30 to $40 was the going rate. An Uncirculated three-dollar gold piece of 1854 cost $25, while a Proof of the same year was valued at $150. Twenty-dollar gold pieces of many years could be obtained for just $36 to $37 each, just a dollar or two over their bullion value at the time.

A large collection was apt to sell in the $5,000 to $10,000 range in 1953. Indeed, the purchase of a collection of this value would be a feather in any dealer's cap. Collections valued at $100,000 or more were virtually unheard of.

The needs of collectors and dealers were served by *The Numismatist*, official journal of the American Numismatic Association, *The Numismatic Scrapbook Magazine*, published by Hewitt Brothers in Chicago, Illinois, and the newspaper *Numismatic News*, founded in 1952 by Chet Krause in Iola, Wisconsin.

There weren't many full-time dealers at the time. And, of the dealers who were in business in 1953, most

went in other directions by 25 years later, 1978. Of the approximately 300 dealers advertising in a summer 1978 issue of *The Numismatist*, fewer than ten had been advertisers in the January 1953 issue of the same publication!

In this arena James F. Ruddy, later to become my business partner, began his career in rare coins. At the time in 1953 he was an employee of Ansco, an important photographic supply company located in Binghamton, New York. In between duties in physics research he began buying, selling, and trading coins.

Individual transactions were small, not only on Jim Ruddy's part but with other dealers as well. His first price lists, printed on a duplicating machine in 1953, brought in numerous orders mostly for several dollars each, although an occasional $10 or $20 payment would be received. His first national advertisement, placed in *Numismatic News* in the summer of 1954, brought its first order from Miss Phyllis Ritter who sent $3.95 plus 15c postage to order the following items: 1853 three-cent silver piece Very Good 50c, 1833 half dime Fine 75c, 1845 half dime Fine 70c, 1858 half dime Fine 50c, 1861 half dime Fine 50c, and 1871 half dime Very Fine $1.00. From the same *Numismatic News* advertisement could be ordered a Brilliant Uncirculated 1909-S Indian cent at $30, a Brilliant Uncirculated 1909-S V.D.B. Lincoln cent at $17.50, or a complete set of Jefferson nickels in an album for $7.

Jim Ruddy's first office was in his home, a white-painted two-story wooden frame structure located at 25 Spruce Street in Johnson City, New York. During the time little thought was given to electronic burglar alarms, security systems, and the like. Indeed, at conventions it was common practice for dealers and collectors alike to store coins in hotel rooms while they were eating dinner or otherwise occupied. There were few thefts. Likewise, most collectors kept their coins at home where they could be taken out during evenings and Sunday afternoons to be studied and enjoyed.

In response to local and nationwide advertising and to price lists Jim Ruddy's business, soon named the Triple Cities Coin Exchange, moved to a second floor office location at 257 Main Street in Johnson City, New York. At the end of a corridor of lawyers, insurance agents, and others was a room in which Jim and a secretary held forth with their business. Two large safes contained the inventory with particularly rare pieces being kept nearby in a vault at the Marine Midland Bank.

Johnson City was well known as a manufacturing center for shoes. The Endicott-Johnson Company was located there, with the firm's red-brick factories with tall smoke stacks dominating much of the town. Endicott-Johnson years earlier was a paternal company: immigrants, mostly from Europe, were employed at low wages to stitch, mold, and form all manner of boots and shoes. Entertainment was provided by company picnics and outings as well as by company-provided facilities including a park (complete with a Herschell-Spillman merry-go-round and accompanying Wurlitzer Model 146A military band organ), theatre, and municipal auditorium. At the entrance to Johnson City at the line separating that village from adjacent Binghamton was a concrete arch which read: "Gateway to the Square Deal Cities." The "square deal cities" were Johnson City and neighboring Endicott. "Square deal" referred to the supposedly fair treatment given to workers by the town's dominant industry.

Binghamton, New York, in the 1890s was a leading area for cigar manufacturing and, later, furniture making. Years later in the early 1950s it had many industries including International Business Machines, General Electric, Ansco, and Link Aviation. Interestingly enough, IBM, the giant multinational corporation and darling of stock market investors, and Link, prominent in the field of aviation trainers, both had their beginning years earlier in the same building located on Water Street.

Main Street in Johnson City was a comfortable, quiet place, hardly a seeming locale for the growth of what was to become the world's largest rare coin firm. Near the small coin office was Woolworth's five and ten cent store, with wooden floors and with the enticing smell of fresh candy at the entrance. A penny scale near the front door provided extra revenue. Woolworth's was a convenient place to buy notepaper, stationery, and small-office supplies.

Directly across the street was the Crystal Tea Room, run by Onofrio "Tony" Tona. Years earlier in 1925 patrons in the high wooden booths in the Crystal were entertained by a newly-installed Mills *Violano-Virtuoso* violin-playing machine, a deluxe model with two violins. Unfortunately, by 1953 the instrument had long since disappeared. Offered for sale at the Crystal was a wide variety of tempting morsels, mostly priced from 50c to $1.50 and including pork chops with Italian sauce, hamburgers prepared several different ways, and other specialties. Further up the street was the Baptist Bible Seminary which in later years provided a handy source for part-time clerical help.

During these early times Jim spent one night a month as secretary of the Triple Cities Coin Club which met in the local Moose Lodge. "We can only let your organization use our hall if one of the club members is a Moose," Jim Ruddy was told. Upon checking, Jim could find none, so he became one.

The world scene in 1953-1954 presented a kaleidoscope of events. In June 1953 Queen Elizabeth II was crowned. I remember listening to the event on my Hallicrafters shortwave set. While some families had television at the time, ours did not. Those families that

James F. Ruddy, who began business in 1953, placed his first display advertisement in "Numismatic News" in 1954. Today the publisher of "Numismatic News," Krause Publications of Iola, Wisconsin, has expanded to produce several different periodical publications as well as many important references and price guides.

At the upper right James F. Ruddy in 1953 works with a group of coins.

PHONE 7-0411

JAMES F. RUDDY   NUMISMATIST

25 SPRUCE STREET
JOHNSON CITY, N. Y.

DEALER IN U. S. COINS

Numismatic News

Published For Collectors

By A Collector

FIRST SECTION

NUMISMATIC NEWS, IOLA, WISCONSIN, MONDAY, JULY 5, 1954

FOR SALE

1797 G Half Cent Plugged	$ 4.00
1800 F Large Cent	5.50
1809 VG-F Rare	20.00
1821 G Close Date	3.00
1823/22 VG Sm. Ob. Rim Dent	8.00
1826 G plus Close Date	.75
1831 G plus Large Letters	.75
1837 VG Beaded Cord	1.00
1839 G Booby Head	.75
1839 G Silly Head	2.00
1845 VF	1.50
1848 F	.75
1850 VF	1.50
1853 VF	5.00
1857 OB VF, REV. Small Pits	9.50
1908 S Unc Indian	1.00
1909 S Red Unc Indian	50.00
1909 S Brill. Unc Indian	28.00
1909 S Br Unc slight spotting	.50
1909 Unc Lincoln	.35
1909 S V.D.B. unc	17.50
1909 S V.D.B. Br Unc	17.00
1909 S V.D.B. Red Unc.	4.50
1909 S Br Unc	4.00
1853 VG 3 Cent Silver	.50
1865 VF 3 Cent Nickel	.40
1833 F plus Half Dime	.75
1845 F plus Half Dime	.70
1858 F Half Dime	.50
1861 F	.50
1871 VF	1.00
1913 I Ex.F Nickels	.50
1913 II Ex.F Nickels	1.00
1914 Ex.F Nickels	2.00
1916 Ex.F Nickels	1.50
1939 D Unc Nickels	2.50
1875 S VF 20 Cent	6.00
1875 CC VG 20 Cent	5.00
1948 Unc Half Dollars	2.00
1953 Unc Half Dollars	1.00

SPECIAL - 3 Complete Sets to 1953 of Jefferson Nickels, V.G. to Unc in new holder. Each $7.00

Satisfaction guaranteed or return within 3 days for full refund. Postage included in price.

JAMES F. RUDDY

25 Spruce St.
JOHNSON CITY, N. Y.

Kinda strong for cleaning coins ain't it.

did were more apt to see what looked like a snowstorm in Alaska than a clear picture of the coronation or any other event. In the same year Josef Stalin, the Russian dictator, died, and was succeeded by G.M. Malenkov. Dag Hammarskjold of Sweden was elected secretary-general of the United Nations. Eisenhower was inaugurated as President of the United States, ushering in what many hoped would be an era of prosperity. Earlier, Eisenhower, non-political by nature, had vacillated between joining the Democratic or the Republican ticket and finally chose the latter.

Julius and Ethel Rosenberg, sentenced in 1951 as atomic spies, were executed amidst a tremendous public outcry reminiscent of the Sacco-Vanzetti situation of several decades earlier. In far-away Egypt, playboy-king Farouk was ousted from the throne and replaced by Colonel Nasser who became premier. Farouk fled into exile, leaving behind him a fabulous collection of coins, stamps, art, and pornography.

Senator Joseph R. McCarthy in 1954 elevated the sport of Communist witch-hunting to the point that television sets displaying the congressional hearings were a prominent fixture in stores, lest business be lost if prospective buyers stayed home to watch the exciting activities. Later McCarthy was formally censured and condemned by a Senate resolution.

New books of the era included Edna Ferber's *Giant*, a tale of the Texas oil fields; Thomas B. Costain's *The Silver Chalice;* Leon Uris' *Battle Cry;* and Charles Lindbergh's biography, *The Spirit of St. Louis.*

On movie screens throughout the United States, most of which were expanded considerably in size for new CinemaScope film projection, were to be seen such offerings as *From Here to Eternity, The Robe, The Living Desert* (a Walt Disney nature film), *On the Waterfront,* and *Rear Window.*

Down at the local soda fountain one could put a nickel in the Wurlitzer Model 1450 jukebox and hear such tunes as *Doggie in the Window, I Believe, Ebbtide, Stranger in Paradise, I Love Paris, Hernando's Hideaway, Mr. Sandman, Hey There,* and *Young at Heart.* For the numismatist, I suppose, the popular 1954 song *Three Coins in the Fountain* may have had special appeal.

In 1953 Mount Everest, the seemingly impregnable goal of mountain climbers, was scaled for the first time by Hillary and Tenzing. Sir Edmund Hillary, upon being asked why he did it, replied with the comment: "Because it is there." It was reported that lung cancer was directly attributable to smoking cigarettes, thus paving the way for the ending of cigarette commercials featuring athletes and others who smilingly proclaimed that cigarettes increased their feelings of well being, social popularity, and many other things. Perhaps even

more gloomy was another "first," the United States test of a hydrogen bomb on Bikini Atoll. The United States submarine *Nautilus* was converted to atomic power, thus marking a new era in ship propulsion. Dr. Jonas E. Salk, who developed a successful antipolio vaccine, began inoculating schoolchildren in Pittsburgh, Pennsylvania, thus establishing himself as one of the greatest modern benefactors of mankind.

At the time Jim Ruddy's business continued to prosper. Collections, usually in the range of several hundred dollars to a few thousand dollars each, were purchased, classified, priced, and then resold to eager buyers both through the mail and to visitors who stopped by in person. Ed Lenga, a local collector, requested unusual coins, pieces which were misstruck. Strangely enough, he would pay a premium for them. Jim sought mint errors in buffalo nickels, Mercury dimes, and many other series, and Ed formed a nice collection.

Mint errors were not in the mainstream of numismatics then. Indeed, many sold for less than regular issues—just the opposite of the situation today. This philosophy prevailed in some areas for many years thereafter. In the early 1960s D. Wayne Johnson, first editor of *Coin World,* wrote that he was perplexed why anyone would want to pay a premium for a mint error coin. If a reader were given a misprinted book he would return it to the publisher, he reasoned, so why shouldn't it be the same with coins? Today, of course, the situation is vastly different, and certain rare mint errors sell for fabulous sums.

It was an error of a sort which provided Jim Ruddy with an interesting situation in 1955. One day at the Philadelphia Mint a coinage die was being prepared for a Lincoln cent. During the preparation of the working die, the hub die was impressed several times in order to sharpen the definition. During the last punching with the hub die there was a slight misalignment. The result was a 1955 cent die with the letters and numerals on the front sharply doubled, almost blurred in appearance. Under a low-power magnifying glass, or even to the sharp unaided eye, each digit or letter was repeated. Instead of 1955 the coin read 11995555. Instead of IN GOD WE TRUST there appeared a nonsensical IINN GGOODD WWEE TTRRUUSSTT.

The die, with its error undetected, was put into service along with a number of other cent dies. All were soon busily at work stamping out a coppery cascade of bright Lincoln pieces. Late in the afternoon a mint inspector looked once, could hardly believe his eyes, and looked again. The oddity was discovered!

What to do? By that time over 40,000 cents had been produced by the error die, and of this number about 24,000 had been mixed together with production from other presses.

The decision was made to destroy the 16,000 error coins still near the press and to let the other 24,000 or so go into circulation. Otherwise nearly a day's production of cents would have been lost.

As noted, oddities were not in particular favor at the time, and apparently mint employees were not aware that the curious 1955 pieces would ever cause a stir.

The 1955 Double Die cents, as they came to be known, were put into bags and shipped for use in the channels of commerce. As luck would have it, most if not all pieces were released in just two locations: in Massachusetts and in upstate New York near Johnson City.

At the time a pack of cigarettes sold in Johnson City for 23c. To purchase a pack in a vending machine the buyer would deposit a quarter and receive a pack of cigarettes plus, under the cellophane in the cigarette package, a refund of 2c. When these coins were packaged by the cigarette distributor many 1955 Double Die cents were used!

Soon these oddities were discovered, and people brought them into Jim Ruddy's coin office. At the time there was little numismatic interest in them. A notice appeared soon thereafter in *Numismatic News*. This sparked some activity, but still most collectors, including Lincoln cent specialists, ignored them. At first Jim cheerfully paid 25c each for the curious cents, but then fearful of accumulating too many he stopped buying! By 1979 Brilliant Uncirculated specimens similar to the ones he bought back in 1955 would command close to $1,000 per coin!

During the next several years 1955 Double Die cents were to become a specialty of the firm. The original stock was soon sold, and more were acquired at ever-increasing price: $5, $10, $20, $40, and upward. At one time around 1960 over 800 pieces were in stock! These coins, being later purchases, were mostly in Extremely Fine to AU grade. They made quite a display housed in brown National brand album pages.

In nearby Binghamton, Claude R. Collier, a long-time collector, was the proud owner of one of the largest and finest groups of United States coins and stamps ever assembled. Upon Mr. Collier's death, his widow, recognizing her late husband's friendship with the young dealer, awarded the coin and stamp collection to Jim Ruddy to sell at auction.

On July 18, 1956, the coin section of the Collier estate was sold, thus marking Jim Ruddy's full-time entry into the coin business on a grand scale.

The illustrated catalogue featured many numismatic classics. The silver dollar section, for example, possessed a 1794, an Uncirculated 1851 original, a Proof 1852, the rare Proof 1858, and a complete run of Proof Morgan silver dollars from 1878 through 1904. Other highlights included different denominations of United States coins, ancient Greek and Roman pieces, and world crowns. The event attracted nationwide publicity. On the sale date bids poured in from all corners of America. The Collier Collection auction was a tremendous success.

In the meantime in Forty Fort, Pennsylvania, a two-hour car ride south of Johnson City, I was beginning my interest in coins. A high school student at the time, I avidly pursued many hobbies.

Reptiles and amphibians in particular were interesting to me. I eagerly devoured all I could read by such authors as Raymond L. Ditmars, curator of herpetology at the Bronx Zoo in New York City, Ross Allen, reptile specialist in Florida, Archie Carr and others. Ditmars in particular was a fascinating author. I enjoyed very much reading of his trips to South America, including the zoologically-isolated island of Trinidad which was the source of many varieties of frogs and snakes not to be found elsewhere in the world.

On October 21, 1952, for my 14th birthday my parents gave me a copy of the classic reference book in the field, *The Reptiles of North America,* by Ditmars. I read it avidly. "The crocodilians are huge lizard-like reptiles, amphibious in habits. They are of direct relationship to races of great antiquity, as crocodilians of similar form and size existed many millions of years ago, during the Mesozoic era, in association with monster reptiles of the dim past..."

I was fascinated by the fact that while North America was populated with several major types of reptiles such as snakes, lizards, and turtles, these could be scientifically broken down further into hundreds of sub-categories. For example, Ditmars related that only one specimen had ever been seen of the rare reptile known as Strecker's hook-nosed snake, an example found close to midnight, July 13, 1930, on a highway three miles east of Rio Grande City, Texas.

Ditmars loved reptiles and delighted in treating them as if they had personalities. When Mrs. Margaret A. Gruner, of New York City, donated a specimen to Ditmars it was accompanied by a letter which he quoted:

"Relative to the age of the box turtle I had you send for, and for which you have at the Park now, I wish to say that when I was a girl at the age of six or seven, which is nearly 33 years ago, I remember this turtle walking about my father's farm, which was then where the Yankee Stadium now stands. It was the only box turtle ever around the place and it kept itself in and around the glass-covered hotbeds.

"When our house was torn down and the steam shovel started work there was some deep digging for a garage. It was then that my father, George Einberger,

saw our turtle crawling between the curb and the sidewalk. Father took him to our store. Since then we sold the store and I have had him in the apartment here for over a year. Now I hope he will spend a long time at the Bronx Zoological Park.''

It was from reading Ditmars that I learned that a scientific pursuit could be romantically and historically interesting as well. While Ditmars could assign Latin names such as *Masticophis fragellum frenautum* to a reptile, he could with equal facility describe it in interesting terms which I, a young schoolboy, could understand and appreciate. In later years when I was to become involved in numismatics I particularly enjoyed reading the works of Dr. William H. Sheldon and Dr. Edward Maris. Writing about his favorite specialty, Dr. Sheldon in *Early American Cents* took the reader through his childhood days when he looked through family heirloom coins by the fireside, told anecdotes of buying, selling, and trading cents, and otherwise enchanted the reader, just as Ditmars did. It would have been a very unfeeling person who after completing the Sheldon book did not feel an affinity, even an affection, for these dark brown and black early coppers. Likewise, one could easily be charmed by Dr. Edward Maris, who studied 1794 large cents and rather than just assigning numbers or dry catalogue listings to them, gave them such interesting appellations as *Venus Marina, Scarred Head, Bent Hair Lock,* and *Shielded Hair,* each descriptive of the coin's appearance.

I often wish that more coins had nicknames. Among later date large cents one can find the curiously-named *Booby Head* and *Silly Head* pieces of 1839. I have always wondered where these names originated. Apparently they were in use as early as the 1860s. Among copper coins of the states dated in the 1780s there are several interesting instances of nomenclature; the *Hercules Head, African Head,* and *Muttonhead* Connecticut coppers, the *Serpent Head* and *Fox* New Jersey pieces, and the *Baby Head* Vermont coppers being examples.

Indeed, perhaps it is within the purview of present-day numismatists to create descriptive names, if for no other reason than to make our hobby more interesting. In the 1960s, Les Zeller, specialist in world coins with my firm, was cataloging a crown which showed a rough storm, waves and other meteorological phenomena. Why not call it the *Wrath of Nature* crown? He did this, and subsequently described it in one of our catalogues as such, without further comment. Much to his elation, he later saw in a competitor's offering another coin nonchalantly described as the *Wrath of Nature* crown! Imitation is the sincerest form of flattery, so it is said.

Following my interest in reptiles I became attracted to rocks and minerals. I subscribed to *Gritner's Geode,* a hobby publication on the subject, sent for catalogues from Ward's Natural Science Establishment in Rochester, and otherwise mailed as many coupons and inquiries as I could. I soon learned that the fountainhead of mineralogy knowledge was a series of learned volumes compiled by a scholar named Dana and which was available only in large libraries and universities. Seeking to gaze upon these volumes myself I took the bus (I was too young to drive a car at the time) to nearby Wilkes-Barre, Pennsylvania, and visited the Osterhout Library. I was told that, yes, the library did have a set of the prized Dana volumes, but being younger than 16 years of age I wasn't allowed to see them. No, not even to peek at them for a brief moment, the librarian told me in no uncertain terms. Disappointed, I went away.

My home town of Forty Fort, a community of about 6,000 people located on the north bank of the Susquehanna River, is deep in the heart of northeastern Pennsylvania's anthracite coal region. My father, a civil engineer by profession, rented and then later purchased a white-painted concrete home located at 64 Yeager Avenue. On the second floor at the front on the left-hand side was my bedroom, which looked at various times like a scientific laboratory, a radio station, and during my phase of reptile collecting, a zoo! A pet alligator, reverently named Ditmars, lived in the closet.

In 1953 I visited Robert Rusbar, the town tax collector, after hearing that he possessed a very fine collection of mineral specimens, including crystals.

Arriving at the Rusbar home by bicycle, I dismounted and ran down a short flight of stairs to the cellar entrance. There was Mr. Rusbar's office as well as his collection. One specimen after another he showed me—delightful minerals such as crystals, bright yellow sulphur ''flowers'' (from Sicily), and other treasures. Then he showed me another collecting interest: coins.

I wasn't a complete stranger to coins. Earlier I was given an 1893 Columbian half dollar by my maternal grandfather, Chester A. Garratt of Honesdale, Pennsylvania. In a moment of enterprise I traded it to a youthful companion, Bob King, for a scrapbook of airplane pictures, another childhood interest.

I was particularly impressed with Mr. Rusbar's album of Lincoln cents. ''See that coin? It is a 1909-S V.D.B. cent. I paid $10 for it,'' he told me. I was amazed that a coin could sell for 1,000 times its face value. I wanted to learn more! An hour or two later I left Mr. Rusbar's office with a handful of blue Lincoln cent folders and a lot of inspiration and enthusiasm.

Fourteen years old in 1953, I sought to increase my knowledge. I visited another local collector, a Mr. Pugh, who sold me an Uncirculated Indian cent for $1 and some worn ones for a few cents each. I was thrilled for I had never seen an Indian cent before!

I subscribed to the *Numismatic Scrapbook Magazine* and read every issue from cover to cover as soon as it arrived. Sharing my boyhood interest in coins at the time was Richard Shemo, who was in my high school class.

I avidly searched through pocket change for specimens I needed. Within a few months I had folders for every series from Lincoln cents through silver dollars. Perhaps a bit optimistically I purchased folders for Barber dimes, quarters, and half dollars, Indian cents, and Liberty nickels, hoping to fill them from circulation finds.

The Forty Fort State Bank, the main financial institution in my town, was particularly helpful to me. I would take $10 or $20 to the bank, exchange it for wrapped rolls of cents, nickels, or dimes, take them home, and then bring them back the next day for additional rolls. Never was there a complaint that I was a nuisance or a bother. I've always gratefully remembered this, and today whenever a young collector writes to me I always reply with interest, believing that encouragement by an adult can really stimulate a child's hobby interest.

On one memorable afternoon at the bank I looked through many rolls of half dollars and completed from circulation one of each date and mintmark variety in the Liberty walking series from 1916 through 1947 inclusive. I didn't bother to save several duplicate 1938-D half dollars obtained, for what would I have done with them? Today, of course, this seems unbelievable in view of the present high value of this issue.

Around the same time I made several visits to another Forty Fort collector, Edmund Karmilowitz, and was rewarded with the sight of dazzling Uncirculated Mercury dimes, commemoratives, and other issues. Mr. Karmilowitz introduced me to rare paper money and showed me, among other things, a pair of one-dollar notes with the bright red letters "R" and "S" on the front. "At one time the Treasury was experimenting with different types of paper," he said. "The 'R' is for 'regular' paper, and the 'S' is for 'synthetic' composition." I was fascinated.

Collecting turned to dealing in a modest way, and by 1954 I was a regular attendee at the Wilkes-Barre Coin Club, of which my friend George P. Williams was secretary. George, a veteran collector, gave me much advice on collecting and dealing. His sense of fairness and equity served as models which are still an inspiration today. Any attorney or estate executor who asked him for advice concerning the disposal of a rare coin collection was assured of an authoritative and honest recommendation. By that time I had a modest trading stock of coins which I would exchange with other club members. Augmenting my stock were purchases made at the club auctions.

The early club meetings were quite exciting. Typically, the meeting would be called to order, and the collectors who had been exchanging coins and stories would take seats around a long table. Then there would be a discussion of current numismatic events, often led by George Williams. Coin auctions would be the subject one month, Lincoln cents another month, and Proof coins still another. The leading collector was Dr. Albert Thomas, who showed from time to time such treasures as a set of flying eagle and Indian cents (complete with the extremely rare 1856, which I saw for the first time), large cents, and a set of commemoratives. These made a vivid impression on me. One of my sorrows concerns the sale of Dr. Thomas' collection in later years. Remembering his connection with me earlier, a few years ago Dr. Thomas wrote to me and said that his collection was for sale. Would I like to buy it? As luck would have it, the letter arrived a day or two after I left for an extended European trip. Upon my return I eagerly telephoned Dr. Thomas only to find that, believing I wasn't interested and therefore did not reply, he sold the collection elsewhere.

After the educational part was over an auction would be held. Rules of protocol were set up. When a coin was put up for bidding it usually had a minimum price. Dealers, of which I was considered one at the time, were not supposed to bid unless the coin failed to elicit interest from a collector.

My first auction experience was with a Brilliant Uncirculated 1879 half dollar. I examined it during the viewing before the club meeting and was amazed with its beauty. The coin was as frosty as the day it had been struck! I was further intrigued by the low mintage of the coin. Although no figures were published at the time in my trusty red-covered *Guide Book of U.S. Coins,* George Williams informed me that only a few thousand had been made. The catalog value was $10, and yet the starting bid was just half that, $5. Surely this great bargain, a rarity in beautiful, perfect condition, would be snapped up as many collectors competed for it!

George Williams, who was also the club's auctioneer, held the coin up for everyone to see.

"I have here an 1879 Uncirculated half dollar. I need $5. Do I have $5?"

"Again, I need $5. Is there any interest?"

There wasn't any interest, fortunately for me, so I hesitatingly put my hand in the air. "Sold for $5!" The coin was mine! I often wonder what happened to this piece. Although it would sell for more than $1,000 today, chances are that I passed it on to a new buyer for $7 or $8 shortly after I acquired it. I don't remember.

Seeking to broaden my purchase opportunities I ran advertisements in the *Times-Leader,* the Wilkes-Barre evening paper. Soon my telephone was ringing with all sorts of offers. I would go down to the bus stop at the

corner of Yeager and Wyoming avenues in Forty Fort and ride to Kingston, Wyoming, Wilkes-Barre, and other nearby communities. I was rewarded with many coins, no great rarities, but many of modest value at the time. Indian cents of 1871 and 1872 turned up as did an occasional 1877. Once I made an offer for a small boxful of Indian cents, paying the prices listed in the *Handbook of United States Coins,* the blue-covered book I took with me. In the group was a nickel-size coin of a yellowish color with Russian inscriptions. I didn't know what it was so I offered just 5c for it, thinking that it was a foreign coin equivalent to an American five-cent piece. I put the coin aside. A year later I found that it was an 1898 Russian five-ruble *gold* coin and was worth $6! I felt guilty about this, but by that time the address of the person from whom I purchased the coin had been forgotten.

Another time I traveled for over an hour to visit the family of the owner of a local bus line. There in a cigar box were hundreds of Indian cents, including many rare dates. I took out my reference book, added them up, and proudly announced my offer. "We don't want to sell them now, we just wondered what they were worth," was the reply. This was my first appraisal, and a free one at that.

One of the most interesting events from this early period involved an elderly gentleman who invited me to come to see him at his drugstore located on Market Street in nearby Kingston. Arriving there early in the evening, I walked up to a one-story wooden frame structure with a large glass window in the front. Entering the store, I found that little had changed from what it must have been like when it first opened for business in the 1890s. Lining the walls were wooden display cases fronted with glass, behind which were dusty old bottles, tin boxes, and other relics of more active days. It turned out that the owner was retired and was putting the property, long closed, up for sale.

During earlier years he was intrigued by two-cent pieces. Each time he took one in over the counter in change he tossed it aside in a box, accumulating several hundred of them over a period of time.

"Do you buy two-cent pieces?" he asked me. I had never seen a two-cent piece before, not even at the coin club, so with a lump in my throat I said, "Yes, I do, I am very interested in them." One by one he counted them out, and I arranged them in little piles by date. Paying the *Handbook* price, I parted with about $25 and became the owner of a treasure trove! I subsequently sold the coins for 25c to 50c each.

As a child I had been been fascinated by the romantic history of Colorado. Pikes Peak, of which I had a colored postcard, was especially alluring. There must be lots of **gold nuggets** around there, and in the nearby towns

there were probably many old coins still in circulation. I took out a modest coin-buying ad in the Denver *Post.* The mailman would soon bring me dozens of letters from old miners, and I would buy many treasures. Alas, it didn't work out that way, and all I had to show for this venture was my cancelled advertising check!

In April 1955, using the address of my father's civil engineering business, 203 Second National Bank Building, Wilkes-Barre, Pennsylvania, I ran my first advertisement in the *Numismatic Scrapbook Magazine.* The ad noted, in part:

"Announcing my coin service—specializing in the purchase and sale of United States issues. If you have a collection, accumulation, or duplicates for sale, write or call. My buying price for choice coins are tops. Let me hear from you and see what you have to offer. I will travel anywhere if warranted."

Offered for sale were many items, including the following: Brilliant Uncirculated 1878 quarter eagle $13, 1847 Brilliant Uncirculated silver dollar $22, 1917 Type 1 Brilliant Uncirculated quarter $6, 1929 and 1930 Uncirculated quarters $5 each, 1916-D dime Good $7, a complete set of Barber dimes (except 1894-S) Good to Very Fine grade $95, 1807 Fine quarter $6. And then there was a solitary foreign coin in the group, the 1898 five-ruble Russian gold coin for which I had paid 5c a year earlier, offered in Very Fine grade at $6.25.

To finance my business I sold my personal collection, which by 1955 included a set of Proof Indian cents, a run of Proof half dollars of every date from 1892 through 1915, and a type set of 48 different commemorative half dollar designs. Earlier my first purchase through the mail was made by sending Maurice M. Gould of the Copley Coin Company in Boston $11 for a Proof 1859 Indian cent.

My first *Scrapbook* advertisement attracted the attention of Dr. Edward W.W. Lewis, a Congregational minister who lived in Norwich, Connecticut. He offered me the chance to purchase his magnificent collection. What an exciting prospect!

My father, Quentin H. Bowers, took an interest in my youthful business activities. He loaned me several hundred dollars, then $1,000, then at one time $5,000 to help finance my inventory during the early years. Believing that I should learn the rules of conducting a trade in a proper manner, he prepared a set of books and told me how to make up a balance sheet. When the time came to run my first advertisement in the *Scrapbook,* the proprietor of that publication, Lee Hewitt, wrote to my father to secure a letter of parental responsibility for my transactions. Several years ago I saw Lee at a convention and he gave me as a souvenir the letter my father had written to him many years earlier.

Q. David Bowers' first display advertisement appeared on page 533 of the April 20, 1955 issue of "The Numismatic Scrapbook Magazine."

Advertisements from the 1950s offered a wide variety of pieces for sale, all at fractions of today's values.

Although I could never interest my father in collecting coins as a hobby, he did invest in coins from time to time, reaping a handsome profit in each instance. Later, in the 1970s, he did become an avid collector—but not of coins. He assembled a definitive collection of hand-crafted brass andirons and co-authored a book (with Henry J. Kauffman), *Early American Andirons.*

With my father I made the long car trip from Forty Fort, through New York, to Dr. Lewis' home in Norwich. There displayed before me were coins of a quality and quantity I had never seen before. Silver dollars by the hundreds, gold coins, commemoratives, and many other pieces were there in dazzling profusion. After two days of careful examination and negotiation we agreed on a price for the magnificent group: $6,000!

Dr. Lewis was a connoisseur. Included were many superb Uncirculated and Proof coins plus some rolls and groups. I was particularly pleased to buy a cigar box full of Uncirculated 1931-S cent rolls. At the time each roll of 50 coins was worth about $150.

Stocked with the Lewis Collection and other purchases, including a collection of gold coins purchased from a Wilkes-Barre pawnshop owner, I began to run large advertisements in the *Numismatic Scrapbook Magazine* and *The Numismatist.* By mid-summer 1955 the quality and rarity had escalated to include such items as Proof 1856 and 1857 gold dollars, the pair at $225; a beautiful Uncirculated MCMVII High Relief double eagle at $145; and a Proof 1833 quarter eagle at, amazingly enough, just $85, less than one-hundredth of the price I would sell the same coin for 20 years later!

During the summer I attended my first American Numismatic Association convention at the Sheraton-Fontenelle Hotel in Omaha. I was the proud renter of a bourse table, the youngest dealer in American Numismatic Association history to have one. The attendance was excellent, and by the show's end a record of 500 conventiongoers was announced!

At the August 1955 convention the auction was held by Aubrey Bebee. I purchased for $610 a Brilliant Proof 1867 with-rays shield nickel, a staggering price, by far a record at the time.

"You'll never sell it!" was heard more than once, and I became a bit frightened. But, along came O.L. Harvey, a collector from Seminole, Oklahoma, who offered me a modest profit for it, and the coin was his. At the same time I was shown a prooflike Uncirculated 1796 quarter by Aubrey Bebee who stated that he had just paid $200 for it. Offered the coin for a modest markup, I turned it down. Today this same coin would bring in the range of $30,000!

Jim Ruddy and I became close friends. In 1955 I was 16 years old and had just begun to drive. Johnson City, Jim's home, was located two hours away and was the destination of my first solo long-distance trip. Conversely, Jim would visit me at my Forty Fort home each time he came to Kingston, Pennsylvania, to visit his parents who lived just five miles away. Both businesses grew rapidly.

In 1957, Jim Ruddy, representing a bid from me, purchased at auction for $4,750 an 1894-S Barber dime. This was a world record price at the time, and the numismatic fraternity was stunned. The event was picked up by the nationwide news services and was carried in hundreds of newspapers throughout the United States, plus Ripley's *Believe It or Not* and other features. I appeared on the "Teens in the News" page in *Seventeen* magazine.

NBC's *Today Show* telephoned me and invited me to appear as a guest to be interviewed at length about rare coin buying and selling. The NBC representative, a member of Dave Garroway's staff there, told me that NBC would take care of all expenses. I wouldn't be paid for my appearance, but to make the trip a pleasurable one, I was to be treated to a three-day all-expense-paid stay at the Waldorf Astoria Hotel. "Have a good time, and eat well," was NBC's suggestion. I invited Walter Breen, a numismatist friend who lived in New York City, to join me for lunch. Without alcoholic beverages (Walter didn't drink and I was under age), the tab came to about $20, a very high price at the time—probably, inflation considered, like paying $100 for lunch today. We were both very impressed!

As a result of all the earlier newspaper publicity related to the 1894-S dime thousands of letters poured in from people all over the United States who had coins for sale. Unfortunately there were no 1894-S dimes included. A typical letter would run something like this:

"I read that you paid $4,750 for an 1894 San Francisco Mint dime. I have an even better dime, mine's earlier and is dated 1892. How much will you pay for it?"

Jim Ruddy received a good deal of publicity from the event as well. A feature article at the time showed Jim holding the dime. For comparison purposes, in front of him were stacked dollar bills, 4,750 of them, representing an equivalent value. The article, after discussing the 1894-S dime and why Jim bought it, changed to a personal observation:

"A reporter asked Mr. Ruddy what he thinks motivates coin collectors. He became one himself only five years ago, and only two years ago he quit his job in physics research to become a full time coin dealer.

"In reply he said coin collecting is educational—stimulating interest, for example, in history. Possible investment benefits are important, too, he said."

REPUTATION - - -

A good reputation is an enviable honor. It cannot be bought, sold, traded, or otherwise acquired part way through life, or in the midst of a business career. It is elemental, and exists or does not exist at the beginning. A good reputation grows. It starts with the first person to whom you are known or with whom you deal, and expands throughout your career as you come into contact with more people. It must be maintained at all times or it ceases to exist.

•

I enjoy numismatics, and my pleasant dealings with the increasing number of you who write to buy or to sell is a constant inspiration. I buy and sell coins on the basis of fairness and my best judgment of value to both parties. If you have coins to sell, I will be pleased to buy at a price which reflects the true quality and value of your material, and will pay cash immediately. Your correspondence is invited.

•

If you are not already on my mailing list, send me a card and you will receive my periodical bulletins as they are issued, listing choice coins for sale.

•

Q. DAVID BOWERS

203 Second National Bank Bldg.   Wilkes-Barre, Pa.
Tel. VAlley 3-8478

One of Q. David Bowers' advertisements; October 1955 in "The Numismatist." From the beginning, emphasis was placed on an enjoyment of numismatics combined with a close relationship with clients.

My first major business venture with Jim Ruddy was the Penn-New York auction which we jointly held on July 27, 1957. A beautifully illustrated catalog containing 955 lots was prepared.

A run of rare Proof half cents in the 1840s sold for record prices of $150 each upward, a 1795 Very Fine *Jefferson Head* cent sold for $362, a Proof 1857 large cent sold for $181, a 1909-S V.D.B. cent in Brilliant Uncirculated condition rose to a new price level of $66, an Extremely Fine original 1852 silver dollar sold for $360, and a superb collection of Gem Uncirculated bust-type half dollars sold mainly in the $10 range per coin with a couple of exceedingly rare Proofs bringing $90 each.

An 1877 Proof twenty-cent piece, the rare Proof-only date, brought a record of $175. When all was said and done many new prices had been established. The auction had created a sensation.

Early in the spring of 1958 Jim and I were staying at the old Park Sheraton Hotel in New York City attending an auction. Seated in the Mermaid Room and with a musical combo playing nearby on an elevated platform we discussed future plans. The Penn-New York auction had been a smashing success, and the excitement of another joint venture beckoned. Why not merge the two businesses? The thought was discussed eagerly. The result was the formation on April 1, 1958, of Empire Coin Company, Inc. Several other names were considered including Continental Coin Company and Penn-New York Coin Company, but Empire prevailed, named after New York which is known as the Empire State.

In the following month, May 1958, the first Empire Coin Company advertisement appeared in the *Numismatic Scrapbook Magazine*:

"James F. Ruddy, Triple Cities Coin Exchange, and Q. David Bowers, Bowers Coin Company, announced the opening of Empire Coin Company, Incorporated. The Empire Coin Company will provide the past clients of the Triple Cities Coin Exchange and Bowers Coin Company with a complete numismatic service. Further announcements will appear in all leading numismatic publications. Your inquiries are invited."

The premises at 257 Main Street, Johnson City, New York, Jim's one-room office, were vacated and newly carpeted and paneled offices on the second floor of 252 Main Street, across the street from the old location, were moved into at the seemingly luxurious rent of $325 per month. Early employees included Louise Tibsherany and Ros Ferrante. A student at the Pennsylvania State University at the time, I spent my summers at Johnson City as well as many weekends other times of the year. My function was to prepare catalogs and advertising. Jim did most of the buying, selling, record keeping, and general administrative tasks.

Within a couple years the entire four-floor structure at 252 Main Street was purchased from the owner, Harold Rawlins. We redecorated the structure inside and out and renamed it the Empire Building.

By the early 1960s Empire Coin Company offered a truly complete numismatic service. Over a dozen staff members bought and sold coins, held auctions, issued catalogs, traveled to conventions, and performed many other duties.

Les Zeller, a numismatic student with a cheery personality and whimsical sense of humor, capably managed our World Coin Department. Henry ("Hank") Spangenberger managed our United States Department and took care of appraisals, evaluating collections, and other duties. In later years Hank went on to operate his own business and to become official historian of the American Numismatic Association.

David Nethaway of Cobleskill, New York, was a traveling salesman and field representative during the early 1960s. Dave would attend club meetings, visit collectors, and attend conventions to promote good will and sales.

Ray Merena joined our staff in 1961 to become general manager. Ray, not a numismatist, learned quickly and became one of our most valued employees. In later years he went on to become general manager of Paramount International Coin Corporation.

Nancy Conklin, who was to become Mrs. James F. Ruddy in the late 1960s, managed our Order Department. Sharon Roberts and Shirley Hawley were among the other important staff members during the early years.

In 1958 the first issue of *Empire Topics* made its appearance. In magazine format this publication offered for sale a wide variety of coins in all categories. Spicing up the issues from time to time were research articles by such numismatic notables as Kenneth Bressett (who later joined the Whitman division of Western Publishing Company to supervise the publication and pricing of *A Guide Book of U.S. Coins*), Eric P. Newman, Walter Thompson, and Walter Breen.

By the late 1950s Jim Ruddy and I both developed a keen interest in rare coin investment. Sensing a need, we offered the first periodic program in the investment field, our Executive Investment Program, whereby a busy professional person or executive could, by means of regular monthly payments, assemble a choice group of coins with price appreciation in mind.

In 1963 came another innovation, the first privately-issued coin investment newsletter, the *Empire Investors Report*. This publication, a success from the start, became widely quoted throughout the numismatic field. Included among other things were the first report ever

TRIPLE CITIES COIN EXCHANGE

presents an

Auction Sale
of
Rare Coins

July 18, 1956

To be sold by
mail bid only

257-259 Main Street
Johnson City, N. Y.

THE PENN-NEW YORK AUCTION COMPANY

Presents an

Auction Sale

of

Rare United States Coins

July 29, 1957

To be sold by
mail bid only

257-259 Main Street
Johnson City, N. Y.

EMPIRE TOPICS

Issue No. 1   May - June   1958

Empire Topics is the publication of
Empire Coin Company, Inc., 252 Main Street, Johnson City, New York.
Telephone 9-3101   Empire Topics is mailed free to all interested collectors.

Empire Coin Company, Inc., was formed on April 1, 1958 by James F. Ruddy and Q. David Bowers. Triple Cities Coin Exchange and Bowers Coin Company were combined to form the new company. Perhaps a brief history of the two combining companies would be of interest.

Triple Cities Coin Exchange was formed in 1953 by James F. Ruddy. Jim specialized in early American coins at first, but soon widened his operations to include the entire United States series as well as a complete offering of numismatic supplies. Advertising on a nationwide basis was started, and soon several thousand customers were being served. In the early part of 1956 the company moved to an office in downtown Johnson City, N.Y. The addition of a secretarial staff made possible an increased sales volume. In the years since 1953 ever increasing sales and a growing list of customers made Triple Cities Coin Exchange one of America's foremost coin companies.

Bowers Coin Company of Wilkes-Barre, Pa., was formed by Q. David Bowers. Dave specialized from the beginning in choice United States coins. Like Jim, Dave soon established a mailing list of several thousand customers. Since 1954 Dave has done a considerable amount of numismatic research and has handled most of the great American numismatic rarities.

DAVE BOWERS

Dave and Jim first combined their efforts in the summer of 1957. Their Penn-New York auction attracted wide attention and was an outstanding success. Realizing that a combination of their two companies would result in a complete numismatic service for collectors, steps in this direction were taken in late 1957 and early this year. Empire Coin Company was incorporated on the first of April, 1958. The combination of facilities, numismatic knowledge, reference libraries, and customer mailing lists made possible a complete numismatic service.

JIM RUDDY

First page of several different publications from the 1950s. The July 18, 1956 auction sale featured the beautiful collection of Claude R. Collier, which included a superb collection of United States silver dollars as well as other scarcities and rarities. The July 27, 1957 auction was remarkable for its high quality pieces including Uncirculated early American silver and many early (pre-1858) Proof coins. "Empire Topics," issue number one, marked the first in a series of magazines produced by Empire Coin Company during the late 1950s and early 1960s.

JC Dealer Pays $4,750
For Just One Thin Dime

By JOHN F. MOORE
Binghamton Press Writer

JAMES F. RUDDY, JR., of Johnson City is a coin dealer. Lots of coins arrive in his mail. Yesterday's delivery included an airmail package containing a dime.

The dime cost Mr. Ruddy $4,750.

Rare coins as everyone knows are expensive. And as everyone knows who knows Mr. Ruddy, he is a young man who wears a hat when it's raining and a topcoat when it's cold, and pays a lot of attention to business.

So there obviously are good reasons why a dime should be worth 47,500 times the amount the U. S. Treasury backs it for.

To understand the big price tag, it helps to know a few facts about gaudy old San Francisco.

Also helpful is a bit of insight into the psychology of great and growing numbers of people who, as coin collectors, "like to finish things."

★ ★ ★

PRIOR TO UNPACKING the small, heavily insured package today, Mr. Ruddy described how he purchased it last Wednesday in an auction at a New York City coin house.

Five other persons vied with him for the purchase. Bidding had begun at $4,200. Afterwards, the Johnson City man ordered the coin shipped to avoid traveling with the expensive package.

The dime as he proudly showed it off today carries the head of Miss Liberty on its front together with inscriptions, "United States of America," and "1894." The back carries the words "One Dime," surrounded by a wreath, and a tiny "S."

Because of the "S," only seven or eight dimes like it are known to exist. Its great value derives from the fact that coin men long to own complete sets of all dimes, or of a series like the Liberty or Mercury-head dimes, or dimes from a particular mint.

The "S" stands for the San Francisco Mint.

★ ★ ★

CALIFORNIA in 1894 was a land of plenty and San Francisco was in a lavish mood. The men at the mint evidently joined in the spirit of prodigality by producing in the year 2,648,821 quarters, 4,048,690 half-dollars and 1,260,000 silver dollars.

But with an un-Californian restraint which owners of the "1894 S" dime have been admiring ever since the mint

—Binghamton Press Photo.

THING OF SOME VALUE—A rare dime is examined with warm regard by its new owner, coin dealer James F. Ruddy, Jr., at Workers Trust Office in Johnson City. The $4,750 he paid for coin is greater than the dollar-bill hoard which bank employes stacked on table for comparison.

men stamped out only 24 dimes.

According to collectors' catalogs the 10-cent pieces likely were minted as "presentation" coins and given to distinguished visitors at the mint. None of the known specimens appear to have undergone the wear and tear of being circulated.

Mr. Ruddy had a customer for the rare dime lined up before he purchased it. He is Q. David Bowers, of Wilkes-Barre.

But until he ships the coin to the Pennsylvania man, Mr. Ruddy is the possessor of an example of the second rarest dime issue in U. S. history. The rarest dime was minted in 1873 in Carson City, Nev., and only one specimen is known to exist.

MR. RUDDY LIVES at 25 Spruce Street and operates his business at 259 Main Street in the village.

A reporter asked Mr. Ruddy what he thinks motivates coin collectors. He became one himself only five years ago, and two years ago quit as a lab technician at Ansco's physics research department to become a full-time coin dealer.

In reply he said collecting is educational — stimulating interest, for example, in history. Possible investment benefits are important too, he said.

Then he commented, "I guess it takes a particular type of person—someone who likes to finish things, to see a job done."

Above: Results of the 1961 Professional Numismatists Guild election. In the top row are Harold Whiteneck, Aubrey Bebee, and Earl Parker. On the bottom row, from the left, are Sol Kaplan, Max Kaplan, and James F. Ruddy, who was secretary of the PNG.

Right: James F. Ruddy's purchase of an 1894-S dime for the unheard of price of $4,750 created much ado in the press.

Below: "Photograde," released in 1970, created a sensation. Within a few years it became the best-selling book on coin grading ever published. By holding a coin up to a clear photographic illustration a numismatist, beginning or advanced, could instantly grade a coin with accuracy.

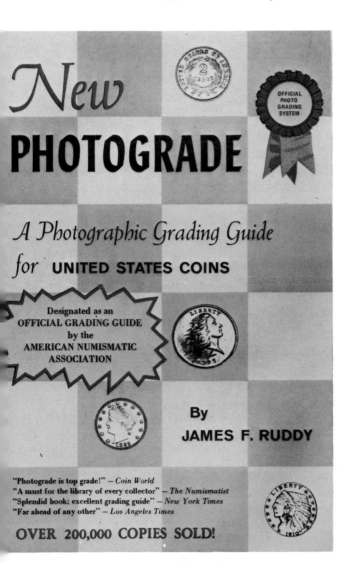

New
PHOTOGRADE

OFFICIAL PHOTO GRADING SYSTEM

A Photographic Grading Guide

for UNITED STATES COINS

Designated as an
OFFICIAL GRADING GUIDE
by the
AMERICAN NUMISMATIC ASSOCIATION

By
JAMES F. RUDDY

"Photograde is top grade!" — *Coin World*
"A must for the library of every collector" — *The Numismatist*
"Splendid book; excellent grading guide" — *New York Times*
"Far ahead of any other" — *Los Angeles Times*

OVER 200,000 COPIES SOLD!

done on the market fluctuations and cycles, studies of the United States and world coin market in depth, and analyses of many specific coin dates, mintmarks, and designs.

Sales grew by leaps and bounds. In 1961 we announced that we had achieved a sales level of over $1,000,000 in rare coins for the year. This figure, staggering at the time, prompted a well-known competitor to telephone and say "that can't be so, no firm has ever sold a million dollars in rare coins in a single year!" But it was true. All of this is, of course, a far cry from the present day when often during one of our auction sales rare coins will change hands at the rate of nearly $1,000,000 *per day*.

During the 1950s emphasis was on collecting United States coins by dates and mintmarks. Noting the rapid price rise around 1960, we became the first firm in numismatics to seriously study the collecting of coins by design types. We reasoned that with the escalating prices of rare dates and mintmarks, collecting by designs would become increasingly popular. Also, it had the tremendous advantage of making many different coin designs available to the collector, as opposed to concentrating on one speciality containing coins differing from each other only by date and mintmark. We encouraged our investment clients to spend money in this area. Those who did were to see their investments multiply many, many times.

We were also a pioneer in the field of world coins, with issues of the British Commonwealth being a particular speciality. By means of many visits to England we obtained the largest stock in this country of British coins. Included were many prizes such as specimen Proof sets of 1826, 1831, 1839, 1853, and so on. From noted British author C. Wilson Peck we obtained the unique 1808 and 1954 British pennies. Two specimens of the 1937 threepence of King Edward VIII were handled. Specimens of the exceedingly rare 1952 shilling and half crown, many examples of the famous 1839 Una and the Lion five-pound piece, and other rarities passed through our hands.

During these trips to England Jim Ruddy and I would rent a suite or pair of connecting rooms at the Dorchester Hotel or, later, the London Hilton. Advertisements would be placed in *The Exchange and Mart* (the only British weekly collectors' publication featuring rare coins at the time), as well as magazines circulated to employees of Lloyd's, Barclay's, and other leading banks. In addition we obtained mailing lists with addresses of private collectors and sent announcements stating that we would be visiting England to buy individual coins and collections.

Most appointments were made with collectors in and around the London area who would come to the hotel. Jim Ruddy, equipped with buying lists for Maundy sets, specimen Proof sets, gold rarities, and the like, would spend tens of thousands of pounds sterling in London while I, accompanied by a chauffeur (I found it risky to drive on the left side of the road as per the English custom, and, besides, the chauffeur knew directions better than I), would travel around the northern and western parts of England to make "house calls."

I have always been impressed with the manners and traditions of England, particularly those handed down from older times. It was always a treat to stay in a small country hotel and to make friends with the innkeeper and overnight guests. Often these houses would be hundreds of years old and would have tiny glass windows and thatched roofs.

Other times I would stay at larger places. One incident I'll never forget. During the week before Christmas my driver and I arrived at eight in the evening at the Grand Hotel in Torquay, a seaside resort on the southern coast of England. The Grand Hotel, a huge rambling structure dating from Victorian times, accommodated hundreds of guests.

We signed the guest register of the day and noticed that despite the rather late hour for checking in, no other names were on the list. I inquired about this and was told that my driver and I were the only guests in the hotel that evening, the week before Christmas being rather quiet!

After settling into my room on the third floor I walked down to the main lobby to locate the restaurant. Finding it, I walked into a room containing many tables, each covered with linen and sporting several place settings. A uniformed waiter snapped to attention and stood against one wall. Presently, he came over, showed me a seat, and handed me a menu. I was impressed by the fact that the menu had the date printed for that particular day. I asked the waiter about the economic efficiency of such a practice, considering I was the only dinner guest, and he said "It's tradition, sir." I invited him to sit down at the table, but he said he couldn't mingle with a guest, it was against policy. So, after serving me he resumed his stiff position against a far wall.

After dinner I began to explore the ground floor of the huge structure. Finally I took a copy of *Time* magazine, which I had brought with me, settled into an overstuffed chair in the lounge, and began to read. A gentleman who had been sitting nearby, a hotel employee I presumed, sprang to his feet and walked up to a piano on a nearby stage. Sitting at the keyboard, he began to play.

Sensing a diversion, I walked over and said, "Are you practicing?"

A Selection Of Priced United States

Coins Offered For Sale By . . .

EMPIRE COIN COMPANY, INC.

Special November — December Listing

A Personal Message From Q. David Bowers and James F. Ruddy

Welcome to our special supplement of the Coin World! As Dick Johnson and other members of the Coin World staff can attest, many long hours went into the preparation of this special feature. We hope that you will find the result to be worth the effort!

We are personally familiar through correspondence with about ten or fifteen thousand of the eighty thousand plus readers of the Coin World. To our past customers we need no introduction. The people who know us will order coins with confidence from the listing to follow. Our reputation is our most important asset. We endeavor to treat others as we would like to be treated ourselves. Numismatics is not only a dollars and cents business with us . . . it is our main interest.

If you have not corresponded with us before, we would

like to make your acquaintance. We invite you to order any items of interest in the pages to follow. We will give you a guarantee of satisfaction on any items purchased. Any item may be returned within three days of receipt for a full and prompt refund. To eliminate the possibility of any controversy, you may return a coin for any reason whatsoever. Our record is quite satisfactory to date . . . less than 1% of the coins we ship are returned.

For our research and for the convenience of our customers, we have one of the finest American numismatic libraries in existence today. Numismatic research has always been one of our specialties. This research has not been without its rewards. Many new and important varieties have been discovered or identified on our premises. If you have any questions or inquiries concerning early United States coins, particularly in the 1700's and 1800's, please write to us.

As you look through the following pages you will find coins of all denominations, types and price ranges . . . something for everyone. Whether you specialize in half cents or double eagles or are assembling a type set, we are sure you will find many items to your liking. You may wish to save this Empire supplement for future reference and ordering. Prices will remain in effect during November and December, or until the items are sold.

We will look forward to making your acquaintance through the mail. Write to us soon.

Q. DAVID BOWERS — JAMES F. RUDDY

Q. DAVID BOWERS

JAMES F. RUDDY

TERMS OF SALE

1. Enclose remittance with order. If possible, list alternate choices. Alternate choices will only be used in instances when the first item(s) requested have been sold. As many items are one of a kind, the use of alternate choices eliminates the mutual disappointment of an unfilled order. If you are ordering a coin for a type set and the date is not of major importance, just indicate the type desired as your second choice and we will substitute a coin of equal or greater value if the first item has been sold.
2. There is no minimum order. Please include an extra 50c for handling on orders under $5.00. An immediate refund will be given for any part of an order unfilled. We do not issue credit slips.
3. Orders to all points over 300 miles distant will be sent via air mail. Postage and private insurance costs on all orders will be paid by us.
4. Satisfaction is guaranteed on all purchases. Fewer than 1% of the coins we ship are returned to us. Any item not satisfactory for any reason may be returned within three days for a full refund.
5. Order from Empire Coin Company with confidence. We are justly proud of our fine reputation for fair and honest transactions.
6. We have included an order blank which may be cut out for your convenience in ordering.

THIS SUPPLEMENT IS A NUMISMATIC FIRST!

This special Empire supplement is the first private supplement in the history of any numismatic magazine or newspaper. To our knowledge it is also the first multi-colored (three colors plus black) advertisement to appear in any numismatic publication.

PATTERN COINS AND COLONIALS

This supplement contains a selection of United States gold, silver and copper coins from our inventory. Due to space limitations, we could not include pattern coins or colonial coins.

We have the finest stock of United States patterns in the country. We have prepared a special priced catalog of patterns that will be sent to interested persons requesting it.

Our stock of colonial coins is second to none. It is resplendent with many "finest knowns", unlisted varieties and rare pieces. We are preparing a listing of colonials and hope to have it ready for inclusion of the next issue of our magazine, The Empire Review.

THE EMPIRE REVIEW

The Empire Review is our own magazine issued from three to five times per year, as time permits. Our last issue was dated August—September, 1961. Copy is now being prepared for the next issue, slated for publication in early January.

The Empire Review is printed on high quality coated paper and is profusely illustrated (our last issue, No. 14, contained over one hundred illustrations). It has been our policy to illustrate many of the rarer coins and die varieties, often with close-up photographs illustrating overdates, recuttings, and other interesting details. We have always honored requests for photographs appearing in our publications. As a result many have been used by Whitman Publishing Company and the leading numismatic newspapers and magazines.

The size of The Empire Review varies. Issue No. 14 was thirty-six pages from cover to cover.

Each issue contains numismatic comments, news, a coin quiz, questions from readers column and an extensive presentation of priced coins for sale. As we have always stressed numismatic research and knowledge, you will find much useful information in the Empire Review that may not be obtained elsewhere. We have always believed that our best customers were numismatically educated customers.

In each issue is a research article of lasting value. Our last issue contained hitherto unpublished information (compiled by Walter Thompson) concerning the Confederate States of America's operation of the New Orleans Mint. Other contributors in the past have been such well-known numismatic authorities as Eric P. Newman, Kenneth Bressett and Walter Breen.

We charge a subscription fee of $1.00 for six issues to help defray the costs of making an address plate and preparing, printing and mailing the issues to you. Needless to say, our actual cost is much higher than the subscription fee. If you become an active customer, your subscription will be renewed with our compliments.

We would like to have you join America's leading numismatists as a subscriber to the Empire Review. If you would like to see a sample copy first, request this and we will send a free sample copy of issue No. 15 when it is ready.

We would like to mention here that the informational material and the coins for sale in the Empire Review are mainly choice United States coins before 1940 . . . much the same nature as the material offered in this Coin World supplement. If you collect only recent rolls, proof sets and medals your subscription dollar would probably be better spent elsewhere.

WHAT TO LOOK FOR

This special Empire Coin Company, Inc. supplement contains priced offerings for sale of the following U. S. coins:

HALF CENTS . . . A choice selection.

LARGE CENTS . . . Dozens of different dates and varieties, including some magnificent rarities.

SMALL CENTS . . . Flying Eagle cents, Indian Cents (don't miss the complete set listed in a later part of the supplement), Lincoln cents. A nice offering.

2c, 3c . . . Choice 2c including an 1864; complete set of nickel 3c in Proof, etc. All conditions, all prices.

NICKELS . . . from 1866 to 1939-D; a selection sprinkled with many rarities and choice items

HALF DIMES . . . From the first year, 1794 to the last year, 1873. Many different varieties of interest.

DIMES . . . A select group of Bust type, Liberty seated, Barber and Mercury types and varieties.

TWENTY CENTS . . . 1875, 1876 (1876-CC too).

QUARTERS . . . Starting with an Uncirculated 1796 and ending with Washington quarters in the 1930's.

HALF DOLLARS . . . A splendid array of hundreds of different dates, varieties and conditions. Including rarities of all descriptions . . . Commemoratives . . . C.S.A.

DOLLARS . . . Type coins, scarce dates, Proofs (incl. 1895). A few nice trade dollars too.

GOLD COINS . . . From popular type coins to great rarities. An attractive selection.

TRANSITIONALS . . . 1858 Indian cent, 1882 Liberty nickel, etc.

HAWAIIAN COINS . . . Confederate States of America coins . . . Miscellany.

CURRENCY . . . Including some bargains.

AND, FINALLY, if you are in a selling mood, rather than a buying mood, see the back page of this supplement.

PREPARED BY EMPIRE

This special supplement to the Coin World was paid for and prepared by:

EMPIRE COIN COMPANY, INC.
Q. David Bowers — James F. Ruddy
O'Neil Building
Binghamton 3, New York
Tel. RA 3-5474

Members of: Professional Numismatists Guild; International Association of Professional Numismatists; American Numismatic Association (life members); American Numismatic Society; other leading numismatic organizations.

First page of the multiple-page advertisement by Empire Coin Company which appeared in the November 24, 1961 issue of Coin World. This was the largest advertisement ever run in a numismatic publication.

"No, I am playing just for you. What would you like to hear?"

I told him that it was unnecessary to play just for me and that he could go back to his chair and relax.

"Our advertisements say that there is musical entertainment each evening, so I must play. How about some selections from *South Pacific*? Americans seem to like those tunes."

The next morning I arose and drove a short distance to visit a collector in the area. A couple hours later I was the pleased owner of what was probably the finest collection of British shillings ever to be assembled. The famous 1798 Dorrien and Magens shilling was represented by a virtually perfect specimen. Highlighting the collection was a Proof 1952 shilling of King George VI, one of just two known to exist. I brought this collection back to the United States in due course. A few months later Douglas Liddell, managing director of Spink & Son of London, visited our firm in Johnson City and purchased the collection intact. So, back to England it went!

On another occasion I stopped near the town of Huddersfield in Yorkshire to visit a Mr. Hadley, an aged collector. Upon my arrival to his beautifully furnished home I was told to wait in the living room. Mr. Hadley, it seemed, was in the library gathering his coins together so he could show them to me. I was immediately impressed by the decorations and accessories in the room, including a magnificent grandfather's clock standing in a corner. Through its case, with glass windows on three sides, could be seen ornate brass workings, musical chimes, and an elaborately engraved face. It was truly a work of art!

Mr. Hadley came into the room a few moments later and noticed me admiring the clock, obviously one of his favorite possessions. He then talked about it for a short time, whereupon it was forgotten and we settled down to the business I had come for: examining his rare coins.

It was a custom at the time for British collectors to keep their coins in cabinets containing many different trays. Coin envelopes, while sometimes used, were not popular, and plastic holders were virtually unknown. Traditionally each coin would be kept in a circular opening within a tray. At the bottom of each opening was a felt disc, usually green. The Hadley collection was no exception.

After due discussion I became the proud owner of an 1880 United States Proof set (which through some unknown process had migrated to England years earlier), an 1826 British Proof set, and a fine collection of British copper coins including farthings, half pennies, and pennies. After writing a check on my London bank account I bade Mr. Hadley farewell.

A few weeks later I received a letter from one of his relatives. It seemed that Mr. Hadley became ill a week or two later and had subsequently died. Prior to his death he expressed the wish that the grandfather clock, which I had so lovingly admired, be given to me. I was deeply touched and wrote my acceptance to his heirs, offering to have it appraised and to pay fair value for it, although it was intended as a gift. At the same time I made arrangements with Davies, Turner & Company, my London shipping agents, to travel to Huddersfield to collect the prize.

Later I received a brief note from the would-be shipper informing me that upon calling for the clock it was learned that the heirs had decided to sell it elsewhere. I was unknown to them, and Mr. Hadley's friendship with me made little difference. So, where the clock is now, I don't know.

Among British pennies there are two scarce modern issues: the 1950 and 1951, of which just 240,000 and 120,000 were minted of each, respectively. It was learned that most of these coins had been distributed in the Atlantic island of Bermuda. Fascinated by this knowledge, Jim Ruddy and Ray Merena of our staff traveled to Bermuda, ran full page advertisements in the local newspapers, and created a sensation by setting up a land-office business paying out cash to hundreds of Bermudians who came in bearing rare pennies! At the same time, Robert Bashlow, a competing New York dealer, also ran advertisements. Each day one camp would try to outdo the other! This great adventure netted thousands of these rarities, probably most of the supply in collectors' hands today.

Meanwhile, in the field of United States coins my firm became well known for handling important collections as well as individual scarcities and rarities. The collection of Edward A. Gilroy, one of the finest ever formed in the field of United States and British coins, was purchased intact. The Kenneth Fuller collection of United States large cents was another prize.

In 1961, through the efforts of Abner Kreisberg and Jerry Cohen, we purchased intact the magnificent collection of United States pattern coins formed by Maj. Lenox R. Lohr, former president of the Columbia Broadcasting System and, later, director of the Museum of Science and Industry in Chicago. This collection numbered nearly 1,500 different pieces and represented the largest number of pattern coins ever to be priced and offered for sale in numismatic history. There were seven different patterns of the year 1792 alone!

The 1894-S dime purchased in 1957 for $4,750 became the first in a series of four or five of that rare issue we were to handle. By 1974 the price had climbed considerably, and one offered in a catalog at close to $100,000 was sold immediately.

Empire Coin Company, Inc.
offers choice U.S. silver & copper coins

Special offering of Liberty Standing Half Dollars. We have just acquired a large group of Liberty Standing half dollars 1916-1947. The following half dollars, all attractively priced, are Brilliant Uncirculated.

1916 First Year. Br. Unc. $18.00
1916-D Br. Unc. 19.50
1916-S Br. Unc. 74.00
1917 Br. Unc. 8.00
1917-D mintmark on obv. BU 35.00
1917-D mintmark on rev. BU 79.00
1917-S mintmark on obv. The most desired coin in the entire series. Br. Unc. 325.00
1918 Br. Unc. 48.50
1919 Br. Unc. 67.50
1920 Br. Unc. 28.00
1921 B.U. Rare only 246,000 coined Br. Unc. 167.50
1927-S Br. Unc. 42.50
1929-D Br. Unc. 19.00
1929-S Br. Unc. 21.00
1933-S Br. Unc. 27.50
1934-S Br. Unc. 32.00
1935-D Br. Unc. 15.00
1935-S Br. Unc. 30.00
1936-S Br. Unc. 16.00
1937-D Br. Unc. 15.00
1937-S Br. Unc. 14.00
1938-D Br. Unc. really scarce 30.00
1939-S Br. Unc. 6.00

Special set of Lib. Standing halves Complete 1934 to 1947, every date and mintmark in Br. Unc. condition. Thirty-nine coins. An excellent buy for 195.00

Complete set of Proof Lincoln cents, 1936 to 1957—fifteen coins. One set only for $97.50

Complete set of nickel three-cent pieces 1865 to 1889 including the overdate 1887/6. All in Proof condition. This set catalogs $779.50 in the new 12th edition Guidebook, however many of the coins sell over the cata., listings—1865, 1877 and 1878 for example. A beautiful set to own, and at our price of $765.00, a good investment too.

Complete set of Liberty Standing quarters 1916-1930-S, with the exception of the overdate. The 1916 is fully Fine with a sharp date. The obv. shows a few light scratches. The dates from 1917 to 1919 are F to XF, all nice coins. From 1919-S to 1930-S they run G to XF. The 1921 and the 1923-S have weak dates, but may easily be read. This set is housed in an album and cat. about $275. Our price is 147.50

1783 Draped bust Wash. cent. Proof restr., from original dies 15.00

1795 Half Cent. Letd. ed. VF 49.00

1794 Cent. Sheldon variety #26. A splendid coin in ExF condition. Square, sharp edge with perfect edge lettering. Perfectly centered. 1794 cents as nice as this one are rarely found 79.00

1955 "double die" cent. The unusual error with complete doubling of the obv. features; two dates, two of each letter, etc. Scarce, becoming difficult to locate in top condition. ExF $22.00; Br. Uncirculated 37.50

EMPIRE COIN CO., INC., Continued on next page

1868 Two cent pc., Br. Proof 25.00
1855 Silver three-cent pc. Rare date Fine $9.00; VF 15.00
1877 Shield Nickel. Br. Proof. Here's the date everyone needs 260.00
1885 Lib. Nickel. The rare date of the Proof Lib. Nickels. Brill. Proof 92.50
1918/7 Overdate Buff. nickel. VG to Fine, sharp. Rare 77.50
1937-D nickel. 3 leg variety. F $10; VF $15; Ex Fine...... 21.00
1820 Dime. The ra. variety with rev. error STATESOFAMERICA crowded together as one word. Br. Unc. The first we have seen in this condition 60.00
1915 Barber Dime, choice Prf 150.00
1916-D Merc. Dime. Abt G $17.50; G $25; G-VG $27.50; VG.. 35.00
1859 Quarter, choice Proof.. 35.00
1863 Quarter, choice Proof.. 35.00
1872-CC Quarter. VG obv. Gd rev. One of the extreme rarities in the quarter series 85.00
1911 Quarter, choice Proof.. 49.50
1921 Lib. Stand. quarter BU 75.00
1926-S Liberty Standing quarter. Br. Uncirculated, rare 85.00
1857 Half Dol. perfect gem Prf. One of about twenty 1857 Prf half dols. in existence. Ext. ra. and well worth our price of 295.00
1857 Silver Dollar. Delicately toned Proof. According to estimates, one of about fifty Proofs of this date known to exist. Vra 145.00

1957 Proof sets. Ten sets for 24.50
1934 Phila. Mint quarters. Half roll (20) coins) Br. Unc.... 67.50
1940-P Mint quarters. Half roll (20 coins) Br. Unc. 59.00
1934-P Mint half dollars. Half roll (10 coins) Br. Unc. ... 29.00
1934-P Mint silver dollars. Half roll (10 coins) Br. Unc. ... 25.00
1935-P Mint silver dollars. Half roll (10 coins) Br. Unc. 25.00

Order from Empire Coin Co., Inc. with complete confidence. All items are guaranteed to be as represented. Any item found unsatisfactory, for any reason, may be returned within three days. Prompt refund given on unfilled orders. No credit slips or deferred payments. We want all of our customers to be fully satisfied with their purchases.

A Reminder: The closing date for the Empire Topics Auction is November 26th. Airmail your bids today, if you have not already done so.

Empire Topics is our bi-monthly publication listing items for sale, numismatic inquiries and questions, original research articles, plus numismatic information and new discoveries. Empire Topics is mailed free to all requesting it. If you are not presently on our mailing list, send us a postcard today. The next issue of Empire Topics, issue #4, will be ready in a few weeks.

EMPIRE COIN CO., Inc.

Q. DAVID BOWERS — JAMES F. RUDDY
252 MAIN STREET   JOHNSON CITY, NEW YORK
Telephone 9-3101

Above: Empire Coin Company advertisement of November 1958 in "The Numismatic Scrapbook Magazine," the most active monthly publication at the time. The prices seem like unbelievable bargains today!

Right: Dave Bowers explains a coin variety to two young collectors at a convention in 1961.

Issue No. 2   JULY-AUGUST-SEPTEMBER   1958

Empire Topics is the publication of
Empire Coin Company, Inc., 252 Main Street, Johnson City, New York.
Telephone 9-3101   Empire Topics is mailed free to all interested collectors.

Q. DAVID BOWERS   JAMES F. RUDDY

SECOND 1894-S DIME ACQUIRED!

It was a great pleasure near the end of last year when, outbidding a large field of collectors and dealers from all parts of the United States, we purchased at auction the "Empire" specimen of the 1894-S dime. This coin is now a part of one of America's finest collections.

Fortunate, indeed, is the dealer who can offer one 1894-S dime in a lifetime. We are now proud to offer another 1894-S dime; the second specimen we have handled within a year! The specimen here offered, one of six or seven known specimens remaining from the twenty-four coined in 1894, is the specimen originally sold to James Stack by the collection of John Clapp. Like its predecessor, the "Empire" coin, it is brilliant uncirculated. Here is an opportunity to acquire one of the very rarest of United States coins—an opportunity which may not be repeated for a long time. Serious inquiries invited.

Thank you for all the nice letters and comments received about our first issue of EMPIRE TOPICS. It must be popular as some requested as many as three additional copies! Incidentally, we will continue to send out copies from our supply of several hundred extras. If you would like an extra copy of Issue No. 1 or would like one for a friend, let us know.

Sales from EMPIRE TOPICS No. 1 were excellent. We're sorry we didn't have several dozen Confederate restrike half dollars in stock, or for that matter, a few more Hard Times Tokens or rolls of 1916-D dimes. Interest was strong in all series. Even colonials, which are usually neglected, received great interest. Check our extensive listing of colonials in this issue.

We received our first copy of the new 12th edition "Guidebook" several weeks ago. Prices, following the market trend, show a steady increase. Price changes were most noticeable in the proofs; particularly the Barber series where increases in some instances were 100%. All series showed a general advance. That's the way it goes when there is an ever-increasing demand and a diminishing supply. Rare coins will never be any cheaper.

Features such as "From Our Research Department" and our "Coin Quiz" received much attention. As soon as the write-up of the new Massachusetts cent variety Ryder 4-J appeared several specialists in the series called wanting to buy it! This subsequently resulted in the cent finding a home in a fine New Jersey collection of colonial coins. We received quite a few numismatic questions from our readers. Some of these are printed in question and answer form in this issue. If we can be of assistance in answering a numismatic problem or question, do not hesitate to write. Questions of reader interest will be printed in EMPIRE TOPICS. Some said the "Coin Quiz" last issue was too difficult. It seems the questions most often missed were No. 1 and No. 5. What did you think? Give the quiz in this issue a try.

SALES CHART

1

Issue No. 3   OCTOBER-NOVEMBER-DECEMBER   1958

Empire Topics, Copyright 1958, is the publication of Empire Coin Co., Inc., 252 Main Street, Johnson City, New York. Tel. 9-3101. Empire Topics is sent free to all collectors on the Empire Coin Co., Inc., mailing list.

Q. DAVID BOWERS   JAMES F. RUDDY

EMPIRE COIN COMPANY AUCTION

This issue of EMPIRE TOPICS features something new: a mail bid auction. The auction, though containing a relatively small number of lots, is remarkable for the quality of the items offered. The unique pattern ten-dollar gold piece by Bouvet, the infrequently seen pattern half dollars of 1877 in silver, a trial impression of the first double eagle die of 1849, a proof specimen of the rare 1836 half dollar with 50¢ over 00¢, a Confederate States of America copper cent, an 1882 Liberty Nickel and an 1858 Indian cent are just a few of the items included. Outstanding also is the offering of Civil War cents and merchant's tokens of the period. Look over the auction carefully. Send your bids early. A bid sheet and a business reply envelope have been included for your convenience.

Thank you once again for all of the nice letters and comments concerning our publication. The sales response from our last issue was excellent, too. Interest in the colonial and state coinages was more than we expected. The encased postage stamps were a complete sellout. The interest in the regular United States series; half cents, Indian cents, dimes, quarters, etc., indicates the strength of today's numismatic market.

We are proud to announce our life memberships in the American Numismatic Association. At the recent A. N. A. convention in Los Angeles, Q. David Bowers was awarded LM #336; James F. Ruddy, #337.

"Blundered Dies of Colonial and U. S. Coins" by Walter Breen which started in issue #2 and concludes in the present issue is the first of a number of articles we plan to publish. Articles by various authors on a wide range of numismatic subjects will appear from time to time. Coming up soon are features about United States transitional coins and territorial gold coinage of California.

A number of people have written to us concerning consignments for inclusion in EMPIRE TOPICS. We welcome worthwhile consignments for our publication; either for offering at auction or for listing at a set price. Our rates for listing are reasonable. You will be assured of our usual careful cataloging and the illustration of rare or important pieces. Your inquiries are welcomed.

Take advantage of the services offered by Empire Coin Company, Inc. They include the following:

- Large stock of United States coins, colonial and state coins, tokens and other items of numismatic interest constantly maintained.
- Complete line of numismatic books and supplies.
- Complete reference and research facilities. Numismatic research is a specialty with us.

Empire Coin Company, Inc., will attend the large regional conventions of the 1958-1959 season. Be sure to stop by at our bourse table to buy, sell or say "Hello."

1

Above left and right: Front pages from two early issues of "Empire Topics," published by Empire Coin Company.

Below right: An auction sale of the 1950s featured pattern half dollars of 1877.

Below: This listing from the 1950s offers silver dollars. Note that the exceedingly rare Proof 1895 is offered at $695, about 1/20th of the price it would sell for two decades later!

1914 rare date. G. $8.00; VG $12.00; Brilliant Proof	435.00
1915 G-VG. scarce	9.00
1915-D Fine $5.00; Brilliant Uncirculated	18.50
1915-S Fine $3.50; AU with lustre	27.50

Liberty Walking Type

1916-S Brilliant Uncirculated	85.00
1917 Brilliant Uncirculated	9.00
1917-S with obverse mintmark. Brilliant Uncirculated	365.00
1917-S on reverse. VF $4.75; AU, brilliant	32.50
1918-S Fine $3.75; VF-EF	7.00
1920 EF with lustre	5.75
1933-S Brilliant Uncirculated	39.00
1934-S Brilliant Uncirculated	37.00
1935 Brilliant Uncirculated	3.50
1935-D Brilliant Uncirculated	16.00
1936 Brilliant Uncirculated	2.35
1938-D scarce. Brilliant Uncirculated	45.00
1939 Brilliant Uncirculated	4.50
1939-D Brilliant Uncirculated	2.50
1940 Brilliant Uncirculated	2.25
1942 Brilliant Uncirculated	1.50
1944 Brilliant Uncirculated	1.35

Franklin Type

1948 Brilliant Uncirculated	3.50
1949 Brilliant Uncirculated, scarce date	12.75

1878 eight tail feathers. Brilliant Proof	53.50
1878 7tf/8tf. Extremely Fine	4.00
1879 Brilliant Proof	53.50
1881 Brilliant Proof	53.50
1881-S Brilliant Uncirculated	2.00
1882 Brilliant Proof	48.00
1883 Brilliant Uncirculated	2.00
1884 Brilliant Proof	58.00
1885 Brilliant Proof	51.00
1885-CC Brilliant Uncirculated	9.50
1886 Brilliant Proof	56.00
1890-O Brilliant Uncirculated	3.50
1890-S Brilliant Uncirculated	2.75
1891 Brilliant Proof	68.00
1892 Brilliant Proof	48.50
1894-S Brilliant Uncirculated	12.75
1895 Brilliant Proof. One of the most popular coins in American numismatics	695.00
1898 Brilliant Uncirculated	2.00
1899 Brilliant Proof	58.00
1901 Brilliant Proof	58.00
1902 Brilliant Unc. $2.25; Brilliant Proof	61.50
1904-S Brilliant Unc.	12.00
1920 Wilson dollar to commemorate the opening of the Manila P.I. mint.—in silver. Brilliant Unc.	120.00

13

Lot number	Description	Estimate

96.	1877 Half Dollar, in silver. AW #1510. Morgan obverse. Reverse similar to that of the 1878 Morgan dollar. Like the other 1877 silver half dollars here offered, it is of extreme rarity. Proof	($400.00)
97.	1877 Half Dollar, in silver. AW #1522. Obverse: Morgan design with circle of beads surrounding Liberty. Reverse: Eagle with fanlike wings, small feathers. Proof	($400.00)
98.	1877 Half Dollar, in silver. AW #1524. Similar to above lot, except the eagle's wings have larger feathers. Proof. We do not know where you could obtain duplicates of these coins, even at twice our estimated prices. A rare opportunity	($400.00)
99.	Bids will be entertained for the above five lots, #93 to #97, AW #1506, #1508, #1510, #1522 and #1524 to be sold as a group. If the bid for this lot exceeds the total individual bids for the individual lots by 5%, the coins will go to this lot. An attractive custom plastic holder for the five pieces will be included	($2,100.00)
100.	1875 pattern trade dollar. Obverse: Liberty seated, facing left; Reverse: the adopted design. Similar to AW #1426. This piece is struck in copper and was unknown to Adams and Woodin. **Unlisted.** Of extreme importance to any pattern collector. Proof	($200.00)

| 101. | (1857) Uniface die trial in white metal for the pattern quarter eagle obverse as used for AW #218 and #219. Rare. The Longacre estate is said to contain several similar trials of this die. Items of this nature are extremely rare and appear on the market infrequently | ($75.00) |

19

Price Near $18,200

Rare $20 Gold Coin Bought by JC Firm

Two Johnson City coin dealers have purchased one of America's rarest coins from Yale University for "close to" the coin's catalogue list price of $18,200.

The 1907 "very high relief" $20 gold piece was purchased from the Yale collection by the Empire Coin Co., Inc., which is operated by James F Ruddy and Q. David Bowers.

The transaction was completed last week in Washington, D. C. Mr. Ruddy said the payment was one of the highest ever made for a single U. S. coin.

He said rare coin authorities consider this particular coin one of the most beautiful U. S. coins ever minted, because of its design and because of the very high relief on the face of the coin.

Only about 20 of the gold pieces were minted, and most of the original ones were given to high government and business leaders when minted.

One was owned by former President Theodore Roosevelt, and currently is on display at the Smithsonian Institution.

The coin was purchased for resale by the Johnson City coin dealers.

GOLD SOLD—This is front of 1907 $20 gold piece bought for about $18,200 by Empire Coin Co., Inc., of Johnson City from Yale University.

Above: This August 1962 clipping illustrates a rare 1907 double eagle purchased from Yale University by Q. David Bowers and James F. Ruddy. Although $18,200 was a world record price at the time, by 15 years later a similar coin was to sell for $250,000.

Upper right: Empire Coin Company advertisement from the late 1950s.

Right: Empire Coin Company handled hundreds of 1955 double die cents. Here they are advertised in quantity, including Brilliant Uncirculated coins for just $60 each if three were bought at one time! By the next decade, in the 1970s, the price had risen to over ten times the earlier level.

Numismatic Depth Study

Collector Should Stop, Think Before Cleaning

By Q. David Bowers

Last week we interrupted our serial discussion on United States coins to touch upon some dos and don'ts of cleaning coins. Among other things we mentioned that cleaning differs from "processing" inasmuch as the function of cleaning is to change the color or brightness of the surface of a coin. Cleaning does not change the condition of the coin. On the other hand so-called "processing," "whizzing," and other such treatments are attempts to falsely improve the condition of a coin — so that a lower-grade coin can be made to appear like a higher-grade coin.

Bernard Blatt, a New York collector, posed several questions — including "What is a coin collector supposed to do with his valuable coins which have tarnished?" and "How can a dealer tell whether or not a coin has been cleaned?"

Before cleaning any coin I recommend that you give the matter some thought. The presence of toning on a piece results from years of exposure to the atmosphere. Toning can often be quite beautiful — and catalogs are full of such picturesque descriptions as "lilac toned," "sea-green coloration with rainbow overtones," etc.

We are speaking now of naturally acquired toning — and not some type of coloration applied as part of a treatment process. Most old-timers — collectors and dealers alike — prefer coins with toning. Most newcomers like them to be nice and bright.

Coin dealers can tell whether or not coins have been cleaned simply by looking at them. To cite but one area of numismatics, half cents which have been cleaned by "dipping" become an unnatural bright orange color completely unlike original Mint brilliance.

On the other hand, a coin which is naturally brilliant will be a reddish color, often fading to a light brown in the fields. The color is "warm" and "natural" (for want of better adjectives) — although this description certainly is not precise.

Seeing one coin is worth a thousand words of text — so my recommendation concerning how to tell a cleaned coin from an uncleaned one would be to enlist the aid of your friendly local dealer or visit a coin club and try to arrange a symposium on the subject.

Almost any dealer or old-time collector can tell a cleaned coin from an uncleaned one — so you should not have any problems in this regard.

Cleaning copper coins is something best not done in my opinion. Far better it is to have lustrous brown or red and brown coins in your collection that it is to have brightly cleaned pieces.

Cleaning silver and gold coins is a different matter entirely. Properly cleaned, a gold coin or a silver coin can be restored to its original coloration at the time of mintage — a bright silver or a bright gold color.

While I personally might prefer a toned silver coin I am in the minority in this field. If you like your commemorative half dollars or Liberty standing quarters to be "bright" then you can accomplish this by cleaning them judiciously — being careful, as noted earlier, not to use abrasives.

Cleaning is all well and fine — except that each cleaning process inevitably takes something, however microscopic, away from the surface as cleaning is based upon a chemical reaction. 500 years from now if a coin has been cleaned 97 times during its history the coin will have a dull surface.

In fact, not even 500 years are required — we often see Proof coins of a few decades ago which have been "cleaned to death" as one cataloger has put it.

To clean or not to clean is not so much of a problem. The problem is "processing" and "doctoring" coins — the situation discussed in last week's column. You will recall that Carl McClerg wrote some lucid comments concerning his experiences in ordering coins in this regard.

"Processing" a coin is an attempt to take a lower-value piece and to artificially give it the appearance of being in a higher grade than it actually is.

As stated last week, grading refers to the amount of wear that a coin has received — not to the surface coloration. There are many ways of "processing" coins — and I am mystified by how some are done.

The most common method is what collectors refer to as "whizzing." An Extremely Fine coin is subjected to abrading of the surface — either by a series of stiff wires, by a stiff brush, or by a process similar in concept. The resulting coin has many parallel furrows in the surface. These are quite pronounced under even fairly low magnification — say 10 or 20 power.

The furrows when viewed at a distance give the appearance of "cartwheel" Mint lustre — something which is found on normal Uncirculated coins.

On a regular Uncirculated coin this "cartwheel" frost is caused by small raised ridges also — the ridges caused by the flow of metal during the striking process. However the ridges are so small as to be almost microscopic on a regular Uncirculated coin. On a "whizzed" coin they are large and deep.

Often the furrows in a "whizzed" coin are applied in a series of arcs tangential to the rim of the coin. This gives the surface a "cartwheel" appearance when the piece is slowly turned in a bright light. The result can be quite deceptive to the uninitiated.

There are several ways to detect a "whizzed" coin. The first is to look at it with a magnifying glass to see if these furrows can be detected. The furrows will appear in the field of the coin as well as on the higher spots. The second is to compare the coin with a known Uncirculated piece which has not been "whizzed" — an Uncirculated piece taken from a fresh Mint roll, for example.

However, even this has its pitfalls — as Ray Merena's comments (in the Coin World "Trends" section a month or so ago) indicated. You may recall that Ray Merena said that 1941-S half dollars, processed coins of lower grades, were "whizzed" and being sold as "BU rolls."

Although this advice might seem hackneyed, your best bet is to deal with an established dealer. By established dealer I do not mean one who necessarily runs the largest advertisements — for many old-time dealers are so busy with their clientele that they don't have time to write advertisements. They have all the business they can handle as it is!

Members of the Professional Numismatists Guild — to name one organization — have agreed not to sell "processed" coins. Any reader of this publication who receives "processed" coins from a PNG member is urged to report this member to the secretary of the PNG: John Smies, P. O. Box 371, Courtland, Kansas 66939. The PNG is not going to be namby-pamby on this subject: any member who knowingly sells processed coins as "Uncirculated" or "Proof" is liable to suspension from the organization.

Do not expect your dream to come true when you see a coin offered at half price. Competition is fierce for top quality pieces. To cite but one example, I would be delighted to pay $125 for any strictly Uncirculated Barber half dollar. I might not be the top bidder in this regard, it is fair to add. Possibly other dealers would pay more. As 2 plus 2 must equal 4 then it would not be reasonable to expect a truly Uncirculated coin for a price which is a mere fraction of this figure!

In a recent issue the "Coin Dealer Newsletter," a publication mainly circulated to dealers, pondered this very point when it noticed that certain advertisers were having a field day selling "bargains" at much less than the buying prices posted by other reputable dealers. Of course, the loser in this regard is the collector — not the dealer.

"There is a sucker born every minute" said P. T. Barnum — and the dealer who sells processed coins makes use of this axiom.

The mathematics of this are simple — and are quite enticing to the vendor who has not scruples in the matter. As a hypothetical situation let us take a Liberty nickel of the year 1900. I pick this example out of the air — there are hundreds of others. Also I must say here that I am not referring to any other offering of this particular coin — I have just selected it at random.

In the current issue of the "Guidebook" this piece catalogues for $5 in Extremely Fine and $25 in Uncirculated condition. For purposes of our illustration here let us assume that each of these grades bring full catalog when accurately described.

In other words let us assume that an Extremely Fine coin, when described as such, readily sells for $5 and an Uncirculated when described as such, readily sells for $25. Let us a l s o assume — and this is not much of an assumption for I would be happy to buy them at this price — that a strictly Uncirculated 1900 Liberty nickel is worth $20 wholesale. Now the plot thickens . . .

Our unethical vendor sees a chance for a profit. He buys an Extremely Fine 1900 nickel wholesale — say for $3 — he then "whizzes" it and offers it for sale at the super "bargain" price of just $15. This actually works out quite well for him. He is selling the coin for FIVE TIMES over what he paid for it! This certainly beats coin dealing by the "old fashioned method" — whereby we pay $20 for a real BU and sell it for $25 — a nominal markup.

The purchaser of one of these "whizzed" coins is happier also. He buys for $15 a coin which he believes to be worth $25 — so he is tickled pink for the moment. On the other hand the purchaser of a really Uncirculated coin at $25 pays $25 with the knowledge that he is buying a coin at the going price.

Lincoln Popular

Art Goupel, of Detroit, who does a realistic impersonation of Abraham Lincoln, is a popular speaker at area coin clubs.

Endorsed System

Robert Morris, Superintendent of Finance 1781-84, drew up a plan for a mint and endorsed the decimal system of coinage presenting both to Congress.

Several 1876-CC twenty-cent pieces (including a group of four Brilliant Uncirculated coins at one time), several 1838-O half dollars, two MCMVII Extremely High Relief 1907 double eagles (including a specimen sold to us in 1962 by Yale University), and other important pieces were to come our way in the early years. Later we were to complete our "list of accomplishments" by handling in the mid-1970s the rare 1913 Liberty head nickel and the 1804 silver dollar.

By the early 1960s Empire Coin Company had a staff of close to two dozen people. A popular diversion for our employees was to visit our company-owned lake, probably unique in the history of professional numismatics. Named, appropriately enough, Lake Empire, this 50-acre body of water was situated on 212 acres of forested land. Water skiing, motor boating, hiking, fishing, camping, and other activities could be enjoyed at various times of the year. Later Lake Empire was sold to the State University of New York which currently operates it as a recreational facility under the same name.

From the earliest years a close relationship was established with the American Numismatic Association. We supported with donations, both personal and corporate, the many projects developed by that group: the Home and Headquarters established in Colorado Springs, the Certification Service, the Museum, and many others. Today our firm offers its Research Department services free of charge to government agencies, numismatic periodicals, organizations, and groups (including the American Numismatic Association Certification Service) for performing authentications and attributions.

Attendance at the yearly American Numismatic Association convention began when I attended my first show in Omaha in 1955. Chicago in 1956, Philadelphia in 1957, Los Angeles in 1958, Portland 1959, Boston 1960, Atlanta 1961, Detroit 1962—the list goes on and on. Countless memories linger today of the many coins bought and sold during those conventions and the many fine collectors and dealers I have met.

The Professional Numismatists Guild has likewise occupied a great deal of my interest, attention, and effort. I joined the PNG in 1960, becoming at the time the youngest member ever to belong to that elite group.

Jim Ruddy, who also joined in 1960, served without compensation for five years as the secretary of the Guild and handled nearly all correspondence between members, relations with the public, and so on. For this he received the Professional Numismatists Guild's Distinguished Service Award.

In recent years I have been a member of the Professional Numismatists Guild Board of Directors. In 1974 I was delighted to receive the Founders' Award, the highest honor given by the organization. In 1977 I was elected by the membership to serve as president for the 1977-1979 term.

In 1964 Empire Coin Company joined with the Honorable Michael V. DiSalle, a former governor of Ohio; Max Humbert, formerly an executive with Presidential Art Medals; James Kelly, a prominent Dayton rare coin dealer; and several others to form Paramount International Coin Corporation. A public stock issue was released with shares selling at $1,000 each. The businesses of Empire Coin Company and James Kelly were merged into Paramount, giving the firm a head start in the numismatic profession. Today Paramount is a major factor in the rare coin business, particularly in the fields of modern Proof sets and commmemorative issues. Jim Ruddy and I left the organization in 1967.

During the same year Jim and I moved to California, each setting up businesses which joined to become the present day Bowers and Ruddy Galleries.

The 1970s have seen many important events. Outstanding among them was the publication of *Photograde*, written by Jim Ruddy in 1970. Following several years of work and the taking of over 5,000 individual high-quality photographs, *Photograde* was ready for publication. Now for the first time in numismatics a collector, beginning or advanced, could instantly grade a coin accurately simply by comparing his piece to a sharp photographic reproduction in *Photograde* and reading the accompanying text. Jim being conservative in nature, printed just 2,000 copies. They were sold out in a matter of days! Overnight the book earned enthusiastic reviews and became a runaway best seller! Soon it was recognized as an official grading guide by the American Numismatic Association. By 1976 over 200,000 copies had been distributed, making it the best-selling grading guide in numismatic history. Curiously enough, the publication in early 1978 of another grading guide by the American Numismatic Association accelerated sales of *Photograde* even further, due, I am sure, to the sharply increased interest in grading.

Jim Ruddy, with his background in physics research, early became interested in die varieties and technical points of coins. Among the many significant pieces discovered by him were the famous 1888/7 overdate Indian cent (first publicized in 1971), the 1867 large 7 over small 7 Indian cent, and several other overdates, including pieces in the British series.

The 1888/7 Indian cent was discovered one day when Jim was looking through a batch of coins obtained from a hiding place in a Virginia mansion. Untouched for nearly a century, they probably were put away at or near the time of issue. Interestingly enough there were two 1888 Indian cents in the group, and both were overdates! The variety, now listed in the *Guide Book of U.S. Coins* and other references, was previously unknown.

In addition, our Research Department at first identified or has verified many other significant varieties over the years sent to us by others.

Following a brilliant numismatic career culminated by his being president and chief executive officer of Bowers and Ruddy Galleries, Jim Ruddy resigned in 1977.

For many years I have had an intense interest in numismatic writing and research. During the first 15 years, until the late 1960s, I wrote virtually every catalog, advertisement, and other word about my organization which reached print. In addition I found time for other writing projects as well, including *Coins and Collectors,* a nostalgic look at the coin collecting hobby published in 1964. This volume, subsequently reprinted by Crown Publishers, sold tens of thousands of copies. *High Profits from Rare Coin Investment,* first published in 1974, became the best selling book on coin investment ever issued. Following close on its heels was *Coin Collecting for Profit,* published by Harper & Row. My *How to be a Successful Coin Dealer* monograph was incorporated into the "Numismation" series of studies published by *Coin World.* A specialized monograph, *A Tune for a Token,* won the coveted Sandra Rae Mishler Award given in 1975, the highest honor conferred on a book by the Token and Medal Society.

I have written for many other publications and publishers, including the *Encyclopedia Americana* and, to mention just one popular magazine, *Reader's Digest.*

On a different subject, but still in the field of collecting, was the mammoth 1,008-page *Encyclopedia of Automatic Musical Instruments,* published in 1972 by the Vestal Press. This volume earned the rare distinction of being designated by the American Library Association as "one of the most valuable reference books of the year."

There is an old-time song, *Today is Yesterday's Tomorrow.* While it is always fun to reminisce about the "good old days" of the early 1950s, when I bought the unwanted 1879 Uncirculated half dollar for $5, when a Proof 1859 Indian cent cost $11, and when a Proof 1913 Barber half dollar cost $25 it is important to enjoy the present. In recent years I have participated in the cataloging of some of the most outstanding collections ever to be sold at auction. The 1973 sale of the magnificent holdings of Matt Rothert, distinguished past president of the American Numismatic Association, contained many rarities which 25 to 50 years from now will probably seem like incredible bargains.

The marvelous collection of Julius Turoff, winner of the "Best in Show Award" given by the American Numismatic Association; the Getty Collection; the Stanislaw Herstal Collection, the largest collection of Polish coins ever to be auctioned in America; the Armand Champa Collection, remarkable for its United States pattern coins; the Dr. Curtis R. Paxman Collection, sold in two parts, featuring some of the finest British Commonwealth coins ever auctioned; the Stanley Scott Collection, featuring coins and medals of George Washington; the Dundee Collection, held with Spink & Son of London, the largest collection of Scottish coins ever sold in America; the 1715 Spanish Treasure Fleet Collection brought up from the depths off of the Florida coast and sold by order of the Real Eight Corporation; the Charles M. Johnson Collection, featuring the holdings of one of America's most distinquished numismatists; the Dr. Ivan Meyer Collection, and others in time will probably become legends.

In 1977 we were awarded the Fairfield Collection, the most valuable rare coin collection ever to be sold at unrestricted public auction sale. Then, too, the Robert Marks Collection comes to mind as do the unforgetable Austin Collection, the Terrell Collection, the superb River Oaks Collection, the James Doolittle Collection, the Donald Herdman Collection, the breathtaking Kensington Collection, the George A. Merriweather Collection, and dozens of others. Indeed, a collection of our past auction catalogs and other publications makes an impressive numismatic library in itself!

In retrospect it would be difficult for me to have picked a profession more enjoyable, stimulating, or rewarding than professional numismatics. And, I don't mean from a profitability viewpoint. To be sure, the profits were there, but I feel they were earned by lots of study and plain hard work, not to mention a sense of responsibility and fair dealing.

To me the fondest memories deal with people I have met and the history and romance surrounding individual coins I have handled. Indeed, it has been a wonderful adventure.

Above: Q. David Bowers and James F. Ruddy weigh and examine a coin in 1974.

Right: George Bennett, auctioneer for many Bowers & Ruddy Galleries sales, awards a silver dollar to a floor bidder as James F. Ruddy records the information in the auction journal.

Just a few of the dozens of Bowers & Ruddy Galleries auction catalogs issued over the years. Featured have been some of the most important private and museum collections ever to cross the auction block.

Covers of three of the many numismatic references written by Q. David Bowers. "How To Be A Successful Coin Dealer" has been distributed for many years by "Coin World." It gives tips and ideas on building a professional dealership. "A Tune for a Token" garnered the coveted Sandra Rae Mishler Award gold medal awarded by the Token and Medal Society. To the right is the cover of the German translation and edition of "High Profits from Rare Coin Investment," the most popular book ever written on the subject of buying rare coins with price appreciation in mind.

Collecting And Investing

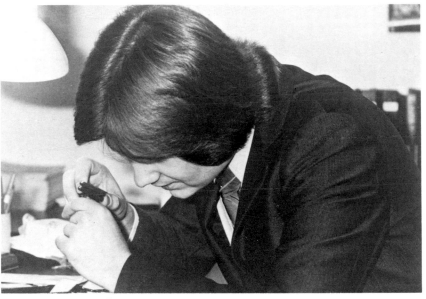

Kent Loose of Bowers & Ruddy Galleries checks the mintmark of a 1932-D quarter.

9

A few years ago John Peterson conducted in-depth interviews with many authorities and personalities in such diverse fields of collecting as violins, Tiffany lamps, coins, and stamps. The result emerged as a chatty and informative book, *Investing for Pleasure and Profit*, published by Dow Jones & Co.

"Hard data suggest the shrewd and capable collector is well prepared to weather very nearly any economic storm," wrote Peterson. "Simply put, all you do is buy the best you can afford of the rarest gems, coins, furniture, classic cars, Persian rugs, Samurai swords, paintings, glassware, figurines, stamps, books, clocks—and at a fair price. Then you wait and values increase. It doesn't take long, not with the manner in which the collectors' markets have been running in the 1970s. Millions of people are making big bucks."

The respected Wall Street investment firm of Salomon Brothers published a study which showed that several different collecting categories, rare coins being prominent among them, showed price appreciation of ten to twenty percent per year, far outstripping comparable investments in the stock market during the 1960s and 1970s, even when dividend earnings produced by stocks were considered.

Edwin T. Sewall, a collector of antique music boxes, estimated in 1978 that the investment return in his hobby area averaged 17 percent per year.

The Commodity Investors Research Group, as quoted by John Peterson, reported a well-documented study which showed that rare United States coins yielded a 19% compounded annual rate of return from 1947 through 1973 and an even higher 27.3% return during the 1969-1973 period.

While success has been there for the *prudent* collector of artifacts, not every garden has been full of roses. There have been some skunk cabbages too. For example, John Peterson summarized one field by writing: "The goal of acquiring art is for aesthetics, not profit. One expert says that only one percent of contemporary paintings sold currently are worth the asking price, and they may never be of greater value than when originally sold."

In a similar vein an Arizona investor, apparently with a lot of money in the bank and not much time to seriously study his investment situation, poured $50,000 into modern limited edition medals during the early 1970s. He was extremely distressed a few years later to find that his holdings could only be sold for a fraction of the price he paid. In one instance a limited edition set of medals which he originally purchased for over $1,200 was worth just $400.

The catch, of course, is that these and other "limited" editions were limited only to the numbers of people willing to order the collections—and those numbers often were immense. Once the original demand, fueled by massive advertisements, had been met, there simply was very little aftermarket.

The key to investment success, in my opinion, is to buy classic items of *proven* rarity and value. Sure, there is a chance that a new medal minted this year, a "limited edition" first day cover of a postage stamp, or a "limited edition" lithograph recently marketed may increase in value, but it has been my observation that for every one of these items, things called "instant collectibles" by one authority, that go up in value within a reasonable amount of time there are a hundred which will drop in value.

Over the years I have studied collectors' items in many different fields. My personal interests, as related throughout the text earlier, are quite varied. And, like most collectors, my interests are constantly changing. There are always new things to be discovered, new fields to be explored.

In the 1950s when I was a student at the Pennsylvania State University I saw at an antique show a display of woven coverlets. A typical coverlet, woven with an ornately patterned design on a Jacquard loom, measures about seven or eight feet long by five or six feet wide. In the corners are prominent squares giving the name and location of the weaver and the time the weaving was done. As these were produced one at a time, often on special order, occasionally the name of the customer would also be woven into the product.

Playing an Aeolian Orchestrelle

No Musical Knowledge Necessary

Style V. Price, $1500

EADING AN orchestra is quite different from personally playing any musical instrument except

The Aeolian Orchestrelle

The orchestral conductor experiences none of the wearying slavery of scales and exercises—and yet his temperamental control is just as pronounced. He throws himself into the spirit of the music in a far greater degree than does, for instance, the pianist, who is compelled to devote so large a proportion of his mental capacity to the mere sounding of the notes. This exacting technique is not necessary to the conductor of an orchestra. A wave of his baton introduces the different voices, swells or diminishes the tone or volume, produces the delicate pianissimo, the thunderous fortissimo.

The player of an Aeolian Orchestrelle can be likened to no one so much as to the conductor of an orchestra. The notes are sounded for him. He controls the registration of the tones, the shadings of tempo, the phrasing, the tone-coloring, all the orchestral effects are at the command of the owner of an Aeolian Orchestrelle. It can easily be learned by anybody and yet allows the greatest possible scope for study and improvement.

The Aeolian Orchestrelle is a home orchestra.

We would be glad to have you come and hear it play your favorite music—Wagner, Beethoven, Bach, Handel, Schubert, a delicious waltz, a stirring march, a bright two-step. The wonderful versatility of the Aeolian Orchestrelle makes it the most universally interesting musical instrument for the home.

We would be glad to have you come and try it yourself—you can learn to play it in ten minutes, master it in a month.

Aeolian, $75 to $750.
Aeolian Orchestrelle, $1,000 to $2,500.
Pianola, $250.
Call at any of the below addresses, or send for Catalogue **M**.

THE AEOLIAN COMPANY

18 West Twenty-third Street, New York

500 Fulton Street, Brooklyn, N. Y.   124 East Fourth Street, Cincinnati, O.

Chicago, Lyon & Healy
Philadelphia, C. J. Heppe & Son
St. Louis, Bollman Bros. Co.
Boston, M. Steinert & Sons Co.

Baltimore, Wm. Knabe & Co.
Cleveland, B. Dreher's Sons Co.
Buffalo, H. Tracy Balcom
San Francisco, Kohler & Chase

Pittsburg, C. C. Mellor Co.
New Orleans, Ph. Werlein, Ltd.
Detroit, Grinnell Bros.
Portland, Ore., M. B. Wells

Washington, Wm. Knabe & Co.
Newark, Lauter Co.
Montreal, L. E. N. Pratte & Co.
Minneapolis, Metropolitan Music Co.

(Fleming & Carnrick Press, New York)

The Aeolian Orchestrelle, popular around 1910, sold for $1,000 to $2,500 for most models, with particularly elaborate varieties bringing up to $5,000—in an era when factory workers often made no more than $10 per week. Foot-pumped in the manner of a player piano, the Aeolian Orchestrelle contained hundreds of tuned organ reeds. The result was a versatile instrument which could play classical numbers as well as marches and two-steps.

In the early 1960s an instrument such as the Style V, pictured above could be purchased in unrestored condition for about $200 to $300. Today the price is ten times that or more, a nice investment return for the collector.

Prices at the time were about $75 to $125 each, more than my college budget could afford for a luxury. Still the desire to own one persisted.

Recently my wife Christie and I went to an antique show. On display were several coverlets. My earlier interest was reawakened.

For $450 I selected a rich red, white, and blue coverlet woven by Henry Miller of McCutchenville, Seneca County, Ohio, in 1848. Accompanying my purchase was a descriptive tag which noted that "Henry Miller was born in Pennsylvania about 1814 and probably served his apprenticeship with a weaver there. He was in Ohio by at least the early 1840s. The 1850 census lists him as a coverlet weaver with $250 worth of real estate, living in McCutchenville with his wife and six-year-old daughter."

Obviously coverlets have been an attractive investment over the years, rising in value by four or five times during the 1960s and 1970s.

In 1915 one of the best selling slot machines made by the Mills Novelty Company of Chicago was the *Cricket,* a tall floor-standing device which offered the patron a chance to win a jackpot worth several dollars if a nickel put in the coin slot would fall down through the right combination of metal pegs. Made of quartered oak with handsome nickeled fittings, the gambling device was a popular attraction in places where it was originally used, the Grand Hotel in Trinidad, Colorado, being one of many examples.

In 1969 a Las Vegas, Nevada, collector, Roy Arrington, discussed the Mills *Cricket* with me. "They are very rare today, and I have only seen a few of them," he related. Coming from one of America's most prominent collectors (and later a dealer) of gambling equipment, this was an impressive statement. At the time he offered one for sale for $1,200.

By a decade later collecting gambling machines had become popular with hundreds if not thousands of enthusiasts. Whereas antique gambling machines could be openly bought, sold, and traded only in the state of Nevada in 1969, by ten years later enlightened legislators of many other states had made it possible for collectors to own antique gambling machines so long as the devices were not currently used for gambling purposes. Interest grew by leaps and bounds. Two publications specifically devoted to the hobbyist appeared, *Loose Change* and *The Coin Slot.* A decade after Roy Arrington's original comment a Mills *Cricket* was sold to a collector for $13,000! At the same time a strong market developed for later gambling machines, devices such as the Watling Rol-A-Top and Treasury made in the 1930s.

In 1870 William S. Wooton established in Indianapolis a furniture manufactory. In 1874 the United States Patent Office issued patent number 155,604 to Wooton for an "improvement in secretaries," consisting "of a secretary constructed in three parts, two of which are together equal in width to the other, each part being provided with compartments or pigeonholes suitable for storing books, papers, etc., and the two lesser parts hinged to the greater part, to serve as doors to the secretary. . ." Thus came into being the Wooton Patent Secretary, advertised as "The King of Desks."

By the early 1960s collectors were beginning to rediscover Victorian furniture. Carved chairs and sofas made of walnut, quartered oak, and other richly-patterned woods, formerly sold for a few dollars each in flea markets and antique sales, began to bring $50, then $100, then more. Wooton desks, a high point in Victorian furniture elegance and complexity, were in the spotlight. With its locks, seemingly countless pigeonholes, ornate hinges, carved top, secret compartments, and overall impressive appearance the Wooton desk was a "natural" for anyone inclined toward relics of a century ago.

At first Wooton desks could be found for a few hundred dollars each. Then knowledge of them caught on and the price rose to $1,000. Then came the publication in 1969 by the Smithsonian Institution of *The King of Desks, Wooton's Patent Secretary,* by Betty Lawson Walters. Advertisements began to appear in the *Antique Trader* and elsewhere seeking these prize items. One seller, imaginatively capitalizing on the interest in western Americana, started calling these "Wells Fargo desks" which further heightened their appeal. The demand increased. The price crossed the $2,000 mark, then $3,000. Morton's, a New Orleans antiques firm, obtained over 20 Wooton desks in a marvelous group and sold most in the range of $4,000 to $5,000 apiece in the mid-70s. By the late 1970s prices had gone even higher.

A classic in its field, an item of proven scarcity, rarity, and desirability, each Wooton's Patent Secretary has handsomely rewarded its owner—rewarded in many ways, as a useful and attractive piece of furniture at the same time as a profitable investment.

During the early 20th century one of the most delightful attractions to the eye and ear was the merry-go-round or carousel. Such manufacturers as the Philadelphia Toboggan Company, C.W. Parker, Allan Herschell, Spillman Engineering Company, William F. Mangels, Gustav A. Dentzel, and Charles I.D. Looff produced hundreds of merry-go-rounds ranging from small portable units with fewer than a dozen horses to a gigantic "mass of gold and glitter" (in C.W. Parker's words) complete with dozens of carved horses, lions, giraffes, and other animals, with music being provided by an automatic organ made by Wurlitzer, Gavioli, Bruder, Ruth, Limonaire, or the North Tonawanda Musical Instrument Works.

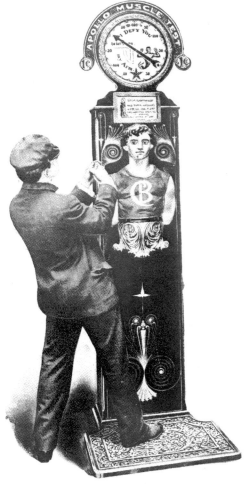

Around the turn of the century the one-cent piece, or "penny" as it is familiarly known, opened a world of entertainment in the penny arcade. Most such arcades, the "Vaudette" shown above being an example, featured dozens of different machines, each of which hungrily devoured Indian cents. And, for the "wealthy" visitor there were usually a few nickel-operated devices on hand as well.

Today arcade machines of the early 20th century are very popular with collectors. Unfortunately, these devices, once made by the tens of thousands, are quite elusive today. Most are made of quartered oak with ornate nickeled finish.

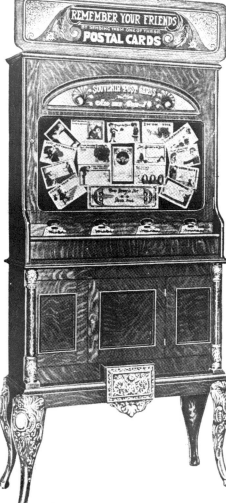

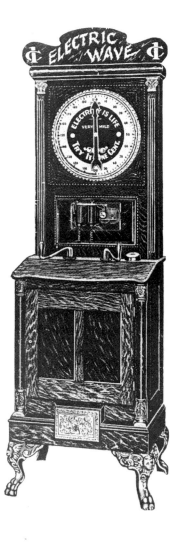

In 1964 Frederick Fried wrote *A Pictorial History of the Carousel*. For the first time a popular reference told how the merry-go-round industry developed, gave stories of individual woodcarvers and other artists, and brought to the forefront of modern day America the nostalgia of bygone carnivals, and amusement parks. Interest increased. Soon a collectors' group, the National Carousel Association, was established. By the late 1970s a single finely-carved Dentzel carousel horse, an item which was worth $250 in 1960 and $1,000 in 1972, had climbed in value to over $2,500. Even this was apt to be on the cheap side, for one collector offered a "Dentzel outside row jumper. Handsome harness and draped cloth on one side. $4,700."

In carousel artifacts, as in other fields, classic items of proven scarcity and in excellent condition have performed marvelously as an investment. And, if the dreams of Barbara Charles and other carousel historians are realized, future years will see more serious historical attention focused on these natural art treasures, with leading museums and institutions adding carousel figures or, even better, intact carousels to their exhibitions. At the same time prices will undoubtedly increase.

In 1886 the Sidney Advertising Clock Company of Sidney, New York, marketed a very unusual timekeeping device. Designed for use in hotel lobbies, railroad stations, and other public places, the Sidney Advertising Clock featured a six-foot-high oak cabinet containing at the top a calendar clock which showed not only the hours of the day but also the days of the month. The main attraction, however, was to be found at the bottom of the device. Behind a clear glass panel there were three rotating drums. "Cards change every 5 minutes," a notice read. Each five minutes a gong would sound and the three drums, geared together, would turn one-third of a revolution. Displayed to the observer would be a set of three advertisements. Another five minutes would pass, the gong would sound again, and three different advertisements would be shown.

In Paris, Illinois, jeweler J.H. Reed ordered one of these fantastic clocks. Advertising space was rented to local merchants. Jay the Photographer, located on the southeast corner of the town square, advertised "Children's pictures a specialty, come rain or sunshine." D.M. Wieder, merchant tailor located on the east side of the public square, invited patrons to "Come and see me." Another sign read: "Advice to traveling men: Stop at the New Eagle Hotel, where you get the best room, best bed, and best meal in the city."

A clang of the bell and three more advertisements would come into view: one for the City Roller Mills (manufacturer of roll process flour, meal, and feed), an advertisement for J.H. Reed (owner of the clock), and a third card which advertised that A.A. Piper was a "manufacturer and dealer in saddles, harnesses, bridles, whips, ropes, and horse-furnishing goods."

A third sounding of the gong would produce a final three sets of cards advertising P.C. Parker's Variety Store, L.C. Mullins' Meat Market, and H. Dollarhide's dealership in farm machinery and fine buggies.

In 1968 a finely-preserved Sidney Advertising Clock was valued at $1,000, if you could find one. A decade later the same type of clock, specifically the one used by J.H. Reed in Paris, Illinois, was sold for $4,000 by a collector in Columbia, Missouri. The purchaser thought it to be quite a bargain.

Shortly before the turn of the century the Regina Music Box Co. introduced several styles of music boxes which changed tunes automatically. The music was programmed on steel discs measuring 15½ inches, 20¾ inches, or 27 inches in diameter, depending on the model. Twelve discs were stored in a device resembling a toast rack. With the drop of a nickel or flick of a switch any one of the 12 discs could be selected for playing, or if left unattended all 12 tunes would play in sequence automatically.

This early day version of the jukebox is recognized as a collectors' classic. By 1960, when antique collecting began to become popular in a big way in America, a fine specimen of a 27-inch-disc *Regina Corona* was sold by Arthur Sanders of Deansboro, New York, for $400. By 1965 the value had reached the point at which an Ohio collector who asked $800 for a comparable instrument sold it instantly. In 1970 another one changed hands at $3,600. By 1975 the value stood at the $5,000 mark. Three years later the valuation had more than doubled to over $10,000, with one sale reported at $14,000. Here again, a classic item of proven scarcity performed superbly as an investment.

In the field of rare coins there have been many investment success stories. Indeed, the numismatist who has built a collection carefully and who has acquired items of proven quality, rarity, and demand has profited superbly. The supply of rare coins has remained static, the demand has increased, and the inevitable result has been a long-term price trend upward.

In June 1955 I ran one of my first large display advertisements, an extensive listing which appeared in the *Numismatic Scrapbook Magazine*. In the intervening years each and every coin has *multiplied* in value at least five to ten times, and for many issues even this dramatic figure is conservative!

For example, the following Proof gold dollars were offered for sale: 1867 $80, 1868 $40, 1870 $42.50, 1873 $30, 1875 $260, 1878 $37, 1880 $57.50. The 1979 *Guide Book of United States Coins* listed the same pieces as follows: 1867 Proof $2,750, 1868 Proof $2,750, 1870 $2,750, 1873 $2,750, 1875 Proof $12,500, 1878 Proof

So There You Are . . .

and here am I with more nice items. You sent so many orders for the gold I listed last issue that I am obligated to offer more at the same liberal prices. You asked for them — here they are:

GOLD

DOLLARS

1849-O AU	$11.00
1851 AU	8.50
1852-O AU	12.00
1853 Unc.	9.50
1854 Ty. II EF.	9.00
1855 EF	8.00
1856 Unc.	10.00
1862 AU	9.25
1862 Unc.	10.75
1867 Proof	80.00
1868 Proof	40.00
1870 Proof	42.50
1873 Unc.	10.75
1873 Proof	30.00
1874 Unc.	10.75
1875 Proof	260.00
1878 Proof	37.00
1880 Proof	57.50

QUARTER EAGLES

1804 EF	65.00
1829 Proof	100.00
1830 Proof	95.00
1833 impaired proof	85.00
1834 AU was proof	17.00
1838 EF	13.50
1839 AU	20.00
1843-O EF	12.50
1844-D Abt. Fine	12.50
1850 VF	11.25
1851 VF	11.25
1852 AU	12.00
1853 VF	11.50
1861 VF	11.00
1869 AU	17.50
1878 Unc.	13.00
1878-S EF	12.00
1884 Unc.	20.00
1889 Unc.	18.00
1896 Unc.	12.75
1902 Unc.	12.00
1904 imp. proof	15.00
1905 Unc.	12.25
1906 Unc.	12.25
1906 AU	9.00
1906 Proof	35.00
1907 AU	9.75
1907 Unc.	12.35
1908 AU	8.25
1910 EF	7.75
1910 AU	8.75
1911 AU	8.50
1911 Unc.	9.00
1912 Fine	6.90
1913 Fine	6.90
1914-D Struck with raised edge Unc.	15.00
1914-D VF	8.50
1915 AU	8.75
1925-D EF	8.25
1925-D Unc.	9.10
1926 EF	8.25
1926 Unc.	9.50
1926 Sesqui	15.00
1927 Unc.	9.10
1928 VF	8.25
1929 Unc.	9.15

THREE DOLLARS

1854 EF	25.00
1855 AU	28.25
1856 VF	27.50
1856 EF	29.00
1856-S (small) G	15.00
1856-S (lge) AU	29.75
1858 Fine	48.50
1860 cleaned Pr.	30.00
1863 EF	30.00
1864 EF	32.00
1874 Unc.	33.50
1874 Proof	97.50
1878 Unc.	34.00
1880 Proof	82.50
1884 Proof	72.50
1885 Proof	82.00
1888 Proof	65.00
1889 Proof	57.50

HALF EAGLES

1803/2 AU	59.00
1804 L-8 Unc. ..	75.00
1804 S-8 Unc. ..	75.00
1806 P-6 AU ...	52.00
1811 Good	20.00
1813 Unc	90.00
1818 Unc.	100.00
1834 plain 4 Unc.	25.00
1834 plain 4 EF	12.50
1835 Unc.	22.50
1836 EF	12.00
1838 EF	15.00
1849 EF	13.50
1851 AU	17.50
1857 AU	15.50
1861 Fine	11.50
1878 Abt. Fine..	10.50
1881 VF	11.50
1881 AU	12.50
1881 Unc.	13.50
1881-S EF	12.00
1882 Fine	11.50
1882 Unc.	14.00
1883 EF	11.90
1887-S EF	11.75
1887-S AU	13.00

Q. DAVID BOWERS — Continued on following page

Half Eagles (cont'd)

1893 Unc.	$13.25
1894-O EF	17.50
1895 EF	11.50
1895 Unc.	14.00
1899 EF	11.75
1899-S Fine	11.75
1900 AU	12.50
1900 Unc.	13.50
1901-S AU	12.75
1902-S Unc.	14.00
1903-S Unc.	13.50
1906 Fine	10.75
1906 AU	11.80
1906 Unc.	13.25
1907 Unc.	13.50
1908 VF	11.25
1908 AU Indian.	12.50
1909-D EF	12.25
1909-D VF	11.85
1911 Fine	11.25
1911 EF	$12.00
1911 Unc.	13.00
1912 VF	11.50
1915 EF	11.50

EAGLES

1797 Unc.	150.00
1799 Proof with slight toning betwen stars rare	158.00
1801 AU	125.00
1870 VF	26.00
1879 EF	27.50
1879 AU	32.00
1880-S Unc.	30.00
1881 EF	20.50
1881 EF	22.25
1888-S EF	21.75
1892 EF	22.00
1893 Unc.	$26.00
1894 Unc.	26.00
1901 Unc.	26.00
1907 Unc.	26.00
1913 Unc.	27.25
1932 Unc.	41.75

DOUBLE EAGLES

1882-S Unc.	47.50
1885-S Unc.	47.50
[illegible] Unc.	48.25
MCMVII High Wire edge struck in high relief Unc.	145.00
1908 Unc. no motto	47.50
1922 Unc.	85.00
1924 Unc.	45.00

I have just acquired one specimen of the **1856 gold dollar** and one specimen of the **1857 gold dollar**—both in **brilliant proof** condition. The catalog value of $90.00 and $60.00 respectively gives no indication of their true rarity. Walter Breen states that only 4 to 12 are known in proof. This pair offered for $225.00.

The **1828 half dollar** with curled base 2 with knob lists at $50.00 Uncirculated in the Guidebook and $100.00 in the Standard Catalog. The Scrapbook of September 1954, states that only nine are known—most of them worn. It is doubtful if more than two or three are uncirculated. I have recently purchased one of these and offer it for $110.00 (Unc.)

As usual I am prepared to buy your collection — none too large or small for my careful attention. Write or call for my prompt consideration. Keep your want lists coming. Ask I may have it!

Q. DAVID BOWERS

203 Second Nat'l Bank Bldg. **Wilkes-Barre, Pa.**

Tel. VAlley 3-8478

June 1955 advertisement in "The Numismatic Scrapbook Magazine." At the time the pieces listed were priced in accordance with their fair market value. Today they seem like unbelievable bargains, for many have increased in value dozens of multiples. Wouldn't you like to be able to go shopping from this advertisement today!

In the 1950s the rare coin business was just a fraction of its present-day size. At the American Numismatic Association convention held in Omaha, Nebraska, in August 1955 record attendance of 500 collectors was announced—a far cry from the over 20,000 collectors which attended some of the ANA shows of the mid-1970s. "The Numismatic Scrapbook Magazine," published by Lee and Cliff Hewitt in Illinois, was the foremost monthly trading medium in the coin field. Supplementing it was "The Numismatist," periodical of the American Numismatic Association. "Numismatic News," published by Chet Krause in Iola, Wisconsin, was of newspaper format and emphasized thousands of classified and display ads—a veritable "convention" in itself. These three publications furnished the thrust of public advertising for Q. David Bowers during the early years. In addition illustrated privately-printed catalogs were sent to interested clients.

$2,750, 1880 Proof $1,900. It is probably safe to say that anyone who would have spent $20,000 to $30,000 with me for select Uncirculated and Proof coins back in 1955 would be a millionaire today!

An 1829 Proof quarter eagle sold by me at $100 in 1955 would bring 100 times that valuation today, and it would be a tremendous bargain. An 1874 Proof $3 dollar gold piece sold at $97.50 in 1955 cataloged at $9,500 in 1979. And, that was not just an isolated example. An 1880 Proof of the same denomination which I sold for $82.50 in 1955 was listed at $6,000 in 1979, an 1884 sold for $72.50 listed years later for $5,500, 1885 formerly at $82 listed at $5,500, 1888 formerly at $65 listed at $5,000, and 1889 formerly at $57.50 listed at $5,000.

A 1797 ten-dollar gold piece Uncirculated at $150 in 1955 commanded a value of $8,000 in 1979. The famous MCMVII (1907) High Relief double eagle which I sold for $145 in 1955 would have brought the lucky owner over $5,000 he had cared to part with it 20 years later!

"Coin collecting isn't just a pleasure for me, it is an *economic necessity*," one of my clients told me recently. Indeed, the astute citizen in today's world is forced to consider rare coins and other non-traditional investments as a means of *economic survival*.

"MAN BECOMES WEALTHY BY INVESTING IN SAVINGS ACCOUNT!" No, you'll never read an article like that in a financial journal. In recent years investing in savings accounts, even those paying generous interest, has proved to be a dismal economic failure when compared to the rate of inflation. For example, in 1978 the national inflation rate was estimated at 8%. At the same time most savings accounts paid 5% to 6%. After taxes, which must be paid on interest each year, most savings account holders would be lucky to net 4% which came to less than half the amount they lost each year by inflation!

In November 1978 a frightening article appeared in *Coin World*. It was noted that in order to keep up with inflation and the increased money supply the Bureau of Engraving and Painting was working three shifts a day. Still, dollars could not be printed fast enough!

The stock market, which certainly has had many success stories, is often elusive to the average investor. Usually the success stories are situations which happened to someone else but not to you. The darlings of one decade are apt to be trampled in the dust the next. In the aforementioned Salomon Brothers study, the return on investment in common stocks, including dividends, did not even keep up with the inflation rate.

So, where does the prudent person invest? There are many areas worthy of consideration. I have investigated and have enjoyed many of them. Perhaps you have had a similar experience.

Traditionally one's home has been a good investment. During the past few decades real estate values in many areas have outpaced the inflation rate. A home which cost $15,000 in 1955 might well sell for $75,000 or more today. In the upper bracket the $50,000 home of 1955 may sell for several hundred thousand dollars now. While buying a home or condominium for living is fine, many do not want to get into the hassles involved with additional properties purchased purely as an investment. The owner of rental properties has to be a specialist. Maintenance, insurance, many different taxes, vacancies, problems with tenants, and shifting areas of desirability and preferences within a given town are all concerns.

What about antiques and other collectors' items? I, for one, really enjoy collecting antique music boxes, nickelodeon pianos, prints, autographs, postcards, clocks, and in conjunction with my main business interest over the years, coins and currency. These have done handsomely as investments, and all indications are that they will continue to do so.

However, for many potential investors larger antiques present difficulties. Financial institutions, pension plans, bank trust departments, and other such investors would have a hard time handling, for example, a dozen 27-inch-disc *Regina Corona* music boxes purchased solely as an investment. First of all, they would be difficult to buy. If one or two per year could be purchased that would be doing well. Even then it would be important to determine if they were in excellent mechanical condition and were well preserved. Once they were purchased, where would they be stored? In a bank lobby? One in your private living room would be fine, but 12 of them in the hands of a pension plan would present difficulties!

In the same vein I have a Wurlitzer Style 165 Military Band Organ made in 1918 and used at Playland-at-the-Beach adjacent to the Cliff House in San Francisco. Producing the sound of a military marching band the instrument provided the musical accompaniment for a gaily-painted, light-spangled carousel. Investment-wise the instrument has done very well. Indeed, it is worth at least three times the price I paid for it several years ago. When restoration is completed what will I do with it? It is too large and too loud to fit into my home. Perhaps a public exhibition or a loan to a museum will be the answer. I don't know. The point is that while it has been an excellent investment, it is hardly the thing for the manager of a bank trust department to consider buying! Even a private collector is apt to have his or her hands full.

In this arena coins stand out as an investment medium with many ideal features. Storage space is not a problem. A small safe deposit box can hold a very valuable collection. When my firm shipped the Fairfield Collection via Brink's from the East Coast to our California offices it

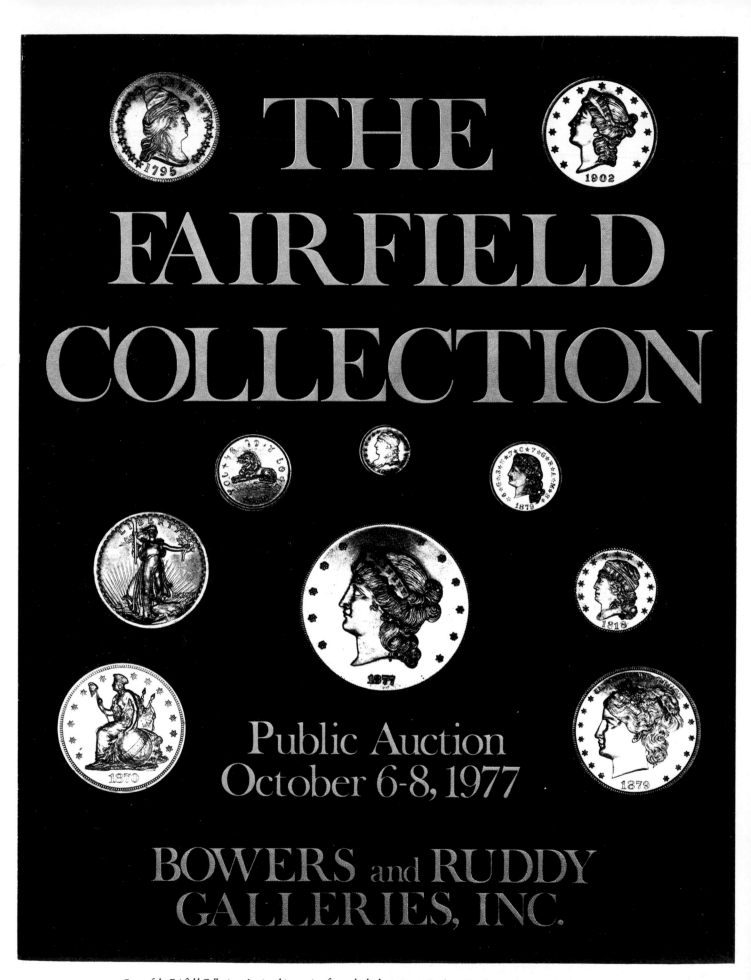

THE FAIRFIELD COLLECTION

Public Auction
October 6-8, 1977

BOWERS and RUDDY GALLERIES, INC.

Cover of the Fairfield Collection. Auctioned in a series of several sales beginning in October 1977, this was the most valuable rare coin collection ever to be sold at unrestricted public auction sale. Worldwide interest centered on the prize rarities offered, gathered over a period of years by a prominent eastern numismatist. Price record after price record fell as pieces found new owners.

was housed in four small metal boxes. The coins, valued at millions of dollars (the collection was the most valuable ever to be sold at unrestricted public auction sale), could be carried by two strong people.

Insurance isn't a problem either. Various underwriters offer insurance policies at reasonable rates for collectors. And, if coins are kept in a safe deposit box rates are even lower.

Handling is likewise simple. Keep your valuable coins and paper money in a dry place, handle them carefully (coins by the edges, paper money in protective plastic envelopes), and you'll have no problem. Transportation is no problem at all. Valuable coins can be shipped easily from place to place by mail. Indeed, insured registered mail is probably the safest way to transport any small valuable object from one location to another. During a quarter century of having thousands of collectors send me tens of millions of dollars worth of coins by insured registered mail no sender has ever experienced a loss.

There is a good market for coins. Year in and year out there has been a strong purchase demand for rare pieces. While many fads have come and gone in the coin market, the classics have always been highly desired. Many years ago I compiled an index of rare coins and charted their performance since 1946. Figured at five-year intervals, the overall trend was always upward, in good economic times and in bad. Of the dozens of coins surveyed there wasn't a single coin—no, not even one—which failed to perform better than other traditional forms of investment such as savings accounts and the securities market. There were many coins which multiplied in value ten to twenty times or more, as the previously-cited figures from my 1955 advertisement vividly illustrate.

"It must be a snap to invest in coins," you might say. "All I have to do is go to a coin dealer, write a check, put the coins in my safe deposit box, and sit back and watch the prices go up." Unfortunately, it is not that simple. If it were, there would be no money left on Wall Street. Anybody who had a spare dollar would invest it in coins!

The truth is that there are pitfalls in coins. Counterfeiting is a big problem. Often coins purchased at "bargain" prices are not genuine. Your best protection is to buy from a dealer who guarantees forever (not just for a limited amount of time) the authenticity of any item purchased. For example, the dealer members of the Professional Numismatists Guild make this guarantee. Another sensible precaution, especially if you are buying a coin "as is" from another collector or seller, is to have the coins checked by the American Numismatic Association Certification Service. For a modest fee you can obtain a photograph and permanent registration of your coin together with a statement attesting to its authenticity or, as sometimes happens, lack of it.

Grading is another area which merits your careful attention. While *Photograde* and the *Official A.N.A. Grading Guide* have made great improvements in this area, there are still many misrepresentations in the marketplace. Often five different sellers will assign five different grades to the same coin, perhaps differing just slightly but still differing, often with important financial consequences. Collectors, who usually have less experience than dealers, are apt to grade coins with even more variation.

Several years ago our firm desired to purchase a substantial quantity of commemorative half dollars. To do this we were willing to pay the going rate for Choice Brilliant Uncirculated coins graded as MS-65 on the A.N.A. scale. We were not looking for bargains nor did we request special discount prices. Over a period of nearly a year we examined $3 million worth of commemorative half dollars sent to us by various sellers! We clearly specified that each coin had to be Choice Brilliant Uncirculated or better. How many do you think met *our* qualifications for this grade? Nearly all of them? Half of them? Wrong, sadly, far wrong. About $400,000 worth, only actually about 8% of those submitted, were graded in our opinion as Choice Brilliant Uncirculated.

As the evaluation of the grade or condition of a coin is largely a subjective matter, experts can legitimately differ. And, to err is human, so even the most meticulous collector or dealer will occasionally make a mistake. However, it has been my experience that grading levels are different from seller to seller. If you do some shopping around you will quickly discover that what one seller calls MS-60 on the A.N.A. scale another seller may call MS-65. The economic implications of this are obvious. For example, let us suppose that seller "A" offers a given coin, accurately and carefully graded, at the following prices: MS-60 $100 and MS-65 $150. At the same time seller "B" offers a specimen graded as "MS-65" at $120, saying it is one of the best bargains ever. This is all well and fine if the coin is truly an MS-65, but chances are virtually certain that it isn't. Why not? Simply because the margin on top-quality coins is so close that large variations do not exist among *comparably* graded coins. Upon inspection the "MS-65" coin offered by seller "B" may prove just to be an MS-60. Thus, you have paid $120 for an MS-60 coin when you could have bought the same coin for less from seller "A."

In 1978 Virgil Hancock, formerly president of the American Numismatic Association, wrote of a firm which profited handsomely by selling vastly overgraded coins to its customers. A logical investigation ensued, and government investigators found that 90% of the company's clients were satisfied! These clients had never learned about grading and couldn't tell the difference!

Any coin buyer who does not take the time to do some serious comparison shopping is foolish, extremely foolish, in my opinion. Comparison shopping can be done only by ordering coins from several different sources and comparing the coins themselves. Comparing the *advertising* for the coins without actually checking the specimens offered is absolutely and completely meaningless. If you have lots of money and aren't concerned about the success of your investment, then bury your head in the sand like an ostrich, order only from one or two places, and do no investigating. You may do well in this regard, but chances are very good that you won't. "Investigate before you invest," in fact, you can't afford not to!

When Ken Bressett and Abe Kosoff compiled the *Official American Numismatic Association Grading Standards for United States Coins* I was invited to write the introduction to the volume. A paragraph in the introduction, "Why is Grading Important?," brought numerous complimentary letters and comments from many different readers, including the two leading weekly numismatic publications, *Coin World* and *Numismatic News*. I quote the paragraph herewith:

"Why is Grading Important? Why are there differences of opinion in the field of grading coins? There are numerous reasons, but the most common are as follows:

"Grading coins can never be completely scientific in all areas. One may weigh a coin and also obtain its specific gravity by mechanical devices, and the results will be factual if accurate equipment is used carefully. There are no scientific means available to measure the surface condition—the amount of wear—of a coin.

"In grading coins, considerations such as striking, surface of the planchet, the presence of heavy toning (which may obscure certain surface characteristics), the design, and other factors each lend an influence. A panel containing a dozen of the foremost numismatic hobby leaders justifiably could have some *slight* differences of opinion on the precise grade of some coins.

"However, it is not *slight* differences which concern us here; it is serious or major differences. The term *over-grading* refers to describing a coin as a grade higher than it actually is. For example, if a coin in AU (About Uncirculated) grade is called Uncirculated, it is overgraded. If a coin in Very Fine grade is called Extremely Fine, it is overgraded.

"What induces overgrading? Here are some of the factors:

"Buyers seeking bargains. The desire to get a bargain is part of human nature. If a given Uncirculated coin actively traded at $100 is offered at $70, it will attract a lot of bargain seekers. The same buyers would reject an offering such as: 'I am offering this stock which trades on the New York Stock Exchange for $100 for just $70 cash,' or 'I am offering $100 bills for just $70 each.'

"In coins, as in any other walk of life, you get what you pay for. If a coin which has a standard value of $100 is offered for $70 there *may* be nothing wrong, but chances are that the piece is overgraded.

"False assumptions. Buyers often assume falsely that any advertisement which appears in a numismatic publication has been approved by that publication. Actually, publishers cannot be expected to examine coins and approve of all listings offered. The person who has no numismatic knowledge or expertise whatsoever can have letterheads and business cards printed and, assuming he has good financial and character references (but not necessarily numismatic expertise), run large and flashy advertisements. Months or years later it is often too late for the deceived buyer to get his money back. The solution to this is to learn how to grade coins and think for youself. Examine the credentials of the seller. Is he truly an expert in his field? How do you know? What do collectors with more experience think of this seller? To what professional organizations does the dealer belong? It is usually foolish to rush and spend your hard-earned money with a coin seller who has no professional credentials and whose only attraction is that he is offering 'bargains.' Think for yourself!

"The profit motive. Sellers seeking an unfair markup may overgrade. For purposes of illustration, let us assume that a given variety of coin is worth the following prices in these grades: AU $75 and Uncirculated $150. A legitimate dealer in the course of business would buy, for example, an AU coin at $50 or $60 and sell it retail for $75, thus making a profit of $15 to $25. However, there are sellers who are not satisfied with the normal way of doing business. They take shortcuts. They pay $50 or $60 for the same AU coin which is worth $75 retail, but rather than calling it AU they call it 'Uncirculated' and sell it for $150. So, instead of making $15 to $25 they may make $90 to $100!

"Inexperience. Inexperience or error on the part of the seller may lead to incorrect grading—both overgrading and undergrading."

So, grading is not only important to the success of your coin investment, it is *vital*.

While bargain hunting is lots of fun, for the investor it is apt to have dire consequences. I have been a collector of many things, as you know. Within numismatics I have had an interest at one time or another in such diverse areas as state and colonial coinage, obsolete currency, tokens, $1 bills, and so on. I have made very, very few *bargain* purchases. I have always had an eye for *quality*, and I learned early that quality does not come cheap-

The first United States cent of 1793 (see above left illustrations) bore on the obverse a depiction of Miss Liberty which, one account said, "appears as if in a fright." The reverse displays a continuous chain of links, hardly a favorable omen for a new country establishing its freedom, so it was observed at the time. The engraver, fearful that the word AMERICA would not fit on the die, abbreviated it to AMERI. At the right above is another variety of 1793 chain cent with AMERICA spelled out in full. To the far right, shown in enlarged illustration, is a marvelous specimen of a 1793 wreath reverse cent. This was the most popular style (in terms of mintage quantities) of the year.

LARGE CENTS were minted continuously from 1793 until 1857 with the solitary exception of 1815. During the first year, 1793, three major varieties were issued: the chain, wreath, and Liberty cap styles. All are elusive today. In later years a wide variety of designs ensued, examples of which are shown at the bottom of this page. Rare dates in the large cent series include the famed 1799, the very rare 1804, the scarce 1809, and among later issues, the scarce 1821, 1823, and 1857.

Large cents can be collected in many different ways. A date sequence forms a fascinating display, as does an assembly of different design types. Some numismatists collect by specialized die varieties, attributing the pieces to "Penny Whimsy," a reference by Dr. William H. Sheldon, which classifies large cents of the years 1793-1814; or "United States Copper Cents 1816-1857," by Howard R. Newcomb, which details varieties of the later series. An organization of large cents enthusiasts, Early American Coppers, issues a periodical, "Penny Wise."

1795 cent illustrating the Liberty cap style used from late 1793 to the early part of 1796.

1796 cent of the draped bust style minted from 1796 to 1807.

1814 cent; classic head type minted from 1808 to 1814.

1837 cent of the general style produced from 1816 through 1839. This variety has plain hair cords.

1838 cent with the two hair cords at the back of Miss Liberty's head in the form of beads.

This 1839 cent variety is familiarly known as the "Booby Head" by collectors.

1839 "Silly Head" large cent depicts a slightly different head style.

In the 1890s John Swan Randall, a Norwich, New York, merchant, acquired a fabulous hoard of thousands of uncirculated cents dated 1816-1820 which had been unearthed from beneath a railway platform in Georgia during the Civil War. Today these issues, known as "Randall Hoard pieces", are highly prized by collectors.

1841 cent of the compact head style, tilted forward, used on certain varieties 1839-1843.

Larger coronet head as used on cents from 1843 through 1857.

ly. Usually you can obtain high quality or you can obtain low price, but not both.

In 1960 I began restoring an automatic musical instrument, an *Electrova* nickelodeon piano which was once used in an arcade in Providence, Rhode Island. In very decrepit condition, the old roll-operated music-maker couldn't play a note. The veneer was peeling off, parts of the mechanisms were gone, and in general it was in a sorry state. Still, by carefully following instructions and seeking the advice of other hobbyists in the field I knew I could restore it. But, first I had to buy some tools. My home workshop at the time consisted of a screwdriver and a pair of pliers. To a local variety store I went, and there before me were many different tools all priced on special sale for 88c each. I bought a hammer, several different sizes of pliers, several wrenches, and several screwdrivers. I was really pleased, for I had assembled a veritible home workshop for less than $20!

Then I began to use what I bought. One of the claws of the hammer broke off on the second or third nail it pulled. One of the pincers on my largest pair of pliers snapped off when I squeezed hard on a metal rod. The end of a screwdriver twisted and bent when I attempted to remove a rusty screw.

Harvey Roehl, an experienced craftsman and historian in the field of automatic musical instruments, came to my rescue. Seeing my predicament, he told me that I could not hope to do a decent restoration unless I had good tools to work with. In the wastebasket went all of the ''bargains.'' With instructions from Harvey I then went shopping for quality tools by Craftsman, Red Devil, Miller's Falls, Stanley, and other makers. I was appalled to see that instead of costing 88c each some of the tools cost $5, $10, and even more. But, the quality was superb, and to this day not a single item has given less than perfect service.

I was once impressed by a sign over a store which read: ''The bitter taste of low quality lasts much longer than the sweet taste of low price.'' So it is with music boxes, with autographs, with hardware and tools, with antique postcards, and, important to the numismatist, so it is with rare coins.

Market trends and fads are another area worthy of thought and consideration. I am not a speculator, and I don't believe in speculation when it comes to financial security or the protection of one's assets. You might call me conservative. As a general rule in numismatics I recommend that you seek out one or several areas of numismatic interest, determine the best condition you can afford in each area, and then carefully buy items of proven rarity and desirability. Along the way there will be many distractions offered by popular fads. Flashy new issues backed by lavish advertising budgets often attract buyers. But, stop and think. Who is *really* paying for the advertising? The ''secret'' is that you are!

If your hometown issues a medal to commemorate its 200th anniversary and sells it for $10, fine, buy one if you want to for sentimental reasons. I would probably do this myself. But, don't mistake this for an investment. Don't buy dozens of them hoping that you are going to pay for your children's college education a decade from now.

In the field of coin collecting there are certain market trends and cycles which are worthy of observation. In January 1975 the Los Angeles *Times* surveyed major dealers and asked their reaction to the gold market. At the time the market was at a peak, following frantic activity during the 1973-1974 years. When gold ownership by the American public became legal on December 31, 1974, I believed that many holders of common gold coins would take profits and that prices would go down. Of the many dealers surveyed by the *Times* I was the only one who did *not* see a sharp upward trend! Prices subsequently plummeted, and I was rewarded with the satisfaction of a follow-up article in the *Times* which pointed out the accuracy of my earlier observations.

Over the years I have written quite a bit on the subject of coin investment. Not all of my words have been enthusiastically received. Once in the early 1960s I wrote an article in *Coin World* stating that in my opinion there was a speculative bubble in certain modern issues. A great furor developed, and one dealer went so far as to take a full-page advertisement condemning my article and stating that *rare* coins were indeed poor things to buy in comparison with modern issues, the issues I called ''speculative.'' Several dozen protests were received by me and by *Coin World*, mainly from people who had a vested interest in the then-rampant speculation. A number of professional numismatists who had been established for many years and who had seen market fads come and go (Harvey Stack of New York City, for example) took my side. Harvey, too, flirted with enmity as at least one dealer stated publicly that from that point onward he would boycott Stack's auction sales unless a retraction was made! The speculative bubble eventually burst, prices dropped, and the controversy was all but forgotten.

I have tried to write in an objective and honest manner and to present all sides of a given situation. It would be easy to brush such problems as counterfeiting and grading under a rug and not mention them to my clients for fear that they might be scared away. Indeed, in some fields (modern art is an example) popular publications rarely mention these subjects. However, I have always believed that an educated buyer is the best buyer. I have always encouraged clients to read as much as possible on

Original 1861 copper-nickel Confederate States of America cent, one of just twelve pieces struck by Robert Lovett, Jr.

Restrike of the 1861 Confederate States of America half dollar, one of 500 made in 1879 by J.W. Scott & Company, using the original reverse die (which was used in 1861 to strike four original pieces in silver).

THE CONFEDERATE STATES OF AMERICA during its brief history was responsible for two coins, the 1861 cent and the half dollar of the same year.

The story of the cent began early in 1861 when the Confederacy contacted Bailey & Company, the Philadelphia jewelers, concerning supplying one-cent pieces for the South. Bailey commissioned Robert Lovett, Jr., a die sinker of that city, to prepare the pieces. In 1860 Lovett had produced a one-cent-size token with an attractive bust of Liberty on the obverse and with his own advertisement on the reverse. This attractive design was deemed ideal for use on the Confederate cent.

Lovett struck just twelve pieces in copper-nickel metal. Then, fearful his assignment would be viewed as illegal by Union authorities, he concealed the dies and twelve coins in his cellar. Lovett nevertheless was quite proud of his Confederate cents, and he carried two of them as pocket pieces. In the early 1870s he accidentally spent one of these in a tavern. This piece, as chance would have it, found its way to Captain J.W. Haseltine, a coin dealer. Haseltine, familiar with the Liberty design from its use on Lovett's earlier advertising token, immediately recognized who made it. He visited Lovett several times in an effort to learn the true story of the Confederate cent, but Lovett remained silent.

One day Lovett pulled out one of his cabinet drawers for Haseltine. There in a tidy row were the ten remaining 1861 Confederate cents! Lovett then told the story, up to that point completely unknown by numismatists, of the origin of the CSA pieces. He sold Haseltine the ten coins and the dies used to strike them.

Haseltine enlisted the help of J. Colvin Randall and Peter L. Krider, also of Philadelphia, to produce restrikes from the original dies. They were careful not to produce any restrikes in the original metal, copper-nickel, thus preserving the integrity of the twelve pieces originally struck in 1861 by Lovett.

The story of the restriking was told in an advertisement used to sell the subsequently-produced coins:

Philadelphia, April 2, 1874

Having succeeded in discovering and purchasing the dies of the Confederate cent, we, the undersigned, have concluded to strike for the benefit of collectors a limited number, and in order to protect those gentlemen who had the [copper-nickel] pieces originally struck in 1861, we determined to strike none in that metal. Our intention was to strike 500 in copper, but after the 55th impression the collar burst and the dies were badly broken. They are now in the possession of Mr. Haseltine and may be seen at any time at his store, No. 1343 Chestnut Street, Philadelphia.

The history of this piece is probably known to most collectors, but for the information of those who are ignorant of the facts we will state that the dies were made by Mr. Lovett, of Philadelphia, in 1861, who says that they were ordered in that year by the South, that he struck but twelve pieces, but probably thinking that he might have some difficulty in reference to them (having made the dies for the South), he mentioned the matter to no one until a few months since, when he parted with ten pieces, struck in [copper-nickel] which he stated were all that he had, having lost two pieces. One of the said two pieces was the means of the dies and pieces being traced. Although the Confederacy did not adopt this piece, it will always be considered interesting as the only coinage designed for said Confederacy...

The notice went on to say that seven restrikes were made in gold, twelve in silver, and finally, 55 in copper. By April 2, 1874, six of the ten 1861 Confederate States of America copper-nickel cents had been sold.

The 1861 Confederate States of America half dollar likewise had an interesting history. In February 1861 the state of Louisiana turned over to the Confederate States of America the United States Mint at New Orleans, which had come under control of the South. It was decided to produce a distinctive Confederate coinage of the half dollar denomination. A.H.M. Patterson, an engraver and die sinker of that city, prepared a reverse die which showed a shield with seven stars (representing the states which seceded from the Union), Liberty cap, and stalks of sugar cane and cotton. Specimens were given to Secretary of the Confederacy Memminger (who gave his to President Jefferson Davis for his inspection), to Dr. E. Ames, to Professor F.L. Riddell of the University of Louisiana, and to Dr. B.F. Taylor, who was the chief coiner of the Confederate States of America Mint.

The existence of the Confederate half dollar was unknown until 1879 when Dr. Taylor made it known that he owned a specimen. In April of that year Taylor sent his coin, together with the original reverse die, to E. Mason, Jr., the Philadelphia coin dealer, with the instructions to tell the public of the coin's existence. Taylor told how the reverse die had been prepared, combined with an official United States of America Liberty seated obverse die on hand from earlier in the year, and used to strike four pieces. It was anticipated that a larger quantity would eventually be made, but silver bullion became scarce and the short-lived Confederate Mint closed its doors on April 30, 1861.

The die subsequently found its way to J.W. Scott & Company, well-known coin and stamp dealers. David Proskey, a former employee of Scott, related the following history of the 1861 restrikes made from the original die:

"J.W. Scott bought the die of the reverse of the Confederate half dollar, together with the Proof specimen of the only known Confederate half dollar, at that time, from E.B. Mason, Jr., of Philadelphia. The United States Government had seized the obverse as its property, and could have seized both sides, as at the close of the war in 1865 the U.S. government became the heir of the Confederacy.

"Scott decided to strike impressions from his die, and he sent out circulars offering silver restrikes at $2 each, agreeing to have only 500 pieces struck. Preparing for this issue, Scott purchased 500 United States half dollars of New Orleans mintage and had the reverses drilled off. Then for fear that the die would break, a steel collar was affixed, and 500 impressions in white metal were struck in order to be able to supply something should the die go to pieces, but the die held intact even after the silver pieces were struck. Each of the latter obverses (Liberty seated) was placed on a blank of soft brass and then struck on a screw press. This helped to keep the obverse from flattening. The writer supervised the process so that the workers kept no specimens for souvenirs. The die was then softened and cut across, so that no more could be struck from the perfect die. The die now reposes in the collection of the Louisiana Historical Society, the gift of Mr. J. Sanford Saltus. A couple of brass impressions exist showing the ridge across. These are now in the collection of Mr. Elliott Smith, New York City.

"When all were struck Scott sent out circulars with the coins to the subscribers offering to pay 50c each over the subscription price for the return of any of the pieces, stating as a reason 'oversubscription,' which was untrue. It was doubtful if over 250 were sold, as Scott had a plentiful supply of them for over 30 years thereafter. He gradually raised the price to $15 each. The original Proof half dollar was several times placed in various auction sales, but always 'bought in.' Finally the writer sold it to Mr. J. Sanford Saltus for $3,000, who presented it to the American Numismatic Society."

the subject, to visit my competitors and to make purchases there if they find better values, and to otherwise "play the field." As my business has grown steadily for many years I haven't taken much of a risk by doing this, so it seems.

It was with great appreciation that I read in the introduction to Harry J. Forman's book, *How You Can Make Big Profits Investing in Coins,* the following paragraph. Even more poignant was the fact that I was the only dealer specifically mentioned by Mr. Forman in this context:

"Anyone can make predictions, and if he does in a field in which he is already well known they are sure to be widely read. Moreover, by waiting until people's memories have been somewhat blurred, and then republishing only his successes, he can often build up a rather good reputation for himself.

"In the numismatic field we have three kinds of forecasters. The first and commonest is the person who makes predictions simply as a promotional device to help sell whatever he has on hand. I don't say that in all or even most cases this involves a deliberate deception. On the contrary, the very fact that a person has invested his own money to purchase one or another item would indicate a certain amount of faith in its market potential. But, such predictions necessarily lack true discrimination and depend for their success, if not on luck, then on the progress of the market as a whole.

"A second type of forecaster is the non-professional numismatist who dabbles in speculation and writes books or articles on market trends. Such an individual is more serious in his selections and understands that there are always widespread differences in the potential of various issues and theories. But for all that, his livelihood is not dependent on his predictions, and even if they should fail he is still reimbursed by his royalties.

"The third and rarest type is the successful full-time dealer who forecasts not for promotional purposes, but simply to share his insights with the general investing public. My good friend Q. David Bowers is one such forecaster, having given much excellent investment advice. . ."

I have always been interested in economics. To me one of the most informative areas of economic study is the field of cycles. While such phenomena as the Kondratieff cycle, the Kitchin cycle, the building cycle, and the Juglar cycle have been noted in the business journals, little attention has ever been paid to cycles in the rare coin market. And yet there seem to be observable trends in this regard.

I believe that most things move in cycles. The person who is not aware of cycles is apt to be doomed to financial failure or perhaps to financial obscurity. Witness, for example, the Dutch citizens who eagerly bought tulip bulbs and even traded their most valuable earthly possessions for them, never dreaming that eventually the market would run out of buyers. And, there were the countless everyday citizens, most of whom had no financial experience, who became stock market "experts" in 1929. Cycles exist almost everywhere.

In 1958 the Ford Motor Company spent many millions of dollars to establish dealerships for the Edsel car. The Edsel was introduced, and initially the public bought as many cars as had been projected. Obviously here was a winner! Then something happened, the Edsel fizzled, and two years later the car was a part of history. Or, do you remember the Hadacol patent medicine fad which saw some of America's leading show business personalities touring America extolling the virtues of this now nearly forgotten elixir? These are examples of short cycles—up and then down, perhaps never to go up again.

Other cycles are longer. In 1925 the most active place in the United States to buy real estate was Florida. Prices rose, speculation was rampant, and tremendous profits were made. Then the bubble collapsed and prices plummeted. Several decades later a new generation of investors was on hand to send prices up once again. Then came government investigations of Florida real estate selling practices, and by the mid-1960s much of the popular investment market for Florida real estate was dead. Then around 1970 Mickey Mouse came along, and the success of Walt Disney World sent Florida real estate prices, particularly those in the vicinity of Orlando, skyward once more.

So it is with coins. All series run in cycles. Fortunately for the numismatist and investor, few cycles are composed of violent upward dashes followed by downward crashes, never to go up again. Coin cycles are generally of a milder nature, often characterized by a spurt of activity, then a leveling off, then another spurt. While the long term trend of rare coin prices has been upward, no individual United States coin or coin series to my knowledge has exhibited a *steady* upward growth rate year in and year out. Often a coin will be quiet for a year or two, active for a year or two, and then quiet for a year or two, then to be followed by another period of activity.

From my beginning days in numismatics I have been an avid reader of coin publications and reference books. The *American Journal of Numismatics, The Numismatist,* and the *Numismatic Scrapbook Magazine* were read issue by issue from the earliest years to the present. I scrutinized articles, studied prices, and observed trends. Certain patterns emerged. In February 1964 in the *Empire Investors Report* I wrote the first article ever published on the subject of cycles in the rare coin market. Since that time scattered references have appeared in the numis-

1892 Columbian half dollar, the first United States commemorative issue. These were sold at $1 each at the World's Columbian Exposition held in Chicago.

1893 Isabella quarter sold at the World's Columbian Exposition for $1. As the Columbian half dollar (see left) was available for the same price, the small quarter was unpopular, so relatively few were sold.

1900 Lafayette commemorative silver dollar, actually struck in December, 1899.

1935 Old Spanish Trail issue was a favorite with numismatists. Just 10,000 specimens were distributed, a low mintage.

1918 Lincoln-Illinois commemorative half dollar.

1928 Hawaiian half dollar commemorating the 150th anniversary of Captain James Cook's visit in 1778. Just 10,000 were distributed, many to non-numismatists. Today this is a highly prized issue.

1922-D Oregon Trail half dollar; one of many bearing this motif issued from 1926 to 1939.

1938 commemorative half dollar observing the founding of New Rochelle, New York, in 1688. 15,266 were distributed.

1936 Norfolk half dollar displays a design crammed with lettering and descriptions.

1936 Cincinnati half dollar, one of three issues offered in a set at $7.75.

1936 half dollar commemorating the 300th anniversary of the founding of York County, Maine.

1934 Texas half dollar representative of the design issued 1934-1938.

From 1892 until 1954 many different commemorative coins were issued. Included were 48 designs of half dollars (which, including mintmark varieties, total 142 issues in all), the 1893 Isabella quarter and the 1900 Lafayette silver dollar. Gold commemoratives were produced in various denominations from the dollar through the $50 gold piece (the latter for use at the 1915 Panama-Pacific International Exposition).

Commemorative half dollars were sold by the mint for face value to issuing commissions which resold them at a profit. For example, 1892 and 1893 Columbian half dollars were offered at $1 each, twice face value. In 1936 a great commemorative fever swept numismatics, and many different issues made an appearance. Supplies were not equal to the demand in certain instances, and in other instances there were charges of favoritism and irregularities in distribution. The result was a speculative fever which saw, for example, a set of three 1936 Cincinnati half dollars (one each from the Philadelphia, Denver, and San Francisco mints), issued at $7.75, rise in value almost immediately to $50!

For the collector today commemorative half dollars and other issues offer a wide variety of fascinating designs depicting many diverse historical situations. Most examples can be acquired in Uncirculated condition.

Various representative types of commemorative gold coins.

1854 pattern cent, slightly
smaller in diameter than the
cent then in circulation and
without stars on the obverse.

1855 pattern cent with the
flying eagle motif resurrected
from Gobrecht's silver dollar
design of 1836. The diameter
is slightly smaller than the cents
then in use in circulation.

1856 flying eagle cent, a
successful experiment which
ended the reign of the large-size
copper cent and paved the way
for a new lighter coinage of
smaller diameter. Specimens
were struck for distribution to
newspaper editors and others in
order to acquaint the public
with new design.

1858 pattern flying eagle
cent with small skinny eagle on
obverse. Reverse exhibits
wreath with ornamented shield.
Never adopted for circulation.

The 1858 Indian cent was a
successful pattern. This design
was subsequently adopted, and
specimens were made in large
numbers for circulation during
the following year, 1859.

1836 pattern two-cent piece
depicts an eagle perched on a
cloud, inspired by a design used
on silver coins during the
1790s.

1863 pattern two-cent piece
with George Washington and
motto GOD AND OUR
COUNTRY.

A pair of 1849 pattern
three-cent silver issues combine
half dime obverse dies with
simple reverse dies stating the
denomination two ways.

1850 pattern silver three-cent
piece bearing a Liberty cap on
the obverse and a palm branch
on the reverse. Silver three-cent
pieces of a different design were
adopted for circulation the
following year, 1851.

J. B. Longacre's beautiful
Indian princess obverse without
stars was used for this attractive
pattern dime of 1871.

This 1879 pattern dime
bears the same obverse design
as used on George T.
Morgan's 1878 silver dollar.
Specimens were struck in silver
and copper.

Charles E. Barber's
"Washlady" design was used
for the dime (shown above) as
well as the quarter, half dollar,
and dollar struck in 1879.

1877 pattern dime with
Miss Liberty wearing a coronet
with a pearl border.

1875 pattern twenty-cent
piece, one of many illustrious
designs proposed this year.

1875 pattern twenty-cent
piece, another in the beautiful
pattern series of this denomination.

1879 pattern quarter featuring Longacre's Indian princess
design.

UNITED STATES PATTERN COINS were made in many different varieties. Today they offer a fascinating field for the advanced numismatist. Pattern coins, it has been said, are the footprints of history. They tell what might have been in coinage, but wasn't. For example, in 1877 Anthony C. Paquet, George T. Morgan, and William Barber competed to produce many designs of half dollars, none of which was subsequently adopted for regular use. In the 1836-1839 years Christian Gobrecht produced an interesting series of pattern dollars. During the early 1860s various mottos were proposed, including GOD AND OUR COUNTRY, GOD OUR TRUST, and IN GOD WE TRUST, the latter being the one finally adopted. Many items included in the pattern series are trial strikings in different metals, either made to test the dies or to provide curiosities for collectors. For example, during the 1870s and 1880s many regular denominations such as quarters, half dollars, and dollars were struck in aluminum and copper. Still other patterns were produced to test experimental ideas. For example, the 1879-1880 $4 gold "stellas" were part of a proposal for an international coinage. In 1913 Edgar H. Adams, using coins in the collection of William H. Woodin (later to become Secretary of the Treasury under President Franklin D. Roosevelt), published *United States Pattern, Trial, and Experimental Pieces,* which for the first time delineated pattern issues and assigned numbers to them. In 1959 Dr. J. Hewitt Judd prepared a revision of this book and gave it a slightly different title: *United States Pattern, Experimental, and Trial Pieces.* Today collectors use Judd numbers for quick identification. For example, the 1871 pattern quarter shown at the lower right of this page is known as J-1093.

An obverse die by Kneass and a reverse flying eagle die by Gobrecht were combined to create this pattern half dollar of 1838. Two or three originals plus several dozen restrikes (probably made circa 1858-1860) are known to exist.

Another style of 1838 half dollar combines Kneass' obverse with a differently-styled eagle reverse by Gobrecht.

1839 pattern Liberty seated half dollar with unadopted reverse design featuring Gobrecht's flying eagle. Struck from a cracked reverse die, probably circa 1858-1860.

1839 pattern half dollar with bust of Liberty wearing a tiara inscribed LIBERTY, similar to that used on the $10 gold piece but facing right instead of left. Reverse is from the regular die used for circulation.

Anthony C. Paquet's design features Liberty seated with a shield and fasces. Like the other pattern half dollars on this page, this design was never adopted for actual circulation.

1859 pattern half dollar by James B. Longacre. In this year over a dozen different pattern half dollars were made, none of which was ever adopted for circulation.

1861 pattern half dollar with experimental motto GOD OUR TRUST. Apart from the added motto the design is the same as that used for circulation.

1869 Standard Silver pattern half dollar, one of dozens of different varieties produced in this series, a type of half dollar intended to replace fractional currency in circulation.

James B. Longacre's beautiful Indian princess design without obverse stars. Of cameo-like appearance, this design, made in various denominations up to and including the silver dollar, is a favorite with numismatists today.

1877 pattern half dollar by George T. Morgan. In this year many different half dollars were made, comprising what Dr. J. Hewitt Judd considered to be "one of the most beautiful and interesting series of all."

1877 pattern half dollar by George T. Morgan bears central motifs similar to those used the following year, 1878, for regular silver dollar coinage. Like all 1877 pattern half dollars they are exceedingly rare today.

1879 pattern half dollar features Morgan's obverse with a large perched eagle on the reverse.

matic press, particularly in the writings of John Kamin, proprietor of *The Forecaster* newsletter, and from the pen of Allen Harriman, owner of the *Coin Dealer Newsletter*.

In recent times I updated my earlier writings about cycles and published them as part of the *Coin World Almanac* published by Amos Press. Much of the information in the paragraphs to follow is from that source.

A microcosm of coin cycles can be exerpted from my *Coin World Almanac* writings, issues of 1976, 1977, and 1978, just by noting a brief commentary in each. In the 1976 issue I wrote that: "Right now gold coins are 'hot' and sell very well. At the same time Indian cents are 'quiet' and there is no rush to buy them."

In the 1977 issue I reported that "gold coins are now 'quiet' and Indian cents are more active!"

In 1978 I wrote that "gold coins have picked up in activity, particularly scarce issues. Indian cents remain active as well."

Sometimes an issue will peak in interest and then subside, perhaps to become hot again many years, decades, or even centuries later. In the long run such things may be good investment, but as one economist has said, "in the long run we are all dead"—so it wouldn't make much difference. For example, during the 1860s, over a century ago, the most active items on the numismatic market were medals honoring George Washington. The Mint Cabinet, the official exhibit of coins displayed at the United States Mint in Philadelphia, considered Washington pieces to be the most important items in its display. Prices reached levels then which have never been reached since! An investor purchasing certain Washington items in the 1860s would still be waiting for a profit!

Modern rolls and Proof sets peaked in 1964 and then dropped sharply in value. By the late 1970s, 15 years later, prices in many instances had not risen to 1964 levels, although the market was warming up. In the meantime over 15 years is a long time to have waited for a profit.

Gold coins, especially common dates, peaked in early 1965, sharply subsided in 1976 and 1977, and then in 1978 were added to the "most active" list once again. Clearly, a sense of timing would have benefited any investor. A given sum invested in such gold coins in 1976 would have brought substantially more eventual value than the same amount invested in late 1974 or early 1975.

Commemorative half dollars have gone through a number of well-marked cycles over the years. Following a craze which was quite reminiscent of the tulipomania, commemorative half dollars peaked in price during the late 1930s. Prices then plummeted to fractions of the highs in many instances. It was not until the mid- and late 1940s that the market recovered. Today, the high prices of the 1930s seem like incredible bargains, so all worked out very well in the end.

The anatomy of a coin cycle can be traced. The performance of coin "X" is typical. It may be a roll, it may be a commemorative half dollar, it may be a common date double eagle, it may be a type coin, it may be a foreign Proof set, it may be one of many different coins or sets which have commanded the attention of investors during the past few decades.

I have divided a typical cycle into several stages. In actual practice the time span of each stage varies. Due to the nature of numismatic communication, cycles prior to 1960 used to take longer than they do now. At the time publications were only available on a monthly basis. Beginning in 1960 *Coin World* was published weekly, and a few years later *Numismatic News* (first issued in 1952) shortened its publication span to the same frequency. The *Coin Dealer Newsletter,* a popular market guide to trends and activity, joined the same schedule.

During the 1960s the teletype, something formerly reserved for newspaper offices and stockbrokers, became a familiar sight in many coin dealerships. The long distance telephone also contributed to the speed at which a coin cycle took place. In today's market a cycle may occur in a matter of months or even weeks.

Stage I. The market for coin X is not particularly active. Some dealers price X for $12 each; some for $11. One dealer offers a group of ten X for $99. At a convention a sharp buyer who knows that a dealer has had trouble selling his large holding of X succeeds in buying 375 pieces of X for only $8 each. In various numismatic publications there are few, if any, dealers stating realistic buying prices for X. In other words, there just isn't much life to X at all!

Popular psychology being what it is, there isn't much support for X from anyone. A dealer is apt to say: "X is dead, so I'm not even interested in discussing buying any for stock." A collector might say: "Why should I bother collecting items like X, there doesn't seem to be much interest in them, and apparently they would be a poor investment—I don't see any buying ads and the last dealer I talked to said that he could care less about X."

Stage II. Some alert persons note that X is selling for $10 to $12 and has been selling at that price for quite some time without any extensive market activity and without any increase in price. In fact, as time wears on the price weakens as dealers give discounts and special deals to move unwanted quantities of X out of stock.

In the meantime item "Y" which is not as scarce as X but which is in a currently popular field, sells for $25. Dealers are publishing many ads offering to buy Y, and many are offering close to the $25 retail price. Item Y is hard to buy in quantities as most people owning Y are

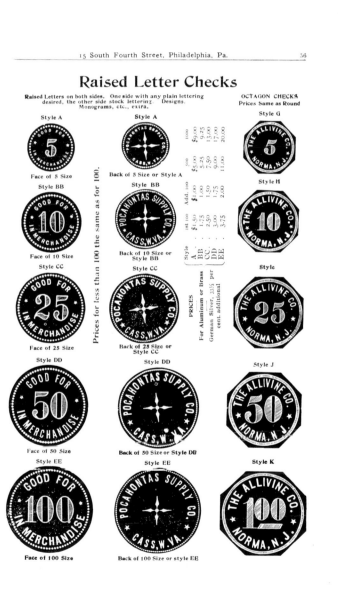

From the 19th century through about 1920 S.H. Quint's Sons Company, die sinkers and engravers of Philadelphia, produced thousands of different tokens. Preparing dies and striking tokens, called "raised letter checks" in the Quint catalog, was a main part of their business which included "stencils, rubber stamps, metallic pattern letters, steel stamps, seals, hotel, baggage, and key checks, German silver and gold badges, burning brands, pew numbers, numbering machines, check protectors, stencil combinations, stencil alphabets and figurines, steel alphabets and figures, indelible inks, stencil colors and brushes, door plates, rubber type, brass main plates for engines and machinery, brass, copper, white metal, aluminum, gold and silver medals, signs, etc."

In the 1960s the author acquired nearly 7,000 original steel dies from the 1880-1920 period plus the Quint ledgers and records pertaining to token production. The records were donated to the American Numismatic Association museum in Colorado Springs, Colorado, so that information would be available to interested scholars. Included in the gift were many dies as well.

Tokens were issued by nearly every type of business imaginable, including hotels, billiard parlors, taverns and saloons, railway depots, streetcar lines, dairies, restaurants, banks, mercantile and dry goods stores, coal companies, breweries, moving and transfer outfits, bakeries, hardware stores, and gambling parlors.

Collecting medals, especially early ones, offers many interesting experiences. The Eight Presidents medal, shown above, is an example. The obverse portrays the central figure of Washington surrounded by cameo portraits of seven other presidents. Issued circa 1840, this medal is of singular interest due to the bungled spelling! On the obverse there are such strange names as JAMES MADDISON and JAMES MUNROE. On the reverse there is JAMES MUNROE again, and someone named ANDREW JACKSONS.

The Token and Medal Society, an organization comprising several thousand enthusiasts, is devoted to the study of medals, old and new, covering a wide variety of subjects. Tokens used in bars, mining company stores, as soap premiums, and even in telephone coin boxes are the subject of articles from time to time, as are modern medals and commemorative pieces.

During the late 19th century many different laminated tokens called "shell cards" were issued. Typically these consist of a brass obverse crimped on the rim around a reverse made of cardboard. Two examples are shown above. The first bears an advertisement for "Treasure Trove," a theatrical production about a buried gold treasure. The second was issued at the Centennial Exhibition in Philadelphia in 1876 in conjunction with an exhibit featuring the Howe weighing scale. Persons weighed would receive one of the tokens with their weight written in on the provided blank space on the reverse.

Russell Rulau made a detailed study of these issues in the 1960s. Since then several dozen additional examples have come to light.

Above are shown three different varieties of tokens issued by Dr. Lewis Feuchtwanger. The central one, a one-cent piece dated 1837 and featuring an eagle killing a snake, was produced by the tens of thousands and saw a wide circulation during the Hard Times era. Examples exist in many different die varieties and are quite plentiful today.

Dr. Lewis Feuchtwanger was especially active during the 1830s, the date of most of his tokens. His first business location appears to have been at 377 Broadway, New York City, where he remained from 1831 to 1837. Thereafter, until 1857, his changes were numerous, and, considering the limits of the city within that period, he may be said to have roved widely. Lyman H. Low, historian of the Hard Times token series, noted that Feuchtwanger during this time was listed at 12 different addresses in the directories, ranging from No. 1 Wall Street to 21 White Street, including three addresses in Maiden Lane.

Feuchtwanger devised a metal alloy of light coloration resembling "German silver," which he hoped to induce the government to adopt for minor coinage. He was a druggist and a chemist, and in 1832 in addition to this business he sold natural curiosities such as rare minerals, gems, preserved reptiles, and so on, a large collection of which he placed on exhibition at Peale's Museum and the New York Lyceum of Natural History.

At his Broadway store, "one door below White Street," he advertised "Nurembergh Salve" and "Kreosote. . .a recent German discovery for preventing toothache." According to Lyman H. Low, these nostrums were highly esteemed in their time.

"Hard Times Tokens," Lyman H. Low's treatise published in 1900 (and the source for the preceding information), gives detailed descriptions of over 100 varieties of political and merchants' tokens issued during the 1833-1844 period. This series is certainly one of the most fascinating of all American numismatic byways.

One of a series of medals issued during the early 19th century by Thomason. The obverse relates to phrenology, a subject later made famous by O.S. Fowler.

1933 Assay Commission medal. For most years since 1860 these medals have been produced in limited quantities annually.

1876 medal issued by the state of Nevada for the Centennial Exhibition.

Lifesaving medal awarded to William Madden.

1826 Erie Canal medal designed by noted medalist and engraver C.C. Wright. Observed was the opening of the Erie Canal on October 26, 1826, following nearly ten years of excavation and construction.

Large silver medal used in the election campaign of 1896.

19th century token of A. Loomis.

Atwood's Railroad Hotel token.

Ferrotype medal from the 1860 election.

TOKENS AND MEDALS comprise literally thousands of different subjects. As the illustrations (some reduced in size) on this page illustrate, the historical connotations are often intriguing. Thomason, an Englishman, produced a series of scientific and philosophical medals illustrating various inventions as well as wonders of the animal and mineral world. The same medalist produced a series illustrating scenes from the Bible. For most years since 1860 the United States Mint has produced a special medal to honor citizens, mint officials, and others who participate in the annual Assay Commission ceremony held at Philadelphia. Designs have ranged from classical to modern, and personages depicted have varied from famous to obscure. The 1876 Nevada dollar shown on this page is one of a series of dollar-size pieces known as "so-called dollars," a specialty which attracts many collectors. The lifesaving medal is one of many 19th century mementoes given to citizens who exhibited special bravery on lakes, rivers, and seas. Most were made of gold or silver. The completion of the Erie Canal on October 26th, 1826, was the occasion for celebrations throughout the length and width of New York state and furnished the topic of the medal shown above. These medals were produced in pewter and silver. Shown in reduced size is one of several different varieties of silver pieces issued during the presidential election campaign of 1896. Some similar pieces were issued for the following election, 1900. Today these are known as "Bryan money."

Tokens desired by collectors include pieces of the Hard Times era 1833-1844, Civil War patriotic tokens and store cards (primarily dated 1863 and 1864), 19th century merchants' tokens of all kinds, transportation tokens for use on ferries, streetcars, and carriages, presidential election tokens and buttons of all kinds, and related items. Indeed, the field is endless.

busy watching the price go up! Other investors who have been watching X stagnate price-wise decide that X is underpriced and start buying. Dealers are contacted by telephone, by letter, by personal contact in shops and at conventions, and by any other feasible means. The formerly unwanted large supply of X is now dried up!

Stage III. Having bought all of the X available at $10 and $12, collectors and investors are now willing to pay $14 and $15, and say so in print and in voice. Dealers run "wanted to buy" ads for X offering $13 for all specimens submitted, knowing that a dollar or two profit awaits them for each X acquired. These "buy" advertisements prompt thousands of collectors, dealers, and other investors to start thinking about X. After all, why is X selling for a super-bargain $15 when Y, which is not as scarce, finds a ready market and a new high price of $30?

Stage IV. X becomes a hot item! Everyone is talking about X! Everyone wants to buy X! There are not enough X to go around! X is exciting! The price of X rises to $20, then to $25, then to $30. Meanwhile, many sell their supply of Y to raise money to buy X. Y drops in value to $18.

Stage V. Those who bought X at prices from $8 to $12 each find the $30 prices very attractive. Some sell. Others hold out for still higher prices. The great activity in X has lessened somewhat as investors turn to other things. X advances to $30.50 and then to $31. Noting that the market is not rising as sharply as before, thousands of X are now sold by many different investors and speculators. The first ones to sell realize $30 to $31 each. Some of the later ones have to be satisfied with $27, and a few are able to get only $25. At the $25 point the supply and demand appear equal, and the price stabilizes—for a short time.

Stage VI. At the new $25 price very few people want to invest in X. It takes fortitude to buy in a falling market, and they have just seen the price of X fall from $31 down to $25. Other investors, who missed the higher profit, are now willing to sell additional X for less than $25. The market is sluggish. X is available in quantity for just $22 each! If you are in the market for a large quantity you may be able to drive a hard bargain and buy some X for $19. A story is told of a large metropolitan convention at which an investor helped a dealer unload 243 pieces of X by offering him $18 each, an unheard of low price in the recent market. In other words, Stage VI brings us back to Stage I. The cycle is complete!

The preceding illustration is typical of many, many past coin price movements, particularly those of the past two or three decades. Each cycle seems to take place at a succeedingly higher plateau. In the next cycle X may start out at $19 and may rise to a new high of $50 before settling back at, say, $35.

While knowledge of cycles may not be critical for the long term investor, it does have the undeniable advantage that such awareness will permit buying "dead" series at favorable prices and will caution the buyer to pass by "hot" coins until they settle in price somewhat. For the short term buyer cycles are of vital importance. Any purchaser who keeps in mind the fact that coins are subject to cyclical variations will have little cause to worry. There is one catch: it takes time to research the investment markets, observe cycles, and to gain insights. This work will pay off in being able to recognize cycles that are yet to come. There is no shortcut to this effort. You will not be able to calculate cycles by reading today's advertisements as very, very few advertisements ever mention price drops! Advertisements can be useful, however, in helping to calculate the up trend in a cycle. When a series becomes super-active the advertisements usually reflect this.

Human nature is often perverse. One of my most valued clients, an important executive with a large public firm, specializes in collecting large denomination gold by date and mintmark varieties. During the 1973-1974 years he was a very active buyer, accumulating at the time many prize scarcities and rarities. Still his want list had many items on it. In 1976 and 1977, slow years in the field of gold coins, I offered him many pieces for 50% to 75% of the cost a couple years earlier. "I'm not interested in buying right now, the market seems dead," he told me. The in 1978 the gold market perked up again. Prices advanced sharply over the 1976-1977 lows. I received a telephone call from my client who said that he wanted to make some major expenditures for items on his want list!

Playing the cycles is apt to be like riding a roller coaster. Up one year, down the next year, always with the feeling of exhilaration, some disappointment, and always an element of fright and surprise. I will leave this to the speculator, of which I am not one.

The speculator, and there are many in coins, believes that a good profit can be made by buying today and selling tomorrow. While this may happen to people fortunate enough to buy at just the right moment in an up cycle, in practice most people are losers. Buying coins in January and selling them in August usually results in making a very nice profit for the dealer but not for you!

And yet I recognize that there is a speculative urge in all of us. Who among us can resist the urge to drop a nickel or a quarter in a slot machine hoping to win a jackpot, and knowing at the same time that the machine is set to pay out less than it takes in? Taking a flyer on a hot stock tip is also a natural. And, in coins, speculating on the swing of gold and silver bullion prices falls into the same category.

My advice is this: if you consider yourself to be an expert on metal and bullion prices, by all means do your research homework in the field and then buy or sell accordingly. However, don't mistake speculation for *numismatic* investment, for they are different.

A few years ago a leading financial columnist telephoned me to get my opinion concerning the price of gold.

"I'm a rare coin dealer, and if you ask me the price, rarity, and desirability of specific rare coins I can certainly help you. But the price of gold metal is something different and is dependent upon such things as the cost of mining, the demand for gold in international channels of commerce, speculative interest, international monetary considerations, and the like, none of which are within the purview of the professional numismatist. Why not ask me the future price of soybeans or plywood, it makes just as much sense?" Amazingly enough, the other dealers solicited for quotations were all too happy to give optimistic and "authoritative" views on the gold bullion market. As it turned out, they all were wrong.

If you must speculate, do it with a small percentage of your coin investment funds. Do it with the idea that the chances of losing are great. Then if you lose you won't be disappointed. If you win you'll be happy. When calculating the return on your investment, don't overlook the cost of money; in other words, bank interest. If a given investment in bullion costs $1,000 and five years later yields $1,200, your profit isn't very spectacular if money in the bank at normal interest rates, and without much risk of loss, would have yielded $1,250.

I have nothing against speculation in gold and silver. In fact, financially I have been amply rewarded by it. No, I have never speculated in it myself. However, when the market for gold and silver is in an uptrend and profits are made by speculators a good share of these profits are spent on rare coins, thus bolstering the sales of our firm and the numismatic marketplace in general. So, I am always happy to see a rise in bullion prices!

Long term investment in high-grade coins of proven rarity and desirability seems to me to be the best way to go. Traditionally, long term investment has not offered much day to day excitement. But, the profit certainly has been there. To my knowledge, every client who has enlisted my help in building a choice collection of United States coins and who has held it as a long term investment for five to ten years or more has made a nice profit upon selling. I have said this in print before, and again I will say that I am not aware of any exceptions to this attractive profit situation, not even one. This is a rather remarkable statement.

While it is certainly possible to invest for the sake of investment alone, and while this can yield nice profits, I recommend building a collection at the same time. The rewards are greater in several areas.

Some time ago at my urging the Professional Numismatists Guild put out a small sticker which read: "Coin Collecting, the World's Greatest Hobby—Art, History, Romance, and Investment." If you concentrate only on investment you will miss the other features. Undeniably art, history, and romance can each bring many hours of pleasure to you. Why overlook them?

At the same time building a collection, unless it is confined solely to a narrow specialized field, serves to diversify your investment. This will smooth out the effects of cycles. Such a diversification will usually mean that your collection as a whole will move upward in value over a period of years.

Within the cycles mentioned earlier, a diversified "portfolio" of coins would have done well. During the fall of commemorative prices in the late 1930s and 1940s, Lincoln cents, Liberty nickels, 20-cent pieces, large cents, colonials, rare gold coins, and many other series were rising sharply in value. A portfolio containing a balanced value in each of these series would have shown a sharp upward trend at the same time commemoratives by themselves were falling. Likewise, in 1964-1965 when the prices of many modern bulk rolls, bags, and Proof sets were dropping, prices of many other issues were rising. During the slow gold coin market of 1976-1977 Barber coins, Mercury dimes, Liberty standing quarters, and Liberty walking half dollars (just to select a few series at random) were increasing sharply in price.

Diversification also lends interest. As they say, "variety is the spice of life." You would not want to have a record collection consisting only of the music of Glenn Miller. You would not want to go only to Niagara Falls each year, year in and year out, for your summer vacation. You would not want to order the same food at the same restaurant each time you went out to dinner. Indeed, it is natural to diversify. So it is with coins.

An ideal way to diversify, in my opinion, is by building a type set of United States coins. Such a set consists of one each of the different major designs produced from 1793 to date. As some of the earlier issues are apt to be expensive, a beginning can be made with coins of the 20th century. Within recent decades several dozen different designs have been produced.

Whereas the date and mintmark specialist will endeavor, for example, to obtain one each of every variety of Barber design quarter dollar made from 1892 to 1916 and will assemble such issues as 1892, 1892-O (New Orleans Mint), 1892-S (San Francisco Mint), 1893, 1893-O, 1893-S, and so on down the line through 1916, the type collector will be satisfied with just one Barber quarter—any date, preferably not a great rarity, within the 1892-1916 range that these coins were struck.

The collector/investor seeking to build a Choice Uncirculated set of 20th century design types will find cer-

tain issues to be elusive. Barber half dollars of even the most common dates are not easy to find in select condition. The Type I Liberty standing quarter minted only in 1916 and 1917 is likewise difficult to locate in really top grade.

In type collecting, as in other branches of numismatic activity, there are many options. For example, within a 20th century type set you may do as most collectors prefer and include just the copper (bronze), nickel, and silver coins from the cent through the dollar. Or, if your budget permits you may wish to include gold coins.

Within the area of 20th century gold coin types there are several options. The simplest and least expensive is to acquire one of each denomination, the quarter eagle, half eagle, eagle, and double eagle, four in all. Or, you may wish to go a step further and obtain one of each major design type. Thus you will have a Liberty head quarter eagle of any date from 1901 through 1907, an Indian head quarter eagle of any year 1908 to 1929, a Liberty head half eagle of any date from 1901 to 1908, an Indian head half eagle from 1908 to 1929, a Liberty head eagle from 1901 to 1907, an Indian head eagle from 1907 to 1933, a Liberty head double eagle from 1901 to 1907, and, rounding out the collection, a Saint-Gaudens double eagle of any date 1907 to 1933.

If you want to add even more coins to your basic type collection there are several additional variations. For example, if your budget permits and you have the inclination you may want to acquire the very expensive MCMVII (1907) High Relief Saint-Gaudens double eagle, a coin of which just 11,250 were struck. Further among Saint-Gaudens double eagles, you may wish to acquire a 1907-1908 issue with the date in regular or Arabic numerals but without the motto IN GOD WE TRUST. Then you will want to acquire another double eagle dated 1908-1933 with the motto.

While most 20th century type set collectors will consider any coin dated from *1900* onward, technically speaking 1901, rather than 1900, was the first year of the 20th century. 1900 was actually the last year of the 19th century. This minor distinction caused quite a bit of fuss around the turn of the century, and doubtless when the year 2000 arrives it will stir controversy again. However, unless I miss my guess most celebrations for the new century will take place in the year 2000 rather than waiting for 2001!

A type set can be as individual as you care to make it. Once you complete your 20th century issues—either a full type set with minor design variations (such as the different varieties of Saint-Gaudens double eagles mentioned above) or a basic type set with just the major varieties (the way most people collect)— you can go back in history to the 19th century. 1860, the year the Civil War had its first stirrings, is the break-off point for

many collectors. A type set of coins from 1860 to date contains a wide variety of Liberty seated and late 19th century issues. Or, you can go further back in history to the first United States Mint issues made for circulation in 1793.

Condition plays a part, too. Few people have the several hundred thousand dollars or more necessary to build a complete type set in Uncirculated grade. And, if a person has the money, chances are that such a collection could not be completed for many years, if ever. Indeed, certain pieces such as the 1793 chain cent, 1796-1797 half dime, 1804-1807 quarter, 1801-1807 half dollar, and 1808 quarter eagle might not be located in Uncirculated grade for many years, or even decades. So, you are faced with choosing grade objectives which are realistic.

Sometimes an Uncirculated specimen of a given issue is available but the price is so high that it might not be a reasonable investment. For example, in the late 1970s an 1853 half dollar with arrows at the date and rays on the reverse was valued at about $250 in Extremely Fine grade. At the same time a Choice Brilliant Uncirculated example sold for well over $5,000. Considering that virtually all of the sharpness and design detail of an Uncirculated piece can be found on an Extremely Fine coin, is it worth paying 20 times more to obtain the higher grade piece? Not everyone, including the most-financially secure collectors, would think so. Extremely Fine might well be an excellent grade in this particular situation.

Analogies could be drawn to other collecting fields as well. For example, if I were seeking a Model A Ford automobile from the early 1930s and if I could afford to buy one in virtually any price category, I might consider an "Extremely Fine" specimen at $4,000, one which was in nice operating condition and which would afford many years of driving fun, to be a better value *for me* than a specimen which was taken from a dealer's showroom in 1931, put up on blocks, covered with a canvas, never driven even a mile, and which might be available now for $20,000. All of this, of course, is a matter of personal preference in addition to financial planning.

Coin collecting is democratic. There are no barriers. Carpenters have collected coins as have kings. Coins do not have to be expensive. I own a very fine collection of music tokens. Prize rarities usually cost in the range of $2 to $5 each, and more than just a few have been obtained for 25c to 50c each in a dealer's junkbox. I am lucky if I can spend $25 to $50 *per year* on the collection, and yet I get just as much pleasure from this as I would from a collection of silver dollars at a hundred times the price. Both collecting areas, tokens and silver dollars, in their own way have been and should continue to be good investment areas.

CIVIL WAR TOKENS. During the middle years of the Civil War official United States coins of all copper, silver, and gold denominations were hoarded. To fill the need for circulating change a variety of substitutes appeared, including the privately minted pieces, called Civil War Store Cards today—as shown on this page. Usually made the same size as a contemporary Indian cent (actual size specimen shown at left; all other illustrations on this page are enlarged), the Civil War pieces featured a wide variety of designs, motifs, and inscriptions. In addition to the store cards, which featured advertisements of merchants, a wide variety of patriotic tokens appeared.

Above are shown pieces advertising such diverse enterprises as that of E. Townley who was a bookkeeper; Straight's Elephantine Shoe Store of Albany, New York; Geo. W. Ritter's Meat Store; Dr. Bennet's Medicines good "if you get sick"; M.B. Xelar who offered wine and beer at his saloon; M.L. Marshall's early rare coin enterprise in Oswego, New York; the Brighton House (which bore the unusual denomination of 5c rather than 1c); and Benjamin & Herrick, fruit dealers in Albany, New York. This latter piece, as illustrated, was struck from dies which were virtually falling apart.

Often ludicrous errors were made, and on the right border of the page are illustrated four of these. C. Runyon's grocery store is stated to be in "Spingfield," rather than Springfield, Ohio. THE FEDERAL UNION, IT MUST AND SHALL BY PRESERVED, instead of BE PRESERVED. THE FLAG OF OUR UNION, IF ANYBODY ATTEMPTS TO TEAR IT DOWN, SHOOT HIM ON THE SPOOT, instead of SPOT. And, in Columbus, Ohio, John Grether was stated to be a "IMPORORTER," whatever that is, of china and queensware.

The Civil War Token Society provides a forum for the many enthusiasts interested in collecting the thousands of varieties of tokens produced during the War Between the States. The research efforts of George and Melvin Fuld, Jon Harris, and others have produced excellent reference books delineating the series.

Interesting Tokens From Our Own Time

Among the most interesting numismatic items produced during the 1970s were the approximately 1,000 different tokens issued by the Patrick Mint to commemorate our nation's bicentennial. Tokens, slightly larger than one-cent size and made of copper alloy, were struck to commemorate a wide diversity of persons, places, things, and events—some of local interest and others of national significance.

Jess Patrick, proprietor of the Patrick Mint, had an ingenious idea. For $22.50 one could order 150 pieces of a personalized design. In the words of his announcement, "We know you will want to be included. Please sketch your design as you wish it to appear on the attached sheet—and select one reverse design (Indian head, Independence Hall, or eagle). Or, simply send us a business card with mention of your specialty and we will design the lettering on the token for you..."

The rates were quite reasonable. For $22.50 one could order 150 pieces (the minimum order). Mr. Patrick's reasoning was quite clever. Due to production requirements, 1,000 of each token would be produced. However, bearing in mind that many clients might want to order just 150 tokens, this obviously left a surplus. The extra pieces were sold to other collectors all over the United States.

At a time in which many medals pertaining to the bicentennial were being offered for sale for $10 to $20 each, the appeal of the inexpensive Patrick Mint tokens was obvious. Further heightening their appeal were the hand-made dies. In Jess Patrick's words:

"In making the dies for the tokens, each letter or numeral was individually punched into the die by hand. This results in a slightly uneven effect—some letters and numerals are punched deeper than others and rest above or below the arc or straight line they are meant to follow. Still others tilt slightly. It was in this fashion that Civil War token dies were made. We think that this method, when employed by our skilled die cutters, lends a great deal of 19th century charm to our tokens. To our mind, excessive mechanization of the minting process has taken its toll, for most modern mass-produced items have little appeal and seem sterile by comparison. We have taken this opportunity to pass on the savings and cost and allow a restoration of this time-honored process of die manufacture. The result has been widespread satsfaction on the part of our customers and enthusiastic collector interest.

"This interest on the part of collectors played a large part in our marketing program. It is necessary to understand this in order to fully comprehend the Patrick Mint series of bicentennial issues, since the marketing principles used were so innovative. If an order was received for less than 1,000 of the same token (the minimum quantity we needed to strike in order to achieve production efficiency), 1,000 pieces were struck and the balance not purchased by the customer went to different collectors. Such tokens were sold in lots of 50 different and also in bulk ... What we have tried to do is to manufacture enough tokens to keep the cost down and to make an interesting, inexpensive series of modern day tokens which anyone can collect and simply enjoy. Not fabricated errors, not off-metal items which only a few people can get, but rather a set of tokens used in this day and age, carrying their own message, and within everyone's reach. The dies for the bicentennial tokens have been cancelled so that no more will be struck with these

designs. This protects interested collectors and makes these tokens valuable to posterity as medallic and token productions of our bicentennial year..."

As noted, at least 1,000 of each token were made. Quite a few of these went to people who ordered a minimum of 150 pieces or, in the very early days of the project, 100 pieces. The remainder went into the Patrick Mint stock for general sale. In other instances (the Norwell, Massachusetts, Bicentennial Ball for example) all 1,000 pieces were sent to the person who ordered them. The greatest quantity ordered was that sent to Jonathon's Coin Shop in Inglewood, California, an order for 10,000 pieces.

The collector of Civil War tokens from the 1860s knows what a tremendous variety of businesses, products, and services can be found immortalized on those pieces. Fish dealers, wine merchants, concert halls, dentists, druggists, fairs, steamboats, bakeries, shoe stores, and dozens of other trades and professions are recalled. Also there are some inscriptions which were undoubtedly important back in the 1860s but which are lost to history now.

The same charm exists with the Patrick Mint tokens produced in our own time. The author became quite interested in the Patrick Mint project and ordered several different varieties personally and for his firm. In addition, following the conclusion of the project, he purchased from the Patrick Mint a bulk quantity of various pieces.

Included were many different and fascinating varieties. Oren C. Russell of Doraville, Georgia, added his sentiments to other citizens of our land by prominently stating on the center of his special token "Happy Birthday America." Frank and Florence Zdebski, address not given on the token, thought up the nice inscription: "A Simple Recognition of This Country's Wonders—Lest We Forget."

Another token has the following inscription: "The Schad Family Spent Bicentennial in Phil. Pa—July 4, 1976." So, hundreds of years from now an obscure numismatist someplace will know what the Schad family did on the important date, although members of the Schad family itself may have long forgotten (unless, of course, they kept some of the tokens!)

While most of the tokens were from the United States, some were from far away places. For example, Taylor's Coins of East Victoria Park, West Australia, advertises that it sells the "Best for Less." Possibly even further away—actually I don't know where it is, perhaps it is an organization right here in the United States—is a token bearing the inscription of the "Confederation of Antarctica."

California's popular wine industry is immortalized by tokens from several different producers, including the Charles Krug Winery in St. Helena; the Pesenti Winery and Tasting Room, which advertises that it is located on Vineyard Drive in Templeton; the Dry Creek Vineyard, Inc. of Healdsburg; the Thomas Vineyards of Cucamonga, which takes space on its token to note that: "California's Oldest Winery, Established 1839;" and the Beringer Vineyards of St. Helena, which notes that it is celebrating its "Hundredth Anniversary, 1876-1976."

On another token Milt Cohen of Secaucus, New Jersey, advertises

that he buys, sells, and trades "Major Error Coins." Unfortunately, close scrutiny with a magnifying glass failed to disclose any die cutting errors or other mistakes on the Cohen token seen by the author. So, Milt Cohen's own token is error-free! Not so with a token issued by the House of Stuart, located in Kansas. The first production run of these tokens had one word spelled as "Housu." The issue was then redone with an appropriate correction, leaving an interesting variety for collectors.

Years ago Civil War and other tokens often had values stating "one cent," "not one cent" (to evade the counterfeiting laws), "good for 25c in trade," or something similar. So it is also with the Patrick Mint products. Some of the denominations are rather peculiar, while others are standard. On one token issued by R.G.A. Coins the value of "half real" is noted. Taking a leaf from the book of Dr. Higley, who produced tokens with this inscription in Connecticut back in 1737, the piece also bears the legend "Value me as you please—I am good copper."

More to the point is the piece issued by Heritage House Rare Coins of Rossville, Georgia, which states that it is good for 25c in trade. Perhaps the world's only 30-cent token is that issued by the Yahara Trading Company. However, as unusual as this value is, it is not quite as unusual as the piece issued by R.W. Colbert of Tucker, Georgia, which states that it is "Good for 33c in Trade." Extremely generous is the token issued by Mac's Coins, address not given on the token, which says that it is worth "$1.00—Good in Trade."

Colonel James W. Curtis of San Antonio, Texas, borrows from Civil War token tradition and values his coin at "Not One Cent." In today's era of inflation and rising prices of commodities, sometimes things are better than money. For this reason the token issued by Hank's Coin Shop might be a particularly good value for it is "Good for One Cup of Coffee."

Chester Clark of Howell, Michigan, a collector of tokens, has this inscription on the piece minted for him: "9 MI. to Hell—Paradise 327 MI." Presumably Hell and Paradise are other towns in Michigan, but who knows? The Gumer Coin Company, located at 328 W. Broadway, Louisville, Kentucky 40202 sounds quite friendly, for its token reads: "The Fair Coin Dealer—With the Customer in Mind." Harold Flartey of New Jersey used his token to observe a prize he won at the ANA convention: "1976 Numismatic Literary Award—Daily Record."

Faith in God is immortalized on tokens by several issues, including the St. John Lutheran Church of Cumberland, Maryland and a piece issued by Pastor E.C. Stumpf in Cicero, Illinois.

A token from Indianapolis was issued by the "World History Class, T.C. Howe High School." Also in the realm of academia is a token bearing the inscription "Bonnie Hepsley, 1976, school teacher." What does she teach? Mathematics? Ancient History? Zoology?

There are quite a few tokens devoted to other trades. Dr. David C. Rockman advertises whimsically that he is a "Dentist—Teeth Ex-

tracted, Bills Exacted." Certainly if we are ever in New York City with an aching molar we will call (212) 358-4448 and get him on the line!

Ole Ramsfield of Shelton, Wisconsin, advertises that he is an "Auto Painter." Ted and Kim Gorman, who for some reason give two addresses, Pasadena, California, and Allentown, Pennsylvania, observe that they are participating in one of America's favorite part-time businesses and are "Tupperware Dealers."

If you are ever in Natural Bridge, New York, you might look up Linda, Dick, and Rhonda Ferris who for at least four years (1972-1976, according to the token—and perhaps still today) have operated what sounds like a nice place to visit: "Wintergreen Patch—Soft Ice Cream, Light Lunches." Or, if you are entertained chairman for your Kiwanis or Rotary Club this month you may be interested in the token which says "Coins, Stamps, Old Pocket Watches—C.H. Phillips, Jr., Lecturer—Coins of this Wonderful Land, America—No Charge." Well, the price is certainly reasonable, and probably with such a diversity of knowledge Mr. Phillips' talk would be entertaining as well.

Several tokens commemorated very important events in people's lives, including "John R. Scoville—Nancy L. Washler—Married June 5, 1976." Best of happiness to them both!

The world's population keeps increasing, as at least two tokens bear out: "Mark Kevin Lorenzo, Born March 1, 1976, San Jose, Costa Rica," and "Diane M. Lyson, Born September 1, 1976, Bicentennial Baby." In another vein we certainly wish a good career to Sally Ann Hornstein who, according to another token, graduated on June 19, 1976 from the University of California at Berkeley.

Certainly we need more love and affection in this world, and perhaps these tokens will help. One token relates that "Tiger Loves Pussycat." Another relates that Judy and Steve, last names not given on the token, were married October 16, 1976. And, sounding a bit like a Will Rogers sentiment is that token issued by J.H. Beasley of Lavonia, Georgia, which proclaims that he is "A Friend to All."

In addition to pieces struck to the order of individuals and merchants, the Patrick Mint in 1976 produced several series. One of them contained 50 tokens and was titled "Great Events of the American Revolution." Another offered "Great Americans," and a third commemorated "Great Events in American Numismatics." In the latter series were such items as the founding of the American Numismatic Society in 1858, the selling of the Stickney Collection in 1907, the establishment of the San Francisco Mint in 1854, the passing on of Virgil Brand (a collector who left a hoard valued at $2,000,000 in 1926), the establishment of the Carson City Mint in 1870, and many others.

Today the bicentennial tokens of the Patrick Mint, produced in fairly limited quantities (nearly all were just 1,000 tokens each, with only an occasional exception) and with the dies forever cancelled, stand as fascinating mementos to the 200th anniversary of American independence. They further stand as a tribute to one man, Jess Patrick, who produced in our modern era pieces with a deep numismatic tradition.

Whether you spend a few thousand dollars or a few hundred thousand dollars, a type set with many numismatic and historical challenges can be put together. Once completed, the type set can be a stepping stone to other series. Perhaps you may want to go on to specialize. A collection of each date and mintmark variety of Morgan silver dollars? Indian cents by date from 1859 to 1909? Commemorative half dollars which observe such diverse events as the 300th anniversary of the landing of the Swedes in Delaware, the 1935 San Diego-California-Pacific Exposition, and the centennial of the state of Texas? Any one of the many diverse pieces in your type set may lead to a specialized interest and activity.

Above all, collect what is *interesting* to you. Jeff Oliphant, who collects antique phonographs as well as coins, told me that among his favorite coins are large cents of the year 1794. Why? Because they are especially interesting to him, mainly due to the unique descriptive names Dr. Edward Maris assigned to the different varieties years ago—the *Venus Marina, Pyramidal Head, Ornate, Egeria* (as Dr. William H. Sheldon, a later scholar in the series, noted: "after the elusive and secretive wife of legendary King Numa of Rome—perhaps because this variety is hard to find in good condition"), the *Abrupt Hair,* and the pleasingly-named *Amiable Face,* to mention just a few.

P.B. Trotter, Jr., a Memphis banker, was fascinated by sailing vessels. He assembled a magnificent collection of hundreds of different coins from many different countries, each coin depicting a ship. Warren Snow, a client in the 1950s, spent countless hours on his two widely separated specialties: Proof United States large cents and Jefferson nickels with sharply-struck steps on Monticello. Dr. Robert Hinkley, a New England friend, assembled a superb collection of Vermont coppers by die varieties. Bob Vlack ordered a starter set of Connecticut copper coins from my firm in the 1950s, became fascinated by it, and went on to do extensive research in the series, culminated by publication of an authoritative reference book covering all United States colonial coins.

Kamal Ahwash has specialized in Liberty seated coins and along the way has found that many issues are more elusive, particularly in Uncirculated grade, than standard reference book prices reflect. Harry Bass, the Texas numismatist, has formed superb collections in two major fields, United States gold coins and patterns. Robert Lubetkin of Iowa competes with me on the purchase of nickel-size tokens once used in nickelodeon pianos and other automatic musical instruments and, at the same time, collects tokens issued by soap companies. Other token specialists may concentrate on issues of a particular state such as Colorado, Illinois, or Connecticut, or, even more specifically, of a certain city such as Cincinnati. Steve Tebo built a beautiful collection of currency from

his native state, Colorado, while K.P. Austin, who now lives in Maryland, built an outstanding display of paper money from his home state, Maine. Dennis Forgue built a superb collection of Illinois paper money and Joe Flynn, Jr. did likewise with currency of his state, Kansas.

James F. Ruddy assembled a nearly complete type set of encased postage stamps issued during the coin-shortage of the Civil War. These colorful and intriguing pieces bear the names of such firms and products as White the Hatter, North America Life Insurance Company, Lord & Taylor, Mendum's Family Wine Emporium, Brown's Bronchial Troches, Ayer's Pills, Ayer's Sarsaparilla, and even Burnett's Cocoaine. Henry Clifford, Kenyon Painter, and Ronnie Carr each built distinguished collections of territorial gold coins. Reed Hawn, a Texas cattle rancher, formed in succession superb collections of United States half dollars and quarters. Another Texan, R.E. Cox, Jr., formed in the 1950s and early 1960s one of the most complete groupings of United States half dollars ever put together, complete with scarcities and rarities as well as an unbelievable array of pattern coins of the same denomination.

Roger S. Cohen, Jr., of Maryland collected half cents, took notes on what he bought and saw, and wrote a book on them. Three decades earlier Howard R. Newcomb did likewise in the field of United States large cents dated 1816-1857. Al Overton, the Colorado dealer, specialized in American half dollars 1794-1836 and in 1967 wrote the standard reference book on the series.

Mint errors, silver dollars, Lincoln cents, gold dollars, commemorative halves, coins of Hawaii, English tradesmen's tokens of the late 18th century, New Jersey copper coins, emergency paper money or scrip issued during the Bank Holiday in 1933, Confederate paper money, streetcar tokens, German inflationary paper money issues of the 1920s, Swiss shooting talers, Hard Times tokens issued 1833-1844, Mexican eight-real pieces, and medals depicting George Washington have been the specialties of still others.

Joining an organization or club will open up additional avenues of interest. The American Numismatic Association, with headquarters in Colorado Springs, is the largest in this country. Its members comprise collectors in all fields from ancient coins to modern, from tokens to paper money. In addition there are numerous specialized organizations. The Liberty Seated Coin Club caters to collectors interested in siver coinage of the mid-19th century. The *Gobrecht Journal,* named after designer Christian Gobrecht, who started the Liberty seated motif with his pattern silver dollars of 1836, is issued regularly and contains research articles, news, and other information.

The Society of Paper Money Collectors publishes *Paper Money,* a periodic journal devoted to the latest news and

discoveries among broken bank notes, large and small size United States currency, foreign bank notes, and related paper. In one issue you might find an article about a long forgotten bank in the wilds of Wyoming in the 1880s; in another issue a treatise on paper money serial numbers.

The *Colonial Newsletter,* a non-profit publication, is available to the numismatist with a fondness for pine tree shillings, Vermont coppers, and Virginia halfpennies. The Token and Medal Society, publisher of the *TAMS Journal,* numbers among its membership thousands of collectors who avidly seek privately-issued tokens, often once used as money.

The Early American Coppers Club with its chatty newsletter, *Penny-Wise,* often discusses such esoteric aspects as the placement of berries on the wreaths of 1802 cents and whether or not 1809 cents are as rare as catalogue prices indicate.

The Numismatic Literary Guild admits writers, columnists, and others with a literary bent to its membership roster. There are many other fine groups as well.

Years ago Farran Zerbe, who later became editor of *The Numismatist* and who assembled one of the greatest collections ever, began his interest as a newsboy in Tyrone, Pennsylvania. A French coin acquired inadvertently in change piqued his imagination, and he sought to learn more about it. From that point the collection grew and grew year after year. At the 1915 Panama Pacific International Exposition in San Francisco Zerbe exhibited his coins, paper money, and related items and also operated a numismatic display which offered coins for sale. His biographer, Frank Morton Todd, wrote:

"Zerbe never cared to acquire a coin or medal for its rarity, but only for what it could tell. In spite of that limitation his collection grew very large. Because of that limitation it became one of the notable collections of the world. He could tell you things about coins and medals you never thought of before; trifling things that might become clues to lost episodes in the lives of nations, economically fundamental things about the essential nature of a medium of exchange, the persistent element of popular valuation found in all media of exchange from the plough beasts of Ulysses to California gold 'slugs.' He knew the mintmarks and the marks of the great designers. He knew the delight the scholar derives from getting hold of a contemporary portrait of Caesar or Alexander, passed by the sitter and stamped by the government; and how when such a portrait is a good piece of art it authenticates the genius of a people that could breed artists capable of such work.

"There were Russian platinum coins minted when platinum was of so little value that it was thought only good to make jitneys with. There was every kind of wildcat note, including money of John Law and his Mississippi Bubble. There were interesting historical and financial documents—checks of many presidents from Washington to Lincoln. There was a check for a half a cent, and a photograph of the government voucher for $40 million in payment for the French interest in the Panama Canal. There were notes redeemable in rum. And there were private coinages such as the $50 slugs of California, beaver coins from Oregon, Mormon issues from Utah, and Bechtler coins from the South.

"In Zerbe's collection there were coins that showed something about the art, architecture, mythology, religion, sports, and pleasures of every period of Greece in her glory, and Rome in her fall. The deterioration and tragedy of a dead empire was reflected in the barbarous crudities of the coins of the Dark Ages. There was siege money in all its variety; devices of besieged cities to carry on business in spite of war. It told sometimes of lost causes, of nations going down; it suggested civilizations destroyed and forgotten.

"The collection aroused great interest in the subject of numismatics, and well it might. It was one of the most definite educational factors of the exposition."

It is perhaps fitting that the American Numismatic Association's highest honor, the Farran Zerbe Award, was named for this man—a numismatist who enjoyed coins for all of their aspects—art, history, romance, and, if the financial aspects were but known to us, undoubtedly investment as well.

As you acquire coins and paper money take time to learn their history. Indeed, the pervasive theme of this book has been to share my interest and enthusiasm about the background of coins and how numismatics can be directly related to such fascinating events as the great California Gold Rush and the later gold mining activity in Colorado, early nickelodeon theatres, the great Treasury silver dollar bonanza of the early 1960s, the Confederate raid on Vermont in 1864, and even the ponderous Corliss steam engine.

The chance finding of a tiny French coin opened the door to a rich treasure for Farran Zerbe. A visit to Robert Rusbar's rocks and minerals collection and the seeing there by chance of a rare Lincoln cent and other coins opened for me a rich and rewarding world of friendship, business activity, and other blessings too numerous to count.

For you, coins offer a passport to art, history, romance, and investment. Numismatics—the opportunities are endless.

An adventure awaits you!

Silver dekadrachm by the artist Kimon, struck in Syracuse, Sicily, circa 1409-1408 B.C. Obverse with quadriga three-quarters left in gallop, Nike flying right and crowning the youthful charioteer. Reverse with female head facing left, sometimes described as Arethusa, with dolphins surrounding. This issue, a landmark among coins of the ancient world, was emitted during the flowering period of high classical art. Several hundred specimens, many of which are preserved in museums, are known to scholars. Issues were engraved by two masters, Kimon and Euainetos.

ANCIENT COINS offer a fantastic field for collecting and research. There are many facets which can be explored: different design types, portraiture and artistry, metallic composition, original buying power of the pieces, and so on. Or, in a more romantic vein, it is interesting to contemplate who possessed and held these pieces.

Coin collecting started in "modern" times with the Renaissance. Although centuries earlier Julius Caesar and Augustus both collected gems, it is not known if they assembled coins on a methodical basis, although specimens were given as gifts. Renaissance and Baroque era nobility had their own coin cabinets and sometimes impressed countermarks in the fields of various specimens, such marks exhibiting the family crest. The coins of ancient Greece and Rome formed the center of interest in such groupings.

Today, ancient coins can be collected in an endless variety of ways with only the imagination of the collector being the limiting factor. Each collection takes on the personality of the formulator, as no one today could have a truly complete collection of all the different coin types of antiquity.

Some traditional ways of collecting ancients include the following:

Greek coins are often collected by city-state. Other numismatists seek to specialize with issues from one specific locality. Another area offering possibilities is collecting by design topics (such as musical instruments on coins) or motifs showing animals or agricultural products. Gods, goddesses, and other figures from mythology form yet another possibility as do specialized collections of different denominations.

Roman coins likewise can be collected in many different ways. Issues of the Roman Republic can be collected by the various moneyers, identified by special markings on each piece. Emperors can be collected by portraits. An established manner is to follow tradition and assemble one piece each of the first 12 Caesars of Rome (Julius Caesar through Domitian). Or, the issues of one emperor can form a speciality. Denominations, figures from legend and mythology (often used as reverse designs), and coins associated with Biblical references form other areas of interest.

One of the most enjoyable ways to assemble ancient coins is to acquire one at a time from a reputable dealer. Learn all that you can from that one piece. Then, when finances permit, acquire another. As a student of ancient numismatics you will then acquire a great perspective of ancient cultures, with specific knowledge of how your individual specimens fit into the large jigsaw puzzle we call the "human predicament," and an awareness where we now stand relative to the past.

(Thanks to Dr. Paul Rynearson for information relating to the ancient series.)

Silver stater, circa 350 B.C., of Acarnania, Leucas (Colonies of Corinth). With Pegasus flying left; head of Athena in Corinthian helmet. These pieces, known as "colts," circulated not only along the coast of the Corinthian Gulf but also in Italy and Sicily. Large hoards of these have been found in southern Italy. The myth of Bellerophon and Pegasus is well known. There was also popular worship of the goddess Athena at Corinth, which accounts for the reverse design.

Silver denarius of Tiberius, circa 14-36 A.D. Obverse with laureate head of Tiberius. Reverse with Livia seated facing right. This is the famous "tribute penny" of the Bible. The silver denarius was the main denomination of Roman commerce for nearly 400 years. During the reign of Tiberius the ministry and crucifixion of Christ took place. Livia, mother of Tiberius, is shown on reverse. A similar piece was probably held while the famous words "Render unto Caesar what is Caesar's . . ." were spoken.

Silver didrachm, circa 400-333 B.C., of Rhodes. Obverse with the facing head of the sun god Helios (who formed the subject for the Colossus of Rhodes, one of the Seven Wonders of the Ancient World). Reverse with rose, a punning allusion to the island's name, as Rhodos in Greek means "rose." The early settlers of Rhodes claimed descendancy from Helios. The gigantic Colossus statue was designed by the architect Chares. Lasting only 56 years after its completion (224 B.C.), it was destroyed by a violent earthquake.

Silver tetradrachm of Alexander III, the Great, circa 336-323 B.C. Obverse with head of young Herakles, wearing a lion skin. Reverse with Zeus seated on a throne. Minted under the authority of one of the greatest military figures of all time, this piece was issued in Cilicia, one of several hundred different city-states which utilized pieces of similar design. This particular piece was struck after Alexander's death.

Silver denarius of Severus Alexander, struck in Rome circa 231-235 A.D. Obverse with laureate head to the right. Reverse with Providentia standing holding corn-ears and anchor. This silver issue of the son of strong-willed Julia Mamaea illustrates an instance of an ancient coin existing in nearly perfect condition.

Silver shekel of Phoenicia, Tyre, struck after 126 B.C. Obverse with laureate head of Melqarth facing right. Reverse with eagle standing to the left, palm over shoulder. This issue is the type most often associated with the "thirty pieces of silver" in the Bible. The reverse design is a style commonly used throughout Greek and Roman times. The illustrated example is nearly in mint condition, an outstanding state of preservation.

Silver antoninianus of Philip I (244-249 A.D.), struck at Antioch. An excellent example of realism in portraiture, this coin shows the ferocity and military might of the Arabian-born emperor who ruled while Rome celebrated her 1000th anniversary in 248 A.D. The radiate crown worn by Philip indicates the value of this denomination as double the worth of a denarius.

Gold stater of Alexander the Great. Although coins of electrum (a mixture of gold and silver) were made in the earlier years, pure gold issues were not extensively issued until these staters of Macedon minted by Philip II and his son, Alexander the Great. Like their silver tetradrachm counterparts, the gold staters circulated throughout the known world.

Silver denarius of Faustina Senior, wife of Antoninus Pius (died 141 A.D.). The Romans issued a full portrait gallery of their emperors by portraying wives, children, mothers, fathers, and even grandparents on their coins! Here is a much-beloved lady, the wife of Antoninus Pius, Faustina Senior. Dying only three years after her husband's accession, she was extensively honored posthumously by the mintage of numerous types and denominations in all metals. The reign of Antoninus Pius is remembered for its great prosperity and virtual absence of civil disobedience and strife.

Silver didrachm of Calabria in Tarentum, issued circa 235-228 B.C. Obverse with Roman soldier on horseback. Reverse with Taras on dolphin, with waves below. Taras, the boy-founder of present-day Taranto in Italy, is said by legend to have been saved by the helping hand of Poseidon, his father, during a shipwreck. Poseidon sent a dolphin on whose back Taras rode into the beautiful natural harbor of Tarentum.

Silver tetradrachm of Athens, circa 430-322 B.C. Of all coins minted in antiquity there are none more famous than the "owls" of Athens. These were issued in various denominations from the tiny hemitartemonion (1/48th drachm) up to the very rare dekadrachm (ten drachms; silver-dollar size, but much thicker). A specimen of the dekadrachm of Athens has the distinction of realizing $312,500 which stood for many years as the highest auction price of any numismatic item. Pictured above is the smaller tetradrachm (four drachms) piece.

1839 pattern 5-pound gold piece featuring young Queen Victoria on the obverse and an allegorical representation of Una and the Lion on the reverse. Engraved by William Wyon, this issue was produced to the extent of several hundred pieces (estimated). Today they are highly prized.

In anticipation of the coronation of the Duke of Windsor, scheduled to become Edward VIII, patterns were prepared of different denominations from the farthing (¼ of a penny) to the 5-pound gold piece. In one of the world's most famous romances, Edward renounced the throne of England to marry his true love, an American commoner, Wallis Warfield Simpson. Above is shown a pattern 1937 penny.

Obverse and reverse of each denomination in a 1953 Maundy set distributed by Queen Elizabeth II.

Obverse and reverse design of 1937 British gold coins (half sovereign, sovereign, two pounds, and five pounds) issued to commemorate the coronation of King George VI.

Interesting die variations, some of which indicate mischief at the mint, exist in British coinage just as they do in various American series. As the enlarged illustration shows, this 1839 Proof halfpenny was struck over a later-dated halfpenny made in 1843! The later numerals are faintly visible beneath the 1839 date.

COINS OF GREAT BRITAIN offer a wide variety of challenges for the numismatist. Most popular with collectors are issues from the mid 17th century to the present, extending from the Commonwealth and Oliver Cromwell down through the various monarchs, including Charles II, James II, William and Mary, William III, Anne, George I, George II, George III, George IV, William IV, Victoria, Edward VII, George V, Edward VIII (patterns only), George VI, and Elizabeth II.

Denominations range from fractional parts of the penny up to immense five guinea gold coins. A wealth of numismatic references are available, including illustrious publications issued in England by Spink & Son, B.A. Seaby, and the British Museum.

Throughout British numismatics there are many interesting sidelights. For example, in 1702 the British Navy captured a fleet of Spanish Galleons in the Bay of Vigo, Spain. An immense quantity of silver (mostly) and gold bullion was captured, and subsequently coins of Queen Anne bearing the commemorative notation VIGO were minted. During the past several hundred years the reigning monarch of England has distributed on Maundy Thursday alms to the poor in the form of tiny specially-minted silver coins of the denominations of 1, 2, 3, and 4 pence. Today these are avidly sought by collectors. Pattern issues, many with fascinating stories, abound throughout British numismatics. Boulton and Watt's Soho Mint (located in Birmingham) introduced steam power to coinage at the dawn of the Industrial Revolution. Many superb patterns were prepared by the Soho Mint, including issues with exquisite workmanship unequalled to the present day.

"Ormonde" emergency crown of Charles I struck from melted down silver utensils. The reverse "V" represents five shillings, the standard crown value.

1653 Commonwealth issue. Specimens were struck from 1649 to 1656 with the exception of the 1650 and 1655 dates.

1696 crown of James III.

1703 Queen Anne crown struck from silver captured in the Bay of Vigo, Spain.

1793 Charles IIII Spanish crown stamped at the center with the bust of George III in an oval, and used as emergency money during a coin shortage.

1817 pattern crown by William Wyon depicts the Three Graces on the reverse. A collector's favorite.

The 1847 pattern Gothic crown is of rare beauty. Depicted is young Queen Victoria.

The 1933 crown of George V has a relatively low mintage of just 7,132 pieces.

ENGLISH CROWNS or five-shilling pieces were made in a wide variety of styles. Shown on this page are just a few of the literally hundreds of different regular issue and pattern varieties. In many instances the crown, the largest circulating silver coin of the realm, was used to commemorate special occasions.

1902 crown of Edward VII, the only regular issue of this short (1902-1910) reign.

This Westphalian billion-mark piece of 1923 was issued during the height of rampant inflation in Germany. At the time it took a wheelbarrow full of currency to buy just the simple necessities of life such as food and clothing.

1613 Saxony taler or dollar-size silver piece, the famous "Eight Brothers" taler.

1754 city view taler of Ratispon (Regensburg) shows the town's skyline as it existed at that time. Many German cities and towns issued similar pieces.

1828 Bavarian crown of Ludwig I, the famous "Blessings of Heaven" or "Family Taler", shows on the reverse his wife and 8 children.

1930 5-mark piece commemorating the 1929 world-encircling flight of the Graf Zeppelin.

GERMAN TALERS or dollar-size silver coins exist in hundreds of different varieties. Prior to the 20th century most issues were produced on a local or regional basis by various church authorities, rulers, cities, city-states, and others. City views of Nuremberg, Regensburg, Munster, Konstanz, and other localities tell us today how these towns appeared centuries ago. Marriages, births, and deaths of many important personages throughout German history are likewise recorded for posterity on coinage. Mining scenes, public monuments, churches and temples, castles, heraldic emblems, allegorical scenes, and other motifs are likewise of interest to the numismatist. Dr. John S. Davenport produced a series of substantial volumes outlining various German talers. These are considered standard references by students of the series today, who often use Davenport's numbers to attribute them.

1842 4 franken piece for the shooting festival at Chur in the canton of Graubunden. 6,000 were minted.

1867 5 franc piece issued for the festival in the canton of Schwyz, whose capital city bears the same name. 8,000 were minted.

1859 5 francs of Zurich, commemorating the shooting festival of that year. 6,000 were minted.

1859 5 francs commemorating the shooting festival held at La Chaux-de-Fonds in the canton of Neuchatel. 6,000 were minted.

1865 5 francs struck for the shooting festival held that year in Schaffhausen, a small canton on the Rhine River. 10,000 were minted.

1861 5 francs issued for the shooting festival at Stanz in Nidwalden, one of two half-cantons which comprise the canton of Unterwalden. 6,000 were minted.

SWISS SHOOTING TALERS were issued over a period of years to commemorate shooting festivals held in various locations. In the 19th century marksmanship was considered to be a highly prized skill, with the tradition of William Tell perhaps serving as an inspiration.

Between 1842 and 1885 17 different varieties of shooting talers were produced. In addition, two others were issued in the 20th century. Of the 19 pieces, 17 bore the denomination of five francs, one was assigned the valued of four francs, and the remaining issue was valued at 40 batzen. Each was given legal tender status.

In addition to the legal-tender shooting talers, many different medals were issued to commemorate these sporting events.

1736 city view taler (not a shooting taler) of Basel, Switzerland.

*1746 "pillar dollar" struck at Mexico City. During the
18th century this was the standard trading coin of the Western
Hemisphere.*

*1914 silver peso inscribed "Muera Huerta" (death to
Huerta), issued by the revolutionist Pancho Villa. General
Huerta in retaliation decreed death to anyone found possessing
one of these coins.*

*1822 8 real piece depicting Emperor Augustine de Iturbide
who reigned just one year.*

*1823 gold 8 escudos struck at Mexico City. Obverse with
cap-on-book design. Reverse with eagle and snake, the national
emblem of Mexico.*

COINS OF MEXICO offer a wide variety of interesting pieces to the numismatist. The Mexico City Mint, one of 14 to
operate under government sanction in that country at one time or another, is the oldest on the American continent, with coinage
beginning in the early 16th century. From this location came pieces which saw use in the channels of commerce throughout the
Spanish Main. Perhaps the most famous is the "pillar dollar" shown at the upper left. Interesting political happenings are evidenced by the short-lived coinage of Maximilian in the mid-1860s and the wide variety of crudely-struck revolutionary issues of
the early 20th century (the Muera Huerta piece shown at the top right being one of many examples).

*1895 Puerto Rico silver peso depicting Alfonso XIII, the
boy king of Spain.*

*1841 silver 8 real piece of the Republic of Central America,
today known as Guatemala. The sun and volcanic range motif
is quite appealing to numismatists today.*

*1925 silver colon commemorative piece issued by the
Republic of El Salvador to observe the 400th anniversary of its
founding.*

*1892 silver peso of the Republic of Honduras. An
allegorical scene of Liberty, Union and the Constitution is on
the obverse.*

COINS OF LATIN AMERICA include issues of many countries, most of which were under Spanish influence in centuries
past. While some were struck in Spain (the 1895 Puerto Rico piece shown at the top left, for example), most were issued by
native mints using bullion mined locally. Certain issues bear the initials of the mintmaster and the chief assayer, a recognition intended to strengthen the metallic reputation and security of the coinage. Like coins of the United States, dollar-size and other
issues of Latin America, particularly those in higher states of preservation, have been excellent investments over the years. Prices
today are many multiples of the valuation just a decade or two ago.

1894 5 mark piece issued for New Guinea, a German possession at the time. The "A" mintmark on the reverse designates Berlin. This piece, the famous "Bird of Paradise crown", is one of the most desired in the world of coinage.

This 1928 Chinese crown is known as the "automobile dollar" for it features a Marmon sedan.

1935 New Zealand "Waitangi" crown. This piece, issued as part of a set distributed to collectors, was struck in Proof condition. The obverse features King George V, observing New Zealand's relationship with England as part of the British Commonwealth.

1866 Hong Kong dollar. During the 19th and 20th centuries this British protectorate issued many different coins.

1915 Cuban peso. Cuban dollar-size coins of attractive design and appearance were issued in several types during the late 19th and early 20th centuries.

1811 French 5 franc piece featuring Emperor Napoleon, France's most famous leader.

18th century Russian ruble of rather crude appearance (in contrast to Western European coinage), typical of that country's coins at the time. The obverse features Catherine.

1963 "Seafaring" 5-pound commemorative piece of Israel, one of dozens of different coins for distribution to collectors issued by this modern nation.

CANADA offers a rich numismatic history. From 1858 to date coins have been made as part of the decimal series, from the cent to the dollar, plus intermittent issues of gold coins. Earlier, coins in circulation consisted of a mixture of pieces struck in foreign countries and pieces issued by various banks (particularly in Montreal), merchants, transportation companies, and others. In addition a rich variety of paper money (two notes of which are shown above) was circulated by private individuals, banks, and later, by the government. Today, in recognition of Canada's bilingual heritage, currency contains inscriptions in French and English.

From 1935 to the present time Canada has issued an attractive series of silver dollars featuring many different motifs relating to the country's history. Four representative examples are shown above.

Two different varieties of Canadian cents, 1891 and 1904, depict Queen Victoria and King Edward VII.

For many years Newfoundland had its own distinctive coinage, as the 1917 half dollar and the 1880 $2 piece illustrate.

Canadian gold coins issued over the years include the 1914 $5 and 1912 $10 piece as shown in the second row above and the sovereigns of 1908 and 1914 shown immediately above. Issued in realtively small quantities, Canadian gold coins were used in bank-to-bank transfers and international transactions. They were not commonly seen in everyday commerce. In recent years Canada has issued gold coins to commemorate the Olympic Games and other events. The main market for these has been with collectors.

Nostalgia Trip...

Romance is where you find it. On pages 289-294 are some 1979 photographs showing the Cripple Creek Gold District. Relate these to the information discussed in Chapter 6.

Mine near Victor

Joseph Lesher is said to have lived here, Victor

Fire station and city hall, Goldfield

Gold Coin Club House, Victor

Faded glory, Victor

Commercial building wall, Cripple Creek

Bibliography

Adams, Edgar H., *Private Gold Coinage of California 1849-1855.* American Numismatic Society, New York, New York, 1912.

Baker, W.S., *Medallic Portraits of Washington.* Robert M. Lindsay, publisher, Philadelphia, Pennsylvania, 1885.

Bancroft, Carolyn, *Gulch of Gold.* Alan Swallow, publisher, Sage Books, Denver, Colorado, 1958.

ibid., *Six Racy Madams.* Johnson Publishing Company, Boulder, Colorado, 1965.

Bancroft, Hubert Howe, *History of California.* The History Company, San Francisco, California, 1888.

Bogue, Dorothy McGraw, *The Van Briggle Story.* Century One Press, Colorado Springs, Colorado, 1976.

Bowers, Q. David, *Coin World.* Various Numismatic Depth Study columns, Amos Press, Sidney, Ohio, 1960 to date.

ibid., *The Encyclopedia of Automatic Musical Instruments.* Vestal Press, Vestal, New York, 1972.

ibid., *High Profits from Rare Coin Investment.* Bowers & Ruddy Galleries, Los Angeles, California, 1974.

ibid., *Put Another Nickel In.* Vestal Press, Vestal, New York, 1966.

ibid., *A Tune for a Token.* Token and Medal Society, Inc., Thiensville, Wisconsin, March 1975.

ibid., "U.S. Gold," article in *Coins Magazine.* Krause Publications, Iola, Wisconsin, February 1971.

Bressett, Kenneth and Kosoff, A., introduction by Q. David Bowers, *Official ANA Grading Standards for U.S. Coins.* Western Publishing Company, Inc., Racine, Wisconsin, 1977.

Brown, Robert L., *Colorado Ghost Towns.* Caxton Printers, Caldwell, Idaho, 1977.

California State Mining Bureau, *9th Annual Report of the State's Mineralogists for the Year Ending December 1, 1889.* State Office, Sacramento, California, 1890.

Coin Collector, The. Babka Publishing Company, Kewanee, Illinois, various 1967 issues.

Coin World. Various issues 1960 to 1978.

Coin World Almanac. Amos Press, Sidney, Ohio, 1977.

Desmond, Adrian J., *The Hot-Blooded Dinosaurs.* Dial Press, New York, New York, 1976.

Druggists' Circular and Chemical Gazette, The. New York, New York, various issues in the 1870s and 1880s.

Feitz, Leland, *Cripple Creek!* Little London Press, Colorado Springs, Colorado, 1967.

Fisher, Vardis, and Holmes, Opal Laurel, *Gold Rushes and Mining Camps of the Early West.* Caxton Printers, Caldwell, Idaho, 1968.

Fossett, Frank, *Colorado.* C.G. Crawford, New York, New York, 1879.

Frank Leslie's Popular Monthly Magazine. New York, New York, various late 19th century issues.

Friedberg, Robert, *Paper Money of the United States.* Various editions, Coin and Currency Institute, New York, New York.

Griffith, Richard D. and Mayer, Arthur, *The Movies,* Bonanza Books, New York, New York, 1957.

Hamilton, Sinclair, *Early American Book Illustrators and Wood Engravers 1670-1870.* Princeton University Press, Princeton, New Jersey, 1968.

Harper, Terrence G., *Vermont Paper Currency and Banks.* Reprint from *Numismatic Scrapbook Magazine*, Chicago, Illinois.

History of Nevada. Thompson & West, Oakland, California, 1881.

History of Sacramento County, California. Thompson & West, Oakland, California, 1880.

How to Detect Counterfeit Bank Notes. Rawdon, Wright, Hatch & Edson, New York, New York, 1856.

Hulfish, David S., *Cyclopedia of Motion Picture Work,* two volumes. American Technical Society, Chicago, Illinois, 1911.

Ingram, J.S., *The Centennial Exposition.* Hubbard Brothers, Philadelphia, Pennsylvania, 1876.

Jackson, Joseph Henry, *Gold Rush Album.* Charles Scribner's Sons, New York, New York, 1949.

Judd, Dr. J. Hewitt, *United States Pattern, Experimental, and Trial Pieces.* Western Publishing Company, Racine, Wisconsin, 1976.

Lee, Mabel Barbee, *Cripple Creek Days.* Doubleday and Company, Garden City, New York, 1958.

Lorich, Bruce, and Andrews, Karen, "The Spanish Treasure Fleet of 1715." Article in Bowers & Ruddy Galleries Auction Catalogue of the 1715 Spanish Treasure Fleet Collection, February 17-19, 1977.

Ludwig, Coy, *Maxfield Parrish.* Watson-Guptill Publications, New York, New York, 1973.

Mackay, Charles, *Extraordinary Popular Delusions and the Madness of Crowds.* Reprinted by L.C. Page and Company, 1932, from the original *Memoirs of Extraordinary Popular Delusions*, London, England, 1841.

Mangan, Terry William, *Colorado on Glass.* Sundance Limited, Denver, Colorado, 1975.

Mast, Gerald, *A Short History of the Movies.* The Bobbs-Merrill Company, Indianapolis, 1976.

McCabe, James D., *The Illustrated History of the Centennial Exhibition.* National Publishing Company, Philadelphia, Pennsylvania, 1876.

McKearin, George S. and Helen, *American Glass.* Crown Publishers, Inc., New York, New York.

Mervis, Clyde, and Coffing, Courtney, and the Amos Press, "1913 Nickel Offers Mystic Aura," article in *The Numismatic Scrapbook Magazine.* December 1971.

Morell, W.P., *The Gold Rushes.* Adam and Charles Black, London, England, 1940.

Mumey, Nolie, *Colorado Territorial Scrip.* Johnson Publishing Company, Boulder, Colorado, 1966.

Murbach, John, description of Lot 1932, Lahainaluna paper money set, "Robert E. Branigan Estate", 1978 ANA auction catalogue, Bowers & Ruddy Galleries, Los Angeles, California, 1978.

Newman, Eric P., *The Early Paper Money of America.* Western Publishing Company, Racine, Wisconsin, 1976.

(continued)

Newman, Eric P. and Bressett, Kenneth E., *The Fantastic 1804 Dollar*. Western Publishing Company, Racine, Wisconsin, 1962.

Niver, Kemp R., *Biograph Bulletins, 1896-1908*. Locare Research Group, Los Angeles, California, 1971.

Numismatic News. Various issues 1952 to 1978.

Numismatic Scrapbook Magazine, The. Various issues.

Numismatist, The. Various issues.

Patrick, Jesse, *The Bicentennial Tokens of the Patrick Mint*. San Francisco, California, 1977.

Peterson, John, *Investing for Pleasure and Profit*. Dow Jones Books, Princeton, New Jersey, 1977.

Roehl, Harvey, *Player Piano Treasury*. Vestal Press, Vestal, New York, 1961.

St. Albans Raid, October 19th, 1864. Franklin-Lamoille Bank, St. Albans, Vermont, 1953.

Sprague, Marshall, *Money Mountain*. Little Brown Company, Boston, Massachusetts, 1953.

Stebbins, L., *Progress of the United States*. Hartford, Connecticut, 1870.

Taxay, Don, *The Comprehensive Catalog and Encyclopedia of United States Coins*, 1976 edition. Scott Publishing Company, New York, New York, 1975.

ibid., *The U.S. Mint and Coinage*. Arco Publishing Company, New York, New York, 1966.

Thayer, William M., *Marvels of the New West*. Norwich, Connecticut, 1887.

Todd, Frank Morton, "The Coin Outlasts the Throne", article in *The Story of the Exposition*, Volume IV, 1921.

Van Allen, Leroy C. and Mallis, A. George, *Comprehensive Catalogue and Encyclopedia of U.S. Morgan and Peace Silver Dollars*. New York, New York, 1976.

Vermeule, Cornelius, *Numismatic Art in America*. Belknap Press, Cambridge, Massachusetts, 1971.

Wallechinsky, David and Wallace, Irving, *The People's Almanac*. Doubleday and Company, Garden City, New York, 1975.

Walters, Betty Lawson, *The King of Desks, Wooton's Patent Secretary*. Smithsonian Institution Press, Washington, D.C., 1969.

Warner, Col. J.J., and Hayes, Judge Benjamin, and Widney, Dr. J.P., *An Historical Sketch of Los Angeles County, California*. Louis Lewin & Company, Los Angeles, California, 1876.

Warren, H.L.J. and Stride, Robert, *Cripple Creek and Colorado Springs Illustrated*. Warren & Stride, Colorado Springs, Colorado, 1896.

Watkins, T.H., *Gold and Silver in the West*. American West Publishing Company, Palo Alto, California, 1971.

Wilde, Adna G., Jr., "Lesher Referendum Dollars, Where Are They Today", article in *The Numismatist*. American Numismatic Association, Colorado Springs, Colorado, February 1978.

Wismer, David C., *The Obsolete Bank Notes of New England*. Quarterman Publications, Boston, Massachusetts, 1972.

Wolle, Muriel Sibell, *Stampede to Timberline*. Sage Books, Swallow Press, Chicago, Illinois, second edition, 1974.

World's Greatest Achievement in Music for Theatres, The. Rudolph Wurlitzer Company, Cincinnati, Ohio, 1916.

Wright, Jim and Nott, Lee, *Colorado Merchant Tokens*. Westminster, Colorado, 1977.

Yeoman, R.S., *A Guide Book of U.S. Coins*. Western Publishing Company, Racine, Wisconsin. Various editions 1946 to date.

ibid., article pertaining to 1848 quarter eagles, *The Numismatist*, July 1953.

Index

Numismatic Literary Guild, 279
Numismatic News, 4, 45, 209, 221-223, 225, 256, 260, 268
Numismatic Scrapbook Magazine, 13, 139, 221, 227-229, 231, 233, 236, 239, 255, 264
Numismatist, The, 12-14, 46, 172, 201, 221, 222, 230-232, 256, 264, 268
Nurembergh Salve, 270
Nutt, Commodore, 187

O

Oatman, Arizona, 277
Obsolete Bank Notes of New England, The, 46
Octopus, The, novel, 198
O'Farrell, Jasper, 122
Official American Numismatic Association Grading Guide, 259, 260
Old Homestead bordello, 149, 156, 166
Old Spanish Trail half dollar, 265
O'Leary, Mrs., 157, 188
Oliphant, Jeff, numismatist, 278
Olsen, Fred, numismatist, 10
Olympia Music Hall, 20
On the Waterfront, film, 224
Onassis, Aristotle, ship owner, 188
Onepapa, Sioux Indian chief, 56, 59
Operator's Bell DeLuxe slot machine, 35
Operators Piano Company, 26, 34
Ophir Mining and Milling Co., 170
Oregon gold coins, 136
Oregon, steamship, 126
Oregon Trail half dollar, 265
Ormonde crown, 283
Ormsby, Dr. J.S., coiner, 132
Ormsby, Maj. William M., 132
Ornate 1794 cent, 278
Osterhout Library, Wilkes-Barre, Pa., 226
Oswald, Lord St., 70
Ott, J.J., assayer, 80
Our Cashier's Scrapbook, 188
Our Trust Is In God motto, 76
Overton, Al, professional numismatist, 278
Owl slot machine, 36
Oysters as a delicacy in the mining camps, 121

P

Pacific Company, coiners, 132, 135
Pacific Mail Steamship Company, 126, 137
Page, M.C., 28
Painter, Kenyon, numismatist, 278
Palace Hotel, San Francisco, 189
Palace token, 35
Panama Canal, 138
Panama-Pacific International Exposition, 138, 145, 172, 265, 279
Panama, steamship, 126
Panic of 1873, 81
Panic of '93, 156, 170
Panprosium, 187
Pantages Theatre, Hollywood, 22
Paper Money, journal, 278
Paquet, Anthony C., engraver, 89, 143, 266, 267
Paramount International Coin Corporation, professional numismatists, 15, 98, 233, 243
Pardee, Colonel, 134
Paris Exhibition (1867), 192
Paris Exhibition (1900), 26
Paris Salon, 152
Paris Theatre, Denver, 22
Park, Boyd, 173
Park Sheraton Hotel, New York, 233
Parker, C.W., 5, 253
Parker, Earl, professional numismatist, 101, 132, 235
Parker, Edward W., 51
Parker House Hotel, Boston, 56, 63
Parker House Hotel, San Francisco, 125
Parker, P.C., 255

Parr Building, Cripple Creek, 154
Parrish, Maxfield, artist, 149, 150
Parrish, Maxfield Jr., 149
Patient Sufferer, A, 20
Patrick, Jess, coiner, 276, 277
Patrick Mint, 276, 277
Pattern United States coins, 6, 8, 9, 67, 73, 75, 78, 90-93, 136, 138, 111, 202, 240, 266
Patterson, A.H.M., engraver, 263
Patterson, Robert M., director of the mint, 6, 73, 74
Patti-Nicolini, Adelina, singer, 33
Paxman, Dr. Curtis R., numismatist, 244
Peale, Franklin, assayer, 6
Peale, Titian, artist, 73
Peale's Museum, 270
Peck, C. Wilson, numismatist, 236
Pedro, Dom, emperor of Brazil, 192
Peerless pianos, 34, 35
Pegasus, 281
Pemigewasset Hook & Ladder Company, 42
Pendleton, F.R., 26, 28
Penn-New York Auction Co., 233, 234
Pennsylvania Society, 207
Pennsylvania State University, 41, 178, 233, 251
Penny arcade, 254
Penny Whimsy, 261
Penny Wise, journal, 261, 279
Penrose, Spencer, 149, 170
People's Bank, Paterson, N.J., 45
Percy, H.C., 188
Perry, P.H.W., 134, 136
Perschke, Walter, professional numismatist, 102
Pesenti Winery, 275
Peter, the eagle, 73
Peters, Jess, professional numismatist, 50
Peterson, John, author, 251
Pfister's Store, Benicia, California, 118
Pharmacist Mining Co., 170
Phelan & Collender, 187
Phenakistascope, 18
Phenix Bank, New York, 49
Philadelphia Mint, 3, 6-8, 12-15, 18, 65, 67-71, 73, 74, 76-79, 81, 89, 91, 94, 96, 100, 101, 103, 109, 114, 117, 124, 136, 138, 140, 141, 143, 174, 200, 201, 204, 208, 212, 213, 216, 224, 268, 271
Philadelphia Toboggan Co., 253
Philip I, King, 281
Philip II, King, 281
Philip V, King, 113
Phillips, Jr., C.H., lecturer, 277
Phoenix Block, Cripple Creek, 157
Photograde, 235, 243, 259
Pianino, 27
PianOrchestra, 27
Pictorial History of the Carousel, A, 255
Piggott Block, Cripple Creek, 154
Pikes Peak, 151-153, 155, 156, 228
Pikes Peak Cog Railway, 152
Pillar dollar, 285
Pinkham, Lydia, 184
Pinnacle Park, amusement park, 157
Pioche, Bayerque & Co., 137
Pioneer Museum, Colorado Springs, 151
Piper, A.A., 215, 255
Piper's Opera House, Virginia City, 84
Pittman Act, 91, 100, 106
Placentia National Bank, California, 56
Placer mining explained, 120, 121
Placerville, California, 122
Playland-at-the-Beach, San Francisco, 257
Pleasant View Ranch, 277
Plymouth Rock Mining Co., 170
Pogo, comic strip character, 4
Poe, Edgar Allan, poet, 112
Polaroid camera, 180

Pole Vaulting at Columbia University, 20
Poli's Wonderland Theatre, New Haven, 20
Polish coins, 244
Pollock, James, director of the mint, 8, 73, 77
Polynesian, newspaper, 125
Portland Hotel, Cripple Creek, 157
Portland Mine, 160, 166, 168
Portsmouth Square, San Francisco, 125
Poseidon, 281
Postage currency (see fractional currency)
Potter's Bar, California, 119
Poverty Gulch, Cripple Creek, 156
Poverty Gulch Gold Mining Co., 170
Praxinoscope-Theatre, 18, 19
Professional Numismatists Guild, 139, 235, 243, 259, 271
Proof coins, 208
Proskey, David, professional numismatist, 204
Provident Loan Society, 100
Providentia, 281
Puck slot machine, 36
Puerto Rican coinage, 285
Pullman, George M., 192
Pyramidal Head 1794 cent, 278

Q

Quarterman Publications, 46
"Quarter union" or $25 gold coins, 136
Quicksilver machine, 120
Quint's Sons Co., S.H., 269

R

Ramsfield, Ole, 277
Randall Hoard, 261
Randall, J. Colvin, numismatist, 263
Randall, John Swan, 261
Rarcoa, professional numismatists, 16, 45, 139
Rare Coin Review, 12
Rawlins, Harold, 233
Rawlins, John, 187
Raymond, William K., numismatist, 56
Real Eight Corporation, 112, 113, 244
Rear Window, film, 224
Reblitz, Arthur, 154
Red Devil tools, 262
Red Light Dance Hall, 166
Red Square, Moscow, 200
Reed, Ira, professional numismatist, 15
Reed, J.H., jeweler, 215, 255
Regina Music Box Co., 255, 257
Reid, Templeton, coiner, 132
Rendell, Kenneth W., antiquarian, 101
Rembrandt, artist, 4
Reptiles of North America, The, 225
Republic of Central America coinage, 285
Rettew, Joel, professional numismatist, 106
R.G.A. Coins, 277
Rice, George W., numismatist, 76
Rich, Laddie, 277
Rich, Wayne S., numismatist, 276
Riddell, Professor F.L., 263
Rip Van Winkle, 20
Rittenhouse, David, director of the U.S. Mint, 3, 4, 70, 73
Ritter, J.W., 275
Ritter, Phyllis, numismatist, 222
River Oaks Collection, 244
Rives, Beverly and John, 43
Robe, The, film, 224
Robert-Morton Company, 22
Roberts, George E., director of the mint, 13
Roberts, Sharon, 233
Robinson, Alfred, 117
Robinson, Hetty Howland, 14
Rockefeller, John D., financier, 188
Rockman, David C., D.D.S., 276, 277
Roe Sale (Mehl), 96